THE PSYCHOPATHOLOGY OF CRIME

THE PSYCHOPATHOLOGY OF CRIME

Criminal Behavior as a Clinical Disorder

Adrian Raine

Department of Psychology
University of Southern California
Los Angeles, California

ACADEMIC PRESS, INC.
A Division of Harcourt Brace & Company

San Diego   New York   Boston   London   Sydney   Tokyo   Toronto

This book is printed on acid-free paper. ∞

Academic Press, Inc.
1250 Sixth Avenue, San Diego, California 92101-4311

United Kingdom Edition published by
Academic Press Limited
24–28 Oval Road, London NW1 7DX

Library of Congress Cataloging-in Publication Data

Raine, Adrian.
    The psychopathology of crime : criminal behavior as a clinical disorder / Adrian Raine.
        p.   cm.
    Includes index.
    ISBN 0-12-576160-0
    1. Criminal behavior.   2. Psychology, Pathological.   3. Criminals--Physiology.   I. Title.
    [DNLM: 1. Criminal Psychology.   2. Social Behavior Disorders--physiopathology.   3. Social Behavior Disorders--etiology.   WM 600 R155 1993]
    HV6133.R25 1993
    364.3'01'9 --dc20
                                                                93-911
                                                                CIP

PRINTED IN THE UNITED STATES OF AMERICA
93 94 95 96 97 98   QW   9 8 7 6 5 4 3 2 1

To John, Julia, and Sally,
and the memory of Anna, Reuben, and Roma

Contents

2   Crime in the Context of Evolution

3   Genetics and Crime

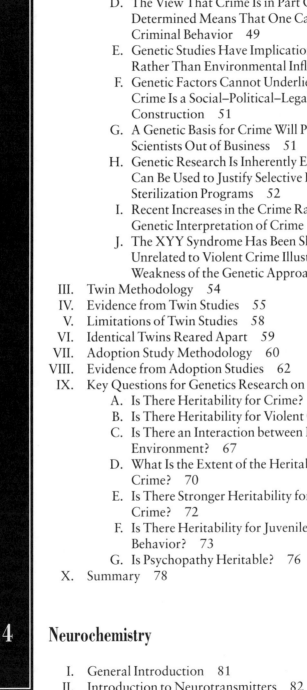

4   Neurochemistry

5   Neuropsychology

6   Brain Imaging

7 Psychophysiology

8 Other Biological Factors: Head Injury, Pregnancy and Birth Complications, Physical Appearance, Hormones, Diet, and Lead

9 Cognitive Deficits

10 Familial Influences

11 Extrafamilial Influences

12 Is Crime a Disorder?

Preface

This book has two major goals. The first goal is to familiarize readers with the rapidly growing and increasingly influential body of knowledge on the biological bases of criminal behavior. Much of this research has been ignored or minimized in more traditional books on crime, yet if we are to fully understand criminal behavior we need to be fully aware of *all* influences that bear on it. By the same token, it is clear that psychosocial and environmental factors are also critically important in the development of crime, and for this reason chapters are also given over to familial and extrafamilial influences on crime. Because these latter processes have been given much more coverage in previous books, more emphasis is given to biological influences in this book; this must not be construed to suggest that social influences are of any less importance.

The second goal of this book is to explore the question of whether crime is a disorder. That is, is serious, recidivistic criminal behavior a disorder or psychopathology in much the same way as depression, anxiety, and schizotypal personality are currently conceptualized as disorders? This question must not be confused with the very different issue of whether mental disorders are frequently found in offender groups, or vice versa. Rather, the key question here is whether criminal behavior, in and of itself, constitutes a disorder. This question does not appear to have been asked previously, at least in such a direct manner, yet it is felt that now there are sufficient grounds in favor of an affirmative answer to this question to warrant further open discussion of this issue.

This question will be addressed in two ways: First, by reviewing definitions of disorder and assessing the extent to which criminal behavior fulfills such definitions, and second, by employing a construct validity approach in which a nomological network of familial, extrafamilial, cognitive, neuropsychological, psychophysiological, brain imaging, biochemical, and genetic predispositions are established for crime. The first of these approaches is outlined in Chapter 1, and the second approach is discussed in Chapters 2 to 11. The final chapter attempts to draw some firm answer to the central question of this book and to discuss criticisms of a psychopathological approach to crime and the wider implications of this approach.

It is hoped that this book will be of interest and value to all those who are concerned with the study of crime and also to those who are interested in psychopathology in general. Although attempts have been made to provide a fairly extensive coverage of research in the areas delineated under the various chapter headings, it cannot be claimed that these reviews are fully comprehensive. To fully review even the biological literature on crime would require a book in itself; to comprehensively cover all psychosocial influences would have taken several books. Instead, important and illustrative studies are highlighted with a focus on conceptual and methodological issues in these areas together with directives for future research. Where appropriate, new hypotheses are developed in these chapters on the basis of the material discussed, although clearly these are only initial hypotheses that require further testing. Summaries are provided at the end of each chapter for the reader to obtain a brief overview of the type of material being discussed and the main conclusions drawn from the material.

This book was not written with the intention of being popular with its readers. Biological research into crime has been, and still is, a controversial area. In addition, the notion that crime may be a disorder is not a neutral topic, as there are important implications for society at large in accepting such a view. Instead, an attempt has been made to write a book with the purpose of presenting controversial material as dispassionately and fairly as possible, to be provocative without being sensational, and to ask potentially contentious questions in the hope that a more open discussion of these issues will result in greater clarification and understanding of the basic causes of and influences on crime.

Charles Hulme at York University first encouraged me to write a book that would provide an overview of the biological bases to crime, although this endeavor is the product of the efforts and encouragement of many others. Gordon Claridge at Oxford University first stimulated my interests in this area of research with Robert Hare's seminal research, while Peter Venables at York University and Sarnoff Mednick at the University of Southern California (USC) have done more than anyone to stimulate and support my work on the biosocial bases of criminal behavior. David Farrington at Cambridge University gave me sound advice on the context of this book and has been a major influence in furthering my knowledge on longitudinal approaches to psychosocial influences on crime. Laura Baker (USC) and Steve Lopez (UCLA) have given me invaluable feedback on individual chapters, together with my students Deana Benishay, Laura Bird, Deborah Kim, and Shari Mills. I also benefitted from many critical discussions on the main thesis of this book with Jenny Dunkin, Frances and Shoki Gupta-Clarke, and Ed and Caroline Locke.

My colleagues Monte Buchsbaum, Jill Stanley, and Jackie Stoddard must be thanked for allowing me to present data on brain imaging in murderers (Chapter 6), and my graduate student, Angela Scerbo, is particularly acknowledged for allowing me to describe in detail her exciting work on temperament (Chapter 7) and neurotransmitters (Chapter 4). Many of the ideas in this book emanated from the many stimulating discussions with the undergraduates taking Criminal Behavior at USC; I owe a great deal to their creativity and boundless enthusiasm, and I have attempted to keep them uppermost in mind as an imaginary audience throughout these writings.

Special thanks are due to my estimable graduate student, Todd Lencz, who spent many hours patiently shaping up my vacuous wit with incisive criticisms and perspicacious advice on many aspects of this book; a less disreputable supervisor might have made him coauthor! Finally, this book would in all likelihood never have been started (and certainly never finished) without my supportive editor, Nikki Fine, whose gentle harassment and clement coercion were the only forces that kept me going.

1

Crime and the Nature of Psychopathology

I. INTRODUCTION

Criminal behaviors range widely in their seriousness and their impact on the public. A few isolated individuals kill people and then eat parts of their victims' bodies, while the bulk of criminal behavior consists of more mundane acts such as theft, burglary, robbery, and assault. The former are bizarre crimes, while the latter are so commonplace as to be almost uneventful except to the victims. Many of the public can easily believe that there is something profoundly wrong psychologically with individuals who murder and then cannibalize their victims, though others would deny this and argue that such people are simply evil.

Whether these criminals, and others who just kill, are "mad" or "bad" represents a judgmental dilemma that society has struggled with for centuries. In contrast, society tends not to be in two minds about crimes such as petty theft and burglary which are mostly, though not always, viewed as wrongful acts and not due to any form of mental disorder.

The purpose of this book is to argue that *many* instances of repeated criminal behavior, including theft and burglary, may represent a disorder or psychopathology in much the same way that depression, schizophrenia, or other conditions currently recognized as mental disorders represent psychopathologies. This argument will in part be based on assessment of the extent to which criminal behavior fits definitions of psychopathology, but perhaps more importantly on empirical data which indicate differences between criminals and noncriminals on biological, psychological, and social variables. This chapter will largely be concerned with the former, while most other chapters deal with the latter. This argument is a very difficult one for society to accept, and the last chapter deals with competing arguments and reasons why accepting this argument is difficult for society.

This chapter will outline nine criteria which have been used to define psychopathology which, when taken together, make up an overall gestalt of psychopathology against which criminality can be compared. A comparative analysis between criminality and disorders currently listed in the Diagnostic and Statistical Manual of Mental Disorders, Third Edition, Revised (DSM-III-R) will then be made to help assess the relative extent to which criminality meets these combined criteria. The construct validity approach, which represents a second important approach to assessing psychopathology, will then be outlined. It will be argued that criminality does indeed meet many criteria for assessing disorder, while the following chapters will help establish initial empirical validity for the view that criminality is a disorder.

Before attempting to view criminal behavior in the context of definitions of "psychopathology," a brief clarification must be made about this term and to whom it applies. There are many terms used to describe psychologically disturbed behavior, including mental disorder, mental illness, mental disease, madness, insanity, maladaptive behavior, behavior disorder, abnormal behavior, and emotional disturbance. The term *disorder* will be used frequently throughout this book because of its simplicity. However, the term *psychopathology* will be more frequently used in this first chapter because in addition to indicating a mental disorder, it also refers to the *study* of psychologically disturbed behavior. The term *mental disorder* conveys much the same meaning however (Coleman, 1972), and throughout this book it will be used interchangeably with the term *psychopathology*.

Those who repeatedly engage in nontrivial criminal behavior constitute the key population to which the psychopathology argument is being applied, whether they are caught offenders who reside in prisons or whether they are undetected, repeated offenders residing in the community. It is important to recognize that, as will be argued at greater length later, disorders are more likely to be dimensional in nature and less likely to form water-tight, discrete categories. Just as there are differing degrees to which an individual may be characterized as depressed or anxious, so in turn there are individual degrees to which individuals express nontrivial criminal behavior. At this stage, drawing very discrete boundaries to whom the psychopathology argument can be applied would be both misleading and inconsistent with the nature of disorder.

There is considerable heterogeneity within the population of repeatedly criminal individuals, just as there is considerable heterogeneity within many established disorders. The psychopathology argument is here being applied to the totality of repeated, criminal behavior. If there are distinct subgroups of offenders, they may be taken to represent subtypes of the general disorder of criminality, just as there are distinct subtypes of the schizophrenias. This issue will be discussed further in Chapter 12.

II. DEFINING PSYCHOPATHOLOGY

Not only is it almost impossible to conclusively demonstrate that crime is a psychopathology, but also it is equally difficult to demonstrate that it is *not* a psychopathology. The reason for this paradox is simple: Experts in psychiatry and psychology have found it exceedingly difficult to outline an acceptable definition of psychopathology. As indicated by Frances, First, Widiger, Miele, Tiley, Davis, and Pincus (1991), "There have never been any very convincing definitions of illness, disease, or mental disorder" (p. 408). DSM-III-R (APA, 1987) states that "no definition adequately specifies precise boundaries for the concept of 'mental disorder'" (p. xxii). If psychopathology cannot be defined, one cannot definitively say whether or not criminal behavior (or any other condition) falls into this category. The difficulties in defining psychopathology will soon become apparent, but these difficulties have not prevented professionals and the public alike from easily accepting the view that conditions such as depression and schizophrenia are clearly disorders or psychopathologies. Although no single definition clearly delineates psychopathology, the many definitions, when taken together, create a general "gestalt" or picture of what constitutes a psychopathology. Seen within the context of this gestalt, depression and schizophrenia appear to be disorders, even though neither can adequately meet all definitions. The key question is whether these definitions provide any degree of "fit" to criminal behavior. To the extent that they provide some fit, the notion that crime may be a psychopathology becomes a possibility. This notion of a gestalt for defining psychopathology constitutes a central idea in this chapter, and although individual definitions of psychopathology will be presented and a critique provided, the argument that must be borne in mind is that, ultimately, it is the overall fit of a condition to the totality of these criteria which may provide the best assessment for what constitutes a psychopathology.

In overviewing how disorder and psychopathology have been defined, it becomes clear that there has been little conceptual progress on this issue in recent years, although paradoxically there have been important advances in our understanding of individual disorders. Part of the reason for this is that the most common stance in psychiatry and psychology is simply to ignore the problem of defining disorder (Kendell, 1986). Nevertheless, at least nine individual criteria of psychopathology have been outlined, although there have been many general definitions proposed. These more general definitions are relatively circular; for example, Kolb (1977) has viewed psychopathology as "abnormal personality functioning" (p. 119), while Goodstein and Calhoun (1982) define it as "a dysfunction of behavior" (p. 11). These definitions tend not to be helpful, as they beg the question of what constitutes "abnormal" or a "dysfunction" and as such will not be discussed further. More precise, specific criteria that have received the most attention in the literature are discussed in turn below. Definitions are first outlined, the "fit" of criminal behavior to these individual criteria is evaluated, and then weaknesses in the definition are outlined. Finally, the overall fit of criminal behavior to the organized whole of these definitions will be evaluated.

A. Deviation from a Statistical Norm

This first definition is a simple and relatively clear-cut attempt to define abnormal behavior as behavior that is statistically infrequent. Generally speaking, many traits are distributed approximately according to a bell-shaped normal curve in which about two-thirds of all subjects fall within one standard deviation either side of the mean score. As an example, IQ as measured by the Wechsler Adult Intelligence Scale has a mean of 100 and a standard deviation of 15, and approximately 2% of the population score lower than 2 standard deviations below the mean (i.e., IQs below 70). Mental retardation is a disorder defined in DSM-III-R (APA, 1987) almost entirely in terms of having an IQ below 70 and represents one clear way in which this criterion for mental disorder has been applied in practice. A less precise formulation of this criterion would be to define disorder as behavior which is unusual and atypical. Schizophrenia, for example, affects approximately 1% of the population and as such would be viewed as a disorder on the grounds that it is relatively rare.

Does criminal behavior meet this criterion? This depends very much on two factors: (1) how crime is defined and, (2) how "statistically infrequent" a behavior should be to count as a disorder. Regarding the first issue, when crime is defined in terms of convictions for standard list offenses (indictable and nontraffic offenses), 28.3% of males and 5.3% of females in England have a registration for crime by the age of 25, or a general population average of approximately 16.8% (London Home Office, 1985). Farrington (1981) estimated lifetime risk for crime (based on indictable or serious offenses) as 43.6% for males and 14.7% for females, or a population average for the United Kingdom of approximately 29.2%. These summary figures are lower for countries such as Denmark, with Visher and Roth (1986) reporting life-time rates of 15.9% for males and 4.7% for females, or a population rate of approximately 10.3% based on data from Mednick, Gabrielli, and Hutchings (1984) from Denmark (the issue of cross-cultural variations in crime and its implication for viewing crime as a psychopathology will be discussed more fully in the last chapter). Rates for countries such as the United States are much higher than those for Scandinavian countries, with McCord (1981) reporting risk for convictions for serious offenses in males by ages 41–50 years at 30.2%. When crime is assessed on the basis of arrest data, Visher and Roth (1986), in an extensive review of participation rates in criminal careers, con-cluded that the best available estimates indicate that 25–35% of urban males will be arrested for at least one index offense during their lives.

These "official" estimates of crime, while high in and of themselves, are very likely to be underestimates of the true crime rate. Self-report studies of crime and delinquency employ the methodology of sampling either random or "high-risk" groups from the general population and asking individuals whether they have committed various antisocial, delinquent, and criminal acts (Klein, 1987). Such surveys have indicated that the majority of participants have committed at least one act that would be regarded as criminal. Self-report studies have been criticized, however, for placing too much emphasis on trivial offenses, and there are nontrivial methodological problems associated with the self-report method (Elliott, Ageton, & Huizinga, 1983). In spite of these problems, it seems that 2–4% of females report involvement in individual, *specific* crime categories (e.g., burglary, car theft, grand theft, and robbery), while corresponding rates for males are approximately four times higher (Visher & Roth, 1986). Clearly, a nontrivial proportion of the population reports having engaged in criminal offenses.

If most of us have at some time in our lives committed what would count as a criminal act, can we say that crime is a psychopathology? Clearly not, but while a relatively large number will have committed a small number of of-fenses throughout the course of their lives, a small minority tend to repeatedly commit offenses and account for the bulk of serious offending. Mednick (1977) reported that about 1% of the male population accounted for more than half the criminal offenses committed by a Copenhagen birth cohort of over 30,000 men. Wolfgang, Figlio, and Sellin (1972) report the same type of finding for the city of Philadelphia. While the average U.S. offender commits only a few crimes each year, the most active 10% of offenders commit crimes at rates that can exceed 100 each year (Blumstein, Cohen, Roth, & Visher, 1986). Self-report studies on inmates in California and Michigan found that offenders who have committed robbery commit this crime when free in the community at an average rate of 15–20 per year; similarly, those who have committed burglary commit an average of 45–50 burglaries per year (Cohen, 1986). Inmates in general report a much higher proportion of offenses than individuals free in the community (Blumstein *et al.*, 1986); this is not surprising given that the more an individual commits an offense, the more likely it is that they will be arrested and convicted. The notion that crime is a psychopathology is best applied to this relatively smaller group of recidivistic, serious offenders because they are more likely to have some intrinsic predisposition to crime relative to one-time offenders whose antisociality may be more transient and situation specific.

Although only a minority of the population falls into this category of repeat offenders, they represent a larger group than some other established mental disorders such as bipolar disorder or schizophrenia, which have lifetime risk rates of approximately 1% (APA, 1987). How statistically deviant should a subgroup be in order to constitute a disorder using the statistical infrequency criterion? There has been no clear answer to this question, but one guideline would be to look at lifetime rates for other behavioral syndromes that are clearly accepted as disorders, and within this context the recidivistic serious offender group would not be out of place. Among the personality disorders, lifetime risk for schizotypal personality disorder is approximately 6% (Baron & Risch, 1987), although other sources estimate it to be higher at approximately 10% (Meehl, 1989). Prevalence rates for major depression range from 9 to 26% for females and 5 to 12% for males, while lifetime risk for alcohol abuse or dependence is approximately 13% (APA, 1987). Prevalence rates for panic disorder, simple and social phobias, and hypochondriasis are listed in DSM-III-R as "common," while the prevalence for nicotine dependence is listed as "large" (APA, 1987). Alcohol intoxication is classified as an alcohol-induced organic mental disorder in DSM-III-R and only requires that a person has drunk sufficient alcohol to produce impulsivity, mood changes, or impaired judgment and that it leads to slurred speech or incoordination. Presumably, a very large proportion of the population would have met these criteria at some point in their lives.

It should be reemphasized that meeting this criterion is by no means a good argument for any condition being regarded as a psychopathology. The statistical infrequency concept has been repeatedly criticized on the grounds that (1) few traits are normally distributed (Duke & Nowicki, 1979); (2) it does not take into account the content of the trait (e.g., outstanding athletic ability would be classified as deviant; Davison & Neale, 1986); and (3) extremes at both ends of the continuum would be labeled abnormal (Goodstein & Calhoun, 1982). Perhaps the major problem with this criterion is that many mental disorders are simply not as rare as most people believe. In this context, repeated serious criminal behavior fares no worse (and no better) than many other disorders when matched with the weak statistical infrequency criterion of mental disorder. Again, it must be remembered that ultimately the key issue will be whether the *gestalt* picture that is being built of psychopathology in this chapter fits crime, rather than any individual aspect of this picture.

B. Deviation from Ideal Mental Health

A parallel criterion to that of statistical infrequency is the notion of deviation from ideal mental health. Under this criterion, an individual would be viewed as abnormal if they deviated from an ideal state of health. The difficulty with this definition is that one needs to define this "ideal" state of health in order to ascertain who deviates from it. The World Health Organization has defined health as "a state of complete physical, mental, and social well-being, and not merely the absence of disease or infirmity." This definition has been evaluated as both comprehensive and meaningless (Lewis, 1953). More specific than this all-encompassing statement are six criteria of positive mental health drawn up by Jahoda (1958), which include self-actualization, resistance to stress, autonomy, competence, accurate perception of reality, and an appropriate balance of psychic forces.

Criminal behavior meets this criterion for disorder fairly easily. Very few criminals could be characterized as being in a state of robust physical, mental, and social well-being, and criminals certainly do not as a group present as self-actualizers who have achieved full realization of their own unique psychological, scientific, and artistic potential (Allman & Jaffe, 1978). As will be seen later in this book, criminals are characterized by major social, cognitive, and biological deficits which clearly preclude them from achieving this ideal state of well-being.

This definition of psychopathology has major weaknesses, however. Defining well-being is almost as elusive as defining disorder and, unless it can be clearly delineated, the definition is not of great practical use. As it stands, only a minority of the general population could be described as being in this optimal state of well-being. This criterion is probably viewed best as a fine goal for society and at worst as a relatively weak criterion for psychopathology.

C. Deviation from the Social Norm

This criterion is again a parallel to the statistical infrequency criterion, but instead of defining abnormality as deviation from a statistical, objective norm, it is defined in terms of the norms laid down by society. Using this definition, behavior that lies outside the bounds of social acceptability and which violates the prevailing social norm is judged to be abnormal or disordered (Gorenstein, 1984; Davison & Neale, 1986). In some senses this is a powerful criterion. Couching disorder in terms of societal deviance makes it a normative concept without absolute boundaries; what is deviant in one society may differ from what is deviant in another. In this sense the floating concept of deviance is just as elusive as the concept of psychopathology, but it also yields insight into why disorder is so hard to define. Scheff (1970) argues that the definition of disorder is elusive because it is based on a concept which is itself elusive, namely social deviance. Social deviance nevertheless has the feeling of being central to the definition of disorder because deviation from the social order is a fundamental concept in society which is understood and shared by almost everyone (Scheff, 1970). A social definition appears to capture some essential ingredient in the way the concept of illness is applied in real terms in society.

Criminal behavior very clearly fits within this definition of disorder. Criminal activities are clearly viewed as lying outside the norm of social acceptability. Those who both break the norm and are caught face being ostracized and isolated from society by being sent to prison. Indeed, criminal behavior probably fits this definition as well as any other mental disorder; while there is an increasing degree of social acceptability to suffering from a disorder such as anxiety, depression, or alcoholism, which makes these illnesses fit less well to this criterion, criminal behavior has become no more acceptable and as such is a good fit.

Despite some strengths to this conceptualization of disorder, like other criteria it has limitations. As Coleman (1972) points out, "It rests on the questionable assumption that socially accepted behavior is never pathological, and it implies that normality is nothing more than conformity" (p. 15). Furthermore, those viewed as deviant in one society at one point in time may later be viewed as benign (e.g., Jesus Christ). Homosexuality has until relatively recently been viewed as a deviation from the norm by society and was classified as a disorder until it was essentially taken out of DSM-III in 1980 (APA, 1980). Alternatively, this last example also illustrates the explanatory power of the social deviance concept; once a behavior is no longer viewed as deviant, it is no longer viewed as a disorder, because social deviance helps define disorder.

D. Distress/Suffering to Self or Others

Using this criterion, individuals who experience suffering, psychological distress, discomfort, or unhappiness are deemed to be "suffering" from a mental disorder. This again is a relatively more powerful criterion because it has a high degree of face validity, stemming directly from the medical model of illness; individuals usually go to doctors because they experience physical discomfort that is interpreted as a direct symptom of some underlying pathology. As such, patients complaining of psychological discomfort (e.g., depression, anxiety) are viewed as suffering from a disorder which produces these symptoms.

This simple definition has been extended to include behaviors that cause distress to others as well as to the self (Adams & Sutker, 1984; Altrocchi, 1980). The reason for this extension is that there are many syndromes that are commonly viewed as disorders yet which do not meet the simple criterion of distress to self. For example, patients suffering from bipolar disorder (mania accompanied with depression) often feel ecstatic, full of energy, feel an increase in goal-directed activity during the manic phase, have high self-esteem, and would not report being unhappy. Indeed, such states frequently tempt patients to stop taking medication so that they can experience these temporary "highs." Those suffering from alcoholism frequently deny any self-distress, though their relatives and friends may well be unhappy and distressed by their behavior. Although some schizophrenics are clearly distressed by their hallucinations, others may experience hallucinations as more benign and stimulating, with their relatives being more distressed by these symptoms than the schizophrenic. Schizophrenics with predominantly negative residual symptomatology (social isolation, blunted emotions, lack of interests, poor personal hygiene) may also not express any particular psychological discomfort or unhappiness.

Criminal behavior fits the extended aspect of this definition in that it clearly creates distress; people do not enjoy being robbed or assaulted. Again, it probably fits the second half of this criterion better than any other established disorder. On the other hand, it is not obvious that criminal behavior fits the first part of this definition. Criminals are not obviously distressed or personally unhappy. However, many criminals may indeed be unhappy and suffering, but deny such distress in much the same way as acting-out behaviors in children may be viewed as reflecting some underlying disturbance or problem which the child cannot or does not wish to verbalize. Such denial is clearly evident in other adult disorders. For example, alcoholics and other substance abusers frequently deny being distressed or emotionally disturbed, although it is fairly clear that at some level they do experience distress. The fact that criminals fail to report distress and discomfort should not therefore be taken as evidence that they are untroubled in their lives.

Although criminals do not verbalize distress in their lives, there is behavioral evidence that in reality they are suffering from distress and are exposed to a high degree of life stress. Later chapters will document a considerable degree of stress and suffering that criminals experience in their childhood, and in later adolescence and adulthood this is supplemented by school and occupational failure, downward social mobility, homelessness, disturbed marital relationships, and social isolation.

The distress/suffering of self or others criterion, like the deviation from social norms criterion, has a high degree of face validity but suffers from four important limitations. The first limitation is that many people are distressed and unhappy, but such distress is appropriate to their life circumstances and is not a sign of underlying pathology. An individual may be greatly disturbed for some time by the death of a spouse, child, parent, or close friend, but most of us would feel that this is a "normal" response to such an event and is not indicative of an underlying disorder. For this reason depressive symptoms following death of a loved one do not constitute a basis for the diagnosis of major depression (APA, 1987). Indeed, not feeling disturbed in such circumstances would be more likely to be indicative of psychopathology.

A second limitation concerns the fact that people differ with respect to how much distress they can put up with before they acknowledge that they are suffering. Criminals may feel distress and unhappiness but do not express it because it does not fit with their macho image.

A third difficulty with this criterion is that some people feel unhappy, frightened, alone, and miserable, but such feelings are produced by being pushed out of the mainstream of society rather than stemming from some intrinsic disorder within the individual. While psychopathological processes may in part contribute to these feelings as well as producing homelessness, it would seem inappropriate to label people as mentally disordered solely because they lie outside of the mainstream of society.

Fourth, the relationship between degree of distress and severity of illness is less likely to be linear and more likely to be described by an inverted U-shaped function. That is, at low levels of mental disturbance, distress is low. At mild to moderate levels of mental disturbance, reported distress increases. At moderate to high levels there is more likely to be a *reduction* in reported distress, since a number of debilitating mental disorders (e.g., Alzheimer's disease, schizophrenia, antisocial personality disorder, anorexia) are associated with a lack of insight into the disorder itself, while distress to *others* may be much higher. Similarly, criminals with a psychopathic personality or who have some of the characteristics of psychopathy lack insight both into their disorder and into their personal state of well-being (Cleckley, 1982).

In summary, criminal behavior fulfills this definition in that it creates distress for those in contact with criminals. In common with many other disorders, it does not fulfill both aspects of the criterion, although there is behavioral evidence that criminals experience more distress than they verbalize.

E. Seeking Out Treatment

This definition is an extension of the distress/discomfort criterion in that it defines disorder in terms of whether an individual seeks out treatment. This is a deceptively appealing definition which again stems from the medical model; just as medical doctors treat individuals with diseases and other physical ailments, psychiatrists and psychologists treat people with psychological disorders. Those seeking out treatment are therefore disordered. A similar criterion is the notion that those receiving treatment in a mental institution represent disordered individuals (Buss, 1966).

Criminal behavior does not meet this criterion, or at best only in those relatively rare circumstances where a criminal turns himself in because he recognizes that he is psychologically disturbed and in need of some form of

quently applied to those who have just started to take drugs, where physiological withdrawal signs tend to be absent (APA, 1987).

4. Pedophilia

This is defined as having intense urges lasting at least 6 months for sexual activity with children (generally younger than 13), with the individual either having acted on the urges or having been distressed by them. The disorder applies to individuals at least 16 years of age and at least 5 years older than the child involved. DSM-III-R reports a worse "recidivism rate" (p. 285) for those with a preference for children of the same sex. As this use of this criminological term suggests, criteria for this disorder would be met by most pedophiles serving prison sentences as well as those who commit undetected sexual offenses against children.

5. Exhibitionism

This disorder is defined as intense urges over a 6-month period to expose one's genitals to a stranger. Again, the individual must act on these urges or be distressed by them. As with pedophilia, however, not all cases of exhibitionism are illegal if they only involve fantasies and urges that are not acted on. Alternatively, many of those convicted and serving sentences for indecent exposure would fulfill criteria for this disorder.

6. Frotteurism

This is defined as recurrent urges to rub oneself up against a nonconsenting person. Individuals must act on these urges or be disturbed by them to be classified as having the disorder. Evidently, victims usually wear tight-fitting clothes, with the frottage often consisting of the offender rubbing his genitals against the victim's thighs and buttocks (APA, 1987). Frottage is often committed in crowded places where the offender can more easily escape arrest and avoid prosecution (APA, 1987). Situations where there is a crush of people in which physical contact would not be too noticeable would also lend themselves to frotteurism (e.g., front rows of indoor rock concerts).

7. Sexual Sadism

Criteria for sexual sadism consist of recurrent urges and sexually arousing fantasies involving acts in which the psychological and physical suffering of the victim is sexually arousing to the person. This category would include a subgroup of sex offenders and potentially other violent criminals serving sentences for nonsexual offenses.

8. Voyeurism

This disorder involves the act of observing an unsuspecting person who is naked, in the process of disrobing, or engaging in sexual activity.

9. Other Paraphilias

Other paraphilias listed in DSM-III-R as "not otherwise specified" and which may constitute criminal behavior included telephone scatologia (lewdness), necrophilia (corpses), and zoophilia (animals).

10. Pyromania

The main features of this disorder are deliberate fire setting, arousal before the act, fascination with fire, and pleasure when setting the fire. The act is not done for monetary gain, nor does it stem directly from a delusion/hallucination.

11. Kleptomania

Criteria include the impulse to steal objects, experiencing tension before the act and pleasure at the time of the act, stealing not being an expression of anger and not being attributable to conduct disorder or antisocial personality disorder.

12. Intermittent Explosive Disorder

This is made up of several episodes where the individual loses control and commits serious assaultive acts or destruction of property. The aggression cannot be explained by previous psychosocial stressors, there are no signs of aggression between the episodes, and it cannot be attributable to conduct disorder, antisocial personality disorder, or psychoactive substance abuse.

The advantage with the DSM-III-R listing criterion of mental disorder is that it is clear cut and has high face validity. The disadvantage is that this criterion is practical rather than conceptual and it provides no clear guidelines regarding what should and should not be included (a definition of disorder suggested by DSM-III-R is however discussed below). Nevertheless, the fact remains that a very high proportion of criminals is likely to fall into one of the DSM-III-R categories described above. This is because many of these disorders largely describe specific criminal acts. It would appear that DSM-III-R has surreptitiously accepted the view that crime is a disorder, but rather than directly face the implications of this view, crime has instead been incorporated into the manual in such a piece-meal fashion that the concept of criminality goes almost unnoticed. It is only when isolated segments of DSM-III-R are reported together as they have been above that it becomes clear that most criminal acts have been incorporated as individual disorders. It should also be noted that these criminal behaviors are not merely listed as associated features of a different disorder. Rather, in and of themselves, these criminal behaviors are viewed very specifically as disorders in their own right. Perhaps the main difference between the conceptualization of crime in DSM-III-R and the proposition being explored in this book is that here criminality is viewed as an overarching disorder which encapsulates heterogeneous aspects or perhaps subtypes of crime; DSM-III-R acknowledges and declares the "subtypes" but is silent on the overarching concept of criminality.

H. Biological Dysfunction

This simple and pragmatic view suggests that a disorder may arise when there has been a disturbance of normal biological regulatory functions (Goodstein & Calhoun, 1982; Roth & Kroll, 1986) and again stems directly from the medical model of illness. In the seventeenth and eighteenth centuries the classification of diseases was modeled on the classification of plants, but during the nineteenth century developments in morbid anatomy and pathology indicated evidence that illness was often correlated with biological disturbances or "lesions" (Kendell, 1986). As knowledge increased over the next century, this notion expanded to include biological and physiological abnormalities.

One unexpected advocate of this position has been Thomas Szasz. Szasz (1960) based his argument that mental illness is a myth in part on the notion that true mental illness stems from identifiable neurological defects. In contrast, he argued that there is no identifiable disease process in most mental illnesses. Consequently, he viewed mental illnesses as stemming from problems of living rather than from bodily disease processes. For example, Szasz (1960) argued that because the delusion that one's internal organs are rotting away "cannot be explained by a defect or disease of the nervous system" (p. 6), then schizophrenia cannot be classified as a mental illness. Szasz was writing at a time before the advent of brain imaging. Subsequent computerized tomography (CT) research in the following two decades clearly demonstrated unequivocal structural brain pathology in schizophrenics in the form of ventricular enlargement and consequently rendered one aspect of Szasz's original argument untenable. However, clear biological pathology has not been clearly identified in many mental illnesses.

Crime meets this definition of psychopathology. Criminals do appear to differ from noncriminals on a number of biological functions which may be etiologically related to crime. Data to support this view are presented in detail in later chapters which deal with genetics, psychophysiology, biochemistry, neuropsychology, neurology, and brain imaging. Although there is fairly clear evidence to support such associations, the question of whether these biological differences cause crime are just as much open to debate as whether many social correlates of crime are causal factors. Consequently, such evidence does not unequivocally confirm that crime meets this biological criterion of disorder. By the same token, almost all mental disorders are in the same position as criminality in that there is no clear evidence implicating clearly defined biological structural or functional deficits in the etiology of disorder.

This last issue outlines the main difficulty with this definition of mental illness. Most mental illnesses simply cannot be defined in terms of some underlying biological difference because the etiology of most illnesses is currently unknown. Furthermore, it is highly unlikely that mental illness is commonly caused by some discrete biological process acting independently of psychological, social, and cultural forces. Many commentators have further argued that this notion of "mental" illness tends to foster an outdated mind–body dualism. As Frances *et al.* (1991) point out, there is much that is physical about "mental" disorders and much that is mental about "physical" disorders; minds do not exist independent of bodies and vice versa. These issues are highly pertinent to criminal behavior. It is highly likely that neither biological nor social forces alone will provide a complete explanation for criminal behavior because such behavior is driven by a complex, interactive system involving diverse biological and social factors. This is probably also true for many mental disorders.

I. DSM-III-R Definition of "Mental Disorder"

The above eight criteria each represent single conceptual units individually attempting to delineate psychopathology. This last definition is more comprehensive in that it aggregates across some of these individual criteria. DSM-III-R (APA, 1987) acknowledged the many difficulties involved in providing a working definition of mental disorder, but nevertheless offered a definition that influenced decision making regarding what should and should not be included in the manual. This definition conceptualizes mental disorder as a "clinically significant behavioral or psychological syndrome" that is associated with distress or disability or an increased risk of suffering death, pain, disability, or an important loss of freedom. This syndrome must not be a response that is expected to a specific event such as death of a relative. It must also be considered a "manifestation of a behavioral, psychological, or biological dysfunction in the person." Finally, conflicts that are primarily between the individual and society are not seen as disorders unless they are a symptom of "a dysfunction in the person, as described above" (DSM-III-R, p. xxii).

Breaking down this definition, criminal behavior must first be viewed as "clinically significant," and second as representing a "behavioral or psychological syndrome." An immediate problem with this definition is that, as with many other such definitions, it does not specify what precisely constitutes "clinically significant" or what is really meant by "behavioral or psychological syndrome." Comparisons with disorders already listed in DSM-III-R (which presumably fit this definition moderately well) can nevertheless guide a decision as to the extent to which criminal behavior meets this definition.

Regarding clinical significance, caffeine-induced organic mental disorder can be diagnosed if an individual drinks the equivalent of two cups of coffee a day and experiences any 5 out of a possible 12 signs, including restlessness, disturbed sleep, nervousness, excitement, and increased energy. In comparison to this listed disorder, criminal behavior would seem to be clinically significant in that it constitutes a behavior which has major implications for the individual and others in society. While caffeine-induced mental disorder is perhaps an extreme example of a disorder whose clinical significance is not great, there are many other disorders listed in DSM-III-R (e.g., histrionic personality disorder, dependent personality disorder) that are no more clinically significant than criminality and that indeed may have less clinical significance.

Crime is clearly behavioral in nature and as such the first part of the next descriptor, representing a "behavioral or psychological syndrome or pattern," is in keeping with criminal behavior. Assessing whether crime represents a "syndrome" is an important and complex issue, and consequently a detailed analysis is required, particularly since it also broaches the issue of categorical versus dimensional conceptualizations of mental disorder. The central issue concerns how one defines a "syndrome" and whether such a classic definition of syndrome fits existing disorders cited in DSM-III-R.

A syndrome is usually viewed as a cluster of signs or symptoms that occur together (Wingate, 1976); for example, if an individual suffers from thought disorder, hallucinations, delusions, catatonic behavior, and flat affect, then these would be signs and symptoms that would delineate the disorder of schizophrenia. Criminal behavior would similarly be viewed as a syndrome if it is made up of a number of symptoms that occur together, for example, the individual steals, is assaultive, uses illegal drugs, and commits sex offenses. Criminal behavior is very heterogeneous, however. Although many criminals take part in many types of criminal activities and while pure "specialization" in a specific crime or delinquent act is rare (Klein, 1984; Hindelang, 1971; Petersilia, 1980; Stattin & Magnusson, 1991), a large proportion would not be expected to steal *and* be assaultive *and* possess illegal drugs *and* commit sex offenses.

On the other hand, few disorders outlined in DSM-III-R meet the classical example of a syndrome. Many nonclinicians might believe that a disorder like schizophrenia is very homogeneous and is defined by the cluster of traits outlined above. The reality is that schizophrenia is almost as heterogeneous a concept as criminal behavior, and few possess all the symptoms outlined above. For example, an individual could receive a DSM-III-R diagnosis for schizophrenia if he or she showed evidence of a single delusion for 1 week (with evidence of the delusion covering a 6-month period) together with some impairment in social functioning (APA, 1987). Hallucinations, thought disorder, flat affect, and catatonia could all be absent. Similarly, many other disorders in DSM-III-R do not represent syndromes in the classical sense.

Not only are many mental disorders heterogeneous, they are also not clearly defined as a category in the usual sense. DSM-III-R endorses this view in stating that "there is no assumption that each mental disorder is a discrete entity with sharp boundaries (discontinuity) between it and other mental disorders, or between it and no mental disorder" (p. xii; APA, 1987), and this suggests that they do not refer to "syndrome" in the way it has been traditionally used in the early psychiatric literature. This may explain the addition of the word *pattern* to the definition, which may be more consistent with the prototypic categorization model that is increasingly influential in the field (Mezzich, 1989). Under the prototypic model, individuals are assessed in terms of the extent to which they resemble the prototype of the category. Under this model no exact set or cluster of symptoms defines a disorder. An example of this prototypic categorization would be conduct disorder in which an individual must show any 3 of 13 different signs. Similarly, schizotypal personality disorder requires any five of a possible nine features for a diagnosis to be given. Under this prototypic approach, two individuals who are both diagnosed as having the same disorder can differ radically with respect to presenting symptoms and possibly with respect to etiology. In the case of schizotypal personality disorder, for example, two individuals diagnosed with this disorder may have only one of the nine schizotypal traits in common. Furthermore, two individuals could differ greatly in terms of the *degree* to which they meet the disorder; one subject may have all nine schizotypal features while another may have only five. In this sense the prototypic approach more closely approximates a dimensional model of mental disorder than the classic categorical model. Prototypic classification is currently represented in DSM-III-R and is likely to be increasingly used in DSM-IV (Frances *et al.*, 1990).

Criminal behavior most easily fits this prototypic approach to disorder. Criminals do differ to some extent with respect to which criminal activities they engage in, but most engage in a range of criminal activities rather than in one in particular. The more dimensional approach to disorder embodied in the prototypic approach is also more in keeping with the view that crime is a disorder in that individuals are not clearly criminals or noncriminals, but rather that individuals in society differ in the degree and extent to which they engage in criminal behavior. To the extent that DSM-III-R views "patterns" in the context of prototypic models of classification rather than in the classical medical sense, criminal behavior fits this definition as easily as schizotypal personality disorder or schizophrenia. To the extent that one defines "syndrome" in the classical sense, there is currently no convincing evidence that criminal behavior meets this definition, but by the same token many established mental disorders also do not meet such a definition. It should be noted that while there is no convincing evidence that criminal behavior can be currently defined as a syndrome in the classical sense, this does not rule out the possibility that it could meet such a definition, since no previous study appears to have assessed this possibility empirically. Factor analytic and cluster analytic studies of criminal populations represent ways in which this issue could be addressed empirically.

Returning to the third aspect of DSM-III-R's definition of mental disorder, criminal behavior must be associated with distress *or* disability *or* an increased risk of suffering death, pain, disability, *or* an important loss of freedom. Crime would fit this aspect of the definition since it clearly increases the risk of an important loss of freedom (i.e., imprisonment). Criminals have also been found to be more prone to physical injury than noncriminals (see Section II on head injury in Chapter 8). Crime is also associated with disability as was described previously in the context of impaired functioning, and it produces considerable distress in others.

The fourth component of the definition requires that the behavior is not an expected response to a particular event, such as a death in the family. Criminal behavior would seem to meet this component, which is intended to rule out (inter alia) depression due to bereavement.

The fifth component stipulates that the behavior must be a manifestation of a behavioral, psychological, or biological dysfunction in the person. Evidence supporting the presence of biological dysfunction in criminals is presented in the subsequent chapters on psychophysiology, biochemistry, neuropsychology, and brain imaging. Evidence for psychological dysfunction is presented in later chapters dealing with cognitive and learning deficits, and social, familial, and extrafamilial social dysfunction are also outlined in later chapters.

Finally, conflicts that are primarily between the individual and society are not seen as disorders *unless* they are a symptom of "a dysfunction in the person, as described above." Criminal behavior can be construed as a conflict between the individual and society, but it would constitute a disorder if it is an outgrowth of biological, psychological, or behavioral dysfunction within the individual. The evidence to support the presence of such dysfunction within the individual is reviewed in later chapters.

Considering DSM-III-R's definition as a whole, criminal behavior meets the various components if one accepts (1) the evidence for biological and psychological differences observed in criminals presented in later chapters, and (2) the modern prototypic approach to classification and diagnosis. Rejection of the first assumption effectively refutes the position that criminal behavior can be viewed as a psychopathology. Rejection of the second assumption leads to the rejection of illnesses such as schizophrenia as a mental disorder. While the DSM-III-R definition is authoritative and relatively comprehensive conceptually, it suffers from the usual limitation that key terms (dysfunction, syndrome) are not defined. Alternatively, there have been few clear definitions of precisely what constitutes a dysfunction, presumably because it is a concept that can be measured well in dimensional terms but poorly in categorical terms. A second important limitation is that it is stipulated that dysfunction must arise *within* the individual. This would appear to minimize the role of external social and environmental factors as causal agents and is not consistent with current views on the etiology of some mental disorders. As will be argued later, there is considerable evidence that social and environmental factors play an important role in contributing to criminal behavior, just as they do for many other disorders.

TABLE 1   Extent to Which Criminal Behavior and Three Other Recognized Disorders Meet Criteria for Disorder

	Crime	Schizotypal personality	Schizophrenia	Caffeine intoxication
Statistical	Moderate	Moderate	Good	Poor
Ideal health	Good	Good	Good	Poor
Deviation from social norm	Good	Moderate	Good	Poor
Distress/suffering	Moderate	Poor	Good	Moderate
Seek treatment	Poor	Poor	Moderate	Poor
Impaired functioning	Good	Moderate	Good	Poor
Listing in DSM-III-R	Good	Good	Good	Good
Biological functioning	Moderate	Moderate	Good	Poor
Definition: DSM-III-R	Good	Good	Good	Poor

III. OVERVIEW OF DEFINITIONS AND THEIR FIT TO CRIMINAL BEHAVIOR

These nine attempts to define disorder vary in their completeness, face validity, and practical utility. The first eight represent more or less single faces of a multifaceted concept, while the ninth draws on several of these single features to obtain a more complete definition.

To provide a general overview of the conclusions drawn from the preceding analysis, Table 1 lists these nine criteria and the extent to which criminal behavior meets them. Because there are no precise definitions of these criteria (e.g., how infrequent is statistically infrequent?) no precise assignments can be given to fit, and as such it must be emphasized that this table is best viewed as *illustrative* rather than definitive. Fit of each criteria to criminal behavior is assessed as "good," "bad," or "moderate."

Criminal behavior does not fit the seeking treatment criterion. It partly meets three other criteria (statistical infrequency, distress/suffering, and biological functioning) and is a good fit for five others (ideal health, deviation from social norm, impaired functioning, listing in DSM-III-R, and definition in DSM-III-R).

To provide some comparisons, Table 1 also provides fit assessments for schizotypal personality disorder, schizophrenia, and caffeine intoxication. Schizotypal personality disorder is chosen as one comparison because it represents a nontrivial Axis II disorder and is a relatively recent addition to DSM-III-R (APA, 1980). Schizophrenia is chosen because it is an Axis I disorder which is a classic illustration of an established, debilitating mental disorder. Caffeine intoxication is chosen because it is a relatively nonserious, ubiquitous condition which may help establish a base level for what may be viewed as a disorder.

Schizotypal personality disorder only partly meets the statistical infrequency criterion because its base rate in the population is approximately 6 to 10% (Baron & Risch, 1987; Meehl, 1989). Schizotypals are not, however, in a state of ideal mental health given their unusual perceptual experiences, ideas of reference, and magical thinking. Schizotypals are odd and eccentric, but they do not break social norms in a major way and are largely accepted in society because they tend to keep to themselves and avoid social contact; they only partly meet the criterion of deviation from social norm. Schizotypals rarely if ever seek help for their condition largely because they have only partial insight into their peculiarities, partly because of their discomfort in social interactions and also because they are not unduly troubled by their disorder. Schizotypals are relatively functioning and only moderately impaired (APA, 1987), and currently evidence for impaired biological functioning is much less than for either schizophrenia or crime (although see Siever, Coursey, Alterman, Buchsbaum, & Murphy, 1984; Lencz, Raine, Scerbo, Holt, Bird, Redmon, & Brodish, 1993).

In contrast, schizophrenia meets all of the criteria well, with the one exception that many paranoid schizophrenics are unlikely to receive treatment. As with any disorder, it must be remembered that there will always be some schizophrenics who as individuals meet these criteria less well, who are much less impaired, who are able to function acceptably well in the community, and indeed who do not come to medical attention.

Those with caffeine intoxication may suffer some degree of distress/suffering, and it is a disorder listed in DSM-III-R, but otherwise they tend not to meet these criteria. Hughes, Higgins, Bickel, Hunt, Fenwick, Gulliver, and Mireault (1991) found caffeine withdrawal symptoms in about 50% of those who drank more than two cups of coffee per day; since 89% of the American population regularly drink coffee or tea daily (Gilbert, 1976), one would expect lifetime risk for this disorder not to be statistically infrequent. The disorder is not severe enough to warrant clinical attention and the degree of distress associated with it is minimal (APA, 1987). It is not viewed as a deviant act, and it does not meet the definition given in DSM-III-R because there is currently little evidence that it stems from a behavioral, biological, or psychological dysfunction within the individual.

If one compares criminal behavior to these three disorders, it does not meet criteria as well as schizophrenia. On the other hand, it meets criteria slightly better than schizotypal personality disorder and considerably better than caffeine intoxication. Again, this analysis is subjective and can only be illustrative of the lines of reasoning outlined earlier in this chapter. It does however illustrate that there are at least some grounds to believe that criminal behavior meets these criteria for disorder at least as well as some other disorders.

IV. CONSTRUCT VALIDITY APPROACH
TO PSYCHOPATHOLOGY

Assessing the extent to which criminal behavior fits proposed definitions of mental disorder is one way of evaluating whether criminal behavior may be a psychopathology. If one cannot agree on a suitable definition, however, one can never unequivocally demonstrate that any particular behavioral or psychological profile does or does not represent a psychopathology. A second approach that can help address this issue and that is gaining increasing importance in the development of DSM-IV is that of empirical validation (Carson, 1991; Frances *et al.*, 1990; Frances *et al.*, 1991; Morey, 1991; Widiger *et al.*, 1991).

Many critics of DSM-III-R have reiterated the issue that there has been an overemphasis on expert opinion and issues of reliability at the expense of construct validity (Blashfield & Livesley, 1991; Millon, 1991; Carson, 1991). For example, Carson (1991) states "there has been and seemingly remains an unaccountable neglect of specifically directed efforts to establish networks or correlated variables that in the aggregate affirm and support the concept to which any proposed diagnosis must be presumed to refer" (p. 306). The argument in favor of a construct validity approach to psychiatric classification lies in the fact that named disorders are constructs in much the same way as IQ or personality dimensions, and as such they are essentially hypothetical constructions. This argument applies much less to those medical disorders where the etiology is known. In the absence of a known etiology, one way to establish the validity of a mental disorder is to establish a "nomological network" of relationships between it and other constructs and observable behavior (Chronbach & Meehl, 1955). To the extent that this can be achieved, the measure of behavior in question could be said to have construct validity.

This approach is certainly not new. An influential paper by Robins and Guze (1970) suggested essentially the same approach, but used the term *diagnostic validity* as opposed to construct validity. This approach is, however, being increasingly used in classification in mental disorders and seems likely to play an even greater role in the future. For example, a major emphasis in the preparation of DSM-IV has been the systematic reviews of the research literature in addition to data analyses and field trials in order to provide rationale and support for current and proposed disorders (Frances *et al.* 1991; Widiger *et al.*, 1991).

Traditionally, the diagnostic validity approach in psychiatry and psychology has emphasized data from family and genetic studies, biological studies, response to drug treatment and course of illness, and psychological test data (Robins & Guze, 1970; Frances *et al.*, 1991). While genetic and biological data are clearly important elements of such validation, it is equally clear that social, environmental, and cultural data are just as integral in any modern-day analysis of the construct validity of a mental disorder.

The remainder of this book will attempt to assess the empirical evidence for the notion that criminals differ from noncriminals on a range of biological and social factors. The extent to which this can be achieved will indicate the extent to which there is some construct validity for viewing criminal behavior as a psychopathology. This empirical level of analysis cannot be divorced from the foregoing discussion of the ways in which criminal behavior meets a number of criteria for mental disorder. Establishing the biological and social correlates of a construct, in and of itself, cannot establish that construct as a disorder. Constructs such as extraversion and intelligence have relatively well-established nomological networks, but they could not be regarded as disorders because neither even begins to fulfill some of the criteria of mental disorder discussed earlier. If criminal behavior is viewed as meeting some of these criteria *and* if a specific network of biological and social factors can be identified which may be of etiological significance to crime, then this would constitute grounds to consider the possibility that criminal behavior constitutes a psychopathology.

This empirical analysis is also necessary to assess some of the assumptions made earlier regarding meeting criteria for disorder. One assumption or argument was that criminals have impaired functioning in cognitive, neuropsychological, and learning terms. Another claim was that criminals have impaired social, educational, and occupational functioning. Another assumption was that evidence exists for biological dysfunction. Some of the following chapters will attempt to support these claims. If these claims cannot be supported, this would effectively disprove the notion that crime can be viewed as a disorder.

Independent of these aims, one particular function of some of the following chapters will be to draw attention to recent biological research in crime, since this corpus of knowledge tends not to have been recognized as much as it might be by other researchers of criminal behavior. Such biological research cannot be viewed in isolation of other important psychological and social knowledge, however, and as such chapters dealing with this knowledge will also be presented. Wherever possible, links will be drawn between biological, psychological, and social phenomena because the author's conviction is that true progress into our understanding of criminal behavior is crucially dependent on a multiperspective approach. Such links will be necessarily more speculative and rest on thinner ice than unidisciplinary perspectives because there has been very little true biosocial research into criminal behavior to date. While most of these chapters will be empirically based, one which underpins biological, psychological, social, and sociocultural research will be largely conceptual in nature. The next chapter concerns the important question of how criminal behavior could have evolved.

V. SUMMARY

This chapter attempts to assess the extent to which crime (particularly re-peated criminal offending encapsulating a large proportion of all crime) may be viewed as a disorder by assessing the extent to which it fits various concep-tions of psychopathology. Most individual criteria of what constitutes psy-chopathology have significant weaknesses, but when combined together they help describe a gestalt picture of psychopathology against which criminality may be viewed. Nine criteria and their fit to crime can be identified as follows: (1) Crime represents some deviation from the statistical norm, although not all criminality can be viewed as statistically deviant; (2) criminality represents deviation from ideal mental health because criminals cannot be characterized as being in a state of mental and social well-being; (3) deviation from the social norm is a criterion clearly met by criminality because crime is socially unac-ceptable; (4) criminals create distress and suffering to others; while criminals may suffer from considerable distress and have experienced significant suffer-ing, they do not generally express this; (5) seeking out treatment is one crite-rion that does not characterize criminals; (6) criminals have impairments in social, occupational, behavioral, educational, and cognitive functioning; (7) different forms of criminal behavior are extensively listed throughout DSM-III-R; (8) a variety of biological dysfunctions are thought to characterize crim-inality; (9) criminality meets the definition of disorder outlined in DSM-III-R. A comparative analysis between criminality and other disorders listed in DSM-III-R suggests that there are grounds to believe that criminality meets these criteria as well as many other disorders. The construct validity approach to psychopathology represents a second approach to assessing crime as a disorder; if a clear nomological network of social, cognitive, biological, and genetic relationships can be established around criminality, and if criminality can be viewed as meeting some of the criteria above, then these two ap-proaches would together raise the possibility that criminality is a disorder. It is argued that criminality does indeed meet many of the criteria for assessing psychopathology, and the following chapters help establish initial empirical validity for the view that criminality is a disorder.

2 Crime in the Context of Evolution

I. INTRODUCTION

Superficially, viewing criminal behavior in an evolutionary perspective seems misplaced. Evolutionary theory has been classically applied to the study of species development and tracing human roots in the wider context of the animal kingdom. Anatomical structures and physiological processes (rather than social behavior) have in the past been the focus of evolutionary theory. Yet one of the key concepts in evolutionary theory is that of "adaptation." To the extent that new anatomical/physiological processes produced through random genetic mutations contribute to an organism's ability to adapt, survive, and reproduce, they will be better represented in the next gene pool and as such will "evolve." By the same token, new *behaviors* evolve to the extent that they confer a selective advantage to those individuals who produce them. Sociobiology, defined by Wilson (1975) as "the systematic study of the biological basis of all social behavior," has explored more closely the evolutionary significance of animal and human social behavior. Yet how can criminal behavior, which appears so *maladaptive* to modern-day man, be viewed in such an evolutionary perspective as an *adaptive* behavioral trait?

The main aim of this chapter is to provide an answer to this question by explaining how criminal behavior can indeed be viewed in an evolutionary perspective; at least in early human history, it is argued that criminal behavior did indeed have adaptive significance. A second important aim is to demonstrate that just as there have been evolutionary pressures for the development of antisocial behavior, there have also been parallel evolutionary pressures favoring the development of behaviors and emotions to oppose such antisocial behavior, a theme which will be returned to in the last chapter of this book.

At the outset it should be noted that the fact that a behavior or structure is no longer adaptive or is no longer currently evolving does not invalidate its evolutionary significance (Crawford, 1987). Furthermore, in early human history there was no police and court system to clearly delineate what we now term "criminal" behavior. Nevertheless, most of the fundamental antisocial behaviors which make up what we now call crime, such as theft, robbery, assault, rape, and murder, do have their analogues in early history, and this behavioral "antisociality" will provide the focus for this chapter.

We will begin with a discussion of the dilemma of whether one should cooperate or cheat, illustrated by the "prisoners' dilemma" developed from games theory and followed by an example of the comparative success of the grudging "Tit-for-Tat" strategy. The question of how cheating can succeed in this context as an evolutionary stable strategy is then outlined, together with the development of subtle cheats and the consequent strategies to counteract subtle cheats. The application of this games theory approach to cheating antisocial behavior is then illustrated in the context of anthropological studies of societies that typify the cheating strategy versus the reciprocal altruist approach, while recent analyses of the sociobiological bases to crime are outlined in the context of two serious forms of antisocial behavior, namely rape and homicide. Finally, evolutionary perspectives on the development of antisocial behavior in humans will be critically evaluated. The key arguments to be made are that (1) criminal behavior in the guise of antisocial, "cheating" behavior has a clear evolutionary basis, and (2) behaviors and emotions have also evolved as a reaction to combat this antisocial cheating strategy. First, however, some specific terms frequently used in sociobiological theory (reproductive fitness, selfishness, kin selection, reciprocal altruism) need to be described.

II. CONCEPTS IN SOCIOBIOLOGICAL THEORY

A. Reproductive Fitness

A detailed elaboration of the sociobiological concepts that will be referred to in this chapter can be found in Wilson (1975). More specifically, seminal discussions of the concepts of kin selection, reciprocal altruism, inclusive fitness, and evolutionary stable strategies may be found in Hamilton (1964), Trivers (1971, 1972), Maynard Smith (1976), and Dawkins (1976, 1989).

An individual's genetic fitness is defined in terms of his or her reproductive success or the number of viable offspring produced. This "fitness," measured in terms of the individual's total genetic representation in the next gene pool, can generally be maximized in one of two ways. The individual either may invest a lot of resources in terms of parental effort in just a few offspring or may maximize number of offspring at the expense of parental effort. A male can successfully adopt this latter reproductive strategy of high offspring–low effort if he "cheats" on female partners by misrepresenting his ability to acquire resources and his long-term parenting intentions. Specific examples of how these reproductive strategies translate into the real world will be outlined later (see Section VII on anthropological studies), but at this point it should be noted that the concept of fitness is central to the evolution of behavior and, as outlined in the next section, it is the driving force behind selfish behavior.

B. Selfishness

A central thesis in Dawkins' innovative and influential book *The Selfish Gene* (Dawkins, 1976; 1989) is that "successful" genes are ruthlessly selfish in their struggle for survival and that they give rise to selfishness in individual behavior. In this perspective, human and animal bodies are merely containers or "survival machines" for armies of ruthless genes. From these machines they plot a merciless campaign of success in the world, where success is defined solely in terms of survival and greater representation in the next gene pool. However, the gene is the basic unit of selfishness rather than the individual (or the group or the species). The individual eventually dies, but selfish genes are passed on from body to body, from generation to generation, and potentially from millenium to millenium.

Inevitably, the selfish gene is responsible for a considerable degree of selfish behavior in the animal world. Blackheaded gulls nesting in colonies will eat one another's chicks when the parents' backs are turned. The female preying mantis devours the male that she mated with immediately after copulation. Emperor penguins in the Antarctic occasionally push each other into the sea in order to check whether a nearby seal is waiting to devour them (Dawkins, 1989). At a less extreme level, birds will readily steal food from one another if given the chance. This selfish, antisocial, and sometimes aggressive behavior has evolved because such behavior confers a selective advantage to the individual in terms of reproductive fitness. Genes responsible for such selfish, antisocial behavior are more likely to proliferate. Certainly in the animal world it is easy to see how antisocial and aggressive behavior has evolved.

C. Kin Selection

At a superficial level it would appear that one quantitative difference between humans and animals is the human capacity for social cooperation, altruism, and selflessness. Yet the human world is not devoid of aggression and anti-social acts, while the animal world is not without heroic acts of apparent unbounded altruism. Indeed, striking examples of altruism in both animals and humans are not easily accounted for by Darwin's concept of "survival of the fittest" (Darwin, 1859), which so readily explains selfish, antisocial behavior. Honeybees sting intruders and give up their lives for the benefit of the hive. Many small birds give alarm calls when a predator is sighted, thereby risking their own lives by attracting the attention of the predator but potentially saving the lives of others in the flock. Vampire bats that have fed on blood at night will on occasion regurgitate blood to feed less successful hungry vampires (Wilkinson, 1984). If genes are truly selfish, why do they endanger themselves for the benefit of others?

Part of the answer to this enigma was developed by Hamilton (1964) in his account of kin selection. Hamilton's argument is that kin selection can account for altruistic acts toward those who are genetically related to the do-gooder. It would "pay" an individual (in terms of reproductive fitness) to die if in doing so a number of close relatives would live and reproduce. This is because the gene(s) responsible for such altruistic behavior are also likely to reside in the bodies of close relatives. Sacrificing oneself to save four siblings would pay handsomely in terms of gene survival; since the genetic relatedness of siblings averages 50%, two genes would be saved for the price of one. Such behaviors are therefore selected for (and would evolve) because they benefit the performer's kin. Such kin selection accounts for, among other things, the high degree of altruism and self-sacrifice shown by parents to offspring in both animals and humans.

Kin selection does not, however, explain why a human may dive into a river to save a drowning stranger, why a vampire bat should feed a nonrelative, or why birds should give warning calls to help nonrelatives. The answer to this puzzle lies in the concept of reciprocal altruism.

D. Reciprocal Altruism

Trivers (1971) argued that such cases of "true" altruism can evolve because in the long run they actually benefit the performer. It pays the individual to help save a stranger if the stranger will reciprocate this help in the future and save the life of the altruist. This assumes that the cost/benefit ratio is appropriate (i.e., that future benefits outweigh immediate costs in the currency of reproductive fitness), that individuals are capable of recognizing each other in the future, and that they are likely to meet again. Vampire bats who share blood typically tend to roost together, and it has been experimentally demonstrated that vampire bats only give blood to bats that they know and recognize (Wilkinson, 1984). Kin selection and reciprocal altruism therefore can be viewed as strategies for a gene to achieve its selfish goals.

The importance of the concept of reciprocal altruism for the understanding of the evolutionary basis to antisocial behavior lies in the fact that this strategy can itself give rise to "cheating," that is, acceptance of acts of altruism from others but failing to reciprocate in the future. Cleaning symbiosis exists among ocean fish in which small "cleaner" fish enter the mouths of the larger "host" fish and clean their teeth and gills of harmful parasites (Maynard, 1968). A continued relationship benefits both fish, and such continued mutual benefits largely explain why the host fish does not make a meal out of its cleaner after having been cleaned of parasites. However, "cheating" by the host fish does take place, as revealed by stomach analyses of these fish (Trivers, 1971). In this example cheating is reflected in direct aggression, but it is important to note that cheating may also consist of the failure to reciprocate altruistic behavior in a relationship where this is expected. In any event, the individual is often placed in a dilemma regarding whether to cooperate or whether to cheat. Somewhat appropriately for an analysis of criminal behavior, the dilemma of whether to cooperate or cheat is nicely illustrated in a game called the "prisoners' dilemma."

III. THE PRISONERS' DILEMMA

Two prisoners, Capone and Clyde, are being held on suspicion of a bank robbery in which one of the bank employees was hit over the head with a baseball bat and subsequently died. They are each held in a separate cell and cannot communicate with each other. The police have no solid evidence to convict either Capone or Clyde of the robbery and murder, though they have good evidence to implicate them in the lesser offense of tax evasion. The authorities are therefore dependent on testimony from one or both prisoners implicating the other in the hold-up and murder. Each prisoner is therefore individually persuaded to betray his partner in crime. Both Capone and Clyde have a prior agreement never to squeal on one another, that is, to remain silent, but their partnership has been a precarious one and neither really trusts the other.

Here's the "deal" that Capone is presented with by the police. If Capone testifies that it was Clyde who killed the bank teller with the baseball bat

TABLE 1   Payoffs in Terms of Prison Sentence for
Capone in the Prisoners' Dilemma[a]

	What Clyde does	
What Capone does	Cooperate (silent)	Cheat (testify)
Cooperate (stay silent)	5 years	30 years
Cheat (testify)	0 years	10 years

[a]Payoffs for Clyde are identical to those for Capone.

(i.e., if he defects, or "cheats" on Clyde), and if this story is rendered plausible by the fact that Clyde remains silent, all charges will be dropped against Capone including those relating to tax evasion and he walks out a free man, while Clyde gets 30 years. On the other hand, if both testify against each other (both cheat), both are convicted but only get 10 years each in prison because both testified. If both stick by their prior agreement and remain silent ("cooperate" with each other), they will both be convicted for the lesser offense of tax evasion (5 years each) and will escape the more severe penalty for the murder. If Capone remains silent (cooperates with Clyde) but Clyde squeals, Capone gets 30 years while Clyde walks out a free man. A mirror deal is also presented to Clyde. These differential payoffs for Capone are diagrammatically presented in Table 1. The payoffs for Clyde are identical to Capone's.

The best solution from the joint standpoint of the Capone/Clyde partnership would be for them both to stay silent and "cooperate" with one another. In this case both would receive only a light (5-year) sentence which, with good behavior and parole, would not be too devastating. The problem is that they cannot communicate with each other and therefore cannot cement their prior agreement to both stay silent. Cognizant of each other's true colors, both are worried that the other will squeal. Under these circumstances, the only rational choice for Capone is to cheat (and perhaps as a notorious gangster, such a decision would come quite easily). The logic here is that no matter what Clyde does, cheating is *always* the best response for Capone. If Clyde cooperates, Capone's cheat response gets him off scott free, which is better than cooperating (Capone would then get 5 years). If Clyde cheats, then Capone's cheat response gives Capone 10 years, which is much better than the 30 years he would get if he played "cooperate" to Clyde's cheat. Rationally, Clyde will come to the same conclusion, and the gangsters will each receive 10 years. Yet if they could communicate and cement their agreement to cooperate, they could both get off with the lighter sentence of 5 years. Cheating is always the best strategy, but mutual cooperation produces the best payoff. Hence the dilemma.

TABLE 2   Payoffs to Suckers and Cheats[a]

	Sucker	Cheat	
Sucker	1	−4	(payoffs to Sucker)
Cheat	4	−1	(payoffs to Cheat)

[a]Reproductive fitness (in arbitrary units) to Sucker (top line) and Cheat (bottom line) as a function of four possible interactions, where the cost of giving = 3, the benefit of receiving = 5, and the cost of time spent in interaction = 1.

This example from games theory highlights the problem of achieving mutual cooperation among individuals and raises the important question of how altruism and cooperation could evolve in an asocial, selfish world. As Axelrod and Hamilton (1981) point out, cheating is not just a viable solution in the prisoners' dilemma game, but it also represents a successful evolutionary stable strategy, at least where individuals only meet once (i.e., play one game).

IV. SUCKERS, CHEATS, AND GRUDGERS

The situation is very different, however, if one assumes that two individuals within a population interact repeatedly (i.e., play several games with each other) and can remember individuals and the outcome of the last game or encounter. Dawkins (1976), working within the context of games theory, compared the relative success of two strategies which he called "Sucker" and "Cheat." Although Dawkins did not assign costs and benefits to each strategy (they are essentially irrelevant as long as the costs of giving are lower than the benefits of receiving), a simple matrix will be constructed to help illustrate the process; this is shown in Table 2. Suckers always help whoever they interact with and give away "resources" at a cost of 3 units, units which can be equated with reproductive fitness or offspring which are worth 5 units to the recipient. They also lose 1 unit in spending time in the encounter, with a total loss of 4 units. Cheats always take resources when they are offered but never give anything away, except that they lose 1 unit due to time spent in the encounter. Suckers do well when they meet another Sucker because they both benefit from mutual cooperation in much the same way as the joint "cooperate" strategy would work in the prisoners' dilemma; while they each lose a total of 4 units, they gain 5, resulting in a net gain of 1 unit. Cheats do poorly when they meet another Cheat because neither gains anything and both lose 1 unit due to time spent in interacting. Cheats do well when they meet a Sucker, because they receive 5 units and lose 1 for time spent (net gain of 4 units). By the same token Suckers fare badly when they meet a Cheat (loss of 4). These payoffs and strategies are similar to those in the earlier game of prisoners' dilemma, but in this game there are repeated encounters or games and each individual makes the same response across all encounters.

In a population made up of all Suckers it is easy to see how a mutant Cheat will be successful, as all its encounters are with Suckers and are hence highly profitable (repeated net gains of 4 units each). When the population is split 50–50, Cheats still do better than Suckers, and they continue to do better than Suckers even when Cheats make up 90% and more of the population. As in the single game of prisoners' dilemma, cheating becomes a successful strategy.

The population outcome became radically different, however, when Dawkins added a third strategy which he termed "Grudger." Grudgers are like Suckers in that they give resources on a first encounter, but if their partner "cheats" on them and fails to reciprocate, they bear a grudge and do not give resources the next time they meet that individual cheat. Dawkins (1976) ran a computer simulation in which the population starts off with a large majority of Suckers and equal-sized minorities of Cheats and Grudgers. Initially, Cheats do extremely well as they take full advantage of all encounters with Suckers and with their initial encounters with Grudgers. Suckers are driven to extinction while the population of Cheats peaks and the number of Grudgers slowly declines. Cheats then begin to do poorly; not only do they fare poorly when they meet one another, but they also get nothing out of Grudgers who have by now been exploited by Cheats in previous encounters and, wiser for the encounter, bear a grudge on future encounters and withhold resources. Grudgers do well when they meet each other, however, and their population steadily increases while Cheats are driven to low levels for a long time until they reach ultimate extinction. In this simulation, therefore, the Grudger proves to be an "evolutionary stable strategy" (i.e., a strategy which, if adopted by the majority of the population, cannot be bettered by alternative strategies).

A similar conclusion was reached when Axelrod and Hamilton (1981) ran a computer tournament for the prisoners' dilemma game in which economists, mathematicians, political scientists, and sociologists submitted computerized strategies. Fifteen strategies competed with each other in games of prisoners' dilemma where each game lasted 200 moves. Although a number of very complex strategies were submitted, the strategy which ended up with the highest number of points was a very simple strategy called "Tit for Tat," which cooperated on the first move of the game and then simply copied the last move of the opponent.

Axelrod then ran a second competition in which 62 entries were received from six countries—again, Tit for Tat proved to be the winning strategy (Axelrod & Hamilton, 1981). Tit for Tat is a similar strategy to that of the Grudger but is more forgiving in that it has a short memory for cheating acts and will forgive a one-time cheat who turns over a new leaf and behaves altruistically. For example, if a one-time cheat turns over a new leaf and gives resources in a later interaction, Tit for Tat will reciprocate this gesture on its next encounter with the reformed cheat. Grudgers have excellent memories however and never forgive an initial cheat response. Axelrod and Hamilton (1981) were further able to demonstrate that cooperation, in the form of a Tit-for-Tat strategy, could be modeled on the concept of an evolutionary stable strategy within the context of the prisoners' dilemma game, showing that it can evolve in an asocial, noncooperative world and can resist invasion from other strategies.

V. THE SURVIVAL OF CHEATS

What does this tell us about the evolution of antisocial behavior? From a traditional perspective these computer simulations emphasize how *prosocial*, not antisocial, behavior develops. From another viewpoint a different picture emerges.

First, Dawkins (1989) points out that Tit for Tat is not strictly an evolutionary stable strategy (ESS) because it can be invaded by a strategy like Sucker which, in a population entirely made up of Tit for Tats, looks and operates entirely like Tit for Tats. Once the proportion of Suckers is high enough, antisocial strategies like Cheat can evolve and get a foothold since they do well against Suckers. Consequently, cheating can to some extent become a successful strategy under these circumstances. Second, Boyd and Lorberbaum (1987) also demonstrated that a "mildly antisocial" version of Tit for Tat (namely Suspicious Tit for Tat) that cheats on the very first encounter before settling on a Tit-for-Tat strategy can invade a Tit-for-Tat population under certain circumstances.

Both of these situations can help model serious and mild forms of antisocial behavior, respectively. Suspicious Tit for Tat at least superficially appears like many people in society, that is, essentially prosocial but with an occasional streak of antisociality. Cheats clearly model the more recidivistic antisocial elements of society, while Suckers model the more genuinely giving, saintly members of society. In many senses, these response strategies are conceptually not too far removed from the real world.

Turning back to Dawkins' (1976) computer simulation of Grudgers, Cheats, and Suckers, it will be remembered that Cheats are eventually driven to extinction. Isn't this a model which demonstrates that antisocial behavior *cannot* evolve as a viable strategy? One important assumption of the model is that individuals are contained within a local environment in which they move around and interact, but only with one another. This assumption is effectively the downfall of the Cheat. Remember that Cheats are driven to extinction because they can no longer get away with one-time "rip offs" of the Grudger who gives once but then withholds assistance on the second meeting. If, on the other hand, Cheats could migrate from one population of Grudgers to another, they could leave the first population when the going gets hot, after they have been recognized by most Grudgers, and then proceed to fleece a new population of Grudgers. Since Suckers can also evolve and succeed happily in populations of Grudgers (the strategies are indistinguishable when played out against each other), these would also provide some rich pickings for Cheats. It is easy to see in this analysis therefore how a small minority of antisocial Cheats could survive strategies such as Grudger and Tit for Tat. The proportion of Cheats within any population would have to stay relatively small—Cheats lose out when they meet one another—but otherwise Cheats can survive, as long as they are prepared to move.

Such a scenario would lead to the prediction that these hard-core antisocials are endowed with wanderlust and drift from population to population. Consistent with this prediction, the modern-day psychopath (or antisocial personality) has been characterized among other things as an impulsive, sensation-seeking individual who fails to follow any life plan and may aimlessly drift from person to person, job to job, and town to town (Cleckley, 1982). Probably the best assessment tool for psychopathy, the Psychopathy Checklist (Hare, 1980, 1985), makes reference to the psychopath's short-term plans and goals, nomadic existence, frequent breaking off of relationships, moving from one place to another, frequent changes of jobs and addresses, itchy feet, and parasitic lifestyle. The "pure" Cheat strategy, therefore, would be consistent with psychopaths and partial psychopaths who manifest a nomadic lifestyle.

In this sense, therefore, models of altruistic and cooperative behavior can also help explain the evolution of antisocial behavior. Furthermore, it also must not be forgotten that cheating itself represents a primeval state which is evolutionary stable since a population consisting largely of Cheats is not easily invaded by Grudgers and Suckers (Dawkins, 1976; Axelrod & Hamilton, 1981). Indeed, mutual cooperation or Tit for Tat will only develop under certain circumstances, for example, where closely related individuals can develop altruism among their kin folk (genetic kinship theory). Given different environmental circumstances, whole populations of Cheats could evolve, a prospect which we will return to shortly.

Even without resorting to this level of analysis, it is clear that cheating can and does take place even when mutual cooperation is the norm. Fischer (1980) describes the case of the sea bass fish which is hermaphrodite, with individuals of a monogamous pair taking turns to provide the eggs (high-investment female) or the sperm (low-investment male). While it is easier and therefore more desirable to play the male role, pairs tend to alternate roles fairly strictly. This provides a good example of cooperation, but it is nevertheless true that some sea bass "cheat" and refuse to take their turn at playing this role (Fischer, 1980). This cheating in turn tends to prompt a Tit for Tat retaliation, leading to the break-up of the pair. The key point however is that cng can to some extent become a successful strategy under these circumstances. Second, Boyd and Lorberbaum (1987) also demonstrated that a "mildly antisocial" version of Tit for Tat (namely Suspicious Tit for Tat) that cheats on the very first encounter before settling on a Tit-for-Tat strategy can invade a Tit-for-Tat population under certain circumstances.

VI. SUBTLE CHEATS

The foregoing analyses have largely dealt with overt cheats who are easily recognized by Grudgers and Tit for Tats. Trivers (1971), in his analysis of reciprocal altruism, distinguishes these "gross" forms of cheating from what he terms "subtle" cheats. Subtle cheats, unlike gross cheats, reciprocate when they receive resources from an altruist, but systematically give back less than they receive. It is easy to see how this can be a profitable strategy. Cheats are easy to detect, but given the difficulty of detecting imbalances in cost/benefit ratios across many encounters with many individuals over a lifespan and estimating whether these are chance imbalances or due to subtle cheating, this latter strategy could potentially be difficult to root out. Even if a subtle cheat was detected, the Tit for Tat reciprocal altruist may be better off maintaining the relationship. Some reciprocal altruism may be better than no altruism at all, and the Tit for Tat may have to switch from one group to another to avoid interacting with the subtle cheater, a switch which may have costs of its own (Trivers, 1971).

Trivers suggests that emotions such as gratitude for receiving and sympathy for those in dire need would be traits which develop to support the system of reciprocal altruism. To the extent that selection will favor the development of subtle cheating, so too will abilities to detect subtle cheating be favored. For example, moralistic aggression and indignation would develop as a strategy to educate the subtle cheater: "Change your ways or I'll have nothing more to do with you." More extremely, Trivers suggests that the Cheat could be exiled, injured, or even killed in order to curb cheating or set an example to others. Conversely, guilt and conscience may develop for a subtle Cheat to show that he is motivated to change his ways. Yet once these genuine traits have developed, selection may favor "mimics" who give the impression of being moralistic, guilty, trustworthy, generous, and friendly in order to continue with their subtle cheating. Although psychopathy and antisocial personality were not terms that Trivers used in this analysis, it is easy to see parallels with these hypothesized characteristics and the pathological lying, smooth talking, manipulativeness, shallow emotions, and frequent verbalizations of remorse and guilt in the absence of any behavioral evidence to support such emotions (Cleckley, 1982; Hare, 1985). The question of whether manifestations of these strategies arise in the real world is the subject of the next section.

VII. ANTHROPOLOGICAL STUDIES

It has been suggested above not only that cheating and subtle cheating can develop as viable strategies *within* a population of altruists, but also that whole populations can develop an antisocial trait or strategy, depending on whether the environmental and local circumstances favor altruism or favor antisociality. Anthropological studies have provided data which lend some degree of support to this proposition. The key strategy of some of these studies has been to compare cultures that differ in their overt levels of antisocial conduct on ecological factors that may give rise to different reproductive strategies and social behaviors. If certain ecological niches can be associated with antisocial behavior, this could provide some support for the notion that antisocial behavior pays in certain environments and that these environments could have led to the development of antisocial behavior in evolutionary terms.

One such model has been developed by Harpending and Draper (1988), who have tried to develop a theoretical framework within which antisocial behavior can make sense in evolutionary terms by comparing the cultures of !Kung Bushmen of the Kalahari desert in Southern Africa with the Mundurucu villagers in the Amazon Basin. There are striking differences in the type of environments that the !Kung and Mundurucu inhabit, and these environments are correlated with altruistic and antisocial behavior, respectively.

The !Kung Bushmen live in a relatively inhospitable desert environment. Because of this inhospitable environment, men need to hunt together and the kill of a wild animal is shared in the camp (Lee & DeVore, 1976). There is a high degree of parental investment in children, who are highly supervised and gradually weaned. Fertility is relatively low, and a disruption of a pair bond by either partner could have fatal consequences for the offspring, who are highly dependent on parental care. This relatively inhospitable environment therefore favors a social framework based on cooperative hunting, sharing of meat, and a nuclear family unit with high investment in a small number of offspring. In turn, the personal characteristics adapted to this environment and lifestyle consist of good hunting skills, reliable reciprocation of altruistic acts, careful mate choosing, and high parental investment in offspring. This "personality" profile is clearly more aligned to altruism than to cheating, antisocial behavior.

In contrast, the Mundurucu are low-intensity tropical gardeners living in a relatively richer ecological niche which allows the women to carry out most of the food production (Murphy & Murphy, 1974). This ecological niche makes for a very different way of life and personality profile in the male. The relatively greater availability of food frees males to engage in male–male competitive interactions centered around talking politics, planning raids and warfare, gossiping, fighting, elaborate male ritual ceremonies and, occasionally, hunting game which will be traded for sex with the village women. In this environment men sleep together in a house separate from the women, whom they hold in disdain. Indeed, females are viewed as sources of pollution and danger. Other types of low-intensity gardeners (e.g., the Gainj tribe in the highlands of New Guinea) also view women as dangerous especially during menstruation and believe that sexual contact is dangerous. In contrast to the !Kung, the Mundurucu mothers provide little care to their infants once they are weaned, and these children must quickly learn to fend for themselves; males play a minimal role in the care of offspring. Personal characteristics of the successful Mundurucu male in this competitive society in consequence consist of good verbal skills for political oratory, fearlessness, skill at fighting and in carrying out raids, bluff and bravado to avoid the risk of battle, and the ability to manipulate and deceive prospective mates concerning the resources he can offer in order to maximize offspring and minimize effort. Furthermore, they should not be gullible, since belief in the folklore regarding the dangers of sex and women as a source of pollution would not foster the passing on of one's genes (Harpending & Draper, 1988). Similarly, successful females living in such a social context of low parental investment are those who can manipulate their men folk by deception over offspring paternity, exaggeration of requirements, and resistance to the development of monogamous bonds (though there is clearly an upper bound to the potential success of this strategy). The Mundurucu's way of life is therefore more clearly associated with a cheating and antisocial strategy than that of reciprocal altruism.

Harpending and Draper (1988) argue, therefore, that the nature of the Mundurucu's social environment favors the expression of what they term the "antisocial trait." Certainly when one considers the fact that the Mundurucu were in the past fierce head hunters who manifested considerable antisocial and aggressive behavior, this appears to be a plausible analysis. What is of particular interest however is that many of the features of the Mundurucu have parallels with some of the features of psychopathic behavior as identified in modern industrialized societies. For example, psychopaths are characterized by a lack of conscience, superficial charm, high verbal skills, promiscuity, and lack of long-term interpersonal bonds (Cleckley, 1982; Hare, 1980). Conversely this antisocial trait is disadvantageous in the milieu of the !Kung Bushmen, which demands high male parental effort, reciprocal altruism, and monogamous relationships as opposed to the strategy of a "cheat."

The anthropological analysis put forward by Harpending and Draper (1988) is of value insofar as it helps to account for the evolution of psychopathic behavior as a successful reproductive strategy in response to specific environmental conditions which confer a selective advantage to individuals with this trait. One weakness of the model is that there is a major inconsistency between the behavior of the male Mundurucu and the Western male psychopath. While the Mundurucu engage in long-term interpersonal relationships with members of their own sex and engage in all-male cooperative efforts for the benefit of the whole settlement, psychopaths do not form long-term relationships with either sex and do not coexist and engage in joint enterprises.

VIII. SOCIOBIOLOGICAL THEORIES OF ANTISOCIAL PERSONALITY DISORDER

In a somewhat different manner from anthropologists, MacMillan and Kofoed (1984) have evaluated a sociobiological theory of antisocial personality in terms of the success to which theoretical predictions made by the theory are substantiated by the empirical data. These predictions consist of (1) a genetic basis to antisocial personality disorder (APD) (cheating is hypothesized to be a genetically influenced reproductive strategy), (2) a graded dimension of antisocial personality (reproductive strategies lie on a continuum), (3) the emergence of antisocial personality at the onset of reproductive age and the "burn out" of antisociality when potential for future offspring decreases, (4) a high sex bias toward male antisocial personality disorder (females have a high biological investment in pregnancy and cannot "cheat" as effectively), (5) a greater genetic predisposition is required in females before manifesting APD (decreased advantage of cheating in females), (6) greater promiscuity and reduced long-term stable relationships in APD, (7) an average level of reproductive fitness in APD (predisposition for the disorder is in genetic equilibrium), and (8) low socioeconomic status in APD (no investment of energy in competition within the social dominance hierarchy for female access). MacMillan and Kofoed (1984) argue that there is a close fit between all of these predictions and the empirical data and that sociobiology has important implications for the understanding and treatment of APD.

This position fits in well with the general argument being made in this chapter that criminal behavior has an evolutionary basis. Several limitations need to be noted however. One limitation of this model is that support for several of its predictions (overall genetic basis, higher female genetic predisposition) is derived from genetic studies of antisocial behavior in general, and not specifically of psychopaths. As will be pointed out in the next chapter, there is little convincing evidence that psychopathic behavior (as opposed to antisocial and criminal behavior in general) has a genetic basis. Other predictions are not as well supported as MacMillan and Kofoed suggest. The prediction of an average level of reproductive fitness in APD made by MacMillan and Kofoed (1984) seems incongruous both with the proposition that APD represents an especially successful reproductive strategy and with the sexual promiscuity of psychopaths. The data cited in support of this prediction is again based on antisocial behavior in general and not psychopathy in particular (Robins, 1966). The prediction of a higher male/female sex ratio in APD is certainly well supported by the general findings in the clinical literature of a 3–5 to 1 ratio in favor of males (Sigvardsson, Cloninger, Bohman, & von Knorring, 1982; Widom, 1978), but it is not completely clear from this analysis why *any* females should exhibit psychopathic behavioral traits since females in biological reproductive terms are unable to "cheat" in the same way as males.

If, as argued by MacMillan and Kofoed (1984), sociobiology does provide a valid account of antisocial personality disorder and psychopathy, it suggests that powers of verbal persuasion, deception, parasitic lifestyle, frequent sexual relationships, irresponsible behavior as parent, and nomadic lifestyle represent the key features of psychopathy while other characteristics are more peripheral (see Hare, 1980; Craft, 1966; McCord & McCord, 1964). Sociobiological theory would predict that individuals assessed on these specific characteristics would show stronger evidence for the role of genetic and biological factors underlying their psychopathy than "psychopaths" defined by other criteria.

The anthropological model proposed by Harpending and Draper (1988) suggests a similar proposition. If competitive societies such as the Mundurucu represent a valid model for psychopathy, one could theoretically use such populations for cross-cultural validation of the biological correlates of psychopathy observed in more developed societies. Such cross-cultural consistencies would constitute strong evidence for the importance of such biological factors in psychopathy or would conversely provide a unique population of noninstitutionalized "psychopaths" free of all the methodological problems which have been associated with the use of institutionalized samples (Widom, 1978).

IX. RAPE AND HOMICIDE

A. Rape

Games theory and anthropological studies provide broad sociobiological perspectives for the understanding of criminal behavior at a general level. Sociobiological explanations have also been developed to account for *specific* crimes such as homicide and rape.

In one sense rape can be viewed as the ultimate "cheat" strategy in evolutionary terms. Rather than striving to accrue resources to attract a female and to invest in the upbringing of the offspring, a male can short-cut this process through the act of rape. Thornhill and Thornhill (1983, 1987) have attempted to argue that rape could have evolved as a strategy to be employed in circumstances in which the individual lacks the resources and social status needed to attract a mate. As an analog from entomology, they present the case of forced copulation in *Panorpa* (scorpion fly). The male normally attracts a female with a dead insect; while the female feeds on the food the male mates with her.

Panorpa who are not successful in competing with other males for a nuptial offering will grab a leg or wing of a passing female with his genital claspers, reposition her in order to access her genitalia, and then copulate.

Thornhill and Thornhill (1987) make a number of predictions regarding human rape based on evolutionary theory and argue that data on rape support these predictions. One key prediction is that rapists will seek out victims with maximum fertility, since this increases the likelihood of offspring resulting from copulation. They argue that examination of rape victim data sets indicate that (1) young women are raped more than old women; and (2) the age distribution appears to follow fertility distribution (peak fertility in females is maximal in the early 20's). They suggest that these data are consistent with an evolutionary perspective, discount alternative more sociological theories of rape, and argue that nonevolutionary perspectives on rape will not provide significant understanding of rape (Thornhill & Thornhill 1987).

These conclusions seem stronger than the data justify. The proportion of rapists who suffer some degree of sexual dysfunction (including failure to obtain an erection and premature ejaculation) in the act of intercourse is substantial (Bartol, 1991); the likelihood of offspring resulting from a single act is therefore small. Rape also has a cost to the perpetrator since the victim could inflict some significant physical harm. These factors reduce the potential benefit of rape as a reproductive strategy. It should be noted, however, that the male scorpion fly is only able to transfer its sperm in 50% of forced copulations, while female scorpion flies escape on about 85% of forced copulation attempts. At least in this species the low probability of success has not prevented forced copulation from evolving as a successful strategy depending on local environmental resources.

Other aspects of human rape are not easily accounted for and indicate that sociobiological theory alone cannot account for all cases of rape. Rape can sometimes consist of oral and anal sex in which there is no chance of reproductive success. Rape is also on occasions committed against women who have passed the menopause. Although Thornhill and Thornhill (1987) predict that rapists and nonrapists alike are expected to prefer attractive women, rape victims are not homogeneous with respect to attractiveness. Indeed, one rapist that the author worked with in prison described how he would always pick *unattractive* women to rape. His rationale that unattractive women are less likely to have a boyfriend and a satisfactory sex life (and therefore would not mind being raped so much) is more in fitting with the notion that faulty cognitions and beliefs may partly account for rape than with sociobiological theory. Finally, sociobiological theory cannot easily account for the fact that a significant proportion of rapists are of high status or else are married and have children (Bartol, 1991); such individuals have no obvious motivation in reproductive terms to commit rape. While a sociobiological theory of rape has some plausibility, therefore, there are many aspects of rape that it cannot easily account for, and sociobiological explanations alone are unlikely to provide an adequate account of the causes of rape.

B. Homicide

Alternatively, a more convincing case has been made for the application of sociobiological theory to homicide. Selfish genes in their strivings for immortality wish to increase, not decrease, their representation in the next gene pool. As such, sociobiological theory would predict that there is an inverse relationship between genetic relatedness and homicide, that is, individuals are more likely to be killed by strangers than by those who are genetically related to them. Support for this hypothesis has been provided by Daly and Wilson (1988a), who point out that the victim is killed by "relatives" in less than 33% of cases in all large samples of U.S. homicides. More telling, most of these cases tend to be accounted for by nonblood relatives, for example, spouses. For example, 19% of homicide victims in Detroit in 1972 were killed by their spouse, whereas only 6% were blood relatives. Corresponding figures for Miami in 1980 were 10% and 1.8%, respectively (Wilbanks, 1984). These data are in line with sociobiological theory, which predicts an excess of non-blood-related perpetrators of homicide.

In order to control for differences in opportunity to kill between blood relatives and nonblood relatives, Daly and Wilson (1988a) compared rates for the commission of homicide by coresidents of the victim who were not genetically related to the victim with that of coresidents who were. Based on data from Detroit in 1972, they found that nongenetic coresidents were 11 times more likely to kill than genetically related coresidents, supporting the notion that genetic relatedness reduces the likelihood of homicide.

Studies of stepchildren also support a sociobiological theory of homicide. Wilson (1980) report data showing rates of validated child abuse reported to the American Humane Association in 1976 as a function of step-parentage. Rates of abuse for children from homes with a stepparent are much higher across all ages (0–17 years) relative to rates for children from homes with two natural parents; as one example, rates of abuse of children aged under 2 years were over six times greater in homes containing a stepparent relative than in homes containing two natural parents. Parents are also more likely to abuse their stepchildren than their biological children. While it could be argued that these striking differences as a function of step-parentage may be due to report bias (i.e., abuse may be more likely to be reported in stepparent homes), data for homicide (in which report bias is a less serious problem) tend to discount this possibility. Data from Canada between 1974 and 1983 for the risk of being murdered by a stepparent versus being murdered by a natural parent as a function of the child's age show that children living with a stepparent are much more likely to be murdered than children living with a natural parent

(Daley & Wilson, 1988b). In England, only 1% of babies live with a stepparent, yet 53% of battered baby cases were killed by their stepfather in a sample of battered babies (Scott, 1973), indicating a large overrepresentation of battering by stepparents relative to natural parents. Data from the U.S. also supports this linkage between abuse and violence; a child in the U.S. living with stepparents is almost 100 times more likely to be fatally abused than a child of the same age living with its genetic parents (Daly & Wilson, 1988b).

Another line of support for a sociobiological theory of homicide stems from infanticide rates as a function of the mother's age. At one level one would not expect any violence between genetically related individuals since it would reduce the perpetrator's inclusive fitness. Trivers' concept of parent–offspring conflict, however, helps to explain family violence, since the level of parenting that is genetically optimal for the parent (in terms of inclusive fitness) rarely matches the parenting needs which would be optimal from the standpoint of the offspring's inclusive fitness. One factor which influences this conflict is the mother's residual reproductive capacity. The older the mother gets, the less likely it will be that she can increase her inclusive fitness with more offspring, and as such she will be less inclined to terminate her genetic investment in her newborn. It would be predicted therefore that likelihood of infanticide by the mother will decrease as the mother gets older. Daley and Wilson (1988a) report data from Canada (1974–1983) which support this prediction. Also shown in this report are data for matricide as a function of mother's age. The mother is more likely to be killed by her offspring when she is older. This age trend would also be predicted by parent–offspring conflict theory; the older and needier and mother becomes, the more likely she will be a net liability to the offspring with respect to their inclusive fitness.

Taken together, these data suggest that homicide may have its roots in evolution insofar as principles derived from sociobiology can explain demographic features of this crime. This does not mean that sociobiology is the only explanation for homicide, and it is almost inevitable that nonevolutionary forces also play a role in causing homicide.

X. EVALUATION OF EVOLUTIONARY PERSPECTIVES

In discussing games theory and the evolution of Cheat, Sucker, Grudger, and Tit-for-Tat response patterns, the impression is given that we are talking about individuals who are "good good" or "bad bad"—either being pure altruists or pure cheats. While such models are helpful in illustrating and testing basic models of the evolution of cooperation, in reality the position may be much more complex. Trivers (1971) suggested that the complex, regulated system of reciprocal altruism will not throw up individual cheats and individual altruists, but instead individuals who differ in the *degree* of altruism they possess and the circumstances in which they will cheat. In this model, many or all individuals will cheat at some point in time, though some will cheat more than others and some will be more altruistic than others.

This issue is important for two reasons. First, dimensional models of antisocial behavior are intuitively more plausible than categorical models, which divide populations into antisocial and prosocial or criminal and non-criminal categories (see Chapter 12 for a further discussion). Almost without exception, most, if not all, of us cheat at some level at some point in our lives. It is also true that some of us "cheat" very frequently while some of us only cheat rarely. The concept of subtle cheating and gradations in cheating allows a more probable and realistic evolutionary model of antisocial behavior to be built.

Second, the more complex regulatory framework which Trivers (1971) puts forward suggests that altruism (and cheating) will not work in a simple, automated fashion. Instead, he argues for "developmental plasticity" of these traits, by which he means that cheating will develop depending on the local environmental and social conditions in which the developing individual finds himself. Just as neuronal plasticity in the early development of the visual cortex of the cat allows its visual system to become fine tuned to better detect features in its environment (Blakemore & Cooper, 1970), so too do environmental factors (e.g., stability of social groups, degree of altruism practiced in the group, conditions under which cheating is detected) shape the extent to which altruist and cheat cards will be played in the very complex poker game of life. If this is true, then it becomes clear that whether or not the evolutionary push to behave as a Sucker, Tit-for-Tat altruist, suspicious Tit for Tat, subtle Cheat, or gross Cheat becomes manifest depends in large part on both broad and specific environmental factors. This in turn suggests a *dynamic* interaction between genetic and environmental factors as opposed to a more *static* and inflexible operation of evolutionary and genetic forces. This is felt to be an important issue and will be returned to in the next chapter and also in the last chapter in the context of differing rates of crime in differing environments (countries).

It must be remembered that sociobiological models of criminal behavior cannot be experimentally tested directly, and instead evidence in support of such models must necessarily be more indirect, consisting of fitting existing patterns of behavior to predictions stemming from sociobiological models. This can give the feeling that the model is being retrospectively "fitted" to the data. Furthermore, a legitimate question can be asked as to what specific types of antisocial behavior a sociobiological approach best applies. Theft and burglary are clearly relevant, as are all criminal offenses in which resources are taken from an individual. Similarly, more white collar crimes involving fraud and effectively any form of "cheating" are applicable. Assault, rape, and murder are also relevant as indicated earlier in this chapter. On the other hand, there are some specific criminal offenses such as arson, pedophilia, taking drugs, and voyeurism which are more difficult to view within this framework.

In general, however, it is argued that an evolutionary perspective of criminal behavior provides a potentially important conceptual approach which can be applied to the majority of criminal acts.

Finally, this chapter has been attempting to explain why antisocial acts of cheating (taking of resources), which may be considered an analog of modern-day criminal behavior, can be understood in the context of evolution. Paradoxically, as Dawkins (1989) has very cogently argued, genes can rather easily be viewed as inherently selfish and antisocial. Attempting to understand how altruistic behavior has evolved provides a much greater challenge to the sociobiologist who will readily accept an evolutionary basis for antisocial behavioral traits.

XI. SUMMARY

This chapter attempted to explain how criminal behavior can be viewed as a successful reproductive strategy in an evolutionary, sociobiological perspective. The prisoners' dilemma was used to illustrate that there can be considerable problems in achieving mutual cooperation and that cheating can instead be a much more viable strategy. Computer simulations illustrate that while a "Tit-for-Tat" strategy of reciprocal altruism can be almost an evolutionary stable strategy, cheating can also represent a successful strategy particularly where Cheats migrate from one population to another. Evolutionary pressures have given rise to the development of subtle cheating (giving back less than what is received) as a strategy, a strategy counteracted by punishing Cheats to discourage their cheating tactics. Anthropological studies indicate that differing environmental niches can give rise to either cheating or reciprocal altruistic reproductive strategies throughout the whole population. Theoretical predictions from sociobiological theory have been applied to the explanation of antisocial personality disorder, rape, and homicide and to some degree are capable of accounting for the observed data. It is argued that (1) criminal behavior in the guise of antisocial, "cheating" behavior has a clear evolutionary basis; (2) behaviors and emotions have also evolved as a reaction to combat this antisocial cheating; (3) this sociobiological perspective can be applied to the majority of antisocial behaviors; and (4) whether or not cheating develops will be a function of both broad and specific environmental factors. As such, antisocial behavior is viewed as a product of the dynamic interplay between environmental and sociobiological forces.

3 Genetics and Crime

I. INTRODUCTION

The sociobiological perspective on crime presented in the last chapter makes the necessary prediction that crime will have a genetic basis. Perhaps the most controversial research on crime has been that which attempts to address this question. This chapter outlines evidence from studies of twins reared together, twins reared apart, and adoption studies which, taken together, indicate a nontrivial role for heritable influences on crime. Seven key questions which have received relatively little attention in the literature will be outlined, and an initial attempt will be made to answer them. In addition to the question of whether crime is heritable, these questions include whether there is heritability for violent crime, whether evidence exists for an interaction between genetic and environmental factors, to what extent crime is heritable, whether there is stronger heritability for female crime, whether there is heritability for juvenile delinquency, and whether psychopathy is heritable. The main arguments to be made in this chapter are that (1) there is evidence for heritability of crime, particularly with respect to nonviolent, adult crime; (2) environmental influences are also clearly implicated by these data; and (3) there are multiple misconceptions on genetic research into crime which have retarded progress on both genetic and environmental influences on crime.

Before presenting and analyzing evidence for heritable influences on crime, it is important to clarify some misconceptions about genetics which have unnecessarily fueled a regressive, dualistic approach to research on the genetics of crime. Although these points may seem to some to be simplistic, it is remarkable how frequently some commentators on the genetics of crime seem to have ignored them, and as such they are laid out in detail below.

II. TEN MISCONCEPTIONS ABOUT THE GENETICS OF CRIME

A. A Gene Is Directly Responsible for Criminal Behavior

The reality is that there are no genes for crime as such; rather, there are genes that code for proteins and enzymes that can influence physiological processes which can in turn predispose an individual toward crime (Bohman, Cloninger, Sigvardsson, & von Knoring, 1982; Venables & Raine, 1987). Furthermore, it is unlikely that a single gene will be found to predispose to crime. Instead, it is more likely that multiple genes, acting in combination, result in varying degrees of genetic predisposition to criminal behavior in the total population.

B. Heritable Influences Imply That All Crime Is Genetically Determined

As will be seen below, there is no evidence at all for such a view, and behavioral geneticists acknowledge both the importance of environmental factors and the interaction between genetics and environment. Criminal behavior is very likely influenced by both environmental and genetic forces and the interaction between both factors. In addition to "additive" effects of the environment (i.e., their separate influences that each explain some variance in criminal behavior), there may be another effect of the "interaction" between genes and environment, meaning that the combination of genetic and environmental influences may be more important than the separate "additive" effect of genetic and environmental influences.

There is a related misconception that because researchers focus on genetic influences in their field of study, they must necessarily deny the role of all other influences. Simply because research has focused on one type of influence on crime does not mean that other influences are not recognized. Behavioral geneticists *do* believe that environmental influences are important, and this is true of psychophysiologists, biochemists, and neuropsychologists. Similarly, most social psychologists do not deny that biological and genetic factors are of importance in influencing behavior; it is simply that their main interest lies in nonbiological influences, and it is very difficult to develop research expertise in both areas.

What is true is that not enough attention has been given by both social and genetic researchers to a biosocial interactive approach. To the author's knowledge, there has been no research to date on what specific environmental factors are crucial triggers for allowing a latent genetic predisposition for crime to express itself. Similarly, there has been no research into how genetic factors can bias an individual to seek out those environments which predispose to crime. If genetic × environment interactions ultimately prove to be central to crime, the omission of such biosocial research will prove to be a major impediment in our understanding of criminal behavior.

C. Genetic Research Can Explain Why Some Specific Individuals Commit Crime

It must be remembered that heritability is a population concept and cannot be applied at the individual level (Carey, 1989). A heritability of .50 for crime would suggest that 50% of the variance in criminal behavior can be accounted for by genetic factors, but this is based on a population of subjects in general and cannot be extrapolated to specific individuals. Such a figure, for example, does not mean that half of one criminal's offenses can be accounted for by genetics while the other half has environmental causes. Nor does it mean that genetic factors account for crimes committed by 50 out of 100 criminals. Some individuals may indeed commit crimes largely due to genetic influences, but currently there is no way to determine who these specific individuals are.

D. The View That Crime Is in Part Genetically Determined Means That One Cannot Change Criminal Behavior

Notions that "crime is destiny" are not supported by behavioral genetic research. Even very specific genetic disorders such as phenylketonuria (PKU), which otherwise result in mental impairment, can be treated by environmental (in this case dietary) interventions. It is highly unlikely that crime can be changed by such simple single environmental manipulations, but it must be remembered that genetic influences do not act in a vacuum—their expression is dependent on environmental parameters. As one example, height is strongly heritable, but an individual with a genetic predisposition to be tall will not reach full height if nutrition is inadequate. Environmental manipulations can in theory be fully successful in reducing the incidence of crime by preventing full expression of genetic predispositional factors. Genetic influences for crime must be seen as a *predisposition* to crime rather than as destiny for crime.

E. Genetic Studies Have Implications for Heritable Rather Than Environmental Influences

The truth is that while genetic studies tend to focus on heritable influences, they also yield valuable information on the role of the environment, a fact which has not received sufficient attention in the literature. Twin and adoption studies not only demonstrate that a substantial amount of variance in criminal behavior can be attributed to genetic factors; they also demonstrate that environmental factors are equally important. For example, while a heritability estimate of .50 indicates that 50% of the variance in criminal behavior is due to genetic influences, it also indicates that 50% of the variance can be attributed to nongenetic (environmental factors). Adoption studies have repeatedly demonstrated the importance of environmental factors such as adverse home environment, institutionalization early in life, multiple temporary placements, and low social class (Cadoret & Cain, 1980; Cloninger & Gottesman, 1987; Crowe, 1974; Mednick & Finello, 1983; Rutter, Boltin, Harrington, Le Couteur, Macdonald, & Simonoff, 1990), though such influences have been rarely recognized by critics of genetic studies. In addition, studies of twins reared apart can potentially yield very important information on environmental protective factors that determine why one twin becomes criminal while the other genetically identical twin desists from crime, though only one to date has been conducted (Grove, Eckert, Heston, Bouchard, Segal, & Lykken, 1990). Rejecting the behavioral genetic approach rejects a powerful strategy for analyzing environmental influences on crime.

Finally, modern statistical approaches to the biometric analysis of twin data allow partitioning of environmental variance into shared (common to both twins, e.g., generalized family influences such as divorce) and nonshared sources (different for the two twins, e.g., different peer groups, differential treatment by parents). Rutter *et al.* (1990) argue that most genetic studies on psychological characteristics of children indicate the importance of nonshared family influences, and the same seems to be true for major personality dimensions in adults (Loehlin, 1992). If such analyses were conducted for crime and delinquency, findings could have important implications for socioenvironmental studies that aim to focus on key environmental influences. One of the few twin studies on delinquency that has addressed this issue confirms the importance of specific environmental effects and the failure to show evidence for a shared environmental component (Rowe, 1985). Further such studies remain to be conducted and are sorely needed.

F. Genetic Factors Cannot Underlie Crime Because Crime Is a Social–Political–Legal Construction

This is a poor but commonly cited reason to deny any role of genetics in explaining crime. The basic argument is that one cannot inherit something that is a construction of the legal system and society. The weakness of this argument can be illustrated with respect to schizophrenia. Schizophrenia is a construct developed by the psychiatric system; it is essentially a construction of what clinicians think this illness is. There is substantial debate about how it should be defined and what factors underlie schizophrenic symptomatology, and its definition keeps changing. Its definition varies in England and the U.S., and base rates for this disorder vary across countries as a function of this definition just as base rates for crime vary across countries. Nevertheless, studies on both sides of the Atlantic have very clearly demonstrated a genetic predisposition for this illness, and this basic finding is not seriously disputed today. With respect to crime, there is evidence for some genetic predisposition to crime notwithstanding the fact that crime, like schizophrenia, is a construction which is open to debate.

G. A Genetic Basis for Crime Will Put Many Social Scientists Out of Business

This viewpoint is most clearly expounded by Gottfredson and Hirschi (1990) when they state:

> Contemporary criminology is highly skeptic of the contributions of biological positivism. Much of this skepticism can be traced to disciplinary rivalries or concerns. Sociologists, psychologists, and economists are naturally concerned with the possibility that biology could leave them with little to explain. [p. 64]

This is probably an understandable and fair reflection of current opinion, but it is almost certain that genetic and biological research could *never* put social scientists out of business. The reasons for this argument are that (1) there is already clear and incontrovertible evidence that socioenvironmental factors play key roles in the development of crime (see Chapters 10 and 11); (2) genetic influences cannot be expressed in a vacuum outside of an environment; (3) the interaction between the environment and genetics may prove to be crucially important in explaining crime; and (4) genetic studies reveal the importance of the environment (see Section II, E above). However it is predicted that there are two classes of researchers who will be put out of business in the next decade: (1) biological researchers who ignore the role of social variables in determining crime, and (2) social scientists who isolate their own research from new findings stemming from the biological sciences. It is anticipated that the most important future challenge for current criminologists lies in who can best integrate social and biological data to explain criminal behavior.

H. Genetic Research Is Inherently Evil Because It Can Be Used to Justify Selective Breeding and Sterilization Programs

Geneticists, like all other scientists, must interpret their data with appropriate caution with respect to practical application. Social scientists in turn must take care not to resort to unnecessary scare-mongering tactics to suppress biological research because it offers another perspective to understanding crime. Again, the source of this specific misconception lies in an overly simplistic and erroneous interpretation of genetic research. Current research indicates a genetic *predisposition* to crime only; individuals are not born to commit crime (see Sections II, A, B, and C above); there is no genetic destiny for crime as such. Eugenic solutions to crime are not supported by the findings of genetic research.

It is sometimes counterargued that while genetic research could not, appropriately interpreted, countenance such malicious social programs, in the wrong hands it could be misinterpreted and used to support such programs. It is true that there are clear examples of this in history, and such examples again demand that both the scientific community in particular and society in general need to interpret genetic research findings with care. On the other hand, despots rarely need to turn to scientific evidence to justify heinous crimes. Man's inhumanity to man has unfortunately been very easy to justify at the time. Hitler's "Mein Kampf," which provided the basis for mass extermination of millions of Jewish people, expounds more a personal philosophy rather than citation of scientific studies claiming to demonstrate the genetic inferiority of Jews, criminals, and other claimed "inferiors," although later such claims were made. Saddam Hussein did not require findings from genetic research to invade and subjugate the Kuwaiti people, nor have other atrocities perpetrated in many other countries required such justification.

Paradoxically, while many are concerned with the consequences of genetic research into crime, few seem to be concerned with possible misdirected interpretations of environmental research. For example, one could argue from social research that extermination of all criminal adults would lower the crime rate in the next generation because such parents exert powerful social predispositions to crime on their children who form the next generation of criminals. It could also be argued that children of criminal parents should be removed from their families to be raised in a crime-free environment (to the extent that there is a genetic predisposition to crime, this would also be an ineffective strategy). Similarly, modeling is a social learning principle that has been used to justify the death penalty as a deterrent against major criminal offenses. In spite of these possibilities and realities, there has been little outcry against social research into crime.

We must not rid ourselves of care in ensuring the humane and socially acceptable use and application of genetic and biological research into crime, but we must rid ourselves of overly protectionist standpoints that stifle research findings and the truth about the causes of crime. We must not forget that society is currently practicing passive eugenic control for serious crime; serious offenders are locked up for many years or most of their lives and denied the opportunity to reproduce. Such policies are *not* the result of misinterpreted genetic or biological research.

I. Recent Increases in the Crime Rate Rule out a Genetic Interpretation of Crime

The argument here is that the proportion of genes thought to predispose individuals to crime would be relatively stable over generations of gene pools; because crime rates fluctuate within a generation, this negates the role of genetic influences. While it is true that such fluctuations may be better explained by social than by genetic influences, one cannot draw the conclusion that genetic factors play no role in crime per se. There are two reasons for this. First, genetic factors may still play a role in determining a constant base rate of crime without explaining crime determined by changing environmental factors. These latter "phenocopies" may show the same phenotype for crime without possessing the genetic predisposition for crime. Second, sudden rises in crime due to sudden changes in the environment may still be partly due to genetic factors which lie dormant until exposed to an appropriate environment, in other words a gene × environmental interaction. Probably for all individuals, an environmental stimulus may be required to trigger an underlying genetic predisposition to crime. Relative shifts in the crime rate from time to time may reflect shifts in environmental triggers for the manifestation of the criminal phenotype.

J. The XYY Syndrome Has Been Shown to Be Unrelated to Violent Crime Illustrating the Weakness of the Genetic Approach

Textbooks on criminal behavior tend to give detailed accounts of early beliefs of an association between violent crime and the XYY syndrome (a genetic disorder in which individuals possess an extra male chromosome) at the expense of twin and adoption studies. The findings of a definitive study by Mednick and associates are cited as evidence against this notion (Witkin, Mednick, Schulsinger, Bakkestrom, Christiansen, Goodenough, Hirschhorn, Lundsteen, Owen, Philip, Rubin, & Stocking, 1977); while XYY individuals are more likely to become criminal than normal controls, they are not more likely to commit violent crime, and the types of offenses they do commit tend to be relatively minor (Mednick & Finello, 1983).

While it is true that there is no good evidence to link the XYY syndrome to violence, this does not embarrass the notion of a heritable basis to crime for three reasons. First, although XYY males are not more likely to commit violent offenses than controls, they do have a raised level of petty property offending (Witkin *et al.*, 1977). This is consistent with data from large adoption studies indicating heritability for petty offending but not for violent offending (see below). Second, while the XYY syndrome represents a genetic abnormality, it is not heritable, stemming instead from random chromosomal mutations at the time of conception. Consequently, XYY research has no necessary bearing on the issue of heritability for crime. Third, even if the XYY syndrome was a heritable genetic disorder and failed to show a relationship with crime, such a failure does not mean that the significant findings of many twin and adoption studies are invalidated or should be ignored. There are many genes other than those on the sex chromosomes which may play a role in criminal behavior.

Clarification of the aforementioned misconceptions must be borne in mind when interpreting the following lines of evidence claiming to support the notion of a part-heritable basis for crime. Before outlining evidence from twin and adoption studies, these methodologies will first be briefly outlined.

III. TWIN METHODOLOGY

The twin method for ascertaining whether a given trait is to any extent heritable makes use of the fact that monozygotic (MZ) or "identical" twins are genetically identical, having 100% of their genes in common with one another. Conversely, dizygotic (DZ) or "fraternal" twins are less genetically alike than MZ twins and are in fact no more alike genetically than nontwin siblings. Many criminology texts frequently state that DZ twins have on average 50% of their genes in common, though this is not strictly true. For example, the reader (irrespective of sex) has about 99% of his or her genes in common with the author. Indeed, both author and reader have about 98% of their genes in common with chimpanzees, who themselves are genetically more similar to humans than to gorillas (Britten, 1986). The majority of genes are said to be "fixed" (sometimes called "structural genes") and make us all fundamentally similar (e.g., we all have two arms, two legs, and a head). What determines the individual variability across humans that we all perceive is the extent to which people share the final 1% of the genes that can vary across individuals. When DZ twins (or brothers and sisters) are said to have 50% of their genes in common, what is really meant is that they have 50% of this remaining 1% of genes in common with each other. Furthermore, it should be remembered that DZ twin pairs won't all have exactly 50% of their genes in common. Some will be somewhat more genetically similar, some less so, with 50% representing an average which could vary considerably.

When the trait being measured is a dichotomy (e.g., criminal/noncriminal), "concordance" rates are calculated for MZ and DZ twins separately. A 70%

concordance for crime in a set of MZ twins, for example, would mean that if one of the MZ pair is criminal, then the chance of the co-twin being criminal is 70%. Similar concordance rates can be calculated for DZ twins. If MZ twins have higher concordance rates for crime than DZ twins, then this constitutes some evidence for the notion that crime has a heritable component. Tetrachoric correlations can be calculated from each of these concordance rates, and the difference between these correlation coefficients, when doubled, gives an estimate of heritability, or the proportion of variance in criminality that can be attributed to genetic influences (Falconer, 1965). More complex, modern, multivariate biometrical models can be fitted to these data and are in more common use today (e.g., DeFries & Fulker, 1985).

IV. EVIDENCE FROM TWIN STUDIES

To date there appear to be 10 studies producing 13 analyses of the genetics of adult crime using twins (see Table 1). Studies vary widely in terms of the country of origin, age and sex composition, sample size, determination of zygosity, and definition of crime. However, all 13 show greater concordance rates for criminality in MZ as opposed to DZ twins. Some of these studies have small sample sizes, and generally speaking the methodologically better studies are the more recent ones of Christiansen (1977) and Dalgaard and Kringlen (1976). Mednick and Finello (1983) point out that two of the earlier studies (Stumpfl, 1936, and Kranz, 1936) took place in Germany and Prussia during the Nazi era and may be politically biased. It should be noted however that MZ–DZ differences in these studies are small relative to some other studies, and Christiansen (1977a) in a detailed methodological analysis of twin studies of crime concluded that Kranz's work was the best of the prewar studies.

If one averages concordance rates across all studies (weighting for sample sizes), these 13 studies result in concordances of 51.5% for MZ twins and 20.6% for DZ twins. In order to assess whether concordance is a function of specific factors (e.g., sex, zygosity determination, small sample sizes, recent versus old studies), total concordance rates were recalculated as a function of the moderator variables shown in Table 2. The MZ/DZ concordance ratios are also calculated, with high ratios indicating greater concordance in MZ twins relative to DZ twins.

Concordances for the two most recent studies (Dalgaard & Kringlen, 1976; Christiansen, 1977a) are lower in both MZ and DZ twin sets, but rates for MZ twins are still more than twice as high as rates for DZ twins (31.0% for MZ and 12.9% for DZ), indicating substantial heritability for crime. This indicates that heritability for crime is not just obtained in old, methodologically inferior studies as some have suggested. Deleting the Germanic studies of Stumpfl (1936) and Kranz (1936) produces concordance rates of 48.1%

TABLE 1 Concordance Rates from Twin Studies of Criminal Behavior

			MZ twins		DZ twins		
Author	Location	Sex	% Concordance	(N)[a]	% Concordance	(N)[a]	Zygosity
Lange (1929)	Bavaria	M	77	(13)	12	(17)	Resemblance
Legras (1932)	Holland	M	100	(4)	0	(5)	Blood
Rosanoff, Handy, & Rosanoff (1934)	U.S.A.	M	76	(38)	22	(23)	Resemblance
	U.S.A.	F	26	(7)	25	(4)	Resemblance
Stumpfl (1936)	Germany	M	65	(18)	37	(19)	Resemblance
	Germany	F	67	(3)	0	(2)	Resemblance
Kranze (1935)	Prussia	M	66	(32)	54	(43)	Blood
Borgstrom (1939)	Finland	M	75	(4)	40	(5)	Blood
Slater (1953)	England	M	50	(2)	30	(10)	?
Yoshimashu (1961)	Japan	M	61	(28)	11	(18)	Blood
Dalgaard & Kringlen (1976)	Norway	M	26	(31)	15	(54)	Blood
Christiansen (1977)[b]	Denmark	M	35	(71)	13	(120)	Questionnaire
	Denmark	F	21	(14)	8	(27)	Questionnaire
Total			51.5%	(262)	20.6%	(345)	

[a]N = number of pairs of twins. Summary figures are weighted for sample sizes

[b]A reanalysis of these data with additional subjects by Cloninger & Gottesman (1987) resulted in correlations of .74 for MZ twins and .47 for DZ twins, indicating a heritability of .54.

TABLE 2 Averaged Twin Concordance Rates Weighted by Sample Size for Selected Twin Studies

Selection criterion	MZ twins		DZ twins		MZ/DZ concordance ration
	% Concordance	(N)	% Concordance	(N)	
Total sample	51.5	(262)	20.6	(345)	2.5
Excluding Stumpfl (1936) and Kranze (1935)	48.1	(212)	14.5	(283)	3.3
Excluding small samples (single-digit studies)	50.8	(242)	20.4	(319)	2.5
Zygosity estimated by blood	53.5	(99)	28.0	(125)	1.9
Males only	53.8	(238)	21.7	(312)	2.4
Females only	29.2	(24)	9.1	(33)	3.2
Post-1975 studies only	31.0	(116)	12.9	(201)	2.4

(MZ) and 14.5% (DZ). This indicates that claims for rejecting results of all twin studies on the grounds of political bias in some of them are unfounded. Twin studies have also been criticized for, in some cases, being based on small sample sizes, but when these studies are deleted, evidence for heritability for crime is still strong (51.0% for MZ, 20.2% for DZ). Twin studies have also been criticized for the way zygosity has been assessed. However, as indicated in Table 2, substantial evidence for heritability is shown from studies where zygosity is determined from blood samples (53.5% for MZ, 28.0% for DZ). Although overall concordance rates are lower for females than for males (as would be expected given the substantially lower crime rates in females), concordance rates in female MZ twins are more than three times those in female DZ twins, again indicating substantial heritability for crime in females in addition to males. Concordance ratios are all greater than 1.9, indicating that even in the worst-case scenario, MZ twins are almost twice as likely to be concordant as DZ twins.

However one views these data, it is difficult to escape from the conclusion that they indicate some degree of genetic predisposition for crime. While some researchers have attempted to reject results from all twin studies on the basis of criticisms which affect only some studies, these criticisms have not been supported by the empirical data presented above. The analyses reported in Table 2 clearly indicate the danger of making such cursory criticisms and drawing negative conclusions without a careful consideration of the importance of these criticisms. Furthermore, the fact that evidence for heritability of crime is found in different countries indicates evidence for cross-cultural generalizability.

V. LIMITATIONS OF TWIN STUDIES

Twin studies have methodological limitations which place limits on the conclusions that can be drawn from individual studies. A very common criticism of twin studies is that MZ twins may share a more common environment than DZ twins. For example, parents may treat MZ twins in a more similar fashion than DZ twins, thus artificially raising concordance rates in MZ twins. If this were true, the greater concordance for crime in MZ twins might be due more to environmental than genetic factors. There is some evidence that this may be the case (Allen, 1976). Criticisms such as these tend to lead researchers to discount results from twin studies as showing evidence for heritability. Such strong conclusions are inappropriate because they do not consider methodological problems with twin studies which can *decrease* estimates of heritability as opposed to artificially increasing them.

One such methodological problem concerns accurate assessment of zygosity. This is frequently assessed in modern studies using blood tests, but DNA fingerprinting is the only certain method of assessing zygosity (Rutter *et al.*, 1990), while zygosity questionnaires are approximately 90–95% accurate. If MZ twins are misclassified as DZ or vice versa, this will result in an *underestimation* of heritability. DNA fingerprinting has never been used in twins studies of crime, and resemblance assessments from photographs and physical examinations have been the more popular (and somewhat less reliable) zygosity assessment methods in the studies reported in Table 1. Future studies using DNA fingerprinting techniques would reduce classification error and possibly produce higher heritability estimates for crime.

Although there is some evidence that MZ twins may share a more common environment than DZ twins, there is also evidence that it is the degree of genetic relatedness (leading to similarity in behavior) that determines the similarity of parental treatment (Kendler, 1983). Furthermore, there is evidence that some twins make attempts to "deidentify" or be different from one another (Schacter & Stone, 1985), while other twin pairs develop opposite (e.g., dominant–submissive) role relationships (Moilanen, 1987). These effects are expected to be greater in MZ pairs, with the result of artificially *reducing* heritability estimates.

Though MZ twins are genetically identical, identical twinning can result in biological differences that can accentuate phenotypic differences. For example, there is a greater discrepancy in the birth weights of MZ twins relative to DZ twins due to the feto–fetal transfusion syndrome, and birth complications have been linked to differences in behavior and cognition. This nongenetic, biological factor will result in an exaggeration of behavioral differences in MZ twins and a reduction in heritability estimates.

It is concluded that methodological problems of twin studies are just as likely to decrease heritability estimates as they are to artificially inflate them. Rutter *et al.* (1990) have suggested that in all probability these effects will tend to cancel each other out. It is important, therefore, not to ignore research findings from twin studies. In spite of its limitations, the study of twins remains a key method in the field of behavior genetics, and future twin studies of crime using up-to-date biometric modeling are likely to make increasingly important contributions to genetic research on crime.

VI. IDENTICAL TWINS REARED APART

The main criticism of twin studies, that MZ twins share a common environment in addition to a common genetic makeup, is circumvented in studies of identical twins reared apart. These are consequently powerful studies for establishing heritability for a trait, but inevitably very few such studies have been conducted to date. One study has been conducted on antisocial behavior in children and adults. Grove *et al.* (1990) studied 32 sets of MZ twins who were separated and reared apart shortly after birth, with zygosity being assessed using a number of techniques (including blood assessment) which result in only a 0.1% chance of misdetermination. A continuous score for antisocial behavior in both childhood and adulthood was derived by interviewing each subject with a standardized interview schedule; as such, this assessment of antisocial behavior was a self-report measure. Statistically significant heritabilities were obtained for antisocial behavior in both childhood (0.41) and adulthood (0.28).

These findings are consistent with eight case studies of MZ twin pairs reared apart in which it was known that one twin was registered for criminality (Christiansen, 1977a). Of these eight pairs, four were concordant for crime, indicating clear evidence for the role of genetic factors. One of the four concordant cases reported by Schwesinger (1952) describes a pair of Mexican MZ twins separated at the age of 9 months and brought up by parents reported to have very different personalities. One twin was brought up in a town after age 9 years, while the other twin remained in the desert. Independently, both twins started to commit juvenile crimes after puberty. Both were separately institutionalized for their crimes.

Studies of twins reared apart, although powerful, also have limitations. Rutter *et al.* (1990) discuss the possibility of bias in sampling given the rarity of such cases, although Grove *et al.* (1990) present evidence against the notion that their subjects consisted of "supernormal" individuals with low rates of antisocial behavior (high rates were observed). The study by Grove *et al.* (1990) differs from other twin studies in that self-report antisocial behavior is being measured as opposed to official measures of crime, though this is probably a strength of the study rather than a weakness, and it is supported by official crime measures in the case studies of Christiansen (1977).

In conclusion, studies of twins reared apart clearly represent an important research strategy for understanding the genetics of crime, but to date the data

TABLE 3   Results of Cross-Fostering Analyses Reported by Mednick *et al.* (1984)[a]

		Are biological parents criminal?	
		Yes	No
Are adoptive parents criminal?	Yes	24.5%	14.7%
	No	20.0%	13.5%

[a]Percentages refer to the proportion of adoptees who had court convictions.

are limited. While the eight case studies are not methodologically strong, they do illustrate the usefulness of this methodological approach and, together with the stronger study of Grove *et al.* (1990), add another important line of support for the notion that there is a genetic predisposition to crime and antisocial behavior.

VII. ADOPTION STUDY METHODOLOGY

Adoption studies also overcome the problem with twin studies because they more cleanly separate out genetic and environmental influences. In this paradigm, offspring are separated from their criminal, biological parents early in life and are fostered out to other families. If these offspring grow up to become criminal at greater rates than foster children whose biological parents were not criminal, this would indicate a genetic influence with its origin in the subject's biological parents.

A variation of this type of study is the "cross-fostering" paradigm which has been used most extensively in animal experimental genetic studies. In this paradigm as applied to humans, the offspring whose biological parents are criminal or noncriminal are fostered by parents who themselves are either criminal or noncriminal. This 2 × 2 design capitalizes on what is effectively a natural experiment and allows for a more systematic exploration of genetic and environmental influences. As will be seen later, this paradigm also allows an assessment of possible interactions between genetic and environmental influences.

A good example of a cross-fostering adoption study is that conducted by Mednick *et al.* (1984). These researchers based their analyses on 14,427 adoptions which took place in Denmark between 1927 and 1947. Infants were adopted out immediately in 25.3% of cases, 50.6% were adopted within 1 year, 12.8% in the second year, and 11.3% after age 2. Court records were obtained on 65,516 biological parents, adoptive parents, and adoptees in order to assess which subjects had convictions. Results of the findings are reported in Table 3.

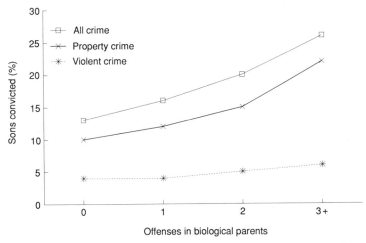

FIGURE 1   Relationship between number of convictions in the biological parents and number of convictions for both property and violent offenses in their adoptees (Adapted from Mednick *et al.* 1984).

When both adoptive and biological parents were noncriminal (neither genetic nor environmental predispositions present), 13.5% of the adoptees had a criminal record. This increased to 14.7% when adoptive parents only were criminal (environmental but not genetic predisposition present). When biological parents only were criminal (genetic but not environmental predisposition present), the conviction rate in the adoptees increased to 20.0%. When both adoptive and biological parents were criminal (both genetic and environmental predispositions present), the conviction rate increased to 24.5%. The effect of having a criminal biological parent was associated with a statistically significant increase in the likelihood of the adoptee becoming criminal.

In addition to these analyses, Mednick *et al.* (1984) present analyses indicating a statistically significant relationship between number of convictions in the biological parents and number of convictions in the adoptees. These data are illustrated in Fig. 1. The more criminal convictions the biological parent had, the more convictions the adoptee was likely to have. This effect was only observed for property offenses however; no such effect was observed for violent offenses.

All of these findings were found to be independent of selective placement of adoptees into adoption homes of a similar socioeconomic status and also independent of the age at which the infant was taken away from the mother. In total, these analyses indicate evidence for a genetic predisposition for crime, at least with respect to property offenses.

TABLE 4   Key Findings from Adoption Studies of Adult Criminal Behavior

Reference	Main finding
1. Danish adoption study	
Mednick *et al.* (1984)	Significant correlation between adoptees and biological parents for property but not violent crimes.
Baker (1986)	Heritable influences for property crimes and antisocial disorders.
Moffitt (1987)	Mental illness and crime in biological parents increases risk of recidivistic, nonviolent crime in adopted-away offspring.
Silverton (1988)	Criminal behavior genetically linked to schizophrenia.
Baker *et al.* (1989)	Convicted females more genetically predisposed to crime than convicted males.
2. Swedish adoption study	
Bohman (1978)	No link between general crime in biological fathers and crime in adoptees.
Bohman *et al.* (1982)	Heritability for petty crime in males.
Cloninger *et al.* (1982)	Interaction between genetic and environmental predispositions for petty crime in males.
Sigvardsson *et al.* (1982)	Heritability for petty crime in males replicated in females; female petty crime requires stronger genetic predisposition.
3. Iowa 1974 adoption study	
Crowe (1974)	Higher rates of antisocial personality in adopted-away offspring of female offenders.
4. Iowa 1978 adoption study	
Cadoret (1978)	Heritability for adult antisocial behavior.
Cadoret & Cain (1980)	Antisocial personality or alcoholism in biological parent predicts antisocial behavior in adolescent adoptee.
Cadoret *et al.* (1985)	Heritability for antisocial personality.
Cadoret *et al.* (1987)	Heritability for adult antisocial behavior and personality.
5. Missouri adoption study	
Cadoret *et al.* (1983)	Interaction between genetic and environmental predispositions for adolescent antisocial behavior.

VIII. EVIDENCE FROM ADOPTION STUDIES

A number of other well-executed adoption studies have been carried out into antisocial behavior in recent years. The main results of these studies are tabulated in Table 4. In total, 15 studies have been conducted from data collected in Denmark, Sweden, and the U.S. These studies are grouped under five different headings corresponding to the five different adoption studies from which they are derived. It should be noted that within each of the five headings some studies are based on analyses of essentially the same or an enlarged data set. For example the findings of an interaction between genetics and environment in males (Cloninger, Sigvardsson, Bohman, & von Knorring, 1982) and the heritability for petty crime in males (Bohman *et al.*, 1982) are based on the same data. Nevertheless, these studies address different issues on the genetics of crime, and studies under one heading are independent of studies in the other.

There are four main points that can be drawn from Table 4:

1. Almost all studies agree that there is some genetic predisposition to crime. Only one of the 15 studies directly contradicts this general finding (Bohman, 1978).

2. Evidence for this genetic predisposition has been found by several *independent* research groups. Replication by an independent research group constitutes a more powerful replication than a within-laboratory replication. These data therefore provide evidence that the basic finding is robust.

3. Heritability for crime has been found in several *different* countries (U.S., Denmark, Sweden). This suggests initial cross-cultural generalizability of the findings, though future studies in non-Western countries are required to establish further the generalizability of the findings. Twin studies conducted additionally in Germany, Japan, England, Holland, Finland, and Norway suggest that positive findings would emerge from such future studies.

4. The three studies that had a large enough sample size to separate violent from nonviolent, petty property crime found that there is heritability for petty property crimes but not for violent crimes (Bohman *et al.*, 1982; Mednick *et al.*, 1984; Sigvardsson *et al.*, 1982). This finding has been observed in both Danish and Swedish samples by independent research groups.

In conclusion, adoption studies provide powerful support for the conclusion drawn from twin studies that heritable influences play a role in criminal behavior.

IX. KEY QUESTIONS FOR GENETIC RESEARCH ON CRIME

The most frequently asked question in the literature concerns whether there is a genetic basis for crime. While not denying that this is an important issue, focusing on this question for the past 50 years may well have retarded rather than progressed this field of inquiry. It seems important to go beyond this relatively simple question to ask seven more complex questions on other key issues in behavior genetics that also have important conceptual and theoretical implications but that have rarely been asked. They are being asked in the following sections because it is felt that the question of whether crime has a heritable basis can be affirmatively addressed and, as such, one can progress to other issues. Nevertheless, there are many criminologists who do not believe that there is a genetic predisposition for criminal behavior, so this fundamental question is addressed first.

A. Is There Heritability for Crime?

The convergence of results from adoption and twin studies, when taken together, would seem to provide substantial evidence for the role of genetic factors in the etiology of antisocial conduct. This basic finding has been vigorously attacked by many criminologists and social scientists, although the most recent and detailed criticisms have been outlined by Gottfredson and Hirschi (1990).

Gottfredson and Hirschi (1990), in a chapter of their book, *A General Theory of Crime*, dealing with biological influences, make a concerted attack on adoption studies of crime and draw the strong conclusion that "the magnitude of the 'genetic effect,' as determined by adoption studies, is near zero" (p. 60). They also conclude that biological studies in general have produced little in the way of meaningful research findings. They base these conclusions on a review of three of the adoption studies that claim to show evidence of heritable factors. Most critical attention is devoted to the study by Mednick *et al.* (1984) which was published in the journal *Science* and which received considerable publicity.

The main criticisms made by Gottfredson and Hirschi (1990) of the study by Mednick *et al.* (1984) are as follows: (1) initial findings on a smaller sample were presented by Hutchings and Mednick (1977), and consequently the findings published in *Science* represent an extension of this study with more subjects added; (2) the initial study should be viewed as a pilot study; (3) the later study should be viewed as a replication study, and cases from the first study should be excluded; and (4) if one excludes these early cases from the second study, findings from the second study are no longer statistically significant. In their Table 2 on p. 55, Gottfredson and Hirschi (1990) incorrectly reported a figure of 24.5% in Mednick *et al.* (1984) as 25.5%, though this error does not seriously compromise their main point.

The key issue lies with independent replication. Gottfredson and Hirschi (1990) correctly argue that the findings by Mednick *et al.* (1990) are not an independent replication of the earlier findings by Hutchings and Mednick (1977). However, Mednick *et al.* (1984) do not make such a claim. Gottfredson and Hirschi (1990) argue that in science, initial findings are traditionally kept separate from later findings. This is not always the case however. Conducting independent studies is largely carried out when the study is relatively easy to conduct; for example, it would be relatively easy to attempt to replicate an initial finding of a claimed association between social class and crime. Where the research is difficult and costly, however, reputable researchers often build on an initially published pilot study and publish a second paper on the final, enlarged sample. One such example can be seen in the field of brain imaging, a costly, technically difficult, and time-consuming area of research (e.g., Smith, Calderon, Ravichandran, Largen, Vroulis, Shvartsburd, Gordon, & Schoolar, 1984; Smith, Baumgartner, & Calderon, 1987). Genetic research is similarly a difficult area of research and it would be quite appropriate to build up a large sample to achieve maximum power. Furthermore, Gottfredson and Hirschi's argument does not apply to new analyses conducted by Mednick *et al.* (1984) that were not conducted on the initial sample (see Fig. 1 above), which in themselves provide strong evidence for some role of genetic factors in crime.

From a scientific standpoint it is also important to take adequate steps to reduce Type 2 errors (concluding that an effect does not exist when in reality it does), and this is achieved by increasing sample size which in consequence increases statistical power. In this context it is quite legitimate to build up a sample size in order to reduce the chances of making such Type 2 errors. While splitting the study of Mednick *et al.* (1984) into two separate samples results in a loss of statistical significance (as shown by Gottfredson & Hirschi, 1990), many published studies would suffer the same fate if they too were split into two, since statistical power is a function of sample size. It would be a major error to conclude that genetic influences exist for crime when in reality they do not. It would be equally erroneous, however, to conclude that genetic effects do not exist when in fact they do, since future research directed into studying solely nongenetic influences would never be able to provide a complete explanation of crime.

Gottfredson and Hirschi (1990) go on to attempt to undermine the scientific credibility of two further adoption studies (Crowe, 1975; Cloninger & Gottesman, 1987) and conclude that there is little or no evidence for heritable or biological influences on crime. As pointed out by Gottfredson and Hirschi, the critical issue lies in whether findings can be independently replicated. As indicated in Table 4 above, there is evidence for such replication of findings in different countries by independent research teams. Gottfredson and Hirschi (1990) critically appraise only 3 of the 15 studies reported in Table 4. They also do not mention findings from the 13 twin analyses reported in Table 1, nor do they cite data on twins reared apart (although the study by Grove *et al.* was published in 1990 and may not have been available to them).

Such omissions seriously compromise the very strong conclusion they draw. No finding in science stands or falls on the findings of one (or even three) studies alone; rather, one must assess all studies whose differing methodologies bear on the issue at hand (in this case studies of twins reared together, twins reared apart, and adoption studies) rather than selective abstraction of individual studies. All studies, biological and social, can be criticized and improved upon, and each has its own individual weaknesses. When a number of independent studies employing different methodologies with their own individual weaknesses converge on the same general finding, however, such data constitute a more powerful base upon which to draw conclusions. This appears to be the case with studies on the genetics of crime.

Gottfredson and Hirschi (1990) proceed also to draw the conclusion that there is little support for the role of biological factors in crime, based on their dismissal of findings from three genetic studies. This is an erroneous conclusion. It is a simple but common mistake for nonbiological researchers to equate "genetic" with "biological." Biological factors may indeed stem from genetic influences but can equally represent direct environmental influences. For example, brain dysfunction is a biological factor that may be genetically mediated, but it can also be caused by environmental factors such as a difficult birth or a blow to the head. If one wishes to argue that biological research has produced little in the way of meaningful research findings, one must systematically review the extensive literature on biological factors and seek to demonstrate nontrivial methodological errors in such research. Taking an example of just one aspect of one of the many fields of biological research into crime, there have been over 150 published studies of electrodermal activity in antisocial and criminal behavior, yet none of these or any other biological studies are mentioned by Gottfredson and Hirschi (1990).

Using the same rigorous critique which Gottfredson and Hirschi (1990) applied to three genetic studies, it may be possible in the future to review studies on environmental influences and demonstrate that these findings are substantive, while findings from biological studies are nonsubstantive. Such a review does not currently exist. Until this is done for genetic and social studies of crime, interested readers are encouraged to read for themselves the twin and adoption studies reported previously and to draw their own conclusions. Given the current evidence, it would seem erroneous to deny the fact that genetic factors play some rule in the etiology of criminal behavior.

B. Is There Heritability for Violent Crime?

One conclusion drawn from adoption studies of crime was that there is heritability for petty property offending but not for violent offending. This seems counterintuitive since one would imagine that violent, more serious offending, being more extreme, would be more "hard-wired" and have a higher heritability than property offending, which one could imagine is more driven by social and economic factors. The fact remains that independent analyses from three adoption studies (Bohman *et al.*, 1982; Mednick *et al.*, 1984; Sigvardsson *et al.*, 1982) that have been large enough to test for heritability have failed to show it.

One twin study draws a somewhat different conclusion from the adoption studies regarding violent offending. Cloninger and Gottesman (1987), in an updated analysis of extensive twin data collected by Christiansen (1977), analyzed for heritability of property offenses only, versus crimes against the person. From these data they estimated heritability to be .78 for property crimes versus .50 for crimes against persons. This suggests that while heritability for nonviolent offending is indeed higher than for violent offending, this twin data (unlike the adoption data) also suggests heritability for violence. What is an even more interesting finding from these analyses is the fact that genetic predisposition for property offending was unrelated to genetic predisposition for violent offending, indicating that separate genetic influences operate for these two types of offending. These results must be tempered by analyses conducted by Carey (1989) indicating only a trend for heritability for violence being statistically significant.

There may be reasons why heritability exists for violence but is not observed. Carey (1989) has suggested that previous studies have relied on official records which may have inaccuracies that lower heritability, though it is difficult to see why inaccurate records should find heritability for property offending but not for violent offending. Certainly the lower base rates for violence reduce statistical power for tests of heritability, and it may be that specific forms of violence (e.g., assault) have heritability while others do not (Carey, 1989). Taking adoption and twin studies together, however, one must conclude that, at the present time, there are no strong data suggesting that there is a statistically significant genetic effect for crimes of violence. This does not negate the possibility that violence may in part have a *biological* basis, and evidence for such a position will be reviewed in later chapters.

C. Is There an Interaction between Heredity and Environment?

Criminologists have tended to focus exclusively on answering the first question at the expense of progressing to ask more interesting and challenging questions that arise from behavioral genetic research into crime. One crucial question concerns whether there is an interaction between heredity (H) and environment (E) (or H $\times$ E interaction). This is an important question because in recent years there has been a shift in focus toward more biosocially oriented research into antisocial behavior (Mednick & Christiansen, 1977; Moffitt & Mednick, 1988; Mednick, Moffitt, & Stack, 1987; Raine, 1989). This trend is at least partially underpinned by the assumption that environmental factors interact with heredity factors in the production of antisocial behavior. An H $\times$ E interaction would suggest that (1) it is when both environmental and genetic factors occur together that an individual is most likely to manifest criminal behavior; and (2) the interaction between heredity and environment accounts for more variance in criminal behavior than either influence alone.

Perhaps the best evidence for an interaction between genetics and environment in accounting for crime is reported by Cloninger *et al.* (1982) in a cross-fostering analysis of "petty" criminality (infrequent minor property offenses which are nonalcohol related). Swedish adoptees ($N = 862$) were divided into four groups depending on the presence or absence of (1) a

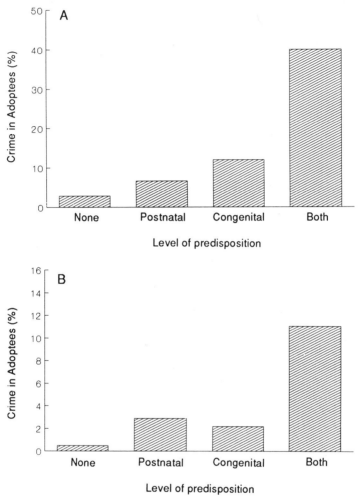

FIGURE 2   Results of a cross-fostering analysis indicating evidence for an interaction between genetic and environmental factors in (A) males (Cloninger *et al.*, 1982) and (B) females (Adapted from Cloninger & Gottesman, 1987).

congenital predisposition (i.e., whether biological parents were criminal), and (2) a postnatal predisposition (variables concerned with rearing experiences and adoptive placement). Results of this study are illustrated in Fig. 2.

When both heredity and environmental predispositional factors were present, 40% of the adoptees were criminal compared to 12.1% with only congenital factors present, 6.7% for postnatal only, and 2.9% when both factors were absent. The fact that the 40% rate for criminality when both biological and environmental factors are present is greater than the 18.8% rate given by a combination of "congenital only" and "postnatal only" conditions is indicative of a nonadditive (H × E) interaction between congenital and postnatal factors. Further analyses indicated that the occupational status of both biological and adoptive parents was the main postnatal variable involved in this nonadditive interaction. Evidence for an H × E interaction is also provided by Cadoret, Cain, and Crowe (1983), who presented data from three adoption studies which again confirm that when both genetic and environmental factors are present, they account for a greater number of antisocial behaviors than a combination of these two factors acting alone. Crowe (1975) found some evidence for an H × E interaction in his analysis of adopted-away offspring of female prisoners, though this trend was only marginally significant ($p < .10$).

In spite of this evidence for an H × E interaction, a clear answer to this issue is clouded on two fronts. One such limitation in the study by Cloninger *et al.* (1982) pointed out by Gottfredson and Hirschi (1990) is that the cell size in the critical category (both heredity and environmental factors present) is small ($N = 10$) compared to the other categories (66, 120, 66), which may give more stable estimates. However, Cloninger and Gottesman (1987) later presented data for females (see Fig. 2 above) with larger sample sizes. As would be expected, these crime rates in female adoptees are much lower than those for males, but the same interactive pattern is present, that is, crime rates in adoptees are greatest when both heritable and environmental influences are present, with this interaction accounting for twice as much crime as both congenital alone and postnatal influences combined. This striking replication on an independent sample give strong support for the presence of an H × E interaction, at least in this Swedish sample.

A more important problem for the notion of an H × E interaction is that some studies simply fail to find evidence for such interactions. For example, Cloninger *et al.* (1978), in their analyses of relatives of 60 probands with felony convictions, conclude that their results ". . . raise serious doubt about the importance of nonlinear gene–environment interaction. Our analyses support additive or linear models without major interactions" (p. 949). These mixed data suggest that the amount of variance accounted for by an H × E interaction is sometimes significant but on other occasions not as large as might be expected. The implications for future research are that interactions between genetic and environmental factors cannot be entirely ignored, but this should not prevent researchers from seeking out direct relationships with crime for both genetic and social factors, or from being critical of the appealing but potentially oversimplistic view that most variance in criminal behavior can be explained by the interaction between environmental and genetic influences.

D. What Is the Extent of the Heritability for Crime?

Overemphasis on the question of whether heritability for crime exists has obscured the more important question of the *extent* to which genetics can explain crime. There has been a tendency for researchers to polarize the issue, with some criminologists arguing for a zero contribution of genetics under the assumption that a study which finds evidence for heritability is making the statement that *all* crime can be accounted for by genetic factors. Certainly no behavioral geneticist in recent times has made such a statement, and there are certainly no data that currently support such a position. But what exactly is the contribution played by genetic factors?

This question has no easy answer, but one can narrow down the range of possibilities. The studies reported above clearly indicate that the contribution of genetics is not zero. At the other extreme it is easy to rule out the notion that genetics fully account for crime. Inspection of Table I showing data for twin studies indicates at a glance that having one MZ twin criminal does not always entail crime in the co-twin. Rather than 100% concordance, the rate for MZ twins is more like 50%. Similarly, studies show that adopted-away children who have a criminal biological parent do not always end up as criminals themselves; rather, rates tend to be below 40%. These rates indicate a substantial role for *environmental* influences.

Some examples from adoption studies help illustrate the point that the proportion of variance in crime that genetic factors explain is not extravagantly large. Cadoret (1978), while arguing for a genetic factor in adoptee antisocial behavior, found that only 3% of the variance in a multiple regression analysis can be accounted for by biological background, with 3% also accounted for by environmental background. Hutchings (1972), in a multiple regression of criminality in 286 probands, reports that 10% of the variance in adoptee criminality can be accounted for by biological background and 3% by adoptive background. Calculations based on data reported by Baker (1986) and Baker, Mack, Moffitt, and Mednick (1989) for property offending in Danish adoptees indicate that the proportion of phenotypic variance accounted for by additive genetic influences ranges from 20.3 to 32%.

These modest rates have their exceptions, however, as twin studies tend to report higher rates. For example, self-report delinquency data in twins reported by Rowe (1983) yield a much higher heritability of .70 relative to the adult official crime data of the adoption studies. The largest of the adult twin studies indicates that 54% of the variance can be accounted for by genetic factors (Cloninger & Gottesman, 1987). Twin studies may give higher heritability estimates than adoption studies because the latter only assess nonadditive genetic factors whereas estimates from twin studies also take into account the effect of dominance (the interaction between alleles at a given locus). Carey (1992) also suggests that twin imitation may be a factor accounting for higher heritabilities in twin studies.

One confusion that arises in establishing how much variance in criminal behavior can be accounted for by genetic factors stems from the fact that rates from adoption studies usually report the amount of *total* variance accounted for by genetic factors. Taking the example of the adoption study by Cloninger *et al.* (1982), only 23.6% of the total variance could be explained by *all* main factors (genetics and environment) and their interaction. However, if one restricts the analysis to *explained* variance (i.e., that part of total variance that is not error variance and is explained by genetic and environmental factors), then 59.3% of the variance could be accounted for by genetic factors alone. Heritability estimates from twin studies, on the other hand, often use Holzinger's h, which is a broad estimate of heritability (Falconer, 1981) and which represents the proportion of *explained* variance attributable to genetic factors. Thus, twin studies may give the appearance of indicating a greater role of genetic factors in accounting for variance, but this can be misleading.

If adoption studies indicate that genetic factors account for less than 25% of the variance in crime, does this indicate that genetic influences are relatively unimportant? In the context of the amount of variance accounted for by *nongenetic* influences, the answer is no. As one example, Cadoret *et al.* (1983) report rather small proportions of total variance explained by *all* factors (i.e., heredity + environment + the interaction between the two) in two of their three adoption samples (total percentages of 12, 16, and 37 in the three studies); environmental factors in these studies are as poor (or as good) as genetic factors in accounting for crime. One reason for this is that there are environmental factors other than having a criminal adoptive parent which contribute to crime and which are not measured in these studies. As such, estimates for environmental influences are conservative, although having a criminal parent is clearly an important environmental influence as well as a genetic influence. Similarly, assessing genetic influences entirely on the basis of having a criminal biological father is equally limiting; some biological fathers may have become criminal due more to environmental than genetic reasons, although it is assumed in all cases that they predispose their offspring to crime. Alternatively, this genetic predisposition may not become expressed until the second generation; for example, the genes in question may be recessive. A source of error variance affecting both estimates is the use of official measures of criminal behavior; self-report measures of crime may in future studies allow for a greater proportion of crime to be accounted for by genetic and environmental factors.

Returning to the original question of the extent of heritable influences on crime, it must be reiterated that discrete quantification at this stage is not possible. One approximate deduction that can be drawn from twin and adoption studies is that genetic influences may well account for roughly half of the *explained* variance in crime. That is, genetic influences are nontrivial and probably account for as much variance as environmental influences in relation to crime.

Genetic factors alone, however, are clearly incapable of providing an adequate explanation for the cause of crime. To place genetic and environmental contributions into a context, it is worth bearing in mind twin data from European countries. The base rate for crime for unrelated individuals in these countries for registered crime is approximately 12% (Bohman *et al.*, 1982; Mednick *et al.*, 1984). Dizygotic twins who have approximately half their genes in common have concordance rates for crime of about 20%. Twins who are genetically identical show concordance rates of about 50%. This indicates a powerful effect of genetic influences. By the same token, 50% of identical twins are discordant for crime, illustrating the powerful effect of *environmental* factors also.

E. Is There Stronger Heritability for Female Crime?

There has been relatively little discussion and research into female crime in general, and this is particularly true of research into the genetics of crime. For reasons discussed below, the question of whether females have a stronger heritability for crime relative to males is a potentially important issue, and consequently the question is worthy of full consideration.

An extensive review of biology and female crime by Widom and Ames (1988) concludes that the genetic predisposition of a woman has to be greater than that of a man in order for antisocial behavior to be manifested. Support for this conclusion stems largely from familial studies which show that antisocial females have a higher incidence of familial crime than antisocial males, from studies of female twins suggesting higher concordance in females, and from some adoption studies that show a doubling of the rate of criminality in biological parents of criminal females relative to criminal males. Similar conclusions are drawn by Cloninger *et al.* (1975, 1978) and Sigvardsson *et al.*, (1982), who suggest that sex typing and greater social pressures toward prosocial behavior in females necessitate a greater genetic predisposition for the manifestation of antisocial behavior.

Caution should be exercised, however, in accepting too readily the conclusion of greater heritability for female crime. While MZ/DZ concordance ratios are somewhat higher for female twins (3.2) than for male twins (2.4), sample sizes in females are much smaller than in males and may therefore be less stable. Additionally, several recent adoption studies not reviewed by Widom and Ames (1988) also fail to support this conclusion. Cadoret (1978) found a slightly higher rate of antisocial personality in the offspring of fathers with antisocial behavior rather than in the offspring of antisocial mothers. Cadoret and Cain (1980) observed no significant sex difference in the genetic predictors of antisocial behavior in adoptees, while Cadoret, O'Gorman, Troughton, and Heywood (1985) found evidence for inheritance of antisocial behavior in male but not in female adoptees. While the twin study with the largest sample size (Christiansen, 1977a) does find higher heritability for females, an updated analysis of Christiansen's data by Cloninger and Gottesman (1987) does not appear to support this conclusion as indicated by data in their Table 6.6 (p. 99).

Set against these negative data, one must also consider positive findings which are additional to those alluded to above. In a large adoption study, Baker *et al.* (1989) found that female criminals appear to be more genetically predisposed to crime than males by virtue of the fact that they are more likely to have criminal adopted-away offspring.

While there is some evidence from some studies of greater heritability for female crime, it is clear that the data are by no means unequivocal. The equivocal nature of this evidence is best illustrated by an interesting and detailed analysis by Baker *et al.* (1989). Despite the evidence supporting the notion of a greater genetic predisposition in female criminals as reported above, Baker *et al.* (1989) also noted that convicted sons and daughters do not differ in terms of the likelihood of their parents being criminal, indicating comparable heritability estimates in the two sexes.

If one was to accept that there is greater heritability for criminality in females, then there are potential implications for biologically oriented research into antisocial behavior. If female offenders represent in an extreme form those who are genetically predisposed to antisociality, then biological investigations of such populations could give particularly clear insights into the way in which such a predisposition manifests itself at a biological level. In practice there has been very little biological research carried out into female offending, possibly because such groups represent a very small percentage of the total criminal population and are difficult to obtain. Nevertheless, findings of such investigations would certainly have applicability to understanding the biology of more prevalent male offending and are consequently sorely needed. Before such research is warranted, there must be a clarification of this important issue by further behavioral genetic studies into female crime and antisocial behavior.

F. Is There Heritability for Juvenile Antisocial Behavior?

Although the central interest of this book lies with respect to hereditary influences on adult crime, there have been some twin studies of juvenile delinquency that are worthy of mention. A number of previous reviews (Eysenck, 1977; Rutter *et al.*, 1990; Carey, 1989; Trasler, 1987) argue that these studies show little evidence for genetic influences on juvenile delinquency. Broadly speaking, these conclusions are largely correct, though it would not be strictly correct to derive the conclusion that there is no evidence at all for heritability for juvenile delinquency.

Previous twin studies of juvenile delinquency are listed in Table 5. It can be seen that concordance rates across twins for juvenile delinquency are much higher than for crime, reflecting the greater base rate for the former. More

TABLE 5   Concordance Rates from Twin Studies of Juvenile Delinquency[a]

Reference	Location	Sex	% MZ concordance	(N)	% DZ concordance	(N)
Rosanoff *et al.* (1934)	U.S.	M	100	(29)	71	(17)
Rosanoff *et al.* (1934)	U.S.	F	92	(12)	100	(9)
Kranze (1935)	Prussia	M+F	69	(16)	59	(22)
Sugmati (1954)	Japan	?	80	(10)	20	(5)
Mitsuda (1961)	Japan	?	73	(15)	75	(4)
Hayashi (1963)	Japan	M	80	(15)	75	(4)
Shields (1977)	England	M	80	(5)	78	(9)
Total			84.3	(102)	68.6	(70)

[a]N = number of pairs of twins. Total figures are weighted by sample size.

importantly, however, there is less of a difference in concordance rates between MZ and DZ twins. Summary figures weighted by sample size across the seven studies yield figures of 84.3% for MZ and 68.6% for DZ, indicating only a modest effect of genetic influences. Though it is clear that the evidence for heritability of juvenile delinquency is weaker than that for adult crime, there does appear to be *some* limited evidence for heritability at this age level.

Table 6 shows key findings from three adoption studies for juvenile delinquency and adolescent antisocial behavior. Bohman (1972) and Cadoret (1978) found no evidence for heritability of juvenile delinquency and conduct disorder. While Cadoret *et al.* (1983) found some evidence for heritability in the form of interactions between heredity and environment, a main effect for heredity was not observed in two of the three samples. These results therefore,

TABLE 6   Key Findings from Adoption Studies of Juvenile Delinquency

Bohman (1972)	No excess of juvenile delinquency (truancy, lying, stealing) in 10- and 11-year-old adoptees in adopted-away children whose biological parents were criminal.
Cadoret (1978)	No evidence for heritability for child diagnosis of conduct disorder (measured by psychiatric interview) in a sample of child adoptees.
Cadoret *et al.* (1983)	Evidence for significant H × E interaction in three samples of adoptees for adolescent antisocial behavior (measured by mothers' report of antisocial behaviors). No evidence, however, in two of these samples for a main effect of heredity using a multiple regression model.
Grove *et al.* (1990)	Heritability of .41 calculated for self-report, retrospective childhood antisocial behavior (pre-age 15 years) in a sample of twins reared apart.

TABLE 7   Other Twin Studies of Antisocial Behavior in Children and Juveniles

O'Connor *et al.* (1980)	Evidence for heritability for "bullying" as rated by mothers' (Holzinger's $H = .60$) in 54 MZ and 33 DZ 7.6 year olds.
Ghodsian-Carpey & Baker (1987)	Heritabilities ranging from .24 to .94 for mothers' ratings of different types of aggressive behavior in 21 MZ and 17 DZ 4- to 7-year-old twins.
Rowe (1983)	Significant heritability for self-report delinquency in both male ($H = .36$) and female ($H = .52$) children in grades 8–12. Heritability as high as .70 suggested by biometrical genetic modeling.

like twin studies, suggest that if there is any heritability for delinquency, it is not marked.

While conclusions from twin and adoption studies are largely negative, there may be significant heritability for *self-report* delinquency and childhood antisocial behavior as rated by mothers from twin studies. Table 7 lists findings from four studies where antisocial behavior is not defined in terms of official measures of juvenile delinquency as used in twin studies. For example, Rowe (1983) reports on anonymous self-report delinquency in 168 MZ and 97 DZ twin pairs in grades 8 to 12 (approximately 13 to 17 years) and found significant heritability for such behavior. Similarly O'Connor, Foch, Sherry, and Plomin (1980) and Ghodsian-Carpey and Baker (1987) find heritability for antisocial and aggressive behavior in children (ranging from 4 to 7 years of age) where childrens' behavior is rated by mothers. The fourth and most recent study is unusual in that it is one of twins reared apart and deserves particular attention. Grove *et al.* (1990), in addition to assessing adult antisocial behavior, assessed child antisocial behavior before the age of 15 from a clinical interview; hence the measure is verbal self-report antisocial behavior. Heritability for this child antisocial behavior was calculated at 0.41.

These discrepancies with other twin and adoption studies may indicate that antisocial behavior is not heritable when legally defined in adolescence, but is heritable when adolescent antisociality is measured by self-report measures or when childhood behavior is assessed by mothers. This again underlies the potential importance of studying milder, potentially more "successful," nonlegally defined aspects of antisocial behavior, an approach that has been largely ignored to date by behavioral geneticists and psychologists, who have largely studied "unsuccessful" delinquents and criminals. The notion that mild forms of delinquency are heritable may be consistent with adult data indicating that milder, petty forms of crime are heritable.

Although it would be erroneous to conclude at this stage that there is no evidence for heritability of early antisocial behavior, one cannot escape from the fact that childhood and adolescent forms of antisocial behavior seem to be less heritable than adult crime. One reason for this is that many children who are antisocial in childhood do not go on to become criminal, though many adult criminals are antisocial in childhood and adolescence. This view would predict that there would be significant heritability for delinquency in that subgroup of delinquents who graduate into adult crime, but not in those who desist from later offending. To date this prediction does not appear to have been empirically tested. A related explanation for the lack of heritability for juvenile delinquency is that peer-group pressures are particularly strong in adolescence. As such, these and other social factors may play a much stronger role in determining juvenile delinquency than genetic factors, whereas genetic factors may be more helpful in explaining adult crime.

An alternative reason as to why evidence for heritability of antisocial behavior is weaker at earlier ages may be that time is needed for the full expression of the genetic mechanisms that underlie antisocial behavior. Data from a twin study of the inheritance of intelligence by Wilson (1983) provides a useful heuristic parallel for this idea. Wilson (1983) found that MZ twins became increasingly concordant for IQ from age 3 months to 15 years, while in contrast DZ twins regressed to intermediate levels of concordance by age 15 years, that is, heritability for IQ is greater at 15 years than in infancy. This indicates that the genetic mechanisms underlying intelligence are dependent on the full development of brain maturational processes which unfold in the context of the individual's living environment. In much the same way, genetic and biological mechanisms underlying antisocial behavior may well require full maturation of the organism to achieve maximal expression. As an example of one factor which will be outlined in more detail in a later chapter, prefrontal areas of the brain do not reach full developmental maturity until early adulthood, and poor functioning of this brain structure has been implicated in criminal and violent offenders. The notion that genes are dependent on maturational and environmental processes to achieve expression comes as no surprise to geneticists, but psychologists, psychiatrists, and social scientists frequently lose track of this fundamental issue.

G. Is Psychopathy Heritable?

It is commonly assumed that psychopathic behavior, in addition to criminal behavior, has a genetic basis. This assumption would seem very reasonable if psychopathy were viewed as a severe form of antisocial behavior (Eysenck, 1977). If mild crime is in part genetically determined, as the evidence cited above would suggest, then surely more "deviant" forms of antisociality such as psychopathy should have an even greater genetic basis. Somewhat surprisingly, there is currently little good evidence for this conclusion.

With respect to twin data, reviews by Hutchings and Mednick (1977), Eysenck (1977), and Reid and Bottlinger (1979) discuss heritability with reference to terms such as "psychopathy" and "sociopathy," yet all samples consist of criminals on whom no good measure of psychopathy has been taken. This extrapolation from "criminality" to "psychopathy" is even more widespread in adoption and familial studies. At least eight of these studies (Schulsinger, 1972; Crowe, 1974; Cloninger *et al.*, 1975, 1978; Cadoret, 1978; Cadoret *et al.*, 1985; Cadoret, Troughton, & O'Gorman, 1987; and Bohman *et al.*, 1982) claim a genetic basis for "sociopathy" or "antisocial personality disorder," yet none of these studies utilizes a convincing or strict diagnosis of psychopathy. Again, the fundamental issue is whether the "psychopathic" behavior referred to in these studies represents anything over and above criminal behavior.

Crowe (1974), for example, used DSM-II criteria for the diagnosis of antisocial personality disorder and allocated this diagnosis to 6 out of 46 adoptees of female offenders as compared to 0 of 46 controls. The difficulty here is that 7 probands had arrest and conviction records, and all 6 of the probands diagnosed as antisocial personality disorder fell into this group. Consequently antisocial personality disorder virtually overlaps with criminality. Similarly Cadoret (1978) diagnosed antisocial personality disorder in the biological families of adoptees if they were convicted felons, while Cloninger *et al.* (1975) define sociopathy as "a personality disorder characterized by the early onset of repeated antisocial, delinquent, and criminal behavior" (p. 13).

This mixing of terms is not the fault of researchers who merely adopt the definition of antisocial personality in DSM-III, which is near synonymous with crime. Such a definition should be contrasted with other methods for assessing psychopathy such as the Psychopathy Checklist (Hare, 1980) which, in addition to the antisocial behavior features emphasized by DSM-III, also contains more clinically derived personality features such as superficial charm, egocentricity, pathological lying, lack of remorse and guilt, and callousness. This is a strict criterion for psychopathy in that it accepts only about a third of prison inmates as psychopathic (Hare, 1983), and it is possible that this measure may form the basis of the future DSM-IV definition of antisocial personality disorder (Widiger *et al.*, 1991; Hare *et al.*, 1991). It is unfortunate that no adoption or twin study has utilized assessment procedures based on Cleckley's conception of psychopathy (Cleckley, 1976), which closely parallels the "antisocial trait" of Harpending and Draper (1988) and which, from an evolutionary standpoint, would be expected to have a particularly strong genetic basis.

Two relatively recent studies attempt to assess analogs of antisocial personality disorder rather than just relying on criminal convictions and suggest that psychopathic behavior may have a modest genetic predisposition. A study by Baker (1986) supports this notion but also suggests that heritability for "antisocial disorder" is considerably less than that for nonviolent property crime. A biometric model-fitting approach was applied to data from 2532 Danish male adoptees and their biological and adoptive parents in order to assess heritability for (1) nonviolent property crimes, and (2) antisocial disorder, where the latter was based on a composite diagnostic variable based on personality disorder, alcohol use, and drug use (previously found by Moffitt, 1984, to be significantly correlated with criminal conviction). Generalized least-squares parameter estimates indicated a relatively small heritability of .27 for antisocial disorder in comparison to a much higher heritability of .45 for property crimes.

The second recent study by Grove *et al.* (1990) employed a dimensional measure of adult antisocial behavior which closely followed DSM-III criteria for antisocial personality disorder in their study of adopted-away identical twins. Heritability for antisocial personality using this measure was calculated at .28, a value very close to that of .27 derived by Baker (1986). While these data suggest that psychopathic behavior may not have a strong genetic basis, "antisocial disorder" is probably only an indirect index of psychopathy in the strict sense of the word.

The implicit assumption to date has been that psychopathy is an extreme form of antisocial behavior which has a strong genetic basis and thus will evidence a very distinct biological profile. In consequence it has become the focus of relatively extensive biological research, perhaps at the expense of research into milder forms of antisocial behavior. A study which more validly assesses psychopathy in an adoption sample would be valuable in clarifying the genetic basis for psychopathic behavior, which is often assumed but which currently can be neither confirmed nor denied.

X. SUMMARY

This chapter evaluates data from twin and adoption studies to assess the prediction generated from sociobiological studies that a genetic predispositoin exists for crime. Ten misconceptions on genetic research are first clarified: (1) There is no single gene capable of producing criminal behavior per se; (2) genetic research does not imply that all crime is determined by genetic factors; (3) behavior genetic studies operate at a population level and cannot determine presence of genetic factors in specific individuals; (4) the notion that crime is in part genetically mediated does not mean that criminal behavior cannot be changed or prevented; (5) genetic studies reveal the clear importance of environmental influences in addition to genetic influences; (6) although crime is a socio–politico–legal construction, this is not inconsistent with an underlying genetic predisposition since other partly heritable conditions are also constructions of society; (7) genetic research does not threaten to put social scientists out of business; this fate awaits biological and social researchers who continue to ignore each others' data; (8) genetic studies cannot be used to support sterilization programs because heritability for crime is not consistent with the notion of destiny for crime; (9) recent increases in crime rates are not necessarily inconsistent with a genetic approach; (10) the failure of XYY research into violent crime does not compromise results of population-based genetic research into crime.

Summary statistics from 13 twin analyses show that 51.5% of MZ twins are concordant for crime compared to 20.6% for DZ twins, indicating substantial evidence for genetic influences on crime. A breakdown of studies indicates that heritability for crime is not a function of age of the study, zygosity determination, sex of subjects, small sample sizes, or bias from studies conducted in the Nazi era. While twin studies have a number of weaknesses that may inflate heritability estimates, other weaknesses exist that will artifactually reduce such estimates. Studies of twins reared apart, while few in number, support heritability for crime. Adoption studies overcome some of the disadvantages of twin studies, and analysis of 14 such studies from three different countries provides strong support for conclusions drawn from twin studies.

Seven key research questions are raised and preliminary answers provided. First, despite strong criticisms from social scientists, empirical data from several sources provide strong converging lines of evidence indicating some degree of genetic predisposition for crime; this conclusion cannot be side-stepped by criticisms of a few selected studies, criticisms of the twin methodology, or erroneous beliefs about the nature of genetic research. Second, there is some limited support for the notion that genetic factors interact with environmental factors in producing crime; one implication of future support for this notion is that criminologists must seek to understand and break down this potentially important interaction. A very tentative and global estimate for the extent of heritability for crime is that genetic influences account for about half the variance in criminal behavior. A stronger genetic predisposition may exist for female crime, and research into females may provide important clues on biological predispositional factors for crime in both sexes. Heritability for juvenile delinquency appears to be less than for adult crime, possibly due to the need for maturational processes to be completed before a genetic predisposition becomes fully manifest. There is no good evidence to date that psychopathic crime has a reliable heritable basis, though future research employing better measures of psychopathy may alter this conclusion. Overall, data from genetic studies support the prediction made by sociobiological theory that heritable influences in part underlie criminal behavior.

4 Neurochemistry

I. GENERAL INTRODUCTION

Brain biochemistry has been extensively researched with respect to disorders such as schizophrenia and depression, and indeed such research is of major importance in understanding the etiology of these disorders. In contrast, brain biochemistry in relation to criminal behavior tends to be overlooked by mainstream criminologists. While many criminology texts and handbooks include critical discussions of the link between genetics and crime, with perhaps some mention of psychophysiological research, research on brain neurotransmitter systems is almost exclusively ignored. One reason for this is that neurochemistry represents an extreme "micro" view of crime, which has traditionally been viewed from a more "macro" perspective. Second, brain biochemistry is a more technical field using unfamiliar terminology that is more difficult to follow and mapping processes that are sometimes difficult to view within the context of broad styles of behavior such as crime. Third, until recently, there have been relatively few studies of neurotransmitters in criminals, and animal research on neurotransmitters and aggression is viewed as even more esoteric to mainstream social science criminologists.

This position is rapidly changing. In an excellent review of neurochemical factors in crime published in 1987, Rubin (1987) was only able to describe four published neurotransmitter studies conducted on criminals. As will be seen below, up to 1992 there have been at least 29 studies published in the area of antisocial behavior and neurotransmitters, with the modal date of publication of studies being 1988–1989 (see Table I). This new, expanding body of literature is becoming increasingly important, and consequently this chapter will focus on neurotransmitters in human antisocial behavior in preference to older and more well-known literatures on sex hormones (e.g., testosterone, progesterone) and other biochemical factors (e.g., hypoglycemia). An overview of these latter biochemical factors will nevertheless be provided in a later chapter in order that a wider perspective on biochemistry will not be lost.

This chapter will first provide an introduction to neurotransmitters and their mechanisms of action before briefly summarizing the main conclusions to emerge from the literature on human pharmacology and antisocial behavior. Focus will be placed on three major neurotransmitters: serotonin, norepinephrine, and dopamine. Results of a meta-analysis of 29 recent studies assessing these three neurotransmitters in adult and child antisocial populations (Scerbo & Raine, 1992) are presented, indicating reduced serotonin and norepinephrine in antisocials. Subanalyses are then presented in an attempt to specify which subgroups of antisocials these findings pertain to. An attempt is then made to integrate these findings into current biological, cognitive, social, and psychopathological research with respect to crime. Finally, recommendations for future research into this area will be outlined. The recurring argument that will be made is that neurochemistry research holds critically important implications for social science research, and vice versa, with reciprocal causal relationships potentially providing the best context for future research in this area.

II. INTRODUCTION TO NEUROTRANSMITTERS

The notion that neurotransmitters play a role in psychological phenomena is not new. Increased dopamine has long been implicated in schizophrenia (Cooper, Bloom, & Roth, 1986), while reduced levels of serotonin, norepinephrine, and/or dopamine have been implicated in depression (Fitten, Morley, Gross,

Petry, & Cole, 1989; McNeal & Cimbolic, 1986). Interest in relating neuro-transmitters to human antisocial behavior, as has been indicated above, has a much more recent history. Other recent reviews of this research may be found in Eichelman (1993), Schalling (1993), and Virkkunen and Linnoila (1993).

Only serotonin, norepinephrine, and dopamine will be reviewed because there are currently too few human studies on other neurotransmitters to allow meaningful analyses. Only human studies will be included because the older animal literature has already been extensively reviewed and because there has been a recent increase in human studies.

A. Basic Mechanisms of Action

Basic neurotransmitters such as dopamine, norepinephrine, and serotonin form the basis for information processing and communication within the brain, and in this sense they underlie all types of behavior, including sensation, perception, learning and memory, eating, drinking and, more controversially, antisocial behavior. Communication systems can be roughly divided into two types, hormonal and neural. Hormones represent biochemical substances that are secreted into the bloodstream by endocrine organs located throughout the body, including the testes (testosterone), ovary (progesterone), and pancreas (insulin). Such hormones are relatively slow in terms of communication speed and will be dealt with in a later chapter.

In contrast, neural signals are electrochemical events that are produced by nerve cells within the brain and are much more fast acting. Neurotransmit-ters are chemicals stored in the synaptic vesicles (small globules) of a commu-nicating cell's axon; this axon carries the nerve impulse of the cell body to other cells. During cellular communication, these chemicals are discharged into the synaptic cleft (the space between two neurons) and are taken up by special receptors in the postsynaptic membrane of the other recipient cell, initiating what is termed a postsynaptic potential and hence the transmission of information throughout the brain.

A specific cell will only produce one transmitter substance, although there are many different neurotransmitters known to exist in the brain. Known transmitters include acetylcholine, the indolamine serotonin (or 5-HT), and the catecholamines (dopamine, norepinephrine, and epinephrine), all of which are classified as monoamines. In addition, amino acids (γ-aminobutyric acid or GABA) and neuropeptides (e.g., β-endorphin and enkephalins) also constitute neurotransmitters. Paradoxically, the well-known and best-studied neurotransmitters (serotonin, dopamine, norepinephrine) account for only a small proportion of cell firing in the brain. For example, serotonin is thought to be the transmitter substance at less than 0.1% of brain synapses. Signifi-cantly, they are thought to be highly important in the context of brain and behavior; for example, serotonin, norepinephrine, and dopamine have been implicated in the etiology of major disorders such as schizophrenia and depression.

While some transmitter systems are distributed widely throughout the brain, others are more localized to specific brain networks. Norepinephrine is largely produced in neurons in the brainstem nuclei whose axons project relatively widely throughout the brain. Dopamine is produced largely by cells in the brainstem which project to the basal ganglia and specific cortical areas. Serotonin is produced by the raphe nuclei in the midline of the brainstem which send projections through the cerebral hemispheres. Norepinephrine and serotonin are implicated in the arousal system and sleep, while dopamine is more implicated in voluntary movement, learning, and memory.

B. Measurement of Neurotransmitters

There are several methods of estimating the central nervous system level of a neurotransmitter. One can measure the level of the particular amino acid precursor which is synthesized to form the neurotransmitter, the particular enzyme known to convert the precursor into the neurotransmitter, the particular metabolite formed when the neurotransmitter is degraded, or an indirect indicator known to covary with changes in the level of the neurotransmitter. Of these, measurement of metabolites provides the most direct measurement of neurotransmitter turnover or usage (see Cooper *et al.*, 1986) and as such would be more likely to yield significant findings.

Each of these indices can be measured from three different bodily fluids: cerebrospinal fluid (CSF), blood, or urine in living subjects. Measurement from the CSF is the most direct measure of a central neurotransmitter. Central neurotransmitters are synthesized in the brain and metabolites first enter into the CSF. From the CSF metabolites go on to enter the bloodstream, which is the next best measure of a central neurotransmitter, although some metabolites may be further broken down by the time they enter the blood. Last, all unused body metabolites collect in the urine, which is the least direct measurement of a central neurotransmitter (Cooper *et al.*, 1986). Further, urine and blood are likely to contain transmitter metabolites coming from various regions of the body rather than simply from the brain. For example, stress may lead the adrenal glands to excrete norepinephrine which then drains into the blood and urine (see Stern, Ray, & Davis, 1980, for a description of sympathetic reactions). Studies using the more direct CSF measure would be expected to produce stronger findings.

III. DRUG MANIPULATION OF NEUROTRANSMITTERS IN HUMANS

If neurotransmitters are causally related to crime and violence, manipulation of these transmitter levels using drugs should lower antisocial behavior. Results of this pharmacological research on humans have not been entirely consistent, however, and are briefly reviewed here (see also Brizer, 1988, and Yudofsky, Silver, & Schneider, 1987).

A. Serotonin

Lithium carbonate, a drug that increases the uptake of the serotonin precursor tryptophan, has been found to decrease aggressive episodes in prison inmates (Sheard, 1975; Sheard, Marini, & Bridges, 1976), mentally retarded patients (Dale, 1980), and conduct- and attention deficit-disordered children (Siassi, 1982). Similarly, administration of the serotonin precursor tryptophan has been found to decrease aggressive episodes in schizophrenics characterized by poor impulse control and high lifetime aggression (Morand, Young, & Ervin, 1983). At least two studies have failed to observe these effects, however (Volavka, Crowner, Brizer, Convit, Van Praag, & Suckow, 1990; Whitehead & Clark, 1970). In general, however, research on the effects of serotonergic manipulation on aggression has shown *decreases* in aggression when serotonin is elevated (Brizer, 1988).

B. Norepinephrine

Drugs that reduce norepinephrine levels (e.g., reserpine) have been shown to inhibit aggressive behaviors (Eichelman, 1986), while drugs that increase norepinephrine levels (e.g., tricyclic antidepressants) have tended to exacerbate aggressive behavior in agitated depressed patients (Rampling, 1978). In general, however, research on the effects of noradrenergic manipulation on aggression has shown *increases* in aggression when norepinephrine is elevated and *decreases* in aggression when norepinephrine is reduced (see Brizer, 1988, and Yudofsky *et al.*, 1987, for reviews).

C. Dopamine

Antipsychotic drugs that act to decrease dopamine levels tend to decrease fighting in patients (Eichelman, 1986; Yesavage, 1984), aggressive delinquents (Molling, Lockner, Sauls, *et al.*, 1962), and individuals with borderline personality disorder (Brinkley, Beitman, & Friedel, 1979). One review, however, indicates that many patients did not improve with antipsychotic medication (Yudofsky *et al.*, 1987). In general, however, *decreases* in aggression are observed when dopamine is reduced (see Brizer, 1988, and Yudofsky *et al.*, 1987 for reviews).

Summarizing these three areas of psychopharmacological human research, serotonin plays an inhibitory role while norepinephrine and dopamine each play facilitative roles in aggression. This literature would therefore predict that antisocial, aggressive populations would be characterized by low levels of serotonin and high levels of norepinephrine and dopamine. Drug manipulation research in humans, however, contains inconsistencies, and studies suffer from methodological limitations such as not using placebo-crossover designs, not considering side effects of the drugs such as sedation, and not considering the concurrent alteration of other neurochemicals due to the drugs. Consequently, the interpretation placed on these studies must be preliminary at the current time.

IV. META-ANALYSIS OF NEUROTRANSMITTER LEVELS IN ANTISOCIAL POPULATIONS

The following analysis is a summary of a more detailed meta-analysis outlined by Scerbo and Raine (1992). Based on the previous human pharmacological literature, it would be predicted that antisocial groups would be characterized by low serotonin levels and high levels of both dopamine and norepinephrine. This review focused on behaviorally defined antisocial and violent behavior to others and did not include violence to self (e.g., suicide attempters) or antisocial behavior assessed using personality measures. The resulting sample of 29 studies yielded 28 serotonin-effect reports, 32 norepinephrine-effect reports, and 19 dopamine-effect reports.

The effect size index used is d, the difference between the means of two groups (experimental and control), divided by the pooled standard deviation. Study outcomes were combined to compute a composite effect size by averaging the d values with each d weighted by the reciprocal of its variance $(d+)$, which gives a stronger weighting to studies with the largest sample sizes. Composite effect sizes were calculated separately for each neurotransmitter (serotonin, norepinephrine, and dopamine) and 95% confidence intervals were computed for each mean effect size.

A. Main Results

A summary of study characteristics is found in Table 1, presented separately for serotonin, norepinephrine, and dopamine. Studies were usually published recently (mode = 1988–1989) and, as expected from this type of biological research, consisted of relatively modest numbers of subjects (mode = 30). The following were also characteristics of these studies: (1) Children were less often studied; (2) absence of psychiatric problems i.e., alcohol abuse, borderline personality disorder, depression, or dysthymia) or suicide history was common; (3) dopamine and norepinephrine were more often measured in urine and CSF while serotonin was more often measured in blood and CSF; (4) measurement of metabolites was common; and (5) use of violent subjects was common.

TABLE 1 Summary of Study Characteristics for the Three Neurotransmitters

Variable	Serotonin	Norepinephrine	Dopamine
Year of publication			
Mean	1985.8	1985.4	1986.8
Median	1987	1988	1988
Mode	1989	1988	1988
Range	1974–90	1977–90	1979–90
Sample size			
Mean	28.5	33.3	33.8
Median	25	30	30
Mode	30	30	30
Range	10–64	11–64	9–64

B. Overall Neurochemical Differences

Table 2 shows the composite (mean) weighted effect sizes and 95% confidence intervals for studies examining serotonin, norepinephrine, and dopamine in antisocial populations as compared to controls. An overall neurochemical difference is indicated when the mean effect size differs significantly from 0.00, which indicates exactly no difference between the experimental and control groups. If the 95% confidence interval includes 0.00, therefore, the effect is considered to be nonsignificant. In the case of serotonin, the mean effect size ($M = -.47$) significantly differed from 0.00 in the direction of lower serotonin in the antisocial groups. The mean effect sizes for norepinephrine and dopamine, however, were not significant.

C. Subgroup Analyses

Subgroup analyses were conducted to assess whether there were additional categorical moderator variables (e.g., age, alcohol use, violence, borderline

TABLE 2 Summary of Neurochemical Effects

| Criterion | Effect size analyses | | |
	Serotonin	Norepinephrine	Dopamine
M weighted effect size $(d+)^a$	−.4680	−.0385	−.0483
95% CI for $d+$	−.61/−.33	−.17/+.09	−.2/+.11
Homogeneity statistic (Q)	150.05	257.06	24.97
Significance level for Q	.000	.000	.126

[a]Effect sizes were weighted by the reciprocal of the variance.

TABLE 3   Tests of Moderator Variables for Serotonin Effect Sizes Using CSF Studies

Variable and class	Between-class effect (Qb)	N	Weighted effect size (d+)	95% for d+	Homogeneity within each class (Qw)
Alcohol abuse	8.54*				
None		4	−1.23	−1.66/−.79	18.99***
Less than half		4	−.38	−.75/−.02	13.68**
Half or more		5	−.77	−1.09/−.46	14.03*
Borderline personality disorder	4.76*				
None		6	−.55	−.83/−.27	32.97****
Half or more		7	−1.02	−1.34/−.7	17.50*
Suicide	21.68****				
None		6	−.32	−.62/ −.03	15.55*
Less than half		3	−1.6	−2.06/−1.14	7.36
Half or more		4	−.89	−1.28/−.5	10.65*
Antisocial behavior	10.59**				
Nonaggressive		2	−.04	−.49/+.4	.01
Violence against person		6	−.89	−1.19/−.58	29.86****
Violence mixed		2	−.98	−1.58/−.38	7.18*
Chemical measured	4.03*				
Metabolite		11	−.85	−1.07/−.62	49.94****
Other (somatostatin)		2	−.23	−.78/+.25	1.28

* $p < .05$.
** $p < .01$.
*** $p < .001$.
**** $p < .0001$.

personality disorder, suicide attempt, depression, type of chemical measured, place of measurement) that mediated the main findings. For example, antisocials could be broken down into subgroups who were either violent or nonviolent, and effects for serotonin may be stronger for the former than for the latter. When only CSF studies were considered, significant effect sizes in the negative direction were found for both serotonin ($d+ = −.75$, $p < .05$) *and* norepinephrine ($d+ = −.41$, $p < .05$) (i.e., significantly reduced central serotonin and norepinephrine in antisocial groups). This result might be expected because CSF measurement provides a more direct estimate of neurotransmitter levels than blood or urine measurements. In addition, however, urine studies showed a significant effect size for norepinephrine in the positive direction ($d+ = 0.19$, $p < .05$), indicating increased norepinephrine in antisocials. Following these initial analyses, further sub-

TABLE 4   Tests of Moderator Variables for Norepinephrine Effect Sizes Using CSF Studies Only

Variable and class	Between-class effect (Qb)	N	Weighted effect size ($d+$)	95% for $d+$	Homogeneity within each class (Qw)
Alcohol abuse	25.06****				
None		2	+1.11	+.43/+1.8	1.94
Less than half		2	−.29	−.7/+.11	7.48*
Half or more		6	−.81	−1.13/−.49	32.20****
Borderline personality disorder	9.43**				
None		4	−.08	−.4/+.24	21.26***
Half or more		6	−.83	−1.19/−.47	35.99****
Depression	6.49*				
None		4	−.08	−.47/+.31	15.29**
Less than half		3	−.78	−1.16/−.41	7.65
Half or more		2	−.5	−1.06/+.06	63.32****

* $p < .05$.
** $p < .01$.
*** $p < .001$.
**** $p < .0001$.

group analyses were conducted only on CSF studies and urine studies of norepinephrine. The following represent the key findings to emerge for each of these analyses:

D. CSF Serotonin (Table 3)

1. Antisocials without a history of alcohol abuse had significantly lower serotonin levels (larger negative mean effect size) than those with a history of alcohol abuse.

2. Antisocials with borderline personality disorder and suicide attempts had significantly lower serotonin levels than antisocials without such histories.

3. Measurements from metabolites exhibited a larger negative mean effect size than measurement of somatostatin (a chemical thought to covary with serotonin levels), whose mean effect size was not significant.

4. Violent/assaultive antisocials had significantly lower serotonin levels than nonaggressive antisocials, whose mean effect size was not significant.

5. No significant differences in effect sizes were found due to age of subjects or presence of depression/dysthymia.

E. CSF Norepinephrine (Table 4)

1. Antisocials with alcohol abuse had significantly lower norepinephrine levels than nonalcoholic antisocials.

TABLE 5   Tests of Moderator Variables for Norepinephrine Effect Sizes Using Urine Studies Only

Variable and class	Between-class effect (Qb)	N	Weighted effect size $(d+)$	95% for $d+$	Homogeneity within each class (Qw)
Alcohol abuse	11.84***				
None		10	+.1	−.09/+.29	62.05****
Less than half		3	+1.25	+.62/+1.88	3.34
Depression	21.82****				
None		7	+.36	+.11/+.61	47.05****
Less than half		3	−.25	−.53/+.04	5.01
Half or more		3	+1.25	+.62/+1.88	3.34
Antisocial behavior	38.47****				
Nonaggressive		3	+1.25	+.62/+1.88	3.34
Violence against person		1	+1.04	+.44/+1.63	0.00
Violence mixed		2	−.93	−1.42/−.43	8.91*

* $p < .05$.
** $p < .01$.
*** $p < .001$.
**** $p < .0001$.

2. Antisocials with borderline personality disorder had significantly lower norepinephrine levels than antisocials without this disorder.

3. Antisocials with depression/dysthymia had significantly lower norepinephrine than antisocials without such histories.

4. No significant differences in effect sizes were found for age, previous suicide attempt, or type of chemical measured.

F. Urinary Norepinephrine (Table 5)

1. Mixed violent offenders (assault against persons or property) had significantly *reduced* urinary norepinephrine, while nonaggressives had significantly *increased* urinary norepinephrine.

2. Antisocials with some evidence of alcohol abuse had significantly *higher* urinary norepinephrine than nonalcoholic antisocials.

3. Antisocials with depression/dysthymia had significantly *higher* urinary norepinephrine values than antisocials without depression.

4. No significant effects were found for age or type of chemical measured.

V. DISCUSSION OF KEY FINDINGS

When studies are pooled together, irrespective of method of body fluid used to assay neurotransmitters, results indicate reduced serotonin in antisocial groups, with no effect for dopamine and norepinephrine. When only CSF studies are examined (providing a more direct measure of central neurotransmitter functioning), results are clearer, indicating reduced central serotonin and norepinephrine activity in antisocials. These findings are only partly expected from the human pharmacological literature but are more consistent with the psychobiological theory of antisocial behavior outlined below.

The averaged effect sizes are not trivial (-0.75 for CSF serotonin and -0.41 for CSF norepinephrine) and are greater for specific subgroups (e.g., -1.23 for CSF serotonin in nonalcoholic antisocials). Furthermore, the averaged effect size for serotonin is 1.8 times greater than that for norepinephrine, indicating greater stability of the serotonin effect in antisocials. As indicated in Tables 3, 4, and 5, however, effect sizes were heterogeneous, indicating that there is wide variability in effect size from study to study. This variability was in part due to variations between studies (e.g., violent versus nonviolent populations, subjects with or without alcoholism). To rephrase this using analysis of variance terminology, the "main effects" for neurotransmitters could not be considered in isolation of "interactions." Two sources of variation, type of antisocial behavior, and affective instability and alcoholism require further elaboration.

A. Type of Antisocial Behavior

A key aim of the meta-analysis was to examine differences between violent and nonviolent antisocial individuals. This assessment was difficult, however, because individuals committing property crimes, which are normally considered nonviolent, were often combined with murderers or other violent offenders in study samples and described as assaultive to either person *or* property. Thus the category of "violence mixed" was created in this analysis to include samples combining violent with property offenders. Only one study contributed reports on a sample of solely nonaggressive antisocials, and those subjects were all gamblers. Results indicated that all violent categories exhibited reduced central serotonin relative to nonaggressives. Urinary results indicated reduced norepinephrine in the violence mixed group but increased norepinephrine in the gamblers. Central norepinephrine could not be compared among the groups because there was only one report in the nonaggressive and violent mixed categories.

Because no studies included samples solely of property offenders, they could not be directly compared to those committing a crime against person. Since central serotonin was significantly reduced in violence against persons, however, while central norepinephrine was not, it can be inferred that central serotonin plays the more influential role in these crimes. Central serotonin was also reduced in the mixed violence group, however, leaving unresolved the role of serotonin in property offenses. Although central norepinephrine was nonsignificant in crimes against person, urinary norepinephrine was reduced in the mixed violence category, suggesting perhaps that the norepinephrine reduction is influenced more by the inclusion of property offenders. Any inference should be made with caution, however, since this category consists of only two reports from a single study.

Last, the increased urinary norepinephrine in gamblers may reflect an overactive behavioral activation system (BAS) (i.e., the activation of behavior in response to cues of reward) in these individuals. Fowles (1980) reviewed studies indicating an increase in heart rate to cues of reward, suggesting that heart rate may reflect activity of the BAS. Since peripheral norepinephrine released from the adrenal glands has a major influence on heart rate, it follows then that individuals with an overactive BAS may also have increased peripheral norepinephrine that drains into the urine. This implies that the mechanism underlying pathological gambling may differ from that of aggressive antisocial behaviors; specifically, gamblers but not aggressives may have an overactive behavioral activating system.

B. Effect of Affective Instability and Alcoholism

Subgroup analyses indicated reduced central norepinephrine in antisocial individuals who had a previous diagnosis of borderline personality disorder, depression/dysthymia, or alcohol abuse. Reductions in central serotonin in antisocials were observed regardless of the presence or absence of such disorder.

These results suggest that the finding of reduced norepinephrine in antisocial individuals may be a function of the presence of individuals with affective instability or alcoholism rather than the antisocial behavior per se. Reduced serotonin on the other hand remains significant across diagnoses, indicating across-the-board reductions in antisocials. One exception is alcohol abuse, which exhibits a larger mean effect size for reduced central serotonin and increased central norepinephrine in nonalcoholics.

VI. INTEGRATION OF NEUROCHEMICAL RESEARCH WITH EXISTING PERSPECTIVES ON ANTISOCIAL BEHAVIOR

Research on neurotransmitters has theoretical and conceptual implications for social scientists, psychologists, psychiatrists, and other researchers interested in a more complete understanding of antisocial and criminal behavior. To date there has been virtually no integration between the fields of biochemistry and the social sciences with respect to crime. One aim of the following analysis is to attempt to foster such a cross-disciplinary integration. At this stage only examples can be given of the potential for such integration, and what follows is best viewed at a heuristic level.

A. Behavioral Activation and Inhibition

Prior to knowledge of the results of the above meta-analysis, Scerbo (1991) predicted reduced central serotonin and norepinephrine in antisocial individuals based on the psychobiological theories of Gray (1975) and Fowles (1988). These perspectives suggest an underactive behavioral inhibition system (BIS) in antisocials. The incorporation of neurochemical results in this theory of socialization is one example of how biological research can be applied to existing theories of the development of antisocial behavior.

Gray (1975, 1976, 1981) has proposed a two-factor learning theory which has application to antisocial behavior. The theory posits the existence of two behavioral systems: the behavioral activation system (BAS) and the behavioral inhibition system (BIS). The BAS is thought to *activate* behavior in response to cues of reward or nonpunishment, while the BIS is thought to *inhibit* behavior in response to cues of punishment or frustrative nonreward. Fowles (1988) has applied this model to antisocial behavior, arguing that reduced BIS functioning may underlie the disinhibitory, impulsive behaviors seen in antisocial individuals. It is argued that an inability to learn to inhibit behaviors from cues of punishment, possibly from reduced conditioned anxiety to punishment, impairs socialization in these individuals.

According to Gray (1987), both systems have neural bases, with the BIS being related to noradrenergic (from the locus coeruleus) and serotonergic (from the raphe nuclei) pathways, while the BAS is related to the dopaminergic pathway. Similarly, Fowles (1980) has suggested a connection between the two systems and psychophysiological response systems. Based upon studies showing an increase in skin conductance in conditions of punishment and an increase in heart rate in conditions of reward, Fowles (1980) suggests that skin conductance and heart rate reflect activity of the BIS and BAS respectively.

Placing Gray's (1987) and Fowles' (1980) theories within the context of neurotransmitter systems, the following would be predicted:

1. Underactivation of BIS: low skin conductance, low norepinephrine, low serotonin.
2. Underactivation of BAS: low heart rate and low dopamine.

Few studies have examined the relationship between neurotransmitters, but these few studies lend initial support for the above neurotransmitter–psychophysiology links. Regarding the BAS system, Mirkin and Coppen (1980) found that depressed patients with no skin conductance orienting responses to auditory stimuli (i.e., nonresponders) had reduced blood platelet uptake of serotonin, indicating that serotonergic functioning is related to electrodermal activity in humans. In cats, Yamamoto, Arai, and Nakayama (1990) showed complete abolition of auditory skin conductance responses after the destruction of the central noradrenaline system in cats, indicating a link between noradrenaline and skin conductance activity. Similarly, schizophrenics with high skin conductance responsivity had higher levels of the norepinephrine metabolite MHPG (Bartfai, Edman, Levander, Schalling, & Sedvall, 1984).

Regarding the BIS system, heart rate may also be interpreted as reflecting the BIS, which Gray (1976) considers to be a substrate of anxiety. In conditions of stress or sympathetic arousal, norepinephrine and heart rate are closely related to each other (Stern *et al.*, 1980; Wessels & Hopson, 1988). Although it is peripheral norepinephrine released from the adrenal glands rather than central norepinephrine that plays the major role in regulating heart rate, Hawley, Major, Schulman, and Linnoila (1985) found a significant positive correlation between heart rate and cerebrospinal fluid MHPG in patients undergoing alcohol withdrawal. While data are limited, they lend some initial support to Scerbo's analysis.

According to Gray's theory, poor socialization may occur due to a decreased ability to learn to inhibit behavior from cues of punishment (i.e., decreased BIS), which may be related to decreased anxiety. Decreased anxiety, in turn, may be reflected in decreased heart rate and skin conductance and thus decreased norepinephrine and serotonin. As will be seen in a later chapter, there is also some evidence that antisocials are characterized by reduced skin conductance and heart rate (possibly reflecting decreased anxiety). Again, these findings are consistent with the notion that decreased anxiety and functioning of the BIS may be related to outwardly directed antisocial/disinhibited behavior.

Placing these data alongside the perspectives of Gray and of Fowles outlined above, the following set of relationships were predicted by Scerbo:

1. Antisocial behavior, underactive BIS: low skin conductance, low norepinephrine, and low serotonin.
2. Activation of BIS: high heart rate and high dopamine.

In this model, therefore, the critical feature is that antisocial behavior is linked to underactivation of the BIS but is not linked in any way to the BAS. According to the psychobiological approach presented above, learning socially accepted behavior is mediated by emotional and psychophysiological reactions to reward and punishment. The primary emotion involved is anxiety, which may be reflected by the psychophysiological indices of skin conductance and heart rate as part of the BIS. Norepinephrine and serotonin, according to the model, are also reflective of the BIS. If reduced functioning of the BIS is related to antisocial behavior, then it is expected that antisocial individuals will also exhibit decreased serotonin and norepinephrine relative to controls. Antisocial behavior is assumed to be mediated by aspects of the BIS rather than the BAS. Dopamine, which is speculated to be related to the BAS, therefore, is not expected to differ in antisocial individuals. These predictions await testing in studies that combine psychophysiological with neurochemical measures in antisocial populations.

B. Psychophysiology and Criminality

As indicated by the above analysis, neurotransmitter findings have implications for the field of psychophysiology. As outlined above, both serotonin and norepinephrine have been implicated in the production of skin conductance responses (Mirkin & Coppen, 1980; Yamamoto *et al.*, 1990), and norepinephrine has been found to be positively correlated with heart rate (Hawley *et al.*, 1985). It is possible that reductions in serotonin and norepinephrine may be mediating the effects of reduced skin conductance and heart rate found in antisocial individuals (Raine, Venables, & Williams, 1990a; Farrington, 1987). It is important, therefore, that psychophysiologists studying crime be aware of the possible biochemical mechanisms underlying the effects of skin conductance and heart rate. Research combining both psychophysiological and neurochemical measures is clearly called for.

C. Environment versus Genetics

Research on neurotransmitters also has potential implications for genetic explanations of antisocial behavior (Scerbo & Raine, 1992). Analyses of CSF studies showed no differences in central serotonin or norepinephrine effects between children and adults. These results suggest that whatever mechanisms led to the reduction of serotonin and norepinephrine in antisocial individuals are in place in childhood and are relatively stable across time. It is unclear, however, whether these neurotransmitter alterations in children and adults are due to genetic or environmental factors. One clue in this regard involves the effects of type of antisocial behavior committed. Property crimes seem to have a genetic basis (Mednick *et al.*, 1984), while violent offending seems to be influenced by environmental stressors such as pregnancy and birth complications (Litt, 1971; Lewis, Shanok, & Balla, 1979), brain damage (Elliott, 1987; Raine & Scerbo, 1991), unstable home environments (Mednick & Kandel, 1988), and child abuse (Widom, 1989a,b).

Scerbo (1991) has suggested that the results of subgroup analyses might indicate that reduced serotonin is influential in crimes against person and property (environment and genetics), while reduced norepinephrine is influential in property crimes only (genetics only). These inferences are indirect, however, and a more powerful conclusion could only be drawn if more studies included samples of purely property offenders. If these inferences hold true, however, they could imply that the serotonin effects may be influenced more by environmental and genetic factors, while the norepinephrine effects may be more genetically mediated.

If the speculation of Scerbo (1991) is true, one would expect heritability in humans for individual differences in norepinephrine assays but less so for serotonin. To the authors' knowledge there are few or no studies on the heritability of central neurotransmitter levels, though the one known study has observed greater environmental than genetic effects for serotonin and genetic effects only for norepinephrine in twins (Oxenstierna, Edman, Iselius, Oreland, Ross, & Sedvall, 1986).

D. Body Build and Antisocial Behavior

Low levels of CSF serotonin may help explain previous claims of a relationship between crime/delinquency and a mesomorphic/endomorphic body build (Glueck & Glueck, 1956; McCandless, Persons, & Roberts, 1972; Wilson & Herrnstein, 1985). Low serotonin levels in disruptive behavior disorder patients may result from decreased concentrations of somatostatin, a peptide which stimulates serotonin release (Kruesi, Swedo, Leonard, Rubinow & Rapoport, 1990b). Somatostatin also influences somatotype as this peptide inhibits the release of growth hormone. As such, reductions in somatostatin could not only reduce serotonin levels but also could increase muscle and body mass in delinquents and criminals. Increased body and muscle mass could predispose to aggression as a result of the social reinforcement obtained from large body size in conflictual social encounters.

Of the two studies measuring somatostatin in this meta-analysis, one found a significant reduction in the antisocial group (Kruesi *et al.*, 1990b) while the other found no significant differences (Roy, Adinoff, & Roehrich, 1988). It is difficult to make conclusions based on these findings, and more research on somatostatin in antisocials needs to be conducted. While these interconnections have yet to be substantiated, they illustrate the way in which brain biochemistry, somatotype, and instrumental learning in a social context may interrelate in predisposing an individual to antisocial behavior.

E. Social Status and Stress

Sociological and psychological studies have frequently implicated low socio-economic status and social stress in the etiology of crime and delinquency, although the precise nature of these relationships is debatable (Gelles, 1982; Mednick, Baker, & Carothers, 1990; Messner, 1988; Thornberry & Farnworth, 1982). It has been argued that low social class/status is related to low serotonin levels in both humans and monkeys, though the relationships are complex and not always consistent with this suggestion (Kruesi, Rapoport, Hamburger, & Hibbs, 1990a; McGuire, Raleigh, & Brammer, 1984; Yodyingyuad, de la Riva, Abbot, Herbert, & Keverne, 1985). Reduced central norepinephrine has also been found in lower status guinea pigs (Sachser, 1987) and animals exposed to external stressors (De Souza & Van Loo, 1986; Lehnert, Reinstein, Strowbridge, & Wurtman, 1984), while blood and urinary norepinephrine in humans tends to increase in stressful situations (Frankenhaeuser, 1971; Frankenhaeuser, Lundberg, Von Wright, Von Wright, &

Sedvall, 1986). Serotonin, however, seems either unaffected or increased by stress in animal studies (De Souza & Van Loo, 1986; Lehnert *et al.*, 1984).

Although speculative, it is not inconceivable that causal/reciprocal connections may exist between these variables, with low norepinephrine and serotonin resulting in stress and downward drift in socioeconomic status due to an antisocial way of life (e.g., via unemployment and imprisonment). It is also possible that other negative environmental factors lead to alterations in neurotransmitter levels.

F. Nutrition

One such negative environmental influence on neurochemistry may be poor nutrition (Scerbo & Raine, 1992). Diets low in or otherwise blocking the uptake of tryptophan or tyrosine (the precursors of serotonin and norepinephrine, respectively) have been found to lower the levels of these transmitters in the brain (see Weisman, 1986). In addition, even when returned to a normal diet, brain serotonin levels are never fully compensated (Timiras, Hudson, & Segall, 1984). Poor nutrition possibly occurring in individuals of lower socioeconomic status, including dietary care during pregnancy, may very well influence neurotransmitter levels throughout life.

Whatever the precise relationship between neurotransmitters and nutrition, stress, and social status, it is clear that neurotransmitters do not influence behavior in an environmental vacuum. In any of a number of directions, social, environmental, and biological factors interact to influence behavior which itself may alter the initial factors. Both biochemists and social scientists working in the area of crime must be cognizant of such possibilities in the explanation of antisocial behavior and work toward their elucidation.

G. Cognitive Factors

It has been suggested that aggressive children may have deficits in social information processing whereby biases in perceiving, interpreting, and making decisions about social information increase the likelihood of aggression (Dodge & Crick, 1990). It is possible that alterations in neurotransmitters may contribute to such information-processing deficits (Scerbo & Raine, 1992). For example, aggressive boys have been found to be more likely than nonaggressive boys to attribute hostile intent in an ambiguous situation (Dodge, 1980) and to make these interpretations impulsively (Dodge & Newman, 1981). If reduced serotonin and/or norepinephrine is related to disinhibition, the deficit in either of these neurochemicals may potentiate the impulsive attributions of hostile intent in aggressive children.

Somatostatin levels may also have an effect on memory. Reducing somatostatin levels in animals have been found to impair memory in passive avoidance tasks (Bakhit & Swerdlow, 1986; Haroutunian, Mantin, Campbell, &

Tsuboyama, 1987), and a reduction of somatostatin has been found in Alzheimer's disease, which is characterized by major memory deficits (Schneider & Emr, 1985; Swihart, Baskin, & Pirozzolo, 1989). If reduced serotonin is a result of reduced somatostatin, it may be that memory is impaired in antisocial individuals with reduced serotonin. Impaired memory may lead to biases in the retrieval of responses and decision-making aspects of information processing, leading to increases in the likelihood of aggression (Dodge & Crick, 1990). For example, if these individuals are exposed to an aggressive environment (e.g., marital conflict, child abuse, gangs), they may develop a response set of aggression. In potentially harmful situations, therefore, aggressive behavior may be the most accessible or readily available response in memory, and deficits in memory will most likely lead to the retrieval of such "automatic" responses. The decision to respond with aggression, therefore, is likely to be facilitated.

Furthermore, an impairment in memory due to reduced somatostatin may decrease the ability to remember cues leading to punishment, thereby decreasing the ability to learn to inhibit behavior in conditions of punishment. This inability would be consistent with the theory of an impaired BIS in antisocial individuals outlined by Scerbo (1991).

While the speculation of neurotransmitter effects on information processing is potentially important and plausible, and while cognitive deficits have been frequently observed in antisocial groups, little work has actually been conducted to examine the relationship between neurotransmitter levels and cognitive functioning. Two studies found neurotransmitter levels to be unrelated to cognitive deficits often observed in antisocials, using the Porteus Maze, the Continuous Performance Test, and the Matching Familiar Figures Test (Kruesi et al., 1990a; Moss, Yao, & Panzak, 1990). One implication of this finding for cognitive psychologists is that cognitive variables may explain variance in antisocial behavior not explained by neurochemical factors. Adding cognitive tests to prospective studies of neurotransmitters, therefore, could help to increase the prediction of later antisocial behavior as well as illuminate the role of neurotransmitters in the cognitive functioning of antisocial individuals. The addition of such tests would be relatively easy to incorporate and would increase the conceptual breadth of neurochemical studies.

H. Effect of Alcohol

Research on the effects of alcohol on crime often shows alcohol consumption to be positively related to antisocial behavior (Cherek, Steinberg, & Manno, 1985). For example, Welte and Miller (1987) found the amount of alcohol consumption in a criminal group to be four times that of the general population. In addition, 46.2% of the criminals (largely violent offenders) reported having committed their crime while under the influence of alcohol. The present results show significantly reduced serotonin in antisocial alcohol abusers.

The effect of reduced serotonin, however, is largest in antisocial groups with *no* alcohol abuse. These results suggest that while reduced serotonin in non-alcoholic antisocial individuals may lead to disinhibited antisocial behavior, the disinhibiting effects of alcohol may provide an extra push toward antisocial behavior for those individuals whose serotonin is not so extremely reduced (Scerbo & Raine, 1992). It is important that researchers be aware of the possibility that there may be a group of antisocial individuals who are not alcoholic but who have a biochemical predisposition to crime, as well as a group who are influenced more by the disinhibiting effects of alcohol. These two groups may differ in terms of their motivation for engaging in antisocial behavior as well as in the etiology of that behavior.

VII. RECOMMENDATIONS FOR FUTURE NEUROCHEMICAL RESEARCH

The following limitations in current research suggest directives for future research in the area of neurotransmitters and antisocial behavior.

A. Indirect Nature of Measures

In contrast to animal studies, methods of estimating central neurotransmitter levels in humans are much more indirect and may or may not reflect actual levels of neurotransmitters in the brain. Furthermore, unlike animal studies, they cannot be localized to specific brain areas. There is little reason to believe, however, that the effects of neurotransmitters on antisocial behavior are uniform across brain sites. To deal with this question, as the technology of brain imaging develops, future studies on the role of neurotransmitters in antisocial behavior could employ imaging techniques, such as positron emission tomography (PET) or single-photon emission computer tomography (SPECT), to examine the functioning of the major brain areas involved in serotonin and norepinephrine production.

B. Control of Environmental Confounds

Measures of neurotransmitters are also based only on single values collected at one point in time and are affected by a large number of potential variables that are rarely controlled for, including diet, arousal, prior aggressive behavior, time of day, global environmental factors, and history of substance abuse. As such, the amount of error variance in neurochemical studies of antisocial behavior must necessarily be large. Alternatively, the fact that significant effect sizes are obtained across studies for central serotonin and norepinephrine attests to the robustness of these findings in the context of this error variance, and in this sense they are striking. Furthermore, some studies (e.g., Kruesi *et al.*, 1990a) controlled for many of these possible confounds either methodologically or statistically and still observed significant effects for serotonin. Although current methodological limitations make for difficulties in making specific conclusions regarding the role of neurotransmitters in human antisocial behavior, it is possible that low levels of central serotonin may reflect a trait predispositional factor for antisocial behavior rather than a factor reflecting state (e.g., diet, time of day). Future research must however be cognizant of a number of environmental confounds.

C. Role of Suicide

Animal and psychopharmacological research on the effect of neurochemicals on antisocial behavior has focused mainly on aggressive behavior. However, the present results seem to suggest a cumulative effect of aggression and suicide with even larger reductions of CSF serotonin found in those antisocial individuals who had attempted suicide. A direct comparison with "nonantisocial" suicide attempters, however, was not made in the above metaanalysis. Such a future comparison would further elucidate the role of serotonin relative to aggression and suicide.

D. Lack of Research in Females

Most of the studies reviewed previously used specialized male populations, that is, criminal adults or conduct-disordered children. The role of neurotransmitters in the modulation of aggressive/antisocial behavior in the general population is largely unknown, and in particular only one study seems to have examined female subjects (Gardner, Lucas, & Cowdry, 1990). In that study, violent and nonviolent females with borderline personality disorder were compared and no significant differences were found in levels of serotonin, norepinephrine, or dopamine metabolites. The role of metabolites found in male antisociality, therefore, may not generalize to females, and future research in this regard is warranted.

E. Self-Report Crime in the Community

A major way that social psychologists and sociologists could usefully collaborate with neurochemists is through the use of self-report crime and delinquency measures on noninstitutionalized, community samples. Such self-report measures have been pioneered by sociologists (Klein, 1989) and are much more sophisticated than questionnaire measures of aggressive personality sometimes used in this field, as they directly tap behavior as opposed to attitudes and have been validated against official measures of crime and delinquency (e.g., arrest data). As mentioned above, few neurochemical studies employ such measures, and findings are therefore restricted to the "unsuccessful" antisocial who comes to the attention of authorities. Such measures would be relatively easy to incorporate into neurochemical studies of antisocial behavior and would add an important methodological dimension to this research.

F. Subtypes of Crime

Animal research has focused on predatory versus affective aggression, while human research has not made an analogous distinction. Similarly, the above results suggest differential roles of serotonin and norepinephrine depending upon the type of crime (committed against person or property), interacting with psychiatric problems and alcohol. Future research might group offenders according to type of crime and presence of various psychiatric disorders (including suicide) in order to test this finding more directly.

G. Treatment Issues

With respect to practical treatment implications, violent crime against persons may be best treated through primary prevention of early environmental stressors, or later by pharmacological or dietary treatment that increases central serotonin activity. In any case of antisocial behavior where reduced central norepinephrine or serotonin is indicated, treatment that raises these neurotransmitter levels (whether pharmacological or dietary) may be beneficial. It is centrally important to point out, however, that no clear cause–effect relationship between neurochemistry and crime has been demonstrated, and therefore it is recommended that treatment interventions based on these findings await further confirmation and extension.

VIII. SUMMARY

This chapter reviewed the literature on relationships between criminal, violent, and antisocial behavior and three key neurotransmitters: serotonin, norepinephrine, and dopamine. Results of a meta-analysis of 29 recent studies assessing these three neurotransmitters in adult and child antisocial populations (Scerbo & Raine, 1992) were presented. Results indicated reduced central serotonin (effect size, ES $= -.75$) and norepinephrine (ES $= -.41$) in antisocials, with no effect for dopamine. Subanalyses were then presented in an attempt to specify to which subgroups of antisocials these findings pertain. These indicated that serotonin was lowest in antisocials with a history of alcohol abuse, borderline personality disorder, and violence, while CSF norepinephrine was lowest in those with alcohol abuse, borderline personality disorder, and depression.

An attempt was then made to integrate these findings into current biological, cognitive, social, and psychopathological research on crime. A disinhibition model was presented which links reduced activity of the behavioral inhibition system with reduced skin conductance, reduced serotonin, and reduced norepinephrine. It was hypothesized that increased body size in antisocials may conceivably be a function of reductions in somatostatin, which would also be expected to result in reductions in serotonin. Social stress and dietary deficiencies in tryptophan may also partly explain reductions in serotonin in antisocials. Alcohol is hypothesized to interact with reduced serotonin in disinhibiting behavior. Finally, recommendations for future research into this area were outlined and include better control over environmental confounds, the use of more direct measures of neurotransmitter functioning, more research on female antisocials, and the employment of self-report measures of crime in community samples. The key argument being made is that neurochemistry research holds critically important implications for social science research, and vice versa, with reciprocal causal relationships potentially providing the best context for future research in this area.

5 Neuropsychology

I. GENERAL INTRODUCTION

One way that a biological predisposition to crime may be expressed is by disruption of the normal neural mechanisms that mediate and control behavior. Criminal and delinquent populations have consequently been investigated using neuropsychological procedures in order to uncover evidence for discrete neurological damage or dysfunction that may account for antisocial and criminal behavior.

This chapter describes a number of neuropsychological theories of violence and crime. The selection of theories described here (frontal dysfunction, left hemisphere dysfunction, left fronto–temporal–limbic damage, reduced lateralization for language) is by no means exhaustive. Theories have been chosen because they represent important neuropsychological perspectives on crime and have been fairly extensively researched, or because they represent relatively new perspectives that have been underresearched but which represent promising lines for future study. More detailed reviews of neuropsychological impairments in various antisocial groups may be found in Yeudall and Fromm-Auch (1979), Yeudall *et al.* (1982), Nachshon (1983), Moffitt (1988, 1990), Kandel and Freed (1989), and Moffitt and Henry (1991), while good overviews specifically of aggressive behavior may be found in Milner (1991). Reference will also be made to studies on specific populations such as psychopaths. These studies are cited because, as will be argued, neuropsychological research into crime increasingly needs to study subtypes of offenders, and the psychopath is one subtype that has been more vigorously researched than others in this area.

The chapter begins with an introduction to basic terms in neuropsychology and a brief discussion of the limitations in the application of neuropsychological techniques to the study of crime. Studies linking dysfunction of the frontal regions of the brain will then be discussed, drawing on both lesion studies and neuropsychological test studies. Neuropsychological studies implicating the left hemisphere and, more specifically, the left fronto–temporal–limbic regions will be outlined, followed by the notion that antisocials may be characterized by reduced lateralization for linguistic functions. Claims for a raised incidence in left-handedness are then examined in the context of this reduced lateralization theory. The much more limited data on posterior brain regions, the right hemisphere, and the corpus callosum will be briefly considered, followed by an analysis of the controversial area of psychosurgery, which has implicated the amygdala in the regulation of violence. Finally, conceptual issues that need to be clarified in future research in this area will be enumerated. It is argued that generalized frontal dysfunction is characteristic of antisocial and criminal behavior in general, but not psychopathic behavior in particular. It is hypothesized, however, that damage specifically to both orbitofrontal and dorsolateral regions of prefrontal cortex may characterize antisocial or psychopathic individuals with features of schizotypal personality disorder, whereas psychopaths without schizotypal features may be characterized by orbitofrontal dysfunction only.

II. INTRODUCTION TO NEUROPSYCHOLOGY

Good introductions to the principles and methods underlying neuropsychological testing can be found in Kolb and Wishaw (1990), Lezack (1983), and Hellige (1993), while very detailed reviews of specific brain areas relevant to crime such as the frontal and prefrontal cortex may be found in Fuster (1988) and Stuss and Benson (1986). This introduction is limited to the very basic principals necessary for the understanding of concepts in this chapter.

Only those key brain areas that are frequently referred to later in this chapter will be discussed here. The brain can crudely be divided into two areas—cortex and subcortex. Cerebral cortex makes up the outer aspects of the brain and is of relatively recent origin in evolutionary terms, while phylogenetically older structures below this level make up the subcortex. Regarding the cortex, each of the two cerebral hemispheres is divided into four different regions or lobes, frontal, temporal, parietal, and occipital. These lobes are outlined in Fig. 1. Most neuropsychological research on crime described below has focused on the left hemisphere, specifically the more "anterior" regions, which constitute the frontal and temporal lobes (delineated by the lateral or Sylvian fissure and the central or Rolandic fissure). Some brief reference will, however, be made to the more "posterior" regions, which include the parietal and occipital lobes. Figure 2 illustrates a medial view (cut along the midline of the brain) and illustrates the limbic region of the brain and also the corpus callosum, a large band of nerve fibers that interlink the two cerebral hemispheres.

An important subdivision to bear in mind in this chapter is the distinction drawn with respect to the "prefrontal" area of the brain. This area is defined in various ways, although one definition is that it is made up of that part of the frontal cortex that receives projections from the mediodorsal nucleus of the thalamus. In general terms, however, it represents the most anterior or front part of the frontal lobe. It is centrally involved in abstract cognitive functions and higher intelligence, planning, behavioral inhibition, and the regulation of emotion and affect, functions which have superficial relevance to criminal behavior. In contrast, the more posterior part of the frontal cortex (premotor and motor cortex) is more concerned with orientation, sensory, and motor functions.

The importance of prefrontal cortex in the control of social behavior and intellectual functions can be seen in the light of comparative studies illustrating that while prefrontal cortex makes up 3.5% of total cortex in cats, 7% in dogs, 8.5% in lemurs, 11.5% in gibbons, and 17% in chimpanzees, it constitutes 29% of total cortex in humans. As will be seen below, prefrontal cortex in turn can be divided into medial, dorsolateral, and orbitofrontal cortex, with the latter region being speculated to be of potentially greater relevance to antisocial and violent behavior.

Subcortical structures are connected to cortical structures by "white matter" or axons (neuronal fibers). An important grouping of interconnected subcortical brain structures is the "limbic system" consisting of the hippocampus, amygdala, fornix, septal region, cingulate gyrus, and mammillary bodies, together with connections to the thalamus and hypothalamus. The limbic system is of particular relevance because it is involved not only in important

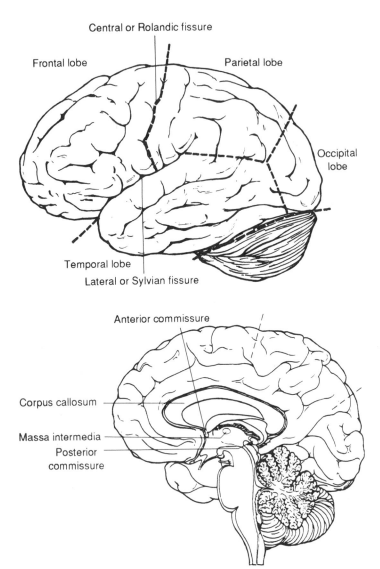

FIGURE 1   Diagrammatic representation of the outer regions of the brain illustrating the four main lobes.

cognitive processes such as learning and memory, but also in emotional and aggressive behavior.

One of the basic principles underlying neuropsychology is the notion that certain functions are, to some limited degree, localized within certain areas of

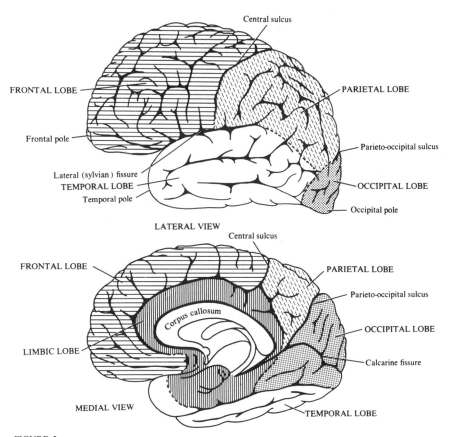

FIGURE 2 Diagrammatic representation of the medial regions of the brain illustrating the limbic areas and corpus callosum.

the cerebral hemispheres, while others are lateralized to one or other sides of the brain. Information on the localization of functions has stemmed classically from studies of patients with lesions localized to specific parts of the brain who then perform poorly on a selected test.

As one example, patients with lesions to the dorsolateral prefrontal cortex have been found to show more perseveration errors on the Wisconsin Card Sorting Task. In this task, patients are asked to sort cards into four piles on the basis of one of three categories (color, form, number). After 10 correct responses sorting cards by their color, the experimenter changes the sorting rule so that cards must be sorted according to the shape of the symbol on them (form), but the subject is not explicitly told this. The subject must then shift response set from color to form in the light of feedback that the previous response was incorrect. Patients with lesions to this part of the brain have difficulty shifting response set and consequently "perseverate" in making the previous (now incorrect) response. Performance on this task (number of perseveration errors, number of categories sorted) is then used to indicate the extent of "dysfunction" of this brain area when administered to criminal and noncriminal subjects. In this way, administration of relatively simple and inexpensive tests can give some, though albeit indirect, information on "dysfunction" or poor functioning of specific brain areas.

III. LIMITATIONS IN THE APPLICATION OF NEUROPSYCHOLOGICAL METHODS TO CRIME

Three points should be emphasized before turning to the neuropsychology of crime. One clarification necessary at the outset is, first, that when neuropsychologists suggest that neuropsychological disturbances underlie crime, the assumption being made is *not* that discrete and clear lesions (structural damage) are to be found in isolated cases of crime. Rather, the assumption is that there are individual differences in the quality of functioning of different parts of the brain, that such dysfunction is in part measured by neuropsychological tests, and that such differences may potentially predispose an individual to commit criminal and antisocial acts. As such, neuropsychological studies of criminals do not attempt to identify a discrete number of criminals with "clinically significant" brain damage, but instead attempt to show that the group as a whole show more dysfunction than controls. The notion then is that a nontrivial number of criminals may suffer some degree of dysfunction. This should not be taken to mean that subgroups with relatively more dysfunction exist within the larger criminal group. This may be the case, and more sensitive indices of brain dysfunction may allow such identification in the future. The present reality, however, is that it is more likely that significant dysfunction may exist in the absence of clear structural brain deficits, and that such dysfunction may be subtle but potentially powerful.

Second, it must not be forgotten that neuropsychological tests are inevitably indirect indices of brain dysfunction, and they vary in the degree to which they are sensitive to such dysfunction. Furthermore, localization of functions throughout the brain is relative and not absolute, and several (not one) brain areas may be involved in one specific form of information processing. As such, it would be naive to expect very strong group differentiation using such measures. The fact that group differences have frequently been observed attests to the strength of the underlying theory rather than the validity of the tests used.

Third, it will be seen in the following sections that neuropsychological studies do not always make distinctions between prefrontal and more posterior frontal brain areas. Part of the reason for this is that currently neuropsychological tests are limited in the extent of their specificity, with some being relatively sensitive to dysfunction localized in one brain site (e.g., Wisconsin Card Sorting and dorsolateral prefrontal cortex) while others are sensitive to damage in almost any cerebral region (e.g., Digit Symbol). As such, finer distinctions cannot always be drawn. This is particularly true with respect to the even finer distinctions between medial, dorsolateral, and orbitofrontal regions of prefrontal cortex which have not to date been accurately "mapped" by neuropsychological tests.

IV. FRONTAL DYSFUNCTION

A. Frontal Lesion Studies

One link between brain dysfunction and antisocial behavior comes from studies of the effects of brain lesions on behavior in normal subjects. One of the first and most dramatic single case studies linking frontal functioning to antisocial behavior is that of Phineas Gage reported by Harlow (1848). Phineas Gage was a dynamite worker for the Great Western Railway who experienced an accident in which an iron tamping rod measuring 3'7" long by 1.25" wide was blown through his head, entering at the lower cheek and exiting from the upper forehead. Amazingly, Gage survived the accident, but he underwent a dramatic personality change. Prior to the accident he was a capable foreman and reliable worker who displayed no obvious antisocial behavior. After the accident he was described as impulsive, irreverent, profane, obstinate, capricious, and antisocial. The brain area damaged in the accident was the left frontal lobe extending from the medial orbital region up to the precentral area.

More recent studies examining damage to the frontal cortex have shown a pattern of changes including argumentativeness, lack of concern for consequences of behavior, loss of social graces, impulsivity, distractibility, shallowness, lability, violence, and reduced ability to utilize symbols. This pattern of deficits is known as the Frontal Lobe Syndrome (MacKinnon & Yudofsky, 1986; Mesulam, 1986; Silver & Yudofsky, 1987). An interesting feature of patients with dorsolateral frontal lesions is that behaviorally they make perseveration errors (repeating responses they know are incorrect) on cardsorting tasks even though at a verbal level they are fully cognizant of their errors and realize what the appropriate response strategy is (Milner, 1963). This bears an interesting parallel to a similar dissociation between the psychopath's verbalizations about the correct prosocial life strategies that he should adopt and his actual discordant antisocial behavior, a feature which has been termed "specific loss of insight" (Cleckley, 1976).

While lesion studies of noncriminal populations suggest potentially important links between the frontal lobes and crime, it should be noted that one study by Virkkunen, Nuutila, and Huusko (1976) failed to find any increase in criminality in a follow-up of 507 Second World War Finnish soldiers with damage to either frontal or temporal lobes. Virkkunen *et al.* (1976) did not break down frontal lobe lesions into those affecting prefrontal areas as opposed to more posterior frontal areas, and such an analysis may have resulted in a more specific link between prefrontal damage and crime.

B. Frontal Neuropsychological Studies

More direct evidence for frontal dysfunction in crime (Flor-Henry, 1973) comes from neuropsychological studies that have implicated anterior and frontal dysfunction in violent criminals. Yeudall and Fromm-Auch (1979), for example, compared 86 violent criminals to 79 normal controls using the Halstead–Reitan Neuropsychological Test Battery (HRNTB) and found significantly more anterior neuropsychological dysfunction in the violent group. Yeudall, Fromm-Auch, and Davies (1982), however, failed to find differences between violent and nonviolent delinquents on the HRNTB and 12 other neuropsychological tests, indicating that frontal dysfunction may be specific to adult offenders.

While Yeudall's findings are impressive, they have been criticized by Hare (1979) and Nachshon (1983), the most important criticism being that subject samples utilized by Yeudall *et al.* are preselected clinical patients suspected of having neuropsychological impairments. It may not be surprising therefore to find a high proportion of these antisocials with neuropsychological impairments. On the other hand, although this group is selected, it is of interest that the neuropsychological deficits are localized to a particular brain region as opposed to being scattered across different brain sites.

In a study using the Luria–Nebraska Neuropsychological Battery (LNNB), Bryant, Scott, Golden, and Tori (1984) found violent crimes in 73% of subjects classified as brain damaged compared to 28% of those classified as normal. In addition, significant impairment was found in violent relative to nonviolent groups on LNNB tasks that have been described by Luria (1980) as associated with adult-onset frontal lobe disorders. In contrast to these findings, Brickman, McManus, Grapentine, and Alessi (1984) compared violent and nonviolent subjects on the LNNB and found impaired functioning for the violent group to lie in tasks more indicative of temporal rather than frontal lobe dysfunction.

Psychopaths have also been studied to examine deficits in frontal lobe functioning, with inconsistent results. Schalling and colleagues (Schalling, 1978a) found initial support for this proposition using the Porteous Maze (Schalling & Rosen, 1968) and the Necker Cube (Lidberg, Levander, Schalling, & Lidberg, 1978). Newman, Patterson, and Kosson (1987) provide support for response perseveration in criminal psychopaths using a card-playing task incorporating monetary rewards; in that response perseveration is a symptom of frontal dysfunction, these findings would be consistent with frontal dysfunction in psychopaths. Further support for frontal dysfunction in psychopathic criminals was observed by Gorenstein (1982), where frontal functioning was assessed by the Wisconsin Card Sorting Test (WCST), Necker Cube reversals, and a sequential matching memory task.

Despite these positive findings, there are a number of negative findings that must be considered. Hare (1984) failed to replicate Gorenstein's findings with the same three measures of frontal dysfunction but using a more stringent and reliable procedure for assessing psychopathy. A similar failure to replicate using psychopaths was reported by Hoffman, Hall, and Bartsch (1987). Similarly, Sutker and Allain (1983) failed to find any differences in perseveration between psychopaths and controls on the WCST, which would support Gorenstein's findings. Raine, O'Brien, and Scerbo (1991a) found significantly *better* performance on the WCST in a group of psychopathic conduct-disordered adolescents relative to conduct-disordered controls.

C. Comments on Frontal Findings

These latter findings cast serious doubt on the frontal lobe hypothesis of psychopathic behavior. It should be pointed out however that failures to observe WCST perseveration errors in psychopaths may not be entirely unexpected if orbitofrontal (rather than dorsolateral) dysfunction provides the major basis for psychopathic personality since lesions to this area do not produce cognitive deficits. Furthermore, if frontal dysfunction acts as a predisposition for crime in general, comparisons between psychopathic and nonpsychopathic criminal offenders would not be expected to produce significant differences.

In addition, frontal dysfunction may be specific to violent criminal offenders. Although psychopaths are more violent than nonpsychopaths, many psychopaths are nevertheless nonviolent, and studies of psychopaths would constitute only an indirect test of this hypothesis. Moffitt and Henry (1991) argue that while evidence for dysfunction in juveniles is mixed, adult violent offenders show more consistent evidence for neuropsychological dysfunction, including frontal dysfunction.

It is also possible that female antisocials may be more characterized by frontal dysfunction than males. The only study that assessed sex differences in frontal dysfunction among delinquents was reported by Moffitt (1988). This study assessed 750 13-year-old normal male and female children in New Zealand on self-report measures of delinquency and on a neuropsychological test battery that included several measures of frontal lobe functioning (WCST, Trail Making Test, Verbal Fluency, WISC-R Mazes, Rey–Osterreith Complex Figure Test). Male delinquents did not differ from nondelinquent male controls on a composite index of these frontal lobe tasks, but female delinquents were found to have significantly lower frontal lobe scores than female nondelinquents. These findings would be consistent with the notion that female antisocials require a stronger biological (neuropsychological) predisposition to antisocial behavior for such behavior to override socialization forces against the expression of such behavior in females.

D. Frontal Lobe Dysfunction in Schizotypal Antisocials

Raine and Venables (1992) have argued that frontal lobe dysfunction may be of particular relevance to a subgroup of criminals having both schizotypal and psychopathic features. At a clinical level the region of the frontal lobes that may be of stronger relevance to psychopathy consists of orbitofrontal cortex, whereas damage to dorsolateral regions of frontal cortex may be implicated in schizophrenia (Weinberger, Berman, & Zec, 1986; Raine, Lencz, Harrison, Reynolds, Sheard, & Cooper, 1992a). Damage to orbitofrontal regions results in impulsivity, reduced guilt, reduced concern and other emotional feelings, less inhibited sexual behavior, indifference, emotional outbursts and aggressive behavior, uninhibited social behavior, and "Witzelsucht" (puerile jocularity), personality changes which bear some close parallels to the clinical concept of psychopathy (Elliott, 1978). The fact that orbitofrontal lesions produce no clear deficits in intelligence is also consistent with the lack of intellectual/cognitive deficits in psychopaths (Hare, Frazelle, Bus, & Jutai, 1980).

Damage to dorsolateral prefrontal cortex on the other hand may be more relevant to schizophrenia and schizotypal personality, as such damage results in a somewhat different syndrome consisting of impairments in abstract reasoning and concept formation (such as response perseveration as measured by the WCST), loss of foresight and ability to plan ahead, poor motivation and work capacity, flat affect, social withdrawal, a lack of insight, poor sustained attention, and poor concentration. Such deficits have been observed in schizophrenics and schizotypals using regional cerebral blood flow (RCBF), PET, and magnetic resonance imaging (MRI) measures of prefrontal structure and function (Buchsbaum, Nuechterlein, Haier, Wu, Sicotte, Hazlett, Asarnow, Potkin, & Guich, 1990; Raine et al., 1992a; Weinberger et al., 1986). One study (Weinberger et al., 1986) has specifically implicated the dorsolateral prefrontal area in schizophrenia using both RCBF and WCST measures of frontal lobe functioning. Individual differences in schizotypal personality have also been related to prefrontal structural deficits measured by MRI, with higher schizotypal scores being associated with smaller prefrontal area in nonhospitalized subjects (Raine, Sheard, & Reynolds, 1992b).

It may be that schizotypal psychopaths represent a subgroup of criminals that is characterized by both dorsolateral and orbitofrontal dysfunction. Hare (1984), in discussing the failure to observe frontal lobe impairments in psychopaths, nevertheless suggests that criminals who show some features of psychopathy but who fall short of the complete psychopathic syndrome (schizotypal psychopaths) show greater evidence of neurological impairment.

Similarly both Elliott (1978) and Damasio (1979) have suggested that frontal lobe patients appear as "partial psychopaths." Raine (1992) found that a group of partial psychopaths (medium scorers on the Psychopathy Checklist) are characterized by higher scores on DSM-III Schizotypal Personality Disorder and self-report measures of schizotypal personality. These individuals are particularly characterized by features of psychopathy relating to an impulsive, unstable, nomadic lifestyle, a lack of life planning, a trivial sex life, and an inability to maintain long-term relationships, features which bear several close parallels to Heston's (1966) description of adopted-away criminal sons of schizophrenic mothers. At the same time these individuals possess social withdrawal, isolation, and a degree of perceptual and cognitive disturbances that bear parallels to the more negative features of schizophrenia (Andreasen & Olsen, 1982).

It may be that schizotypal psychopaths constitute a syndrome which most clearly represents the genetic relatedness between schizophrenia and psychopathy (Silverton, 1988) and which is in part determined by dysfunction of both orbitofrontal and dorsolateral areas of the frontal lobes, with orbitofrontal cortex contributing to the psychopathiclike personality features and dorsolateral prefrontal cortex contributing to the cognitive and social withdrawal features of schizotypal personality. Initial support for this proposition comes from Devonshire, Howard, and Sellars (1987), who found impulsive and socially withdrawn "secondary psychopaths" to show frontal lobe damage as indicated by more perseveration errors on the WCST, whereas "primary psychopaths" demonstrated no such deficits.

It will be noted in a later chapter that reduced skin conductance orienting responses, a psychophysiological measure that has been related to frontal structural and functional deficits in two recent brain imaging studies, is particularly characteristic of antisocials with features of schizotypal personality, a finding which again lends some support for the link between frontal dysfunction in antisocials with schizotypal personality. Future neuropsychological studies of antisocials that use measures of schizotypal personality to subdivide antisocials would be capable of providing more direct tests of this theory.

E. Conclusions on Frontal Dysfunction Theory

It is concluded that at the present time there is some evidence linking frontal dysfunction to antisocial and violent behavior in general, though the findings specifically for psychopathy are inconsistent. Frontal dysfunction may represent a general feature of antisocial behavior per se rather than being specific to a subtype of criminals such as psychopaths. However, it is hypothesized that antisocial or psychopathic individuals who also have features of schizotypal personality may be particularly characterized by prefrontal dysfunction, specifically orbitofrontal and dorsolateral dysfunction.

It is possible, however, that criminals have deficits in certain areas of the frontal lobes whose functions are not detected by traditional neuropsychological tests thought to reflect frontal functioning. It is in this context that future MRI and PET measures of frontal structure and function hold promise for a breakthrough in this area. Furthermore, several studies find frontal deficits to coexist with temporal deficits, and it may be that disruption to fronto-temporal connections may play a key role in mediating violent behavior (see below).

V. LEFT HEMISPHERE DYSFUNCTION

Flor-Henry (1973) developed an influential and important theory which argued that criminal psychopaths were characterized by left hemisphere damage, and in particular by disruption to frontal and temporal cortical-limbic systems. In support of this theory, detailed and extensive testing on neuropsychological test batteries by Yeudall and Fromm-Auch (1979), Yeudall, Fedora, Fedora, and Wardell (1981), and Yeudall *et al.* (1982) revealed evidence for a frontotemporal locus of dominant hemisphere damage in a wide variety of criminal groups including criminal psychopaths, sexual offenders, male violent criminals, adolescents with conduct disturbances, and behavior-problem schoolchildren. A number of other studies have observed that where neuropsychological deficits are observed in violent groups, they tend to involve left hemisphere functions of language (Mungas, 1988; Tarter, Hefedus, Winsten, & Alterman, 1984), verbal comprehension (Hart, 1987), and expressive speech (Brickman *et al.*, 1984).

These data are consistent with a large number of studies on delinquent and conduct-disordered children indicating that lowered IQ in these groups is a function of lowered verbal IQ as opposed to lowered spatial/performance IQ (Quay, 1987; Moffitt, 1990). The same pattern of deficits has also been fairly consistently observed for adult criminal offenders (Wilson & Herrnstein, 1985; Nachshon, 1983). Verbal IQ deficits tend to be linked to left hemisphere dysfunction while performance IQ deficit (nonverbal, spatial skills) is associated with right hemisphere dysfunction. Although verbal–performance IQ discrepancies are not perfect indicators of lateralized hemispheric dysfunction, these findings are certainly consistent with the notion of selective hemisphere dysfunction in criminals in general.

In a series of reviews of the previous literature and new empirical studies, Nachshon (1982, 1983, 1988, 1991) has also argued for left hemisphere dysfunction in violent offenders. Nachshon's theorizing differs from other theorists in two important ways: (1) in contrast to frontal theories (see above) and left fronto–temporal–limbic theories, Nachshon (1988) argues for a generalized functional as opposed to a specific structural disruption to the left hemisphere; (2) he bases evidence for this view not on EEG or traditional neuropsychological test data but instead on studies of lateral preference (Nachshon & Denno, 1987), skin conductance asymmetries (Hare, 1978), divided visual field studies (Hare & Jutai, 1988), and dichotic listening studies (Hare & McPherson, 1984; Nachshon, 1988). Nachshon (1988) argues that left hemisphere dysfunction predisposes to violent offending by disrupting normal left hemisphere control over impulsive behavior.

There are a number of limitations to this specific version of the left hemisphere dysfunction theory of violence. First, results of hand asymmetries in SC responding are clouded by the fact that brain–hand connections for skin conductance responding have not to date been clearly identified. As such, it is difficult to draw firm conclusions regarding lateralized hemisphere dysfunction from these data. Second, although Nachshon (1988) invokes the concept of impulsivity as a mediator between left hemisphere dysfunction and violence, none of the above studies have tested this notion using measures of impulsivity. Third, Nachshon's dichotic listening data that are used to support the notion of a global left hemisphere deficit are not easy to interpret. For example, Nachshon (1988) argues that a left ear advantage on a dichotic tone task in violent offenders is abnormal and reflects a left hemisphere deficit, whereas most other researchers would view such a pattern as normal for nonverbal material (Bryden, 1982; Beaumont, 1983). Fourth, this theory should predict EEG and ERP abnormalities over the left hemisphere, but to date such findings have not been observed (Hare, Williamson, & Harpur, 1988; Harpur, Williamson, Forth, & Hare, 1986; Raine & Venables, 1988b). In spite of these criticisms, left hemisphere dysfunction in criminals does receive substantial support from more traditional neuropsychological test data.

Left Fronto–Temporal–Limbic Damage

Yeudall (1978) and Yeudall *et al.* (1981) have argued that crime and violence are in part determined by damage to left frontal/anterior temporal cortex and left hippocampal/amygdala areas. Empirical evidence for this view is based on an extensive number of neuropsychological studies of habitually violent and aggressive subjects. As one example of many such studies carried out by Yeudall and his colleagues, Yeudall and Flor-Henry (1975), in an extensive neuropsychological investigation of aggressive criminals, found that 76% of such subjects had dysfunction localized to the frontal and temporal regions of the brain. Of these, 79% showed frontotemporal abnormalities lateralized to the left hemisphere. Similar localization to the dominant temporal lobe in violent-aggressive adolescents has been reported by Yeudall (1978).

Yeudall (1978; Yeudall *et al.*, 1981) has used this neuropsychological evidence of anterior temporal dysfunction to implicate the limbic regions of the temporal lobe, in particular the amygdala and hippocampus. Lesion studies in both animals and man are cited to support the role of the amygdala in generating violence, as are studies linking temporal lobe epilepsy to violence.

The episodic dyscontrol syndrome (Monroe, 1970) is also invoked to link temporal–limbic systems with frontal inhibitory control mechanisms. Specific brain areas argued to be dysfunctional by Yeudall include dorsolateral prefrontal cortex, orbitofrontal cortex, temporal cortex, basal ganglia, hypothalamus, amygdala, and hippocampus.

Although at one level the evidence in favor of this theory appears substantial, there are three important criticisms that Yeudall's left fronto–temporal–limbic theory faces. First, many of Yeudall's subjects are drawn from courts who refer patients for neuropsychiatric assessment, and as such the population is a preselected one in which one would expect a high incidence of neurological damage. Second, the aspect of the theory involving temporal–limbic systems is largely speculative and based on inferential data only. In particular, there are no specific neuropsychological tests of hippocampal and amygdala functioning included in his test battery. Third, most of the empirical tests of Yeudall's theory have been carried out by Yeudall and his associates, and there is a clear need for his findings to be replicated in an independent laboratory.

In spite of these criticisms, the left fronto–temporal–limbic theory of violence is potentially important and further empirical testing of this theory is warranted. Any such future research would usefully (1) conduct testing on unselected samples of violent individuals; (2) employ MRI or PET scans in addition to more traditional neuropsychological tests to more clearly pinpoint damage/dysfunction to key structures such as the hippocampus and amygdala; and (3) utilize EEG mapping techniques as a further line of converging evidence.

VI. REDUCED LATERALIZATION FOR LINGUISTIC FUNCTIONS

The traditional left hemisphere dysfunction theory of violence essentially argues for a type of structural damage to the left hemisphere that can be detected by neuropsychological tests validated against patients with brain lesions. A more subtle, recent, and potentially more plausible theory of violence concerns the notion that violent individuals are less lateralized for speech processes. Evidence for this viewpoint to date stems largely from studies of psychopaths. A striking clinical feature of psychopaths is their unusual use of language. Not only is their language unusual in the sense that they are loquacious and deceitful, but also because of the curious dissociation between what they say about themselves and how they actually behave. Cleckley (1976) argued that a form of deep-seated aphasia may represent this characteristic of the psychopath.

Several recent studies have lent some experimental support for this view. Gillstrom and Hare (1988) found that psychopaths not only make more hand gestures than nonpsychopaths during an interview, but in particular make more "beats" (nonsemantic, language-related gestures). Jutai, Hare, and Connolly (1987) found psychopaths to show a larger vertex-evoked potential slow wave in a dual-task phoneme discrimination condition, a result they interpreted as reflecting "unusual speech processing in psychopaths under conditions of distraction" (p. 175). Raine and Venables (1988a) found that psychopaths showed faster rise time of the skin conductance (SC) response to consonant–vowel stimuli than nonpsychopaths. This effect was specific to speechlike stimuli in that it was not observed to orienting or aversive nonspeech stimuli. Furthermore, SC rise time to these consonant–vowel stimuli was significantly related to psychopathic traits reflecting linguistic peculiarities, but not to nonverbal psychopathic traits. These studies provide some support at a general level for the view that psychopaths have unusual speech processes.

The notion of abnormal linguistic processing in psychopaths has been placed on a more specific footing by two dichotic listening studies. Hare and McPherson (1984) administered a verbal dichotic listening task to adult prisoners divided into three groups (high, medium, and low psychopathy) on the basis of scores on the Psychopathy Checklist and DSM-III-R criteria for antisocial personality disorder. A significant Group × Ear interaction was observed whereby the high-psychopathy group was less lateralized than the low-psychopathy group (see Fig. 3). Hare and McPherson (1984) interpreted their results as indicating reduced lateralization for language in psychopaths.

A similar and more recent study confirms that these findings are not spurious. Raine, O'Brien, Smiley, Scerbo, and Chan (1990d) administered a verbal dichotic listening task to juvenile offenders aged 13–18 years. Four self-report and behavioral measures of psychopathy were used to define psychopathy using cluster analytic techniques. Results of this study are also shown in Fig. 3. It can be seen that while nonpsychopaths showed the expected normal right ear (left hemisphere) advantage for verbal material, psychopaths evidenced a reduction in this lateralization. This was confirmed by a significant Group × Ear interaction; while right ear performance was significantly greater than that for the left ear for nonpsychopaths, no significant ear differences were observed for psychopaths. Between-group analyses also indicated that psychopaths had higher left ear and lower right ear scores than nonpsychopaths. Although subjects in the two studies (Hare & McPherson, 1984; Raine *et al.*, 1990d) differed in age, ethnic background, type of dichotic listening task, and method of psychopathy assessment, it can be seen from Fig. 3 that the pattern of results in the two studies is strikingly similar, indicating robustness of the effect.

This reduced ear asymmetry again indicates that psychopaths are less lateralized for linguistic processes. A number of counterexplanations to this conclusion can be ruled out. Since the verbal dichotic listening paradigm used by Raine *et al.* (1990d) is not affected by directing attention to one ear (Repp, 1977), the reduced asymmetry is unlikely to be due to psychopaths selectively

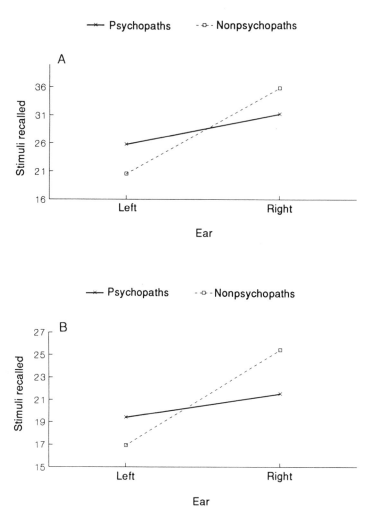

FIGURE 3 (A) Verbal dichotic listening data in adult psychopaths (Hare & McPherson, 1984) and (B) juvenile psychopaths (Raine *et al.*, 1990d) illustrating a reduction in the right ear advantage for psychopaths and potentially reduced lateralization for linguistic functions.

attending to the left ear. Since left-handed subjects were excluded, the reduced asymmetry cannot be a function of a greater proportion of left-handers in the psychopathic group. Although psychopaths were younger than nonpsychopaths, the significant Group × Ear interaction remained after entering age as a covariate. Since the lack of a main effect for Group indicates that overall performance did not differ between the two groups, the reduced ear asymmetry cannot be explained by poorer overall performance in the psychopaths.

Rather than being less lateralized for language processes, it could be argued that psychopaths have either left hemisphere dysfunction or an interhemispheric transfer deficit. The first possibility, however, would not predict raised left ear performance found in psychopaths relative to nonpsychopaths, whereas the second alternative cannot explain the reduced right ear performance in psychopaths (see Fig. 3). A selective reduction in left hemisphere arousal is also an unlikely explanation since several EEG and event-related potential studies have failed to observe such an effect (Forth & Hare, 1990; Harpur et al., 1986; Raine & Venables, 1988b). The data are, however, consistent with the notion that linguistic processes are less lateralized in the left hemisphere in psychopaths and perhaps receive greater cortical representation in the right hemisphere relative to nonpsychopaths. This effect does not seem to be modality specific; the same reduction in hemisphere asymmetries has been recently observed in the visual modality in psychopaths (Hare & Jutai, 1988).

An important advantage of reduced lateralization theory over traditional left hemisphere dysfunction theories is that reduced lateralization is likely to be developmental in nature and not itself caused by violence. For example, it is quite possible that damage to the left hemisphere could result from violent behavior rather than left hemisphere damage causing violence. This counterexplanation, however, cannot easily explain the more subtle process of reduced lateralization for linguistic processes that is likely to be neurodevelopmental in nature.

Left-Handedness and Conclusions on Reduced Lateralization

Studies of lateral preference in criminals and delinquents also provide some support for the notion that criminals tend to be less lateralized for speech processes than noncriminals. Most people (approximately 90%) are right handed (defined by writing hand), and this is due to the fact that the left hemisphere is "dominant" in most people. Contralateral pathways tend to predominate between hand and brain, with the left brain controlling the right hand. Furthermore, the vast majority of right-handers are left hemisphere dominant for language. Left-handed subjects are less clearly lateralized for language processes, with approximately 70% having language lateralized to the left hemisphere, about 15% being lateralized in the right hemisphere, with the remaining 15% having representation for language in both left and right hemispheres. As such, handedness can be taken as a crude indication of lateralization for language, with left-handedness indicating relatively weaker lateralization for language.

The prediction that would be generated by a speech lateralization theory of crime would be that criminals should be more likely to be left-handed, since left-handers are more likely to have bilateral language representation. Several studies have observed this finding. Gabrielli and Mednick (1980), in a prospective study of 265 Danish children, found that a left-side preference measured at age 11 was predictive of delinquency measured at age 17. Importantly, left-handedness in delinquents could not be accounted for by low verbal IQ, suggesting that gross left hemisphere dysfunction does not account for the effect. Ellis (1990) reports that there have been at least seven studies finding significantly higher left-handedness in criminal and delinquent groups.

There are however failures to replicate. Hare and Forth (1985) failed to find differences between criminals and controls, although criminals with intermediate levels of psychopathy were found to have significantly higher left-handedness than noncriminals. Ellis (1990) reports that although West and Farrington (1977) failed to find a link between handedness and delinquency in their longitudinal study of delinquency, West communicated to Ellis in 1978 that there was a significant relationship between recidivistic delinquency and left-handedness in the expected direction. Two studies reported the opposite results of higher *right*-handedness in black offenders (Denno, 1985; Nachshon & Denno, 1987), although as noted by Ellis (1990) these two studies are based on overlapping subject pools.

While the data on handedness and crime/delinquency are mixed, there is still a preponderance of findings indicating more left-handedness in antisocial groups, and some nonsignificant findings are not entirely negative. In total, these studies tend to support the notion that antisocial groups are characterized by reduced lateralization for language. Because left-handedness is only a crude index of reduced lateralization for language, the positive findings are particularly striking, and the nonsignificant results more to be expected given the indirect nature of the measurement of lateralization. Reduced lateralization for speech processes is not the only explanation of the crime–handedness link, and a review of other explanations that implicate the role of emotion, attention, and hormones may be found in Ellis (1990).

In conclusion, findings from dichotic listening and handedness studies provide initial support for a theory of crime involving reduced lateralization for language, but further research is required to establish precise relationships between crime per se and abnormal linguistic processes. In addition, an unresolved issue concerns the way in which reduced lateralization for verbal material translates itself into criminal and violent behavior. A number of alternatives seem feasible. If reduced lateralization for language results in poorer verbal comprehension and communication, this in turn could contribute to misinterpretation of events and motives in an interpersonal encounter, which in turn could precipitate violence. Similarly, a child with poor linguistic skills may be less able to talk himself/herself out of trouble with parents or peers. Poor verbal abilities and communication skills per se could contribute to peer rejection in childhood which, in combination with other later social and situational factors, could predispose to alienation and violence. Alternatively, linguistic abnormalities could result in verbal deficits that lead to school failure, which in turn could predispose to later alienation and violence. Future lateralization research should be conducted within the context of other cognitive and social research to better tease out these possible explanations and confirm the importance of linguistic processes and speech lateralization in predisposing to crime.

VII. OTHER BRAIN SITES AND CRIME

As indicated above the focus of neuropsychological research into crime has been on left frontal, left temporal, and limbic dysfunction. In contrast, there has been almost no research at all into damage to more posterior parietal and occipital cortex, the right hemisphere, or other brain structures such as the corpus callosum. Isolated studies suggest that these brain structures might benefit from more exploratory research.

Regarding posterior cortex, Virkkunen *et al.* (1976), in their study of open head injury in Finnish soldiers, indicated that the highest rates of crime occurred to those with open head injuries to the occipital cortex (10.9%). This lies in contrast to the finding that only 4.2% of those with frontal damage developed criminal behavior; the same percentage of crime was found for soldiers with parietal lobe injuries. Raine and Venables (1988b) found that psychopathic criminals had significantly higher scores on neuropsychological tasks associated with right parietal dysfunction relative to nonpsychopathic criminals, although another way of viewing this finding is that nonpsychopathic criminals have right parietal dysfunction.

Although much of the evidence favors left hemisphere dysfunction in violent crime, right hemisphere dysfunction may be more characteristic of nonviolent crime associated with depression, and with delinquency in females. For example, Yeudall (1977) found that while 72% of violent criminals had left hemisphere dysfunction, 79% of *nonviolent* offenders had right hemisphere dysfunction. Furthermore, Yeudall *et al.* (1982) found that while 84% of persistent delinquents showed neuropsychological deficits, these deficits were greater in the right hemisphere than in the left. This pattern was especially true of female delinquents, which is of interest given the greater rates of depression in females in general. With respect to the corpus callosum (a band of nerve fibers interlinking the two cerebral hemispheres), Schalling (1978) made the suggestion that psychopathic criminal behavior may represent a partial interhemispheric disconnection syndrome, but there have been few data reported either confirming or disconfirming such a model in delinquents and criminals. One dichotic listening study considered and ruled out this possibility given the pattern of findings observed (Raine *et al.*, 1990d), though Schalling's hypothesis is an interesting one warranting closer scrutiny.

Further research into these brain sites would appear warranted, particularly if such research attempts to assess interrelationships between these mechanisms. Because the corpus callosum is central to the transfer of information between the right and left hemispheres and because it also plays an important inhibitory function, damage to callosal fibers may possibly mediate lateralized hemisphere dysfunction and the functional predominance of one hemisphere over the other. Similarly, the parietal and occipital lobes have important cortico–cortical connections to other cortical structures more directly linked to criminal behavior (e.g., frontal and temporal lobes) and as such may play a contributory role in predisposing to crime.

VIII. PSYCHOSURGERY AND CRIME

The use of psychosurgical techniques to control antisocial and aggressive behavior has been, and continues to be, an extremely controversial area. In one review of 15,000 psychosurgical cases, 2.5% of operations (or 375) were conducted for the control of antisocial behavior (O'Callaghan & Carroll, 1982). While small in comparison to the total number of cases in this review, the use of nonreversible surgical techniques to control antisocial behavior is clearly of significance. Not only is this of ethical and moral concern, but it is also of significance in that such studies can potentially contribute to knowledge of brain mechanisms that may be implicated in antisocial behavior.

Psychosurgery on prefrontal areas was first conducted by a Portuguese neurologist, Egas Moniz. Moniz had attended a conference in London in 1935 in which it was reported that prefrontal leukotomy had a quietening effect on two chimpanzees who had been previously emotional and difficult when experimentally frustrated. One participant who asked the question of whether such a technique could be used on humans to good effect prompted Moniz to attempt an experimental study. He developed a technique called leukotomy in which holes were drilled through the skull, allowing a leukotome to be inserted through the side of the head. When swiveled, this instrument cut through the white fibers connecting the frontal lobes with other cortical and subcortical structures, effectively disconnecting the frontal lobes from the rest of the brain. Moniz's report of success with this technique on humans the following year led to large-scale and somewhat indiscriminant use of this technique and the development of other psychosurgical techniques including orbital undercutting, lobectomy, and lobotomy (Beaumont, 1983). One neurosurgeon alone (Walter Freeman) in the United States is "credited" with over 3500 lobotomies.

It should be made clear that psychosurgery has most frequently been performed on patients with psychiatric disorders, and as noted above its use on antisocial and aggressive subjects has been relatively small (O'Callaghan & Carroll, 1982). Nevertheless, this sample of approximately 375 is large enough to give some indication of its effectiveness. Regarding operations on the frontal lobes, outcome studies indicate that such surgery is relatively ineffective in controlling antisocial and criminal behavior (Scoville, 1972; O'Callaghan & Carroll, 1982). This is not entirely surprising, and indeed one can seriously question both the theoretical and the empirical grounds for expecting success from such surgery. Empirically, it has been established that frontal lesions in primates and cats actually lead to an *increase* in aggression and the inability to deal with aggression (Singh, 1976; Miller, 1976), although apathy and indifference have also been reported with total ablation of prefrontal cortex. This increase in aggression is not surprising given the case of Phineas Gage in which destruction of prefrontal cortex *increased* antisocial behavior. Theoretically, one would also expect that after destruction of prefrontal cortex, the normal inhibition exerted on limbic structures would be lost, resulting in more emotional and aggressive behavior since these structures are involved in the facilitation and regulation of aggression. The failure of surgical interventions involving prefrontal cortex is not therefore surprising.

More consistent results have been observed for less wholesale, more selective psychosurgery performed on more carefully selected cases. Initially conducted in Japan, amygdalectomy (removal of the amygdala, an almond-shaped part of the brain which is part of the limbic system) was thought to be successful in making aggressive patients more passive. This operation was then taken up in the United States, and altogether outcome data from 185 such operations have been reported in four studies (Narabayashi & Uno, 1966; Kilo, Gye, Rushworth, Bell, & White, 1974; Vaernet & Madsen, 1970; Balasubramaniam, Kanaka, & Ramamurthi, 1970). Using the outcome categories developed by O'Callaghan and Carroll (1982) for this series of cases, outcome is as follows: marked improvement, 39%; some improvement, 35%; no improvement, 21%; worse, 5%. Setting these data in dichotomous terms, some "success" is achieved in 74% of cases while "failure" is found in 26% of cases.

One reason why human amygdalectomy studies have had variable outcomes is because it is very likely that the amygdala has both excitatory *and* inhibitory effects on aggression. For example, in cats the cortical and medial nuclei of the amygdala suppress predatory attack while the basolateral complex *facilitates* such attack (Siegel & Mirsky, 1990). Ablation of the whole of the amygdala would therefore be less expected to show a selective effect in reducing aggression.

It is difficult to draw firm conclusions from psychosurgery data. As O'Callaghan and Carroll (1987) point out, psychosurgery studies are of notoriously poor quality. Furthermore, success is sometimes short termed or not independently assessed. On ethical grounds it is not easy to justify interventions that are not reversible and that one cannot easily give consent to (Beaumont, 1983). Not surprisingly, therefore, outcome for amygdalectomy has been viewed in various ways. O'Callaghan and Carroll (1987) concluded that results are "decidedly unremarkable" (p. 318), whereas Beaumont (1983) suggests that modern amygdalectomy "appears effective in reducing emotional excitability, and improving the patient's social adaptation, without significant effects on cognitive abilities" (p. 157).

Perhaps it is easier to draw a conclusion from psychosurgical studies if the question of "Should psychosurgery be performed to control aggression?" is separated from the question of "What do these studies tell us about neural mechanisms underlying aggression and antisocial behavior?" Bypassing the first question allows for a more dispassionate answer to the second. Regarding prefrontal psychosurgery, it is clear that studies do *not* indicate that frontal lesions lessen antisocial and aggressive behavior, though given the animal data this does not mean that this structure is not involved in regulating such behavior. Regarding the amygdala, psychosurgery studies seem to indicate some involvement of this structure in the mediation of aggression, though the limited nature of the evidence must be borne clearly in mind. Modern psychosurgery uses more refined surgical techniques and is performed on a few selective, intractable cases. There have been no full-scale assessments of these isolated cases in the past decade, and it may be that, conducted in this manner, amygdalectomy may be more effective than earlier studies indicate.

IX. CONCEPTUAL ISSUES IN NEUROPSYCHOLOGICAL RESEARCH ON CRIME

Before summarizing the main points of this chapter, several conceptual issues surrounding neuropsychological research into crime require discussion. Though these conceptual issues are not all specific to the neuropsychological issues raised here, they do nevertheless bear on future neuropsychological research in this area.

The first of these issues concerns the inevitably heterogeneous nature of crime and violence. The preceding discussion of neuropsychology has not made a clear distinction between crime and violence. This is largely because studies indicate that violence in particular and crime in general is associated with neuropsychological dysfunction, although there is a general belief in the literature that neuropsychological dysfunction may be more associated with more serious violent offending. Even when specific comparisons involving violent offenders are taken into account, most studies tend to compare a group of "violent" incarcerated offenders with nonviolent offenders or noncriminal controls. Such research tends to ignore the fact that violence itself is heterogeneous in nature. Individuals who have committed a single serious violent offense with no previous criminal convictions may differ considerably from recidivistic criminals with a history of assault in terms of underlying causal mechanisms. The issue of recidivism in delinquency was highlighted above with respect to West and Farrington's (1977) findings on left-handedness. Alcohol-associated crime and violence may differ considerably from crime committed when the perpetrator is sober. The neuropsychological correlates of sexual violence may be very different from those of nonsexual violence. Although some researchers have been cognizant of the heterogeneous nature of violence, others have not. In this respect criminological researchers tend to be more aware of this issue than psychologists and biologically oriented researchers. The global nature of the theories reported below needs to be challenged in future research, although the obstacles are considerable.

A second issue concerns the way in which crime and aggression are measured. Almost all research reported above is concerned with incarcerated offenders where violence is defined using official court records. Such research ignores the large numbers of individuals in the general population who commit nontrivial violence yet are never featured in research studies. Such bias may be overcome through the use of self-report measures of violence. As argued at other points in this book, use of such measures is essential for a more unbiased theoretical perspective of the neuropsychology of crime and violence.

A third conceptual issue concerns the problem of demonstrating cause–effect relationships in the neuropsychology of crime and violence. The problems related to establishing causality are common to many fields of study in the behavioral sciences, but social scientists tend to mistakenly think that an advantage of biological research over social research is that problems of causality are fewer. The reality is that such problems are particularly acute in the area of the neuropsychology of crime and violence. Theories based on these data which argue that damage to certain brain areas may cause violent behavior are open to the criticism that violent behavior may cause brain dysfunction. To take one example, due to their location in the skull frontal brain areas are particularly susceptible to damage from closed head injuries (Lewis, 1976; Adams, Mitchell, Graham, & Doyle, 1977). This introduces the question of whether frontal dysfunction causes crime and violence, or whether a criminal lifestyle causes frontal damage, or indeed whether causality works in both directions. This issue may be best resolved by prospective neuropsychological studies of crime and violence (e.g., Denno, 1989; Moffitt, 1990), but relatively few studies have utilized such study populations.

A fourth and related conceptual issue concerns the fact that most of the research reported above collected neuropsychological measures concurrently with measures of crime and delinquency. Prospective studies on the other hand are capable of making more powerful statements on the etiology of violent behavior. Although they can never demonstrate causality, they are capable of helping to rule out some possible relationships through temporal ordering of events. For example, neuropsychological dysfunction at age 5 cannot be caused by fights, accidents, and injuries taking place in adolescence and early adulthood. Unfortunately, few such studies have been conducted. Until the neuropsychology of crime and violence is viewed within a more developmental perspective, it will be difficult to conduct substantial tests of the neuropsychological theories reported above and to generate new perspectives for such behavior.

A fifth conceptual issue that has received very little attention in the neuropsychological literature on crime and violence research concerns the issue of whether the correlates of violence differ in any substantive way from the correlates of crime. Violent offenders as a group commit more nonviolent crimes than other offenders and as such tend to be recidivistic criminals. Since most psychological research to date indicates that the correlates of crime tend to be very similar to the correlates of violence, an important question concerns whether or not the etiology of violence differs in any substantive way from the correlates of repeated, nonviolent crime. To answer this question studies must match violent individuals with nonviolent controls on number of nonviolent criminal offenses. None of the studies reported above have used such controls. Without them, it is difficult to draw any clear conclusions on the etiology of violence as opposed to crime per se.

Sixth, it would be easy to conclude after reading a chapter on neuropsychological theories of crime and violence that social and environmental factors play no part in determining aggressive behavior. This is clearly *not* the case. Though attempts have been made to clarify this issue in earlier chapters, it is prudent to reiterate the point in the context of neuropsychological research. One of the problems with such research to date is that it ignores the fact that violence does not take place in a biological vacuum, free of the influences of social, psychological, situational, and more global socioenvironmental influences. While there have been exceptions (e.g., Moffitt, 1990; Denno, 1989), neuropsychologists researching crime have tended to ignore social influences on crime almost as much as socially oriented researchers have ignored neuropsychological influences. In particular, it is quite possible that the interaction between social and neuropsychological factors is more important in explaining crime and violence than either factor alone. Although this position has been established to some degree in research on crime and antisocial behavior (Mednick & Christiansen, 1977; Raine, 1988), the lack of communication between social scientists and neuropsychologists has resulted in relatively few tests of this proposition for violent and aggressive behavior.

Seventh, with some rare exceptions, neuropsychological theories of violence to date tend to take a very limited perspective of the number of biological influences which may contribute to violence. Traditional neuropsychological research on violence has, for example, generally ignored psychophysiological factors, while this research in turn tends to be conducted in isolation of hormonal research. Studies that incorporate measures from a variety of subdisciplines of biology are capable of making more powerful statements regarding violence. Similarly, studies of, for example, prefrontal dysfunction in violent offenders would be strengthened if they took multiple measures of frontal functioning (e.g., standard neuropsychological tests, EEG, event-related potentials, PET). More commonly, theories are tested using a single measure of the brain mechanism presumed to underpin violence.

In spite of the many conceptual issues surrounding neuropsychological research into crime, such work has been valuable and has given rise to a number of potentially important theories of crime and violence which may be usefully pursued. These theories and associated research must, however, be viewed within the context of these conceptual issues.

X. SUMMARY

This chapter reviews evidence from neuropsychological studies indicating that one way in which a biological predisposition to crime may be expressed is through disruption of the neural mechanisms that normally mediate and control behavior. While there is some limited evidence suggesting that the frontal lobes are compromised in criminal and violent offender populations, support for the notion that this brain region is specifically linked to psychopathic criminal behavior is inconsistent. However, it is hypothesized that damage to both orbitofrontal and dorsolateral regions of prefrontal cortex may particularly characterize antisocial or psychopathic subjects with features of schizotypal personality disorder, whereas psychopathic criminals without schizotypal features may be characterized by orbitofrontal dysfunction only. While there is some evidence favoring disruption to the left hemisphere (and left fronto–temporal–limbic structures in particular) in violent and criminal populations, a number of limitations to this argument are noted. There is some evidence from dichotic listening and divided visual field studies that adult and juvenile psychopaths are characterized by reduced lateralization for linguistic processes, and this notion is lent partial support by some evidence for a higher incidence of left-handedness in criminal and delinquent populations. There are very little data on the corpus callosum in offender groups, but it is speculated that structural or functional disruption to this fiber tract may be partly responsible for hemispheric asymmetries found in these groups. Psychosurgery on the frontal lobes is an ineffective intervention for crime and violence. While it is hard to draw firm conclusions from the limited evaluation studies of psychosurgery on other brain regions, there is some evidence suggesting an overall inhibitory role of the amygdala on aggression. The conceptual issues facing neuropsychological research on criminal behavior that need to be addressed in future studies include the need to study more homogeneous groups, the need for more research on self-report measures of crime, the use of prospective studies to better resolve questions on cause–effect relationships, the need to integrate neuropsychological data with other biological measures such as psychophysiology and brain imaging techniques and, most important of all, the need for neuropsychologists to integrate their findings more closely with social predispositional factors for crime.

6 Brain Imaging

I. INTRODUCTION

Perhaps the most exciting development in clinical neuroscience in recent years has been the development and increased use of several brain imaging techniques. The excitement lies in the fact that these techniques allow for much better visualization of both structural and functional properties of the brain than any other previous technique. As mentioned in the previous chapter, the disadvantage with traditional neuropsychological measures is that they are only indirect indices of brain dysfunction. New brain imaging techniques hold out the promise of an exponential increase in our understanding of the type of brain abnormalities and dysfunctions that may underlie different disorders because they are much more direct measures of central nervous system (CNS) structure and function.

Within the field of crime, these new techniques are just beginning to receive application, and to date there have only been a handful of studies which have applied new methods to further our understanding of crime and violence. It is expected that such techniques will have more widespread application to criminal populations as they become cheaper and more available, and more than with any other methodology there is the potential for a revolution in our understanding of the neurophysiological and neuroanatomical underpinnings of crime and violence.

For these reasons, this chapter will outline the limited knowledge that has been gained to date from brain imaging studies. Findings from computerized tomography (CT), positron emission tomography(PET), regional cerebral blood flow (RCBF), and magnetic resonance imaging (MRI) studies will be reviewed in turn. One recent study on PET in murderers will then be presented which highlights the potential role of prefrontal dysfunction in violent offending. Findings of all brain imaging studies will then be integrated to suggest the hypothesis that frontal dysfunction may characterize violent offending while temporal dysfunction may characterize sexual offending. Prefrontal dysfunction and its role in violent offending will then be placed in a theoretical context, and finally applications and implications of brain imaging research will be outlined. Before outlining empirical studies in detail, a brief overview of brain imaging techniques will be given to familiarize the reader with basic technical aspects of this research.

II. TECHNIQUES IN BRAIN IMAGING

One important point of clarification to be made at the outset is that there are two basic types of information that brain imaging techniques yield: (1) information on brain *structure*, and (2) information on brain *function*. It should be noted that a brain can be structurally impaired without any obvious functional abnormality and, by the same token, there can be brain dysfunction even though the brain appears quite normal structurally. As such, structural and functional brain imaging techniques provide different information about the brain, although structural and functional deficits do also co-occur. The two main structural brain imaging techniques consist of computerized tomography (CT) and magnetic resonance imaging (MRI), while the two main functional brain imaging techniques consist of positron emission tomography (PET) and regional cerebral blood flow (RCBF).

A. Computerized Tomography

Before the advent of CT, pneumoencephalography was the chief technique used to image the CNS, but this technique produced relatively poor resolution of brain structures. CT was introduced in 1973 and resulted in a major increase in resolution of brain structure. In CT, standard x-rays are passed through the brain from one side of the head, and the amount of radiation that is not absorbed by intervening tissue is measured by radiation sensors within the CT scanner. The X-ray source is then moved across the subject's head and the process repeated on 160 locations. The X-ray source is then rotated 1° and the procedure is repeated throughout 180°. A computer is then used to digitize the data stored by the radiation sensors; this data matrix can then be used to reconstruct the subject's brain in the transverse (horizontal) plane. Effectively therefore, CT can be viewed as a three-dimensional X-ray.

CT scanning has had a major impact on our understanding of a number of disorders. The discovery from CT studies that schizophrenics had enlargement of the lateral ventricles was a major finding, clearly establishing that schizophrenia was not simply a product of deviant family processes, but involved a disease process affecting the brain. CT provides a good image of the overall brain in the transverse plane and also of the lateral ventricles, with a ventricle/brain ratio being one of the more commonly derived indices used in research on disordered groups. CT scanning is also very useful for the detection of calcified lesions which are difficult to image using other techniques. Nevertheless, CT has a number of disadvantages, including the facts that the subject is exposed to X-rays, spatial resolution of smaller brain structures is poor, scanning can only be conducted in the transverse plane, and images are affected by spectral shift artifact, which distorts the signals at the skull boundary. Nevertheless, it is a cheap technique relative to other imaging procedures and, not surprisingly, most of the imaging research on crime and violence has been conducted using this technique.

B. Magnetic Resonance Imaging

Most of the limitations of CT scanning are overcome by MRI. This imaging procedure involves the yoking together of magnetism and radio-frequency radiation. Initially, a high-strength magnetic field is used to align atomic nuclei in the brain (these nuclei are otherwise randomly orientated). MRI is most frequently applied to hydrogen atoms because the best signal/noise ratio is found for hydrogen, and fortunately hydrogen protons are the most common element in biological tissue. The second stage consists of applying a radio frequency (RF) signal at right angles to the magnetic field which moves some of the nuclei out of alignment with the magnetic field. The third stage consists of turning off this RF pulse; the nuclei then return to their initial alignment and in doing so a voltage is induced in the electrical field (termed "magnetic resonance"); this voltage change is then detected and measured by a coil of wire around the tissue.

Because the different types of tissue in the brain (white matter, gray matter, CSF, blood, and diseased tissue) all differ in terms of their imaging parameters,

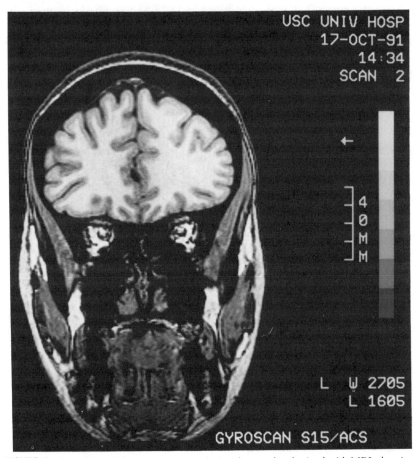

USC UNIV HOSP
17-OCT-91
14:34
SCAN 2

4
0
M
M

L   W 2705
L 1605

GYROSCAN S15/ACS

FIGURE 1   Illustration of the anatomical resolution that can be obtained with MRI, showing a coronal cut of prefrontal cortex taken anterior to the genu of the corpus callosum. This slice is taken with a Philips S15/ACS 1.5 Tesla scanner, using gradient-echo imaging acquisition with TR, 34 ms, TE, 12.4 ms, flip angle, 35°, field of view, 23 cm, and slice thickness, 1.7 mm.

excellent visualization of structures can be produced. For example, T1-weighted images produce very good visualization of gray matter (neurons) from white matter (axons), while a T2-weighted scan will allow optimal visualization of diseased tissue. An example of the type of resolution and gray–white matter differentiation that can be obtained is shown in Fig. 1, which shows a coronal (head-on) slice through prefrontal cortex anterior to the genu of the corpus callosum.

The key advantages to MRI are that (1) visualization of many structures is much superior to CT; (2) there is no exposure to radiation; (3) the brain can be imaged in all three planes; (4) there is no bone artifact; and (5) recent advances in MRI acquisition and computer software allow the brain to be displayed in three dimensions and cut in any plane. Key disadvantages are that the technique cannot be used with patients with pacemakers, aneurysm clips, or ferromagnetic implants, and it is also relatively costly (approximately $1000/subject). In spite of the many advantages, there has been barely one study conducted in antisocial populations to date. MRI is viewed by many as the imaging technique of the future (see Chapter 12 for a discussion of "fast MRI" in this context), so it can only be a matter of time before it receives application in research on violent and criminal populations.

C. Positron Emission Tomography

This functional imaging technique is used to measure the metabolic activity of different regions of the brain. First, a cyclotron is used to manufacture a short-lived isotope such as fluorine-18; the short half-life of the positron emitter helps keep the dose of radiation to the patient relatively low. The isotope is then "tagged" or integrated with an analog of glucose-2-deoxyglucose. This compound (flurodeoxyglucose or FDG) is then injected into the subject just after the start of a psychological task (e.g., Wisconsin Card Sort or continuous performance task). A series of blood samples is then taken from the subject to measure glucose and deoxyglucose. Since glucose is the only source of energy used by the brain, the fluorine is quickly transported to the brain, where the most active regions receive the largest quantities. After about 30 minutes the deoxyglucose uptake is largely completed, so that the radioactivity is "fixed" in the brain at this point.

The subject is then taken to the PET scanner. Positrons emitted by the decay of the isotope interact with electrons to emit two gamma photons that travel in opposite directions. Crystals that detect these photons are positioned around the head, and the origin of the gamma rays can be mapped by a computer to eventually produce a picture of the brain. Because more gamma rays are released by regions of higher metabolic activity, the neural activity in different parts of the brain can be visualized. Because radioactivity is mostly fixed by the end of the challenge task, measures obtained during scanning reflect glucose metabolism at the time of the earlier task rather than at the time of the actual scanning sequence.

The key advantages of PET are (1) it provides a direct measurement of brain glucose metabolism, and therefore of brain activity which can be localized to specific regions; (2) the spatial resolution is reasonably good, that is, PET scanners with a resolution of 10 mm can image structures such as the caudate nucleus, and more recent scanners are able to provide even better resolution than this. Such resolution is better than single photon emission tomography (SPECT) but not as good as MRI; (3) hypothesized dysfunction to a specific brain region can be tested by "challenging" this brain region with a neuropsychological task thought to involve this region and measuring glucose metabolism at this brain site as a function of other brain sites; and (4) PET can now be used to measure neurotransmitter functions. The relative disadvantages of PET are (1) its cost (approximately $3000/subject), (2) exposure of the subject to radioactivity (though this is less than exposure from a CT), (3) temporal resolution is poor, that is, activity levels are averaged over the 30-minute uptake period; recent developments using oxygen-15 with a half-life of only 2 minutes allow for an increase in temporal resolution, and (4) logistic difficulties sometimes involved by the availability of a cyclotron for production of the isotope. Despite these difficulties there have been several studies of violent populations using PET, probably because PET presents the best measure of brain function to date.

D. Single Photon Emission Tomography

Both animal and human studies show that there is good correspondence between blood flow in the brain and glucose metabolic rate. As such, blood flow measured in different parts of the brain has been used as a functional brain measure. SPECT can be used to produce a three-dimensional representation of RCBF in the brain. Typically, a radioactive gas, xenon-133, is inhaled through a face mask. Crystal detectors placed at locations around the head are then used to assess the time course of the appearance and dissipation of the isotope.

SPECT differs from PET in that the tracer emits only a single photon. For this reason, localization of the source of the protons is less precise, so that a disadvantage of SPECT relative to PET is that its spatial resolution is poorer. Furthermore, SPECT cannot easily detect lesions in white matter because clearance rates in white matter are lower than in gray matter. On the other hand, a cyclotron is not required because commercially available tracers can be used, thus reducing the cost of the scan. SPECT also allows data to be rapidly acquired, and because there is less exposure to radiation, the procedure can be repeated to assess differences produced by a challenge task relative to baseline conditions.

III. COMPUTERIZED TOMOGRAPHY STUDIES OF CRIME AND VIOLENCE

Because CT has been in operation since the mid-1970s and because it is relatively cheap, there have been more studies of violent and criminal behavior using CT than any other imaging technique. There appear to be eight studies carried out to date (all Canadian) that report CT data on aggressive offenders. Key findings from these studies are given in Table 1. Most of these studies do not look at CT data in isolation, but in combination with other data such as

TABLE 1 Overview of Key Findings from CT Studies of Offender Groups[a]

Reference	Subjects	Technique	Key finding
Hucker et al. (1986)	39 pedophiles 14 property offenders	CT	Left and bilateral temporal horn dilation; dilation of anterior horn of lateral ventricles in pedophiles
Langevin et al. (1987)	18 murderers 21 assaulters 16 property offenders	CT	No significant differences
Herzbert & Fenwick (1988)	14 aggressive TLE[a] 7 nonaggressive TLE	CT	No significant differences
Hucker et al. (1988)	22 sadistic sex assaulters 21 nonsadistic sex assaulters 36 property offenders	CT	Right temporal horn abnormalities in sadists
Langevin et al. (1988)	91 incest offenders 36 property offenders	CT	No significant differences for main group comparisons, but violence within incest group associated with temporal lobe abnormalities
Langevin et al. (1989a)	84 pedophiles 32 property offenders	CT	No significant differences
Langevin et al. (1989b)	15 exhibitionists 36 property offenders	CT	No significant differences
Wright et al. (1990)	18 pedophiles 12 incest offenders 34 rapists 12 controls	CT	Smaller left frontal and temporal areas in sex offenders

[a] TLE, temporal lobe epilepsy.

EEG or neuropsychological testing. While there is variability in findings, they tend to suggest that temporal areas may be impaired in violent individuals. Each of these studies will be reported in some detail below.

Hucker, Langevin, Wirtzman, Bain, Handy, Chambers, and Wright (1986) compared 39 male outpatients charged with a sexual assault on a minor or who were seeking attention for pedophilia to a group of 14 nonviolent, nonsexual property offenders on CT, intelligence tests (WAIS-R), and two neuropsychological test batteries (Reitan and Luria–Nebraska). CT scans were globally rated for abnormality by a neuroradiologist blind to group membership. Regardless of location of abnormality, a significantly greater proportion of the pedophiles (52%) had some structural brain abnormality relative to the controls (17%). Individual group comparisons on CT data for left temporal abnormalities and right temporal abnormalities were nonsignificant ($p > .20$). A significantly greater incidence of left and bilateral temporal lobe abnormalities was, however, observed in the pedophiles, with the most frequent abnormality being dilation of the anterior temporal horns of the lateral ventricles. Interestingly, while 37% of the pedophiles also showed clinically significant impairment on the Reitan neuropsychological test battery, only 8% had impairments on *both* CT and the Reitan. An unexpected additional finding was that for pedophiles with a history of alcoholism (38% of the pedophile group), left and bilateral CT pathology tended to occur significantly more often in the nonalcoholic group. Group differences in age (pedophiles were significantly older) did not account for the CT findings, nor did illicit drug use. No significant group differences were found for handedness, and although pedophiles were divided into heterosexual, homosexual, and bisexual subgroups, statistical analyses were not conducted on CT data to test for group differences.

Comments. Significant strengths of this early study are that (1) the subjects are an outpatient group and consequently are not institutionalized; (2) attempts are made to deal with the effects of age, handedness, and drug and alcohol use; (3) a criminal control group is used to control for the effects of crime per se; and (4) neuropsychological test data were also available to assess brain function as opposed to structure. These strengths are particularly striking for an early brain imaging study of pedophilia.

Limitations included (1) CT ratings are subjective and not quantitative, and no indication is given as to what constitutes a CT abnormality; (2) pedophiles had a significantly lower verbal IQ than controls, and this was not covaried out of CT analyses; (3) while a criminal control group is used, recidivism per se is not taken into account; and (4) by chance, 19% of pedophiles would be expected to show deficits on both structural (CT) and functional (Reitan) brain measures, whereas in actuality only 7% fell into this group, indicating a *negative* relationship between structural and functional brain deficits.

Langevin, Ben-Aron, Wortzman, Dickey, and Handy (1987) assessed 18 murderers, 21 assaulters, and 16 property offenders (controls) on CT. All subjects were facing charges for these offenses and were examined as part of a pretrial psychiatric assessment. CT methodology was as in Hucker *et al.* (1986) above, and CT scans were assessed for any abnormality, temporal lobe abnormality, and "diffuse abnormality." No significant group differences were found, with CT abnormality rates of 6.7% in killers, 25% in assaulters, and 28.6% in controls. Groups also did not differ in terms of EEG. On the other hand, 33% of killers and 17% of assaulters showed clinically significant impairment on Reitan scores compared to 0% of controls, with a trend ($p < .10$) for significant group differences on this neuropsychological test data. Killers were 7 years older than controls, though this difference was not statistically significant.

Comments. The nonsignificantly *reduced* rate of CT abnormalities is striking given the expectancy that this group should show higher rates than controls. This highlights the fact that a relatively large proportion (28.6%) of property offenders who make up the control group have CT abnormalities. This may suggest that property offenders themselves may have significant structural brain pathology. A normal control group would be helpful in future studies to provide a base rate in the normal population for CT pathology. As in Hucker *et al.* (1986), there was a dissociation between structural (CT) and functional (Reitan) brain measures, and even within the functional measures discrepancies existed between EEG data and neuropsychological test data. While killers were older than controls, this age difference, if having any effect, might be expected to lend itself to more CT deficits in the killer group, but this was not observed.

Herzberg and Fenwick (1988) compared 14 aggressive patients with temporal lobe epilepsy with 17 nonaggressive temporal lobe epileptics. No details were presented of CT methodology. Patients were defined as aggressive if they had shown repeatedly aggressive behavior on the ward according to case notes, and this was further assessed with a 5-point rating scale for aggression. No significant differences were found for CT or EEG data.

Comments. The authors concluded from their negative results that "demonstrable brain damage is unlikely to be an important variable" (p. 54) in accounting for aggression. However, as acknowledged by the authors themselves, the majority of the "aggressive" subjects were not in fact seriously violent as indicated by ratings on a 5-point scale. For example, two of the "aggressive" subjects were verbally aggressive only, and nine subjects were rated as "minimally aggressive" and had no criminal convictions. As such, these negative results should be treated with caution. Furthermore, groups were unbalanced for sex, and no handedness or age data are reported for the two groups. No information was provided on how the CT scans were analyzed or how abnormalities were assessed.

Hucker, Langevin, Wortzman, Dickey, Bain, Handy, Chambers, and Wright (1988) also report CT data for 22 sadistic sexual assaulters, 21 non-sadistic sexual assaulters, and 36 nonviolent, nonsexual controls (property offenders). Sexual offenders were recruited from a forensic unit and had committed rape, attempted rape, indecent assault, or sexual assault on females aged 16 years or over. Controls were selected from either a correction unit or a forensic unit. Groups did not differ significantly on age, education, IQ, or handedness. CT procedures were the same as in Hertzberg and Fenwick (1988), except that two neuroradiologists interpreted scans, agreeing in 92% of cases. While groups did not differ significantly in terms of CT abnormalities per se, sadistic sexual assaulters were more likely to have right-sided temporal horn abnormalities (41%) relative to nonsadistic assaulters (11%) and controls (13%). In contrast, 60% of the nonsadistic offenders had neuropsychological impairments on the Luria–Nebraska test battery compared to 17% of sadistic assaulters and 17% of controls. On this occasion CT results did not differ for alcoholic and nonalcoholic assaulters. The same CT findings were observed by Langevin, Bain, Ben-Aron, Coulthard, Day, Handy, Heasman, Hucker, Purins, Roper, Russon, Webster, and Wortzman (1985), but because the Hucker *et al.* (1988) study represents a larger version of this study with overlapping cases, only the latter study is reported here.

Comments. Again, strengths of this study include consideration of effects of age, education, IQ, handedness, alcoholism, and the effects of crime per se. One limitation is that all sexual assaulters came from a forensic facility, whereas some of the controls came from an ordinary correctional facility. This may bias findings because sexual assaulters are presumably referred because they are suspected of some degree of brain dysfunction. However, such a criticism cannot easily explain why sadistic sexual assaulters had a higher rate of right temporal horn abnormalities than nonsadistic assaulters. Chi-square analyses are only reported on two measures (total and right temporal horn abnormalities), and there is no indication of how many other measures were originally scored; this may lead to capitalization on chance and selective reporting of significant findings. Yet again, dissociations were found between CT and neuropsychological test data.

Langevin, Wortzman, Dickey, Wright, and Handy (1988) conducted CT assessments of 91 male incest offenders facing charges of sexual assault and/ or incest involving a biological relative who had been referred for pretrial assessment to a psychiatry department. The same group of property offenders used in Hucker *et al.* (1986) served as controls. CT procedures and assessments were the same as in other studies by this research group. Rates of generalized CT abnormality were nonsignificantly lower in the incest group (23.5%) relative to controls (30%). Analysis of specific temporal lobe abnormality failed to produce significant group differences. However, when incest offenders were divided into those with and without a history of violence, 35% of the violent group showed CT temporal lobe abnormalities relative to 13% of the nonviolent group. These two groups did not differ on neuropsychological test data (Reitan and WAIS-R).

Comments. While these findings are largely nonsignificant, one interesting exception lies in the greater rate of CT abnormality in the violent subgroup of incest offenders (35%). What diminishes the significance of this result is the fact that this rate of 35% is only 5% higher than that for the property offender control group (30%). This again indicates that noncriminal control groups should also be employed in brain imaging studies. As with the other studies, neuropsychological data led to different findings relative to the CT data.

Langevin, Wortzman, Wright, and Handy (1989a) reported CT data on 84 pedophiles and 32 of the 36 controls (property offenders) that were used in Hucker *et al.* (1988). No significant group differences were observed for either general CT abnormalities or abnormalities specific to the temporal lobe, although the rate of temporal lobe abnormalities was twice as great in heterosexual (26%) and homosexual (28%) pedophiles relative to controls (14%). In contrast, heterosexual and homosexual pedophiles (but not bisexual pedophiles) did show evidence of left hemisphere dysfunction as indicated by verbal IQ deficits and the Halstead–Reitan neuropsychological test battery. Langevin *et al.* (1989a) acknowledged the inconsistency of the CT findings with their previous work.

Comments. One possible source of the nonsignificant findings in this study is the fact that pedophiles were 10 years older than controls, though again, it is not easy to see how such a difference could occlude true differences in brain abnormalities, since the greater age in pedophiles would be expected to create group differences, not occlude them. As in all other CT studies, neuropsychological test data produced a different set of findings from the CT data.

Langevin, Lang, Wortzman, Frenzel, and Wright (1989b) made CT and neuropsychological assessments on 15 male genital exhibitionists convicted of indecent exposure and 36 nonviolent property offenders who had also acted as controls in Hucker *et al.* (1988). CT scans were rated blind by a neuroradiologist. Most subjects were right-handed. Groups did not differ in terms either of any CT abnormality or, specifically, of temporal lobe abnormalities. The only group difference to emerge on neuropsychological tests (WAIS-R, Halstead–Reitan test battery) consisted of more impaired performance in exhibitionists on Tactual Performance, Trails A, and Aphasia Screening. The authors concluded that, while exhibitionists may show soft signs of learning disabilities and some degree of minimal brain dysfunction, they differ from sadists and some pedophiles by not evidencing structural brain abnormalities.

Comments. While age was not controlled for in this study (exhibitionists were 12 years older than controls), the greater age of exhibitionists might be more likely to have produced group differences in CT rather than occluding them. Yet again, neuropsychological testing produced somewhat different findings from CT data, with three tests indicating poorer performance in the exhibitionist group, indicating some degree of neuropsychological dysfunction. However, because 26 different neuropsychological subtests were examined, at least one of the three significant findings would have been observed by chance. An interesting trend not commented on by the authors was the fact that the property offenders had a 50% *higher* rate of CT abnormalities than the exhibitionist group, again suggesting that this offender "control" group may have a raised rate of brain abnormality.

Wright, Nobrega, Langevin, and Wortzman (1990) used CT to assess 18 pedophiles, 12 incest offenders, 34 rapists, and 12 nonviolent, nonsexual offenders (controls). Both area and density were measured in a cut taken at the level of the full length of the third ventricle. Brain area in this study was measured from eight subareas corresponding to left and right frontal, temporal, parietal, and occipital areas. Sex offenders had relatively smaller left hemispheres compared to controls. Specifically, sex offenders had significantly smaller left frontal and left temporal areas relative to controls, with effects for right frontal and right temporal areas being marginally significant ($p < .10$). Of the three types of offenders, the incest offenders had the smallest left hemisphere area. No differences in optical density were observed. The authors suggested that these results supported their earlier findings of temporal and anterior horn dilation in pedophiles and sexually aggressive offenders.

Comments. An important feature of this study is that, unlike many other CT studies, brain area is divided into subregions, allowing assessment of the frontal area to be made. When this is done, structural abnormalities are more specifically localized to frontal and temporal regions relative to more posterior parietal and occipital regions. Unfortunately, the authors did not go on to assess whether it was the rapist group who were most responsible for the frontal effect. Another advantage of this study is the use of quantitative area assessments of brain abnormalities as opposed to more qualitative clinical judgments used in other studies. As acknowledged by the authors, however, many of the subjects in this study overlap with samples from other studies published by this group. As such, it is difficult to judge to what extent these findings provide independent support for previous findings of temporal lobe abnormality.

General Comments on Computerized Tomography Studies

A cursory glance at Table I immediately indicates two things. First, half of the studies do not find any differences between experimental and control groups. This may indicate that offender groups do not suffer from structural brain abnormalities. Alternatively, CT is limited in terms of spatial resolution. While it has been an important technique for visualizing the whole brain, assessing size of the lateral ventricles, and revealing presence of gross anatomical abnormalities, it is not as sensitive as MRI in assessing more subtle reductions in size of specific brain structures. Consequently, lack of significance may reflect a Type 2 error.

The second observation that can be made from Table I is that if there is a difference between groups, it lies with respect to greater temporal lobe abnormalities in the sex offender group, especially with respect to pedophiles and violent sexual assaulters (Hucker *et al.*, 1986; Hucker *et al.*, 1988; Langevin *et al.*, 1988; Wright *et al.*, 1990). On the other hand, the finding of temporal lobe abnormality is clearly not universally found. Specifically, this abnormality does not seem to characterize aggressive, assaultive, and murderous individuals or exhibitionists (Langevin *et al.*, 1987; Herzberg & Fenwick, 1988; Langevin *et al.*, 1989b).

Frontal abnormalities are generally not reported in CT studies because CT does not lend itself to accurate assessment of discrete frontal abnormalities as a slice thickness of 10 mm results in a significant partial volume effect. Indeed, it appears that frontal abnormalities were assessed in only one of the studies in Table I and, in this case, significant differences were found (Wright *et al.*, 1990). Furthermore, anterior temporal horn enlargement would be expected to indicate loss of frontal tissue, and in the study where this was measured, significant effects were again obtained (Hucker *et al.*, 1986). Frontal structural deficits may therefore characterize violent offenders, though CT data are currently limited.

Several other general observations may be made from CT studies. One striking aspect of many of these studies is that there are dissociations between CT and neuropsychological measures of brain abnormality. This may seem contradictory, but it must be remembered that the former is a structural measure and the latter is a functional measure. Such findings may therefore reflect dissociations between structure and function and underlie the need for the assessment of both types of brain abnormality wherever possible. One general methodological issue that restricts generalizability of findings to date is that many of the studies in Table I are from the same laboratory with a common control group; studies from other laboratories are therefore needed to provide a good test of robustness of these findings. Finally, an interesting possibility in some studies is that the lack of significant group differences may conceivably be due to relatively high rates of structural brain abnormality in the control group, where this is made up of property offenders (Langevin *et al.*, 1987, Langevin et al., 1988; Langevin *et al.*, 1989b). It may be erroneous therefore to assume that nonviolent offenders do not have congenital brain abnormalities, particularly since there appears to be a stronger genetic basis for property offending than for violent offending (e.g., Mednick *et al.*, 1984).

IV. POSITRON EMISSION TOMOGRAPHY AND REGIONAL CEREBRAL BLOOD FLOW STUDIES OF CRIME AND VIOLENCE

There appear to have been only four studies reporting data on PET and RCBF in violent offenders (though see below for a recent study by Goyer, 1992, on a

PET study of personality-disordered subjects). The key findings tabulated in Table 2 from each of these studies are reported below.

Graber, Hartmann, Coffman, Huey, and Golden (1982) reported a qualitative assessment of six case studies of male sex offenders who were viewed as mentally disordered. RCBF, CT, and neuropsychological test data were available on all subjects. Three of the cases were pedophiles while three were rapists. RCBF appears to have been measured in a resting state as no challenge task was used. The main pattern to emerge is that four of the six offenders had "abnormal test results" (p. 133), and of these four, three were pedophiles. For RCBF specifically, inspection of the case notes indicates that all three pedophiles showed reductions in overall gray matter RCBF, whereas such deficits were only observed in one of the rapists. Although it was noted that neuropsychological testing (Luria–Nebraska test battery) indicated frontotemporal dysfunction in three of the four cases classified as abnormal, this regional specificity was not analyzed or reported for RCBF measures. It can be concluded from analysis of the case notes that CT and RCBF measures were discrepant in two of the four cases showing abnormality.

Volkow and Tancredi (1987) report data on both glucose metabolism and cerebral blood flow in four psychiatric inpatients with at least three arrests for violence and four normals matched on age, sex, and handedness. Cerebral blood flow was determined using ^{15}O-labeled water, while glucose metabolism was determined using ^{15}flurodeoxyglucose (FDG). While violent patients were assessed on both glucose metabolism and blood flow, the controls only appear to have been assessed on the latter. Three slices centered at the thalamic level were used to assess subjects on left versus right temporal, and frontal versus occipital cortical measures. Ratio measures were computed to assess relative hypofrontality (reduced metabolism and flow in frontal areas) and left relative to right temporal dysfunction. Owing to the small N size, no statistical comparisons were made between groups. However, ratios for both glucose metabolism and blood flow in the violent group indicated relative hypofrontality and left temporal dysfunction. On an individual basis, Volkow and Tancredi (1987) argued that all four subjects showed left temporal dysfunction, while two of the four showed frontal dysfunction. These latter two showed no remorse for their violent acts and did not show CT abnormalities. In contrast, the two who did express remorse were reported to have shown minimal functional abnormalities (measured by PET), yet they showed marked cortical atrophy.

Garnett, Nahmias, Wortzman, Langevin, and Dickey (1988) report data on glucose metabolism in one male sexual sadist and two male controls (university students). Subjects were played a sexually neutral auditory tape or an erotic audiotape for 40 minutes during FDG uptake. The tape manipulation failed to elicit differential patterns of brain activation. In general the sadist was found to show greater bilateral activation to both stimulation conditions, but no differences in activation were observed between conditions, and there

TABLE 2 Overview of Key Findings from PET, RCBF, and MRI Studies

Reference	Subjects	Technique	Key finding
Graber et al. (1982)	3 pedophiles 3 rapists	CBF	Reduced CBF in pedophiles but not rapists
Volkow & Tancredi (1987)	4 violent patients 4 normal controls	PET	Left temporal dysfunction and hypofrontality in violent patients
Garnett et al. (1988)	1 sexual sadist 2 normal controls	PET	Bilateral cortical activation in sadist; right hemisphere activation in controls
Hendricks et al. (1988)	16 child molesters 16 normal controls	CBF	Reduced CBF in child molesters; greatest over frontal areas
Raine et al. (1993)	22 murderers (NGRI[a]) 22 normals	PET	Selective prefrontal dysfunction in murderers
Tonkonogy (1991)	14 violent OBS[b] 9 nonviolent OBS	MRI/CT	Anterior–inferior temporal lobe lesions in 5 female violent OBS

[a]NGRI, not guilty by reason of insanity.
[b]OBS, organic brain syndrome.

were no clear findings for limbic activation. No procedural details are provided for PET quantification and analysis.

Hendricks, Fitzpatrick, Hartmann, Quaife, Stratbucker, and Graber (1988) measured cerebral blood flow in 16 male child molesters incarcerated in a security complex within a psychiatric facility and believed to be "treatable sex offenders." Sixteen normal controls were selected from university staff and would almost certainly differ from the child molesters in terms of IQ, educational level, and social class. Furthermore, three of the controls were female, and controls were 4 years younger than child molesters. RCBF was estimated using a ^{133}Xenon inhalation technique. Child molesters had lower CBF over all brain sites relative to controls for both gray and white matter, although there was an interaction with anterior–posterior gradient, indicating that values in the child molester group were lower particularly over frontal sites. Post hoc tests were not used to further break down this interaction. CT scan data were available for three slices taken at the level of the lateral ventricles. Groups did not differ in terms of overall brain area or in terms of size of the lateral ventricles. Subanalyses on offender subgroups (pedophiles, homosexual hebephiles, and incest fathers) revealed no significant group differences. The authors concluded that findings replicated those of Graber *et al.* (1982).

Comments on Positron Emission Tomography and Cerebral Blood Flow Studies

Because these studies are preliminary, findings must be interpreted with caution, particularly since sample sizes are small and frequently few procedural details are reported. A number of other additional criticisms pertaining to these studies are as follows.

First, only Garnett *et al.* (1988) employed an activation condition (sexually arousing tape). This is potentially an important strength because the investigators attempt to activate or "challenge" those brain areas which they believe may be involved in sexual activity (although in this case the manipulation failed). An additional advantage of such a challenge task is that one has some degree of control over what the subject is doing. In contrast, artifactual group differences may occur in "resting baseline" nonchallenge conditions because one group is differentially engaged in some type of mental activity.

Second, the three studies that measured both structure and function (CT and PET/RCBF) (Graber *et al.*, 1982; Volkow & Tancredi, 1987; and Hendricks *et al.*, 1988) found a dissociation between these measures. This confirms the same dissociation found in CT studies and suggests that caution must be exerted in generalizing from one type of study to another. Clearly, functional deficits can exist without structural deficits, and vice versa.

Third, studies measuring glucose metabolism are inevitably based on small sample sizes, precluding the use of statistical tests of significance. As such, firm conclusions cannot be drawn from these studies. In particular, factors such as head injury, ethnicity, and psychopathology within the experimental group remain uncontrolled. Nevertheless, the study by Volkow and Tancredi (1987) supports CT data in indicating a moderate degree of converging evidence suggesting that frontal and temporal brain regions may be implicated in some forms of criminal behavior.

A fourth issue concerns subject sampling and control groups. For example, subjects in the study by Hendricks *et al.* (1988) were incarcerated in a psychiatric facility. Because other institutionalized groups were not used as controls, differences in RCBF in the child molesters may be a function of generalized underarousal due to institutionalization. Such a criticism does not, however, easily account for their second finding of a Group × Site interaction whereby the offender group had lower values particularly in the frontal lobe. However, the fact that this study contained female controls when all experimental subjects were male may be a nontrivial factor in accounting for higher CBF in controls, since females have been found to have higher CBF than males (Gur & Gur, 1990).

Fifth, a criticism of PET studies that also applies to CT studies is that the extent to which deficits are *relative* is often not assessed. While CT scans may reveal abnormalities in temporal areas, a question remains as to whether these abnormalities are greater relative to another brain area. Similarly for PET data, it is important to establish that a certain brain site shows reduced glucose metabolism relative to another brain site if one wants to establish specificity of findings. Two studies that do demonstrate such a relative deficit (Volkow & Tancredi, 1987, and Hendricks *et al.*, 1988) indicate relatively lower frontal activity, and as such these data constitute more powerful evidence for specific brain dysfunction. Although the advantage of PET relative to CT lies in better localization of dysfunction, localization is very general in some studies (e.g., frontal lobe, temporal lobe), and in some studies findings are not localized at all.

Despite these criticisms, these four studies are important in providing unique information on brain function in criminal samples. While there are clear limitations, such limitations are frequent in ground-breaking studies which at the least provide a basis for methodologically better studies.

V. MAGNETIC RESONANCE IMAGING STUDIES OF CRIME AND VIOLENCE

Tonkonogy (1991) is the only study that has to date included MRI in assessments of offenders. Tonkonogy (1991) used both MRI and CT on 87 patients with disorders such as schizophrenia and bipolar disorder referred for neuropsychiatric examination due to alcohol abuse, cerebrovascular accidents, or head injury. CT, MRI, EEG, and neurological examinations were used to diagnose organic mental disorder in 23 of the 87 patients. Of these, 14 had what was termed "frequent episodes of violent behavior" (p. 190). The main finding to emerge is that the 14 psychiatric patients with organic mental disorder with concomitant violence were significantly more likely to have lesions in the anterior–inferior temporal lobe than the 9 organic mental disorder patients without violence. In four of the five cases lesions were lateralized to the right hemisphere. Three were male while two were female. The authors speculated that violence may result from unilateral tissue loss in the amygdala–hippocampal region of the temporal lobe.

Comment. This study is valuable because it is the first to use MRI on a forensic sample. On the other hand results must be regarded as preliminary for several reasons. First, MRI was only used on a subset of subjects and, of the five violent cases, it appears from the case studies presented that only one is assessed with MRI. Therefore this study is much more representative of a CT study than an MRI study, and consequently these findings should not be weighted more heavily than those of other CT studies since this study does not benefit substantially from MRI methodology. Second, it is clear that all cases are a selected sample of those who have already been shown to have substantial brain pathology as indicated by CT or MRI. However, such selection does not explain why such pathology should be localized to a specific brain area in the subgroup of violent patients. Nevertheless, findings are clearly limited to this selected sample. Third, because all patients had a severe mental illness, deficits might be in part due to illness in these patients rather than to violence per se. Fourth, there are no methodological details of how CT and MRI were conducted. Fifth, there are no details of what constitutes brain pathology, how lesions were localized, and whether whoever rated the scans was blind to group membership. These are significant methodological limitations.

VI. REDUCED PREFRONTAL GLUCOSE METABOLISM IN MURDERERS

One of the themes that arises both from neuropsychological test data described in the previous chapter and from the imaging data described above is the notion that violent offenders may be characterized by frontal dysfunction. At the time of writing, the most recent brain imaging study of a criminal population has tested this hypothesis by assessing glucose metabolism using PET in murderers pleading not guilty by reason of insanity (Raine, Buchsbaum, Stanley, Lottenberg, Abel, & Stoddard, 1993). While it has a number of important limitations in its own right, it also addresses some of the limitations described above for earlier imaging studies and provides some assessment of temporal dysfunction, which has been implicated in earlier imaging studies. This section will briefly describe the methodology and initial findings from this study and then attempt to place the observed findings within a wider etiological context.

A. Subjects

The experimental group consisted of 22 homicide cases tried in the state of California (20 male, 2 female) with a mean age of 35.4 years (SD = 10.4). Twenty were charged with murder while two were charged with attempted murder. Subjects were referred to the University of California, Irvine (UCI) imaging center to obtain evidence relating to an insanity defense (not guilty by reason of insanity, NGRI) or to capability for understanding the judicial process (incompetence to stand trial, IST).

A control group was formed by matching each murderer with a normal subject of the same sex and age (within 2 years with one exception) who had been tested using identical PET imaging procedures in the same laboratory. Three of the 22 murderers (all male) had been diagnosed as schizophrenic according to court-appointed psychiatrists. In order to control for this raised prevalence of schizophrenia in the group of murderers, these three schizophrenic murderers were individually matched on age and sex with three schizophrenics from a larger sample tested under identical procedures at the Brain Imaging Center at UCI. The resulting 22 controls (20 male, 2 female) had a mean age of 34.2 years (SD = 10.9). Normal controls have been screened for health by physical exam, medical history, and a psychiatric interview. No subject was taking any medication, had a history of psychiatric illness in self or first-degree relatives, or had current significant medical illness. Subjects with a history of seizure disorder, head trauma, or substance abuse were excluded.

B. Continuous Performance Task and Positron Emission Tomography Quantification

The FDG tracer was injected into the subject in the test room and taken up by the brain as a tracer of brain metabolic rate for a 32-minute period during which the subject completed the continuous performance task (CPT). A degraded stimulus version of the CPT was employed as the frontal challenge task because it is traditionally viewed as a frontal task in the neuropsychology literature and has been shown to produce increases in relative glucose metabolic rates in the frontal lobes in normals, in addition to increases in right temporal and parietal lobes (Buchsbaum *et al.*, 1990). Subjects were asked to respond with a button press each time that they detected the digit 0 (target stimulus).

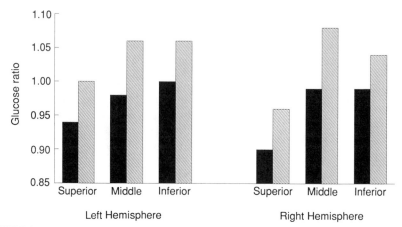

FIGURE 2   Superior, middle, and inferior prefrontal gyri relative glucose metabolic rates in left and right hemispheres in murderers, ■ and controls, ▨ (cortical peel technique).

C. Key Findings and Their Specificity

Significant group differences found in analyses from both box and cortical peel techniques support the hypothesis that murderers are characterized by prefrontal dysfunction. The box analyses indicated strongest effects for anterior medial prefrontal cortex and for the higher, supraventricular superior prefrontal cortex, with significantly reduced glucose metabolism in these areas in murderers. At lower levels, medial prefrontal glucose levels did not differentiate the two groups. At the lowest, infraventricular levels, however, prefrontal deficits were again indicated by reductions in orbitofrontal glucose metabolism in murderers, although this effect was weaker and more specific to the left hemisphere. The peel analyses corroborated the general finding of widespread prefrontal dysfunction in murderers, particularly when values were expressed relative to posterior (occipital) cortex. An illustration of one of several significant group analyses for prefrontal gyri (cortical peel technique) is shown in Fig. 2. Values for nonprefrontal, more posterior frontal motor areas on the other hand did not differ across groups, indicating specificity of findings to the prefrontal area. While both groups show the expected posterior activation in occipital and precuneus areas (reflecting the visual nature of the CPT task), the murderer fails to show the prefrontal activation that is observable in the normal control. Most murders in this sample were single murderers or else committed two murders within the space of 1 to 2 days prior to being caught. One murderer was a true serial killer as indicated by the fact that he murdered approximately 45 people over a number of years. Although the single murderer showed the lack of prefrontal glucose metabolism relative to the normal control, the multiple murderer showed a substantial degree of prefrontal activity. Given the role of the prefrontal cortex in executive functions and planned, forethoughtful behavior, the presence of prefrontal activity in the multiple murderer would be consistent with the planned, careful execution of murders in contrast to the more impulsive acts of the one-time murderer.

The fact that the prefrontal deficit in murderers is relatively specific and does not reflect generalized brain dysfunction is indicated in four ways. First, glucose levels for a particular area were expressed as a ratio of all other brain areas in that slice and therefore reflect *relative* glucose metabolic deficits. Second, one prefrontal area (medial frontal at the level of the lateral ventricles) did not distinguish the two groups, indicating some specificity within prefrontal cortex for the observed deficit. Third, posterior frontal glucose metabolism levels were the same in both groups, indicating that within the frontal lobe, the deficit was localized to the more anterior (prefrontal) region. Fourth, no deficits were observed in temporal and parietal regions, again localizing the deficit to anterior prefrontal regions. As such, the relatively specific nature of the deficit indicates that it cannot be easily explained by general factors such as motivational deficits and underarousal, which have been previously implicated in crime and violence.

Although prefrontal deficits have also been observed in schizophrenia (Buchsbaum *et al.*, 1990), murderers are differentiated from schizophrenics in terms of the extent of this deficit. For example, schizophrenics have been found not only to show reduced frontal glucose during the CPT, they also show deficits relative to controls at right temporal and right parietal sites, areas that are also activated by the CPT (Buchsbaum *et al.*, 1990). In contrast, murderers show deficits specific to prefrontal cortex that do not extend to temporal and parietal regions. In spite of this initial evidence for group specificity of the findings, firm conclusions cannot be drawn until further imaging studies using the CPT are conducted with other psychiatric groups.

A history of closed head injury does not appear to be a major environmental cause of prefrontal dysfunction. Although orbitofrontal damage frequently follows closed head injuries, the medial–inferior surfaces of the temporal lobes are equally susceptible to such injuries (Stuss & Benson, 1986) yet were not found to be dysfunctional in murderers. Furthermore, head-injured murderers were found to have slightly higher, not lower, prefrontal activity than nonhead-injured murderers. Nevertheless, head injuries, while not affecting all subjects in exactly the same brain region, should not be ruled out as playing a possible predispositional role in violence, particularly since early child abuse (linked to later perpetration of violence) can produce significant head injury (Milner & McCanne, 1991).

Group differences in prefrontal activity do not appear to be a function of group differences in age, sex, schizophrenia, handedness, ethnicity, motivation, or history of head injury. Groups were matched on age and sex and contained equal numbers of schizophrenics. Left-handed murderers, ethnic minority murderers, and murderers with a suspected history of head injury were found to have prefrontal values that were slightly *higher* than their right-handed, Caucasian, and nonhead-injured counterparts, indicating that these factors cannot account for *reductions* in glucose metabolism found in the group as a whole. However, head injury affecting a number of different brain areas may still play a contributory role. Reduced motivation in murderers to perform the activation task cannot easily account for reduced prefrontal glucose metabolism since there were no differences in performance on the CPT in murderers.

Taken together, these results indicate selective prefrontal dysfunction in murderers that was not a result of left-handedness, ethnic minority status, schizophrenia, or motivation deficits. It is important to recognize that the findings of this study relate specifically to murderers in whom questions regarding mental illness or organic brain injury have been raised, and results cannot be generalized to other murderers or violent offenders at this stage. Furthermore, the finding for the single case of the multiple murderer suggests that heterogeneity within the murderer group needs to be addressed further.

VII. OVERVIEW OF BRAIN IMAGING STUDIES: FRONTAL DYSFUNCTION IN VIOLENT OFFENDERS AND TEMPORAL DYSFUNCTION IN SEXUAL OFFENDERS?

The number of brain imaging studies conducted to date on offender groups is too small for the conduction of a formal meta-analysis. However, an informal analysis of Tables I and II yields some patterns that can be used to suggest preliminary hypotheses on different brain areas that may predispose to different types of crime.

Of the 14 CT, PET, and MRI studies conducted to date, 8 suggest some specificity of findings. In all cases, selective deficits are found in the anterior region of the brain (either frontal or temporal areas). Although temporal findings are more frequently observed than frontal findings, it must be remembered that the more numerous CT studies frequently do not assess frontal deficits. Furthermore, all three functional brain imaging studies that report specificity of findings indicate frontal dysfunction, indicating that future functional studies may find more evidence for frontal than for temporal dysfunction.

Four of the studies provide evidence for selective frontal dysfunction. One of these studies involved murderers (Raine *et al.*, 1993), one involved violent subjects (Volkow & Tancredi, 1987), one involved sex offenders in which the largest subgroup consisted of rapists (Wright *et al.*, 1990), and one involved child molesters charged with sexual assault (Hendricks *et al.*, 1988). As such, frontal dysfunction tends to be found in violent offenders, child assaulters, or sex offenders containing a large proportion of rapists, who may be more likely to be violent than incest offenders or pedophiles.

Six studies found evidence for deficits partly localized to the temporal lobe. The six samples being tested in these studies were as follows: pedophiles, sadistic sexual assaulters, incest offenders, sex offenders (34 rapists, 18 pedophiles, 12 incest offenders), sadistic sexual offenders, violent offenders, and violent psychiatric patients with organic brain syndrome. As such these six studies contain a larger proportion of sex offenders, including more passive sexual offenders such as pedophiles and incest offenders.

The hypothesis being suggested, therefore, is that there is a tendency for frontal dysfunction to be associated with violent offending and rape, while temporal dysfunction may be more associated with sexual offending including incest and pedophilia. The data are only suggestive of this hypothesis, however, since the studies finding temporal dysfunction also contain samples of violent sexual offenders. It may be that a continuum exists, with frontal dysfunction and violence at one end of the continuum and temporal dysfunction and sexual offending at the other. The middle of this continuum may involve some degree of both temporal and frontal dysfunction and a mix of both sexual and violent behavior. Interestingly, one of the two studies that found evidence for both temporal and frontal dysfunction used a sample made up almost evenly of rapists (53%) and incest offenders/pedophiles (47%) (Wright *et al.*, 1990). The other study found that frontal dysfunction characterized violent individuals who had no remorse for their actions (Volkow & Tancredi, 1987), suggesting the possibility that psychopathy may also be at this end of the continuum.

One recent study, although not assessing violence per se, does lend some conceptual support to the notion of prefrontal dysfunction in violence and aggression. Goyer (1992) tested a total of 17 personality-disordered subjects (largely borderline and antisocial personality disorder) on PET using an auditory CPT as the uptake task; all subjects were also administered a questionnaire measuring life history of aggression. A significant negative correlation ($r = -.52$, $p < .03$) was observed between aggression scores and glucose metabolism in the frontal slice taken 4 cm above the canthomeatal line, indicating reduced frontal activity in those with relatively higher scores. Conversely, no such correlations were reported for temporal lobe glucose metabolism. This study provides some further support for the notion of frontal deficits in relation to aggression and violence.

One difficulty making the hypothesis described above speculative is the fact that, as outlined earlier, many of the CT studies on sex offenders come from the same group of researchers (Hucker *et al.*, 1986; Langevin *et al.*, 1987; Hucker *et al.*, 1988; Langevin *et al.*, 1988; 1989a,b; Garnett *et al.*, 1988). Though these researchers cannot be faulted for being productive, a better analysis would ideally include studies from many different laboratories. While speculative at the present time, this hypothesis may at least provide some basis for hypothesis testing in future imaging studies, since studies to date have been empirically driven rather than theory driven. The following section attempts to provide some conceptual underpinnings for future brain imaging studies of offender populations.

VIII. THEORETICAL INTERPRETATIONS OF PREFRONTAL DYSFUNCTION

Discussion here will focus more on the finding of relative frontal dysfunction because temporal lobe deficits in relation to abnormal sexual functioning have been covered elsewhere. Briefly, both animal and human patient research indicates that changes in sexual functioning are linked with damage to temporal–limbic areas of the brain. A temporal lobe–sexual activity link has also been found in normal humans. For example, early research by Moscovich and Tallaferro (1954) indicated that six normal subjects who masturbated to orgasm showed EEG changes in temporal lobe regions (see Hucker *et al.*, 1988; Garnett *et al.*, 1988, Langevin *et al.*, 1989; and Reiss & Roth, 1993 for further details).

Turning to frontal dysfunction, findings of functional brain imaging studies have implications for theoretical accounts of violence. As indicated in the last chapter, a number of brain deficits have been postulated as potential predispositional factors to violence, including left hemisphere dysfunction, lateralization abnormalities, and temporal dysfunction. Little evidence was observed for temporal dysfunction in studies involving PET and CBF, and three of the four found some evidence for frontal dysfunction. Findings for some nonmedial structures (orbitofrontal, superior, middle, and inferior surface) in Raine *et al.* (1993) indicated that prefrontal deficits were greatest over the left hemisphere, but these must be regarded as suggestive only since laterality effects were not obtained in other analyses. While Volkow and Tancredi (1987) also found some evidence for deficits to be lateralized to the left hemisphere, evidence for lateralization from studies as a whole is weak.

Regarding the interpretation of frontal dysfunction in violent offenders, such dysfunction may be best viewed as a *predisposition* to violence rather than prefrontal dysfunction in and of itself, causing violence. One predispositional model for the link between prefrontal dysfunction and violence would be to suggest that (1) there are a number of pathways by which prefrontal dysfunction can contribute to violence; (2) the greater the prefrontal dysfunction, the greater the likelihood that several of these pathways will be activated; and (c) the more pathways that are activated, the greater the risk for serious violence. These putative pathways can be viewed at neurophysiological, neurobehavioral, personality, cognitive, and social levels. At a neurophysiological level, reduced prefrontal functioning could result in a loss of inhibition normally exerted by the frontal cortex on phylogenetically older subcortical structures which are thought to play a role in facilitating aggression (Gorenstein & Newman, 1980; Weiger & Bear, 1988). At a neurobehavioral level, damage to prefrontal cortex in clinical patients has been found to result in behavioral changes that include risk taking, rule breaking, emotional and aggressive outbursts, and argumentative behavior, which in turn could predispose to more violent acts (Damasio, 1985; Mesulam, 1986). At a personality level, frontal damage has been found to result in impulsivity, loss of self-control, immaturity, lack of tact, inability to modify and inhibit behavior appropriately, and poor social judgment which could predispose to serious violence (Luria, 1980). At a cognitive level, poor concentration, divergent thinking, and reasoning ability could result in school failure, employment failure, and economic deprivation, thereby predisposing to a criminal way of life which in turn could predispose to violence. At a social level, the loss of intellectual flexibility, concept formation skills, problem-solving skills, and reduced ability to use information provided by verbal cues resulting from prefrontal dysfunction (Kolb & Wishaw, 1990) could impair social skills essential for formulating nonaggressive solutions to fractious interpersonal encounters. This model should be viewed from a heuristic standpoint, illustrating that while prefrontal function may be related to violence, it may be essentially a predisposition only, requiring other environmental, psychological, and social factors to enhance or diminish this biological predisposition.

From an etiological standpoint, although the findings of this study implicate a biological factor as predisposing to violence, it is important to emphasize that the cause of this dysfunction could be environmental as well as biological or genetic. Birth complications have been implicated in later violent offending (Mungas, 1983) and represent only one of a number of early environmental agents that could contribute to prefrontal dysfunction. Alternatively, the deficit could be neurodevelopmental in nature. Homicide rates in both whites and nonwhites show a step increase between the ages of 15 and 19 before peaking in the 20s (O'Carroll & Mercy, 1990), an age at which prefrontal cortex is reaching full maturity (Huttenlocher, 1979) and at which there are important environmental demands (e.g., leaving school, starting work, getting married) placed on the individual which require prefrontal executive functions. Breakdown of prefrontal functions at this age, in conjunction with environmental stressors, could in part explain the increase in homicide rates in the late teens and into the 20s.

IX. APPLICATIONS AND IMPLICATIONS OF BRAIN IMAGING RESEARCH

Results of brain imaging studies of violent individuals are potentially of key importance in the contexts of law, psychiatry, and society. While individual murderers are often suspected of some brain dysfunction, the above study is the first indicating that, as a group, murderers show a clear dysfunction of a *specific* cortical brain region. If offenders as a group such as murderers show evidence of a relatively focal brain abnormality relative to control groups, this would have potential implications for judgments in contexts of the insanity defense and competence to stand trial. Tancredi and Volkow (1988) have argued that new imaging techniques offer the promise of giving psychiatric evaluations of dangerousness and violence much greater objectivity.

Applications of brain imaging need to proceed cautiously, however. First and foremost, there needs to be much more extensive evaluation of brain imaging in offender groups, both to establish that certain groups do have clear and significant brain pathology and also to establish reliable normative data to provide a context for the evaluation of such pathology. Even if clear deficits can be demonstrated in certain offender groups, the fact that an individual offender has this characteristic does not demonstrate, in and of itself, that such individuals are legally insane. Brain imaging is necessarily a post hoc test, and questions will always remain as to whether identifiable brain dysfunction existed at the time the offense took place. More importantly, the causal relationship between brain dysfunction and commission of the offense must, in many cases, be very much open to question.

The key question to be asked in an insanity defense is whether the person, at the time of committing the act, was unable to appreciate the wrongfulness of the act due to having a severe mental disease or defect, and as such was not responsible for his or her actions. Brain imaging findings can only provide data that may or may not be consistent with such a state of mind or with a proposed severe mental illness and cannot by themselves provide a clear answer to what is effectively a post hoc legal question. Bearing these limitations in mind, however, brain imaging studies have the potential to make important contributions to such decision making.

Finally, even though brain imaging research into offender groups is in its infancy, researchers need to move away from overly simplistic notions of linking one specific brain region or another to criminal and violent behavior. Such simplistic notions are inevitable in the early phase of any research area and indeed are essential to providing basic information upon which to build. Yet ultimately it is clear that brain mechanisms that underlie such behavior will involve multiple brain sites that form one or more neural networks which contribute to such behavior. It is the mapping of these neural networks that poses the ultimate challenge to future brain imaging researchers in this area.

X. SUMMARY

This chapter highlighted the importance and future potential of brain imaging research for beginning the process of more directly understanding the brain mechanisms that contribute to criminal and violent behavior. The basic principles involved in four main structural and functional imaging procedures, CT, MRI, PET, and SPECT, were first outlined. Findings from CT studies are suggestive of temporal lobe structural deficits in sex offenders, but these findings are not universally found and furthermore these structural findings are not paralleled by temporal functional deficits as measured by neuropsychological test data. Results of functional PET and RCBF studies are difficult to evaluate given the small number of studies, the small N sizes employed, and the infrequent employment of an activation task, but they are suggestive of frontal dysfunction in offenders. The only MRI study is suggestive of temporal lobe structural deficits. One further recent PET study of 22 murderers and 22 age- and sex-matched controls obtained evidence for selective prefrontal functional deficits in the murderer group.

An integration of findings from these studies gives rise to the hypothesis that frontal dysfunction may characterize violent offenders while temporal lobe dysfunction may characterize sexual offending; offenders with conjoint violent and sexual behavior are hypothesized to be characterized by both frontal and temporal lobe dysfunction. A model of frontal dysfunction in violent offending is presented which views such dysfunction as operating at the neurophysiological, neurobehavioral, personality, cognitive, and social levels and emphasizes the importance of not viewing brain imaging findings in isolation of social and environmental processes. While brain imaging research must be applied to forensic issues with caution, it is argued that it holds the promise of revolutionizing our understanding of the neural networks which in part contribute to criminal and violent behavior, and therefore of understanding the causes of such behavior.

7 Psychophysiology

I. GENERAL INTRODUCTION

Since the 1940s an extensive body of research has been built up on the psychophysiological basis of antisocial, delinquent, criminal, and psychopathic behavior. For example, there have been at least 150 studies on electrodermal and cardiovascular activity in such populations, and in EEG research alone there have been hundreds of studies on delinquency and crime (Gale, 1975). This body of research has received little attention in the broader field of criminology and is rarely referred to in textbooks of crime. One purpose of this chapter is to bring this body of knowledge to the attention of this more general audience. For readers who have some familiarity with this area, a second aim is to provide an update on recent findings in this literature, to highlight some of the more salient issues, and to provide some directives for future research.

Within the context of this book, psychophysiological findings are of clear importance in that, if it can be demonstrated that crime has a psychophysiological basis, this would be consistent with a biological predisposition to criminal behavior and adds more weight to the notion of crime as a psychopathology. The fact that criminals have certain psychophysiological characteristics that differentiate them from noncriminals does not prove that crime is a psychopathology, but if such characteristics could be uncovered, they would lend additional support to the notion of a physiological predisposition to crime that may have either environmental or genetic origins.

After a brief introduction to the advantages of psychophysiological research, studies on skin conductance (SC) activity and antisocial behavior will be reviewed with respect to orienting activity, resting arousal, responsiveness to aversive stimuli, and responsiveness to speech stimuli (further reviews on classical conditioning and skin conductance half-recovery time are covered in Chapter 8). After introducing the measurement of heart rate, both resting and phasic heart rate studies of antisocial populations will be reviewed and their theoretical significance examined. This will be followed by a review and theoretical analysis of electroencephalogram (EEG) studies of criminal populations and studies of event-related potentials (ERPs). Recent prospective psychophysiological research will then be analyzed, together with recent findings linking underarousal to an early disinhibited temperament, which may be an early forerunner of antisocial behavior. Finally, future developments in this field of research will be outlined with special reference to the nature of the interaction between psychophysiological and social predispositions for crime.

II. INTRODUCTION TO PSYCHOPHYSIOLOGY

Definitions of psychophysiology vary, but one useful perspective of psychophysiology outlined by Dawson (1990) is that it is "concerned with understanding the relationships between psychological states and processes on the one hand and physiological measures on the other hand" (p. 243). Psychophysiology is uniquely placed to provide important insights into criminal behavior because it rests at the interface between clinical science, cognitive science, and neuroscience (Dawson, 1990). As such, it is sometimes easier to see the relevance of this research for crime relative to biochemistry research because concepts in psychophysiology more easily map on to broader concepts such as learning, emotion, arousal, and cognition.

This is one main strength of psychophysiology. A second main advantage that psychophysiological measures hold over other physiological measures such as hormones, neurotransmitters, and brain glucose metabolism is the excellent temporal resolution of such measures. That is, measures such as skin conductance and heart rate are sensitive to changes in the environment (e.g., experimental manipulations or presentation of stimuli) occurring over periods of 1 or 2 seconds. ERPs have even greater temporal resolution, with detectable electrical changes taking place just milliseconds after the presentation of a discrete stimulus. Enhanced temporal resolution means that an individual's physiological reactivity can be measured to specific and transient events or manipulations. In contrast, assays of hormones and neurotransmitters reflect pooled activity occurring over minutes rather than seconds, while measures of brain glucose metabolism reflect brain processes occurring over a pooled period of about half an hour.

A third and important advantage of psychophysiological recording procedures is that they are relatively noninvasive compared to neurotransmitter assays, which require a spinal tap or the withdrawal of blood, and PET and CT, which involve exposure to radiation. Relative to brain imaging technology, psychophysiological recordings are relatively cheap, though they do require technical skills and equipment, which has meant that they have not been widely used. Recent technical advances in both software and hardware promise to make the technology of psychophysiology available on a wider scale.

Detailed introductions to psychophysiological measures and recording techniques may be found in Cacioppo, Tassinary, and Fridlund (1991), Coles, Donchin, and Porges (1986), and Dawson, Schell, and Filion (1990). The following sections will only provide a very brief overview of these measures and what they reflect. A wide number of psychophysiological measures have been recorded from antisocial populations, but because SC, heart rate (HR), EEG, and ERPs have been more commonly used, this chapter focuses on these four specific psychophysiological systems.

III. SKIN CONDUCTANCE AND CRIME

A. Introduction to Skin Conductance Activity

Skin conductance is usually measured from electrodes placed on two sites of the hand (fingers or palms) and involves the passage of an imperceptible current across the electrodes. Changes in SC activity reflect very small changes in the electrical activity of the skin, with increased sweating leading to an increase in skin conductance activity. These small changes can be detected using a polygraph, which incorporates preamplifier and driver amplifiers that increase the signal changes so that they can be seen and measured either by hand from a polygraph chart or by computer software. Skin potential (SP) is a measure similar to SC but it does not involve the passage of an electrical current and instead measures the resting potential difference of the skin. SP correlates highly with SC, though currently it is not in widespread use.

Galvanic skin response (GSR) is an older term for SC, while electrodermal activity (EDA) is a more generic term that includes both SC and SP. Skin conductance responses (SCRs) usually occur from 1 to 3 seconds after the onset of a stimulus (typically a tone) and provide a very sensitive index of what is termed the "orienting reflex" or "what is it" response. Habituation refers to the normal process whereby after repeated presentations of a neutral stimulus (e.g., 70-dB tone), the subject gives a repeatedly smaller response until the SCR ultimately "extinguishes."

Individual differences in the size of a subject's response to an orienting stimulus have been taken to reflect the degree to which a subject allocates attentional resources to the processing of that stimulus (Dawson, Filion, & Schell, 1989). While being peripheral by virtue of the fact that SC is an autonomic nervous system measure, SC is nevertheless a simple but powerful measure of central nervous system processing. For example, extensive experimental research indicates that SCRs represent a very sensitive measure of the allocation of attentional resources (Dawson et al., 1990; Dawson & Schell, 1985). Arousal is measured by (1) resting skin conductance level (SCL), and (2) the number of spontaneous SC responses given in a resting, "undriven" state where no external stimuli are presented.

Because the autonomic nervous system (ANS) plays an important role in emotional behavior and because SC is a direct measure of sympathetic ANS activity, SC has also been taken to reflect states such as anxiety. It is important to recognize that no unique, one-to-one relationships between psychophysiological measures and specific emotions have been uncovered. Nevertheless, because the sympathetic nervous system is sensitive to stress and emotional arousal, in general terms SC activity can be used to index stress reactivity to aversive or arousing events. In this context, SC is an excellent and direct measure of autonomic arousal.

B. Findings on Skin Conductance Activity

Most previous discussions of SC and antisocial behavior have focused specifically on that subgroup of criminals who are psychopathic (Hare, 1970, 1978; Siddle, 1977; Siddle & Trasler, 1981; Blackburn, 1983; Fowles, 1980; Zahn, 1986), though Venables (1987) provides one exception to this. The most comprehensive review for SC activity has been conducted by Hare (1978), and consequently it is worth reiterating the conclusions drawn for research conducted up to this date. These are that psychopaths are characterized by (1) reduced tonic arousal as measured by SCL [though not nonspecific fluctuations (NSFs)], (2) reduced SCRs to aversive but not neutral tones, (3) reduced SCRs in conditioning and quasiconditioning paradigms, and (4) longer SC half-recovery times to aversive stimuli.

What follows is a review of studies carried out since 1978 for antisocial behavior in general (as opposed to psychopathy in particular), with a view to

TABLE 1   Key Findings for SC Arousal Measured by Skin Conductance Level and Nonspecific Fluctuations

Reference	Subjects	Findings[a]
Significant findings		
Hinton, O'Neill, & Dishman (1979)	Public offenders	Low NSF
Buikhuisen et al. (1985)	Crimes of evasion	Low NSF, low SCL
Venables (1989)	Conduct disorder (age 18)	Low SCL (age 11; males and females)
Raine et al. (1990a)	Crime (age 24)	Low NSF (age 15)
Nonsignificant findings		
Tharp et al. (1980)	Psychopathic gamblers	n.s.d. SCL
Hemming (1981)	Criminals from good homes	n.s.d. NSF
Hare (1982)	Psychopaths	n.s.d. NSF, SCL
Buikhuisen et al. (1985)	General crime	n.s.d. NSF, SCL
Raine & Venables (1988[a])	Psychopaths	n.s.d. SCL
Schmidt, Solant, & Bridger (1985)	Conduct disorder	n.s.d. SCL, NSF

[a]Abbreviations: NSF, nonspecific fluctuations; SCL, skin conductance level; n.s.d., no significant differences.

assessing the extent to which these conclusions drawn in 1978 also hold true for the wider concept of antisocial behavior in studies of more recent origin. Reviews on SC classical conditioning and SC half-recovery time are held over until the next chapter due to their relevance for cognitive theories of criminal behavior. Studies are broken down according to resting arousal, orienting to neutral tones, responsiveness to aversive stimuli, and responsiveness to speechlike stimuli.

1. Skin Condutance Arousal

Arousal in 10 studies has been assessed by measurement during an initial "rest" period of either SCLs or NSFs. Key findings are outlined in Table 1. Four of the ten studies find significant effects, with three of these four finding differences for NSFs. Only one of the four found effects for SCL, although one of these studies found trends for lower SCLs (Raine et al., 1990a). NSFs may produce stronger support for SC underarousal in antisocials relative to SCLs because the latter are more influenced by factors such as local peripheral conditions of the skin and the thickness and hydration of the stratum corneum (Venables & Christie, 1973), factors that are unrelated to autonomic arousal. An interesting finding is that of Buikhuisen, Bontekoe, Plas-Korenhoff, and Buuren (1985), who found effects specific to type of crime, that is, under-

TABLE 2   Key Findings for SC Orienting to Neutral Stimuli

Reference	Subjects	Finding
Significant findings		
Blackburn (1979)	Secondary schizoid psychopaths	Reduced frequency
Raine & Venables (1984a)	Conduct disorder with schizoid personality	Reduced frequency
Raine (1987)	Schizotypal criminals	Reduced frequency
Raine *et al.* (1990a)	Criminals	Reduced frequency
Nonsignificant findings		
Aniskiewitz (1979)	Psychopaths	n.s.d.[a] (% responding)
Hinton *et al.* (1979)	Public offenders	n.s.d. (amplitude)
Schmidt *et al.* (1985)	Conduct disorder	n.s.d. (amplitude)
Raine & Venables (1988a,b)	Psychopaths	n.s.d. (amplitude and frequency)

[a]No significant differences.

arousal characterizes crimes of evasion (e.g., customs offenses) but not other forms of crime. It could be speculated that being autonomically underaroused is particularly conducive to escaping detection of covert crime.

2. Skin Conductance Orienting

Key findings from seven studies that have assessed SC orienting in antisocial groups are given in Table 2. Four out of eight studies find evidence for an orienting deficit as indicated by reduced frequency of SCRs to neutral tone stimuli. Frequency measures of SC orienting appear to produce stronger findings in these studies, perhaps because frequency measures tend to be more reliable than amplitude measures (Raine & Venables, 1984a). This in turn may be because amplitude is more affected by non-ANS factors such as the number and size of sweat glands (Venables & Christie, 1973). The most striking finding from Table 2, however, is that reduced SC orienting appears to be specific to psychopathic, criminal, and antisocial individuals with schizoid or schizotypal features. Three of these four findings are from the same laboratory however, and consequently stronger conclusions await confirmatory findings from other researchers.

This link between reduced SC orienting and antisocials with schizotypal features is of particular interest in the context of the hypothesis developed in a previous chapter on neuropsychology in which it was suggested that frontal

TABLE 3   Key Findings for Skin Conductance Responses to Aversive Stimuli

Reference	Subjects	Findings
Significant findings		
Buikhuisen et al. (1985)	Crimes of evasion	Low SCR (120 dB)
Schmidt et al. (1985)	Conduct disorder	Low SCR (90 dB)
Nonsignificant findings		
Tharp et al. (1980)	Psychopathic gamblers	n.s.d.[a] (95 dB)
Hare (1982)	Psychopaths	n.s.d. (120 dB)
Raine & Venables (1981)	Conduct disorder	n.s.d. (105 dB)
Buikhuisen et al. (1985)	General crime	n.s.d. (120 dB)
Raine & Venables (1988a)	Psychopaths	n.s.d. (90 dB)
Raine (1990)[b]	Psychopaths	n.s.d. (105 dB)

[a]No significant differences.
[b]SC measured at age 15 years and related to psychopathic personality also measured at age 15 in those who became criminal by age 24 years.

dysfunction may particularly characterize this subgroup of antisocials. SC orienting deficits have been found to be related to both structural and functional frontal deficits. Hazlett, Dawson, Buchsbaum, and Nuechterlein (1993) found that schizophrenics characterized by SC nonresponding to orienting stimuli showed significant reductions in glucose metabolism in the frontal cortex relative to responding schizophrenics. In normal subjects, Raine, Reynolds, and Sheard (1991b) found significant relationships between number of SC orienting responses and prefrontal area as measured by MRI in the direction of reduced prefrontal area in those with fewer orienting responses; correlations ranged from .43 to .54 (see also Raine & Lencz, 1993). Consequently, the finding of reduced SC orienting (a measure related to frontal deficits) in schizoid antisocials is consistent with the hypothesis that frontal dysfunction may be one mechanism underpinning this subgroup of antisocials.

C. Skin Conductance Responses to Aversive Stimuli

Eight analyses providing data on SCR amplitudes to aversive stimuli are shown in Table 3. All studies assessed responsivity using auditory stimuli ranging from 90 to 120 dB in intensity. Only two of the eight analyses showed evidence for lower responsivity in antisocials. Three studies testing adult psychopaths all failed to find significant group differences. Two of the studies failing to find effects used stimuli that are unlikely to have been

TABLE 4   Studies on SC Responsivity to Speech or Speechlike Stimuli in Psychopaths[a]

Reference	Subjects	Finding
Lakosina & Trunova (1985)	Violent affective psychopaths	Larger SCR to verbal stimulus
Raine & Venables (1988a)	Psychopaths	Fast rise time to consonant–vowel stimulus

[a]All findings were significant.

strongly aversive (90 and 95 dB intensity). Nevertheless, Hare (1982) used 120-dB stimuli and failed to find significant effects for adult psychopaths, indicating that stimulus intensity cannot easily account for the failure to find effects.

D. Skin Conductance Responses to Speech and Other Significant Stimuli

Two studies that have assessed SCRs to speech or speechlike stimuli both found psychopaths to show evidence of *greater* attentional processing (see Table 4). The first study (Lakosina & Trunova, 1985) showed that Russian psychopaths characterized by violent and affective behavior gave larger SCRs to verbal stimuli. The second study (Raine & Venables, 1988a) showed that English psychopaths showed faster SC rise time (time taken for the response to rise to its peak amplitude) to consonant–vowel stimuli. This finding was specific to the speechlike stimuli since similar effects were not observed to pure tone stimuli. Furthermore, as noted in the previous chapter, SC rise time was correlated with psychopathic traits thought to tap unusual speech processes shown by psychopaths (e.g., glibness and superficial charm, lying and deception, conning), but not those behavioral psychopathic traits unrelated to speech processes (e.g., presence of early behavior problems, committing multiple types of offenses, impulsivity). Given the view that fast SC rise time indicates a more open attentional stance to the environment (Venables, Gartshore & O'Riordan, 1980), the faster SC rise time seen in psychopaths to speechlike stimuli was interpreted as indicating a focusing of attentional resources on speech stimuli, a process consistent with the notion that psychopaths are characterized by abnormal speech processes (Cleckley, 1976; Hare *et al.*, 1988; Raine *et al.*, 1990d).

A study by Damasio, Tranel, and Damasio (1990), while not assessing responsivity to speech stimuli, is of particular interest in that it measured SC responsivity to "socially significant stimuli" (pictures depicting mutilation, social disasters, or nudity) in five patients who had bilateral lesions to orbital frontal and lower mesial frontal cortex and who showed "sociopathic behavior" (defined by severe deficits in social conduct, judgment, and planning following brain damage). Psychopaths with frontal lesions showed reduced SCR amplitudes to the socially meaningful stimuli compared to six control patients with nonfrontal lesions, but showed normal responses to neutral tone stimuli. While preliminary, these results suggest that frontal dysfunction may underlie both psychopathic behavior and deficits in SC orienting to meaningful social stimuli. Such findings are broadly consistent with recent findings implicating prefrontal cortex in the mediation of SC orienting responses (Hazlett *et al.*, 1993; Raine *et al.*, 1991b).

E. Summary of Findings on Skin Conductance Activity

These reviews indicate that (1) there is some evidence for underarousal in antisocials, particularly with respect to crimes of evasion; (2) orienting deficits seem to be specific to antisocials with concomitant features of schizotypal personality; (3) prior findings up to 1978 of reduced SC responsiveness to aversive stimuli have not been observed in more recent studies, either in psychopathic or in nonpsychopathic antisocials; and (4) psychopaths may, however, be more responsive to speech stimuli but less responsive to socially meaningful stimuli. The strongest findings are with respect to classical conditioning and SC half-recovery time, but these findings will be reviewed in detail in the next chapter dealing with cognitive processes.

IV. HEART RATE AND CRIME

A. Introduction to Heart Rate

Heart rate (HR) is in some ways a simpler psychophysiological measure than SC, and in other ways it is more complex. In terms of tonic or resting HR, resting HR level is relatively easy to record and can be measured with portable equipment, as opposed to a polygraph, without significant loss in quality of data. Furthermore, it is one of the few psychophysiological measures that can be easily recorded without any equipment at all, since an excellent measure of resting HR can be obtained from the pulse. Alternatively, the measurement of phasic changes in HR in response to experimental stimuli is more difficult to assess than measures such as SC responsivity, and artifacts such as sinus arrhythmia and prestimulus HR level need to be taken into account. SC responses can also be scored more quickly by hand. In consequence there have been fewer studies of HR reactivity than of resting HR. Both have been less frequently assessed than tonic and phasic SC activity in the context of antisocial behavior.

There are two basic measures of phasic HR activity. In response to the onset of a neutral tone stimulus, the heart normally slows down for a brief period. This "deceleratory" response is followed by a speeding of heart rate, which in turn is termed an "acceleratory" response. Such acceleratory responses are particularly common to aversive stimuli and are thought to reflect sensory rejection and "tuning out" of noxious environmental events (Hare, 1978; Lacey & Lacey, 1974). Conversely, deceleratory responses have been thought to reflect increased sensitivity to the environment or environmental "openness" as part of the orienting response.

Heart rate reflects both sympathetic and parasympathetic nervous system activity, unlike SC activity, which reflects sympathetic processes only. As with SC activity, HR has been commonly used to assess the extent of autonomic arousal and reactivity to both neutral and aversive events. Psychologically, low HR has been thought to reflect "fearlessness"; Venables (1987) cites data showing that both decorated bomb disposal experts and experienced parachutists have lower resting heart rate levels than controls. High heart rates, particularly in infants and young children, have been associated with anxiety and a fearful temperament (Kagan, 1989). Larger heart rate decelerations to neutral stimuli are thought to reflect relatively greater orienting and attentional processing.

B. Resting Heart Rate Findings for Crime and Antisocial Behavior

There is a major contrast in research findings for resting HR for psychopathic criminal behavior on the one hand and milder forms of antisocial behavior on the other. With respect to psychopathy, reviews by Hare (1970, 1975, and 1978) reveal no successes and at least 15 failures to obtain lower resting heart rate in institutionalized, criminal psychopaths. In stark contrast, studies on younger noninstitutionalized populations in which mild forms of antisocial behavior are assessed reveal very clear effects, showing that antisocial individuals are characterized by lower resting HR.

Fourteen studies that have assessed resting HR in these younger, milder antisocial populations are shown in Table 5. These 14 studies report analyses on 18 samples of antisocial subjects. Two of these analyses represent reanalyses or extensions of earlier studies. One by Raine et al. (1990a) represents a 9-year follow-up of those tested at age 15 (Raine & Venables, 1984a). The other by Farrington (1987a) reanalyzes HR data collected by West and Farrington (1977) and presents new analyses for violent offending. One of the studies (Rogeness, Cepeda, Macedo, Fischer, & Harris, 1990) presents HR data for three independent samples of antisocial behavior, while another (Little, 1978) reports findings for three separate age groups. In total, therefore, there are 16 independent samples contained in these 14 studies.

TABLE 5 Studies on Resting Heart Rate Level in Nonpsychopathic, Noninstitutionalized Antisocial Populations[a]

Reference	Subjects	Key finding	Effect size
Davies & Maliphant (1971)	13.6-year-old schoolboys	Lower resting HRL[b] in antisocials.	1.44
Wadsworth (1976)	11-year-old schoolboys	Lower resting HRL (at 11 years) related to delinquency measured from ages 8–21 years. Lowest HRL found in nonsexual violent offenders.	0.39
West & Farrington (1977)	18- to 19-year-old noninstitutionalized males	Convicted offenders more represented in low resting HRL category.	—
Farrington (1987)	18- to 19-year-old noninstitutionalized males	Lowest HRLs in those convicted of violent offenses at age 25. Lower HRLs in children of criminal parents.	0.40
Little (1978)	7-, 9-, and 11-year-old schoolchildren	Lower resting HRL linked to antisocial behavior in 9 and 11 year olds.	—
Raine & Venables (1984b)	15-year-old schoolboys	Lower resting HRL in antisocials.	0.58
Bullock (1988)	15-year-old schoolgirls	Lower resting HRL in girls rated as antisocial.	1.60
Venables (1987)	11-year-old offspring of criminal or control parents	Lower resting HRL in children with criminal parents.	—
Raine & Jones (1987)	11-year-old boys with behavior problems	Lower resting HRL in those characterized by conduct disorder and socialized aggression.	0.63
Rogeness et al. (1990)	12-year-old boys with conduct disorder (unsocialized)	Lower resting HRL in conduct-disordered boys relative to depression and anxiety controls.	0.50
	12-year-old boys with conduct disorder (socialized)	Lower resting HRL in socialized conduct disorder relative to controls.	0.50
	13-year-old girls with conduct disorder (both types combined)	Lower resting HRL in conduct-disordered girls relative to controls.	0.35
Maliphant et al. (1990a)	12- to 13-year-old schoolgirls	Lower resting HRL in disruptive, badly behaved girls.	1.28
Raine et al. (1990a)	15-year-old schoolboys	Lower resting HRL (age 15) in those who are criminal at 24 years.	0.63
Maliphant et al. (1990b)	7- to 9-year-old schoolboys	Lower resting HRL in disruptive, badly behaved boys.	1.91
Bice (1993)	8- to 10-year-old schoolboys	Lower resting HRL in prosocial aggressives.	0.68

[a]All reported findings are statistically significant.
[b]HRL, heart rate level.

One of these studies (Bullock, 1988) has not been formally presented, so details will briefly be provided here. Bullock (1988) assessed 51 15-year-old schoolgirls (range 14–16 years) from two schools in the northeast of England. Subjects were unselected with the proviso that parental permission was granted for subject participation. Subjects were tested by a 25-year-old female and, after filling out questionnaires in an isolated school room, sat quietly while resting HR was sampled using a finger plethismograph in conjunction with a BBC microcomputer B. Antisocial behavior/personality was assessed by teacher ratings of behavior using the Unsocialized-Psychopathic subscale of the Behavior Problem Checklist (Quay & Parsons, 1970), while a self-report measure of socialization was assessed using the socialization scale of the California Personality Inventory.

For the total sample of 51, significant correlations were observed for both teacher rating ($r = -.48$, $p < .001$) and socialization ($r = -.59$, $p < .001$) measures, in both cases in the predicted direction of lower HR in antisocial/undersocialized subjects. These findings replicated across separate high ($r = -.49, -.48$, $p < .01$) and low ($r = -.53, -.70$, $p < .01$) social class groups for teacher rating and self-report measures, respectively. In a group analysis, subjects scoring above the mean on both measures were designated as "antisocial" ($N = 12$) while those below the mean on both were designated as "prosocial" ($N = 24$). HR for the antisocial group (M = 81.4, SD = 12.0) was significantly lower than that for the prosocial group (M = 100.2, SD = 11.6), $t = 4.6$, $p < .001$.

All 14 studies found significantly lower resting HRL in antisocial groups. No failures to replicate this finding have been found to date for noninstitutionalized, nonclinical populations. Out of the 16 independent samples, 15 find significant effects; the only failure comes from the study of Little (1978), who observed significant effects in 9 and 11 year olds, but not in 7 year olds.

Several features of these studies should be noted. Heart rate is measured in these studies between the ages of 7 and 15, with the exception being West and Farrington (1977), who measured HR at age 18. Almost all of these samples are uninstitutionalized, with the one exception being Rogeness *et al.* (1990), who assessed children in a private psychiatric hospital. Twelve of the 14 studies assessed children drawn from the normal population and, as such, subjects were not the severe extremes on a distribution of antisociality. The key differences between these studies and those of adult criminal psychopaths are that (1) mild levels of antisocial behavior rather than seriously psychopathic behavior are being assessed; (2) samples are noninstitutionalized; (3) samples are nonselected and therefore are not restricted to "unsuccessful," caught criminals, and (4) subjects are relatively young.

While relatively homogeneous in some ways, these 18 analyses are heterogeneous in other ways. Resting HR level was measured in a wide variety of ways (polygraphs, pulsimeters, stop watches). A wide number of definitions of antisocial behavior is used, ranging from legal criminality and delinquency to teacher ratings of antisocial behavior in school, self-report socialization measures, diagnostic criteria for conduct disorder, and genetically inferred law breaking. Subjects were assessed in a wide variety of settings (medical interview, study office, school, university psychophysiological laboratory, hospital), and lower HR was found both in males and in females and across both sides of the Atlantic. Such heterogeneity attests to the robustness of the observed effects. Importantly, there has been good cross-laboratory replication of this finding.

C. Effect Sizes for Lower Resting Heart Rate Level in Antisocials and Potential Artifacts

Effect sizes in these studies vary. In the 13 analyses reporting means and SDs, effect sizes vary from .35 (females in Rogeness *et al.*, 1990) to 1.9 (Maliphant, Watson, & Daniels, 1990b). Across the 10 studies, however, the average effect size is 0.84. This represents an unusually strong average effect for any replicated measure, social or biological, in the field of antisocial and criminal behavior. One of the lowest effect sizes (.4 in Farrington, 1987) was for a sample in which HR was recorded at the end of a 2-hour interview, whereas much larger effect sizes have been observed in studies where resting HRL is measured prior to other experiments and procedures. These effect sizes are not trivial. For example, an effect size of .84 found for HR and antisocial behavior is larger than the effect size of 0.80 for the difference in height between 13- and 18-year-old girls (Cohen, 1988). As another comparison, low serotonin in violent and antisocial populations is a strong finding in the area of neurochemistry and violence, yet the averaged effect size calculated in a recent review of this literature is 0.47, or just over half the effect size for low HR. In the guidelines drawn up by Cohen (1988), an effect size of 0.84 as observed for low HR would be classified as "large" (0.8), relative to "medium" (0.5) and "small" (0.2) effect sizes.

Lower resting HR in antisocials does not appear to be an artifact of other factors. Age is negatively correlated with HRL, but many of the studies in Table 5 either controlled age or else subjects were of the same age or were within such a narrow age range (e.g., 14–16 years) that age effects are not expected. Cigarette smoking is not controlled for in many of the studies, but since smoking would be expected to *increase* HR, and since antisocials would be more expected to smoke than prosocials, this cannot account for *reduced* HR in antisocials. Exercise and regular engagement in sporting activities can reduce heart rate. This seems an unlikely explanation of the group effects, however, since exercise effects are largely observed at the extremes of exercise levels; for example, Wadsworth (1976) found no relationship between resting HR and ratings of physical energy, while Raine and Venables (1984b) found no significant relationships between resting HR and adventure-seeking behavior. Furthermore, delinquents are less likely to engage in athletics and sporting activities than nondelinquents (Offord, Allen, & Abrams, 1978; West & Farrington, 1977), though it is still possible that delinquents are more likely to engage in nonstructured, nonofficial activities that promote physical fitness. Since HR levels have been found to be lower in those from homes broken by divorce and separation (Wadsworth, 1976), such early life stress may account for lower resting HR in antisocials. However, Wadsworth (1976) found that delinquents from broken homes, who might for this reason be thought to have particularly low resting HR, did not differ from controls. Alcohol intake is not mentioned in the methodology of most studies, and delinquents may be expected to drink more than nondelinquents. Alcohol *increases* HR, however, and as such this factor again cannot account for the *lowered* HR in delinquents. While food ingestion and circadian rhythms could conceivably affect HR, Raine *et al.* (1990a) tested all subjects at exactly the same time of day and still observed significant effects. Finally, body weight is negatively correlated with resting HR, and delinquents have controversially been thought to have a larger body build (endomorphy–mesomorphy) than nondelinquents (see Chapter 8). Wadsworth (1976), however, found pulse rates to be unrelated to height, shape, and weight.

Taking these factors into consideration, it seems that reduced HRL in antisocials cannot easily be accounted for by artifactual relationships. This seems to be particularly so since skin conductance and EEG arousal measures, which are not affected by factors such as body size and physical fitness, also relate to antisocial behavior (e.g., Raine *et al.*, 1990a), indicating that reduced heart rate reflects generalized underarousal rather than being determined by these artifacts. Nevertheless, future studies need to more carefully assess factors such as body size and physical fitness in order to more conclusively demonstrate that such factors do not mediate the HRL–antisocial behavior relationship. The fact that some of the above artifacts would be expected to *increase* HRL in antisocials suggests that the HRL–antisocial relationship will prove to be stable when artifacts working in both directions are fully accounted for.

D. Theoretical Interpretation of Lower Resting Heart Rate Levels in Antisocials

Lower resting HR levels in antisocials can be interpreted in a number of ways which, though separate, may also be related. First, low HR may reflect lack of fear. As mentioned earlier, field studies indicate that low HR is a correlate of fearlessness. Such an analysis would be consistent with theories of antisocial behavior based on a reduced fear concept (e.g., Mednick, 1977; Trasler, 1978). Reduced fear would predispose to antisocial and violent behavior since such behavior (e.g., fights and assaults) require a degree of fearlessness to execute. Lack of fear, especially in childhood, would help explain poor socialization since low fear of punishment would reduce the effectiveness of conditioning. It should be remembered that while the above studies recorded HR in a "resting" state, this measurement period frequently preceded a series of other experiments or procedures (e.g., medical examination, exposure to aversive tone stimuli). As such, low HR may be viewed as reflecting lack of anticipatory fear to mild to moderate stressors.

A second, related interpretation of low HR is that it reflects autonomic underarousal. Such underarousal might facilitate stimulation-seeking behavior which in turn predisposes to stimulating antisocial acts, which increase autonomic arousal (Quay, 1965; Hare, 1970; Raine *et al.*, 1990a).

A third, more complex interpretation is that low HR reflects a vagal passive coping response to a mildly stressful testing situation. Obrist (1981) presented evidence indicating that increased cardiovascular activity represents active coping in response to a stressor, while reduced cardiovascular activity represents passive coping. Reduced HR in an evolutionary context would be adaptive in preparing the organism for disengagement and inactivity in a threatening situation (Engel, 1977). Furthermore, immobilization via its resulting muscular relaxation attenuated painful experiences, and this may be of particular relevance in that antisocials, by a method of passive emotional withdrawal, may be relatively insensitive to socializing punishments. This interpretation will be discussed in the next section on phasic HR in psychopaths.

A fourth interpretation lies in the notion that antisocial and violent offenders have an ANS that is vagotonically tuned, that is, favoring parasympathetic as opposed to sympathetic ANS processes. Venables (1988) bases this theory on heart rate, hypoglycemia, and EEG data in violent and antisocial individuals. Low heart rate is a direct index of vagotonia or parasympathetic tuning, and hence vagotonia may underlie lower heart rates of violent offenders. This theory and its links with EEG are elaborated in more detail below.

A fifth and more speculative suggestion is that low resting HR in antisocials may reflect enlargement of the lateral ventricles of the brain, which may be precipitated by birth complications. Cannon, Raine, Herman, Mednick, Schulsinger, and Moore (1992) report that low HR in a group of schizophrenics is associated with enlargement of the third ventricle of the brain. Such ventricular enlargement may reflect reductions in the area of periventricular structures such as the hypothalamus, a structure known to be involved in mediating heart rate. Interestingly, enlargement of the third ventricle has also been linked to reduced SC responsivity (Cannon, Fuhrmann, Mednick, Machon, Parnas, & Schulsinger 1988), which in turn has been found in antisocial populations. Such brain deficits, flagged by reduced heart rate, may also lead to cognitive deficits that predispose to school failure and delinquency.

Whatever interpretation is placed on lower HR in antisocials, it is clear that such an effect is not related to psychopathic personality. This is suggested by the fact that, as outlined earlier, studies of adult psychopaths find no differences in resting heart rate. It could be argued that low HR may characterize psychopathic adolescents, but an unpublished study of HR in institutionalized psychopathic adolescents compared to institutionalized conduct-disordered adolescents failed to find this effect (Raine, 1991). Similarly, Venables (1987) found that, while children with criminal fathers had low resting HR, children whose fathers were psychopathic did not show this effect. These data suggest that the finding of low resting HR is specific to young, noninstitutionalized, nonpsychopathic antisocials.

It is important to note that these findings for resting HR in antisocial adolescents probably represent both the strongest and the best replicated biological findings in the field to date. The fact that such effects are obtained for mild antisocial behavior call to attention the finding from genetic studies that heritability for crime is particularly true of petty criminality (Chapter 3). Findings for resting HR make a clear and important statement that one does not have to turn to serious adult, psychopathic offenders to obtain evidence for biological predisposing factors to crime and antisocial behavior. Indeed, such findings also demonstrate the potential importance of researching noninstitutionalized antisocial groups to gain a clearer understanding of factors that predispose to antisocial and criminal behavior. Given the ease and low cost of measuring resting HR, this measure could and should be adopted as a standard measure in future biological and social studies of crime.

E. Findings for Phasic Heart Rate

The literature on phasic heart rate is considerably less extensive than that for resting HR. The most commonly discussed finding is the notion that psychopathic criminals are characterized by anticipatory HR acceleration prior to an aversive event.

This conclusion is based on significant findings from three studies conducted by Hare and colleagues. Hare and Craigen (1974) found that psychopaths gave significantly larger acceleratory HR responses in anticipation of a signaled electric shock, followed by reduced SC responses to the shock itself. Hare, Frazelle, and Cox (1978) again showed larger anticipatory HR acceleratory responses to a loud (120-dB) tone in psychopaths, with undersocialized psychopaths also showing reduced SC responses to the aversive tone. Hare (1982) also demonstrated that psychopaths showed greater anticipatory HR acceleration and reduced SC responses to an aversive 120-dB tone.

Hare (1978) has interpreted these findings as indicating that psychopaths have a very proficient active coping mechanism that allows them to "tune out" aversive events. Hare (1978) points to data from Lacey and Lacey (1974) indicating that increased heart rate is thought to increase pressure in the carotid sinus, resulting in reduction in reticular and cortical arousal, and hence reduced responsiveness to the aversive properties of the stimulus. Because high heart rate helps reduce the impact of the aversive stimulus, psychopaths give a smaller SC response to the aversive stimulus itself.

Siddle and Trasler (1981) have criticized Hare's position on several counts. They argue that while Hare suggests that this mechanism may reduce the impact of cues predicting aversive events, it is difficult to see how a process that follows the warning cue (HR acceleration) can attenuate processing of the earlier cue. Second, they point out that only a subgroup of psychopaths (those with low socialization scores) showed reduced SC responsivity to the aversive tone in Hare *et al.* (1978). Third and perhaps most importantly, they point out that rather than the psychopathic group having an abnormal HR response in this situation, the nonpsychopathic criminal controls appear to be much more abnormal in that they show virtually no anticipatory HR response, since studies of normals show at least a biphasic (acceleratory and deceleratory) response.

This latter point of Siddle and Trasler (1981) is of interest for two reasons. At a general level it illustrates the difficulty of drawing conclusions from research on psychopathy when comparisons are drawn with criminal controls in the absence of data from noncriminal normals. More specifically, their point appears consistent with the notion drawn in the previous section that nonpsychopathic antisocials show *reduced* tonic HR in situations preceding mildly aversive events. That is, Hare's nonpsychopathic criminal controls appear to be responding to the anticipated stressor in much the same way as the noninstitutionalized antisocial groups reviewed earlier. In this context, the *nonpsychopathic* controls in Hare's experiments may be the more abnormal group, responding to the anticipated stressor with a passive coping response as indexed by lower HR (Obrist, 1981).

There are additional complications to a straightforward interpretation of these data. For example one study that aimed to replicate the finding of increased HR acceleration in anticipation of an aversive stimulus failed to do so. Tharp, Maltzman, Syndulko, and Ziskind (1980) tested noninstitutionalized sociopaths and failed to find any evidence of cardiac acceleration prior to an aversive stimulus in the sociopaths. This failure to replicate may, as suggested by Tharp *et al.* (1980), have been due to the fact that a less intense aversive stimulus was used. Alternatively, it may be that the effect is specific to institutionalized psychopaths and does not generalize to noninstitutionalized sociopaths who in this study consisted of noninstitutionalized gamblers.

Findings by Hare (1982) also indicate that clear interpretations of the HR acceleration finding are difficult. When subjects choose to listen to a comedian in preference to a warning tone, psychopaths showed decreases in *both* HR and SC in anticipation of the aversive tone, a finding which Hare (1982) interpreted as indicating that psychopaths only screen out aversive events when the situation forces them to attend to cues predicting punishment. While this is an interesting and potentially important interpretation, it can also be viewed as increasingly restricting the range of the initial finding.

The notion of anticipatory HR acceleration as playing a role in helping psychopaths to tune out aversive events is an interesting one with great appeal and has been cited by a number of other researchers (e.g., Fowles, 1980; Venables, 1987). Given that no further studies of this phenomenon have been reported in the past 10 years, however, interpretation of these data should proceed cautiously.

V. ELECTROENCEPHALOGRAM AND CRIME

A. Introduction to EEG

The introduction given to EEG here will be limited to information needed to grasp later sections, while an excellent overview of EEG may be found in Ray (1990). EEG reflects the electrical activity of the brain and is recorded from electrodes placed at different locations on the scalp according to the standardized International 10–20 system. Although the neurophysiological basis of EEG has not to date been delineated with precision, there is reasonably good evidence to suggest that it reflects depolarizations of the dendritic trees of pyramidal cells. As such, EEG is thought to reflect cortical activity, although it is likely that subcortical structures such as the thalamus and hippocampus are involved in the control of this cortical activity. It should be borne in mind that although group differences may be localized to one area of the scalp, and although the inference is drawn that the brain area underlying this electrode may be dysfunctional, such assumptions are not strong. That is, spatial resolution of EEG is relatively poor and is much inferior to brain imaging techniques.

EEG can be broken down into different frequency components, most commonly delta (0–4 Hz), theta (4–8 Hz), alpha (8–12 Hz), and beta (13–30 Hz), although alpha and beta are also often subdivided into slow and fast components. Alpha frequency is sometimes recorded and refers to the frequency within the 8- to 12-Hz band at which alpha activity predominates; the lower this frequency, the more underaroused the individual is thought to be.

EEG frequency has been aligned with a continuum of consciousness, with delta associated with sleep, theta associated with drowsiness and low levels of alertness, alpha associated with relaxed wakefulness, and beta associated with alertness and vigilance. All frequencies are present in the awake individual, but individuals differ in the relative amount of power existing in these main frequency bands. As such, individuals with a predominance of theta or slow alpha activity would be viewed as having relatively reduced levels of cortical arousal, while those with relatively more fast alpha and beta activity would be viewed as relatively more aroused.

In the studies reported below, EEG is either clinically scored by eyeballing the chart record or otherwise subjected to a more quantitative computerized analysis that more objectively delineates the EEG into different components.

Clinical scoring is more qualitative and subjective, with records being categorized as normal or abnormal depending on the presence of such factors as excessive theta activity and other EEG signs of abnormality. It should be made clear, however, that a nonsignificant proportion of ostensibly normal subjects have abnormal EEGs (10–15%), and this should be borne in mind when considering rates of abnormalities reported below in clinical studies of criminal populations. Computerized, quantitative analyses are to be preferred to the earlier, more clinical EEG assessments, although unfortunately the latter tend to predominate in studies of offender populations.

B. Findings for Resting EEG

There have probably been literally hundreds of studies assessing EEG in criminals, delinquents, psychopaths, and violent offenders. Reviews of these studies may be found in Ellingson (1954), Hare (1970), Syndulko (1978), Mednick, Volavka, Gabrielli, and Itil (1981), Blackburn (1983), Volavka (1987), Venables (1988), Venables and Raine (1987), and Milstein (1988). Since extensive reviews exist, this section will briefly summarize the main points made by these reviews and generate some additional observations.

It is clear that a large number of studies implicate EEG abnormalities in violent recidivistic offending. As examples, Bach-y-Rita, Lion, Climet, & Ervin (1971) and Hill and Pond (1952) examined large samples of violent offenders and observed EEG abnormalities in about 50% of the cases. These findings have been supported by other studies of murderers and other violent offenders (e.g., Mark & Ervin, 1970; Williams, 1969).

Mednick *et al.* (1981) conclude their review with the statement that "a high prevalence of EEG abnormalities exists among persons convicted of violent crimes; this is especially true of recidivistic offenders" (p. 67) and argued that the bulk of this research implicated the anterior regions of the brain. They also suggest that the prevalence of EEG abnormalities in violent individuals ranges from 25 to 50%, with the rate of abnormalities in normals estimated as ranging from 5 to 20%. Similar conclusions are drawn by Volavka (1987) and Milstein (1988) for crime in general and violent crime in particular.

In contrast, reviews of the EEG literature on psychopathy reflect a greater inconsistency. Hare (1970) concluded that psychopaths are characterized by excessive slow-wave activity. A later review by Syndulko (1978), however, which could benefit from later results not available to Hare in 1970, found six studies claiming to show more EEG abnormalities in psychopaths, while four found no group differences. Syndulko concluded that an answer to the question of whether psychopaths have EEG abnormalities was "maybe" and that there was little evidence that psychopaths have more abnormalities when compared to other psychiatric control groups. Blackburn (1983) similarly concluded that there were many data inconsistencies, and found in a study of his own (Blackburn, 1978) that primary psychopaths were *more* aroused than secondary psychopaths.

It is probably fair to conclude that there have been extremely few methodologically good EEG studies that employ a strict criteria of psychopathy. The one study that meets these criteria failed to find any difference between psychopathic and nonpsychopathic criminals (Harpur *et al.*, 1986). Although future studies may reveal EEG abnormalities in psychopaths, there is currently little good evidence for resting EEG abnormalities in psychopaths.

While reviews agree that criminals and violent offenders are characterized by EEG abnormalities, they also agree that there are major problems in the interpretation of these findings. Methodological difficulties with these studies include the lack of adequate control groups, the subjective nature of scoring EEG records, the lack of blind assessment of EEG records, the lack of widely accepted and reliable criteria for defining "abnormality," and the lack of sensitivity to state of alertness of the subject. More rigorously designed studies using recently developed brain mapping facilities are required to confirm these early findings. One relatively recent study by Milstein (1988) along these lines measured EEG from 32 electrodes in 10 violent, aggressive inpatients, with recordings on all subjects taken on 27 separate occasions. This extensive mapping study indicated that while aggressives do not form a unified group with respect to EEG, one general finding was that excessive slow-wave (delta) activity accompanied times when the subject's status became worse.

C. Theoretical Significance

Studies have tended to focus on the empirical issue of whether abnormalities exist in the EEGs of criminals and psychopaths, and the theoretical significance of claimed findings has received relatively little attention. One theory suggests that since excessive theta activity characterizes the EEG of children, excessive theta activity in adult offenders may reflect "cortical immaturity" (Hare, 1970).

More recently, Venables (1988) has attempted to integrate diverse findings of lowered heart rate, hypoglycemia, and EEG underarousal in violent offenders by arguing that the concept of vagotonia can explain all three sets of results. Vagotonia refers to the notion that there is a predominance of parasympathetic over sympathetic autonomic processes, and Venables' theory argues that violent individuals have an excess of vagal tonus. Low heart rate is a direct index of vagotonia or parasympathetic tuning, and hence vagotonia may underlie lower heart rates of violent offenders. Since stimulation of the vagus nerve leads to hypoglycemia via release of insulin from the pancreas, increased vagal tone in violent offenders would also be consistent with findings of hypoglycemia in such populations (Virkkunen, 1984).

EEG findings are integrated into this theory because Gellhorn and Loofbourrow (1963) point out that EEG alpha frequency is low in vagotonics and high in sympathotonic individuals. Since low alpha frequency indicates cortical underarousal, this would be consistent with findings of EEG underarousal in violent offenders. Consequently, the observations of low heart rate, hypoglycemia, and EEG underarousal observed in violent offenders may be underpinned by the unitary process of excessive vagal tuning.

Although the theory is largely based on these three sets of findings, Venables (1988) also outlines the potential relevance of testosterone with his theory. He cites experimental evidence indicating that low EEG alpha frequency can be a function of high testosterone level; a relationship between EEG and testosterone would be consistent with other studies indicating that high testosterone levels may be associated with aggressive and violent behavior (see Chapter 8). The strength of Venables' theory is that, unlike many other theories of violence that are based on a single phenomenon or class of findings, it is based on a diverse set of findings from the areas of psychophysiology and neuroendocrinology that have not been previously integrated.

D. Future EEG Research

Earlier reviewers have focused their recommendations on technical considerations. These include the use of more modern quantitative techniques to assess EEG abnormalities in preference to nonblind clinical ratings, the recording of EEG from a wider electrode montage to localize abnormalities, better control groups, better-defined experimental groups, and the use of new EEG mapping techniques. It is agreed that these are very appropriate considerations.

More generally, however, research in this area clearly needs to be more theoretically driven. The question of whether general EEG abnormalities exist in a particular offender group is no longer particularly interesting. There is sufficient general evidence indicating that such is the case, at least for violent and criminal offending in general. Future studies must instead use EEG methodology to test theories and predictions. As one example, there is evidence that excessive theta activity is relatively localized to more anterior regions of the brain (Mednick et al., 1982; Williams, 1969) and that frontal regions may show specific dysfunction (Monroe, 1974). The notion that frontal dysfunction may predispose to violence and crime has been discussed in earlier chapters (see Chapters 5 and 6). In the context of EEG research, this theory could be tested by recording EEG over frontal and nonfrontal sites during a neuropsychological challenge task that activates the frontal lobes (e.g., Wisconsin Card Sort, continuous performance task). Previous EEG studies have very rarely used such tasks to challenge brain areas thought to be dysfunctional in crime and violence, but are of clear value not only theoretically but also methodologically in that they provide some control for general state of alertness (Syndulko, 1978).

Studies are also needed to explore the possibility that EEG abnormalities may underlie cognitive deficits and school failure, which may be linked to later violence. Most EEG studies have only measured EEG; future studies must also measure other constructs thought to be related to EEG dysfunction (e.g., cognitive and neuropsychological measures) and which may provide important conceptual links to crime. EEG studies in conjunction with brain scan studies are obviously very desirable but unlikely to be practical in the short term.

In a similar vein, an important priority for any future test of Venables' vagotonia theory is to assess heart rate, EEG, and blood glucose levels in the *same* population of aggressives. Further research is also required to investigate the possible causes of vagotonia. If this theory can be substantiated, an intriguing experimental question would be whether manipulations of the balance of sympathetic versus parasympathetic activity could have any effect in reducing levels of aggression.

The issue of causality has also been generally ignored in the past literature, and further research is greatly needed to help identify the direction of causality and rule out potential artifacts. With respect to causality, longitudinal studies are needed to assess whether EEG abnormalities precede crime and violence (see Section VII on prospective psychophysiological research) or whether violence precedes (and possibly causes) EEG abnormalities. With respect to artifacts, reduced levels of sleep and irregular patterns of sleep might be expected to be common in criminals and this would certainly affect EEG, yet no study appears to have taken this possibility into account. EEG abnormalities may have their basis in head injury produced by trauma either at birth or later in life by environmental accidents (see Chapter 8), and future studies need to assess variables such as these in conjunction with EEG in criminal and violent groups to help elucidate the network of relationships between these variables.

VI. EVENT-RELATED POTENTIAL STUDIES

There have been at least 21 ERP studies conducted on psychopathic populations, and a review of this literature has recently been conducted by Raine (1989). The essential points of this review will be reiterated here.

ERP studies of psychopaths can conceptually be broken down into early, middle, and late latency studies. A model was generated to account for these data, and this is shown in Fig. 1.

Early ERP studies observed long latency brainstem averaged evoked responses (BAERs), which psychologically can be interpreted as indicating reduced arousal and excessively high filtering of environmental stimuli. The behavioral consequence of such underarousal and filtering would be stimulus deprivation and chronically low levels of arousal. Findings for middle latency ERPs were much more equivocal, but it was speculated that psychopaths appear to show increased ERP amplitudes to stimuli of increasing intensity (visual cortical augmenting), a phenomena which has been linked to sensation seeking. Results from late latency ERPs were much more consistent and indi-

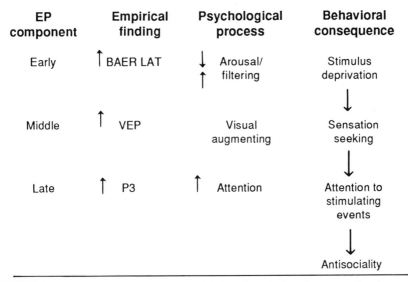

FIGURE 1   Extended stimulation-seeking model of psychopathy based on event-related potential findings.

cated, surprisingly, that psychopaths gave *enhanced* P300 amplitudes, indicating enhanced attention to stimuli of interest, suggesting enhanced attention to stimulating events.

The behavioral consequences of findings from these three ERP levels (stimulus deprivation, sensation seeking, and attention to stimulating events) were argued to be causally linked. That is, individuals with chronically low levels of arousal (possibly caused by excessive filtering of stimuli) would seek out stimulating events in order to increase their levels of arousal to more optimal levels. This stimulation seeking may partly account for the enhanced attention shown to events of interest, as reflected in enhanced P300 ERPs to target stimuli in a selective attention paradigm. Potentially dangerous and risky situations where acts of violence and crime are facilitated may, therefore, represent situations to which such antisocial personalities become particularly attracted.

As with many biological theories of violence, this ERP-based model is only a partial explanation of violent behavior. Whether or not the proposed biological predisposition to violence manifests itself in antisocial personality, crime, and violence may be very dependent on the environmental circumstances in which an individual is placed. For example, given an appropriately high IQ, adequate parenting, and rearing in a family of high socioeconomic status, this risk-taking and stimulation-seeking bent may manifest itself in careers such as those involving risky business ventures, the armed forces, or motor racing rather than crime and violence.

An unusual feature of this model is the argument based on late ERP findings that psychopaths are capable of *enhanced* attentional processing. This contradicts established views of criminal behavior in the biological literature, which almost universally emphasize *deficits* with respect to such populations. Nevertheless, the five analyses that obtained evidence for enhanced P300 ERPs in the review by Raine (1989) are supported by results of two recent studies on adult psychopaths and adolescents with psychopathiclike personalities (Forth & Hare, 1990; Raine, Venables, & Williams, 1990c).

Such findings may have implications from the standpoint of intervention. As one example, psychopaths have been observed to show both larger P300 amplitudes over parietal scalp recording sites and also higher scores on neuropsychological measures sensitive to parietal lobe functioning. These findings are relatively specific in that no differences were observed for ERPs recorded from temporal sites, for neuropsychological tests sensitive to temporal lobe functioning, or for verbal and performance IQ (Raine & Venables, 1988b). These findings suggest that psychopathic criminals may be very skilled at tasks and occupations that involve manipulospatial ability partly subserved by parietal cortex such as artwork, driving, and mechanics. If one could identify violent psychopaths in adolescence, it might be possible to develop the latent abilities that they clearly possess and steer them away from a violent and criminal way of life. Similarly, one may be able to identify work and other situations that are of particular interest to the young aggressive psychopath and that may "compete" with events more likely to elicit violent and criminal behavior (Raine & Dunkin, 1990).

VII. PROSPECTIVE PSYCHOPHYSIOLOGICAL STUDIES OF CRIME

One of the major difficulties in trying to draw conclusions on the psychophysiological basis of criminal behavior is that most studies conducted to date have been nonprospective and have utilized institutionalized populations. In addition, most studies report results from only one of the three most commonly measured psychophysiological response systems (electrodermal, cardiovascular, cortical). Prospective longitudinal research allows for much more powerful statements to be made about predispositions for criminal behavior and for elucidation of cause–effect relationships, but inevitably there are few such studies because prospective research is more difficult to execute.

To date there have only been four prospective psychophysiological studies conducted on crime starting in adolescence or earlier, and none of these have recorded from more than one psychophysiological response system (Wadsworth, 1976; Loeb & Mednick, 1977; Mednick *et al.*, 1981; Petersen, Matou-

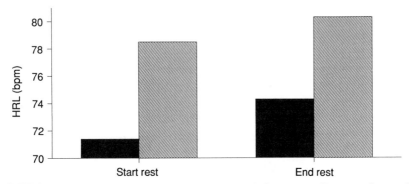

FIGURE 2   Resting heart rate (taken at both start and end of a rest period) measured at age 15 and outcome for crime at age 24 years. Criminal, ■; noncriminal, ▨ (Adapted from Raine *et al.*, 1990a).

sek, Mednick, Volavka, & Pollock, 1982). However, each of these studies provides individual evidence implicating reduced arousal in the development of criminality in the cardiovascular or electrodermal or cortical response system.

One recent prospective study provides relatively strong evidence that underarousal may be critically involved in the development of antisocial and criminal behavior (Raine *et al.*, 1990a). Between 1978 and 1979, a random sample of 101 male schoolchildren aged 15 years was tested in a series of psychophysiological paradigms. Ten years later, in December 1988, searches were made for all subjects at the computerized central Criminal Records Office in London. Subjects found guilty of crimes and sentenced at courts were classified as "criminal." Using this criterion, 17 out of the 101 subjects were found to possess a criminal record. Offenses ranged in severity from theft to wounding, with the most common offense being burglary and theft. Five of the 17 criminals had been imprisoned at some point in time following psychophysiological testing. Crimes recorded at the Criminal Records Office are synonymous with "serious" offending and do not include trivial offenses such as traffic violations.

In the first psychophysiological paradigm (Raine *et al.*, 1990a), measures of skin conductance, heart rate, and EEG were taken during a resting period in order to provide indices of electrodermal, cardiovascular, and cortical arousal. Criminals-to-be were then compared with noncriminal controls on these measures of arousal. Findings are shown in Fig. 2, 3, and 4. Criminals were found to have significantly lower resting heart rate at both the start and the end of the rest period, indicating reduced cardiovascular arousal (Fig. 2). Criminals also had significantly fewer nonspecific skin conductance fluctua-

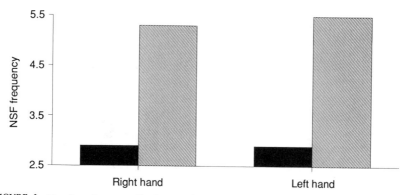

FIGURE 3   Number of nonspecific skin conductance response fluctuations measured at age 15 and outcome for crime at age 24 years. Criminal, ■; noncriminal, ▨ (Adapted from Raine *et al.*, 1990a).

tions during the rest period, indicating reduced electrodermal arousal (Fig. 3). Criminals had significantly more slow-frequency EEG theta activity than noncriminals, indicating cortical underarousal (Fig. 4). Group differences in social class, academic ability, and area of residence were not found to mediate the link between under arousal and antisocial behavior. This is the first study providing evidence for underarousal in an antisocial population in all three (electrodermal, cardiovascular, cortical) psychophysiological response systems.

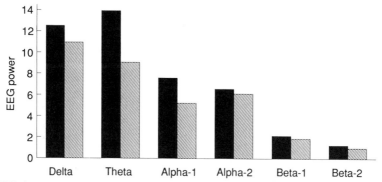

FIGURE 4   Electroencephalographic (EEG) power in arbitrary units across six frequency bands measured at age 15 and outcome for crime at age 24 years. Criminal, ■; noncriminal, ▨ (Adapted from Raine *et al.*, 1990a).

These three measures correctly classified 74.7% of all subjects as criminal/noncriminal, a rate significantly greater than chance (50%). While prediction is by no means perfect, there are reasons to suspect that prediction may be better than this rate indicates. For example, 23% of subjects were predicted to be criminal by virtue of having low arousal but were misclassified as "noncriminal." It is possible, however, that these subjects did indeed commit criminal acts but were not caught for their offenses and were therefore officially counted as noncriminals. Future studies using self-report in addition to official measures of crime would help to address this issue and potentiate the use of psychophysiological variables in the prediction of adult offending.

This study suggests that when data are collected in noninstitutionalized, unselected populations, stronger evidence can be found for links between biological measures and antisocial behavior. Psychophysiological underarousal is a much utilized but complex construct, indicated by the fact that all three measures of arousal are uncorrelated in the general population. The fact that all three independent measures converge in predicting crime in the same sample can be viewed as providing some degree of replication of the arousal–crime link.

The second psychophysiological paradigm in this study concerned the measurement of orienting deficits using skin conductance and heart rate measures (Raine, Venables, & Williams, 1990b). Criminals-to-be were found to be characterized at age 15 by a reduced number of skin conductance orienting responses to a series of 65-dB orienting stimuli. Furthermore, 31% of criminals were characterized by electrodermal nonresponding (no response to any of the orienting stimuli) in contrast to a rate of only 10% in noncriminal controls. These orienting deficits in the electrodermal system were also supported by findings of significantly smaller heart rate orienting responses to the same stimuli. Reduced orienting activity in criminals-to-be is consistent with the notion that antisocials have a deficit in the allocation of attentional resources to external stimuli (Raine & Venables, 1984a). Such a deficit may help explain some early social and cognitive impairments in antisocials, such as poor academic work, antisocial school behavior, and difficulties in sustaining training courses and jobs.

Findings from the third psychophysiological paradigm suggest, however, that these attentional deficits seem likely to be specific to *passive* attend situations. In this third paradigm (Raine *et al.*, 1990c), ERPs were recorded to stimuli that predicted the occurrence of an aversive tone. These events can be viewed as "target" stimuli to which the subject had to respond. Criminals-to-be were characterized by significantly *larger* N100 ERPs to the attend stimulus, a finding suggesting *enhanced* early stimulus-set attention in criminals. These findings are surprising and go against classic notions that antisocial groups are characterized by across-the-board attentional deficits. They are, however, consistent with recent ERP studies of psychopathic and antisocial behavior reviewed earlier in this chapter which indicate that in experimental conditions requiring *active* attention to short-term task-relevant events, antisocials show evidence of greater attentional processing. Overly focused short-term attention to events of interest may relate to the undue emphasis on short-term gratification in criminals and psychopaths at the expense of sustained attention required for a more stable, noncriminal lifestyle. This interpretation is consistent with cognitive measures of attention discussed in Chapter 9. One potentially important implication of these results is that interventions on antisocial populations may usefully focus on the type of attentional abilities and situations that give rise to performance superiorities in such subjects.

In conclusion, prospective psychophysiological studies clearly hold the promise not only of clarifying and extending research on institutionalized populations, but also of allowing for new insights into the psychophysiological predisposition for criminal behavior. It goes without saying that psychophysiological factors alone cannot explain all criminal behavior and by themselves will never be capable of accurately predicting later criminal behavior. Again, it must be emphasized that the value of such studies would be greatly enhanced if such psychophysiological research could be integrated into prospective research on social risk factors for the development of criminal behavior, a point that will be returned to shortly.

VIII. DISINHIBITED TEMPERAMENT AND PSYCHOPHYSIOLOGICAL UNDERAROUSAL

The above prospective research highlights the potential importance of underarousal as a psychophysiological predisposition for violence. Findings to be reviewed in this section in turn suggest that such underarousal may predispose to a disinhibited temperament which in itself may act as one early predispositional factor for criminal and violent behavior. Prospective, longitudinal studies are essential for the examination of this proposition. To date such studies have been limited, focusing on relatively early years, and none have been extended into adult years to clearly establish whether a disinhibited temperament does predispose to violence. Existing studies will be briefly reviewed, however, because there are interesting parallels on the psychophysiological correlates of crime and the psychophysiological correlates of a disinhibited temperament which suggest the potential importance of such research on temperament.

Most of the early research in this area has been conducted by Kagan and colleagues. In these studies (Kagan, 1989; Kagan, Reznick, & Snidman, 1988; Reznick, Kagan, Snidman, Gersten, Baak, & Rosenberg, 1986) children classified as either inhibited or uninhibited at 21 months of age were also found to be inhibited or disinhibited at ages 4, 5.5, and 7.5 years. Consequently early temperament (as measured by a tendency to withdraw or interact across a variety of experimental situations) appears to be relatively stable.

Some support for the notion that temperament may show some stability across time has recently been put forward by Scerbo, Raine, Venables, and Mednick (1993a). The assumption that behavioral inhibition/disinhibition may be a temperament that remains stable over time was tested using a cohort of 1795 Mauritian children tested longitudinally at ages 3, 8, and 11 years. Subjects were rated on theoretically relevant behaviors of inhibition such as approach–avoidance, fearfulness, verbalizations, crying behavior, and sociability. An inhibition index was calculated and used to classify children as extremely inhibited, middle, or extremely uninhibited at each age. Results indicated that subjects classified as uninhibited at age 3 had higher disinhibition scores at age 8 years ($p < .01$). Subjects who were inhibited at both ages 3 and 8 (stably uninhibited) were more likely to remain disinhibited at age 11 years ($p < .02$). These results were independent of sex and ethnicity and were replicated from one sample to another. Consequently, these findings provide some cross-cultural generalizability for the findings of Kagan and colleagues.

Importantly, Kagan and colleagues have provided evidence that inhibited and disinhibited children differ in terms of their physiological responsiveness to novel stimuli (Kagan, 1989; Snidman, Kagan, & McQuilkin, 1991). In particular, uninhibited children have been found to have lower heart rate levels. Low heart rate measured at age 4 was correlated with disinhibited behavior at age 5.5 years, while those with relatively low fetal heart rates had lower levels of motoric activity and crying at age 4 months.

A confirmation and extension of this link between heart rate and disinhibition has been provided in the Mauritius longitudinal study (Scerbo, Raine, Venables, & Mednick, 1993b). Lower heart rate measured at age 3 was associated with disinhibition at age 3 ($p < .0001$), while those who remained stably disinhibited from ages 3 to 8 years were also found to have lower resting heart rates ($p < .002$). Again, these results replicated from one sample to another (see Fig. 5). In addition, children who remained stably disinhibited from ages 3 to 8 years were twice as likely to have lower heart rate *and* lower skin conductance levels measured at age 3 years. Again, these findings were found to replicate from one half of the sample to the other. Importantly, group differences in heart rate could not be attributable to group differences in height, weight, or respiratory complaints.

A disinhibited temperament appears therefore to be relatively consistent across time and underpinned by lower heart rate and possibly lower skin conductance activity. The interesting possibility suggested by this research is that reduced autonomic arousal may in infancy predispose to exploratory behavior and a lack of fear and in childhood to a disinhibited temperament. This temperament may later predispose a child to externalizing behavior problems such as socialized aggression and hyperactivity and in early adulthood to criminal and violent behavior. Clearly, the studies conducted to date

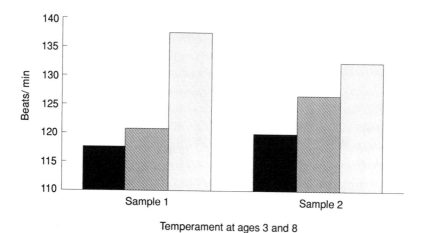

FIGURE 5   Resting heart rate measured at age 3 in stably disinhibited, ■; inhibited, □; and control, ▨ Mauritian children where stable temperament is measured across ages 3 and 8 years (Adapted from Scerbo *et al.*, 1993b).

have only laid the basis for the hypothesis that a disinhibited temperament may predispose to adult violence and that both are underpinned by low autonomic arousal; confirmation and extension in other prospective studies is required. Nevertheless, these early findings linking underarousal to a disinhibited temperament are conceptually consistent with the body of research reviewed earlier linking autonomic underarousal (especially low heart rate) to the development of later criminal behavior.

IX. FUTURE DEVELOPMENTS: THE NATURE OF THE INTERACTION BETWEEN PSYCHOPHYSIOLOGICAL AND SOCIAL PREDISPOSITIONS FOR CRIME

If social researchers maintain their focus on strictly social predispositions for crime, then this will likely lead to some advances in our understanding of crime, just as there will be further modest progress from psychophysiological researchers who focus specifically on some of the issues outlined above. It is predicted, however, that the truly *major* advances will be made by those who make serious and genuine attempts to integrate both social and psychophysiological factors in attempting to understand the development of crime. Unhappily, although many pay lip service to such a principle, there is precious little empirical data upon which to base future studies. Nevertheless, some suggestions in this area for future research are made below based on the current small data base. A more extensive analysis of a social psychophysiological approach to understanding antisocial behavior is provided in Raine (1988) and Raine and Mednick (1989), while practical implications of such integrative research for the treatment of criminal offenders is provided in Raine and Dunkin (1990). Four specific questions can be posed regarding the nature of the interface between social and psychophysiological factors for crime.

The first question concerns whether the effects of social and biological risk factors are additive and independent. That is, do social and biological risk factors for crime *fail* to interact, with each explaining *independent* sets of variance in violent behavior? Although this is a negative scenario and goes against the more general, popular view that social and biological variables may interact, it is clearly possible and needs to be tested. If biological and social risk factors represent additive and independent effects, this would in fact be of considerable importance because it would indicate that using both sets of variables will provide a much better explanation of violence. In a predictive context, it would indicate that because the two sets of explained variance are independent, prediction of future violence will be greater when both social and biological risk factors are entered into the prediction equation. Such an outcome would encourage future multidisciplinary research.

The second question that needs to be asked concerns whether social and biological risk factors interact. That is, is risk for crime particularly magnified in those who possess *both* sets of risk factors? Initial empirical findings suggest this may be the case specifically where violent crime is concerned. In a review of longitudinal studies relating biological variables to violence, a relatively consistent finding emerged: Biological predispositional factors relate most strongly to violent offending when combined with an *adverse* early home environment (Raine & Mednick, 1989). As one example, the presence of minor physical anomalies (reflecting a disruption to fetal neural development in the first trimester of pregnancy) have been related to violent offending (Kandel, Brennan, & Mednick, 1990). This relationship is, however, mediated by family intactness in that the greatest degree of violence occurs in those individuals who have both minor physical anomalies *and* have been raised in unstable, nonintact families (Mednick & Kandel, 1988; see Chapter 8). The rate of violence in those with both biological and predispositional factors is seven times that of those who have only minor physical anomalies. One explanation of this type of interaction is that for violence, early biological deficits can be compensated for by a relatively good home environment (or its correlates such as better postnatal health care services), whereas adverse environmental factors exacerbate the effects of early CNS disruption (Raine & Mednick, 1989). If social and biological risk factors do interact in explaining violent crime, such findings would be of importance in indicating the necessity of taking both sets of factors into account in understanding crime and violence.

A third question concerns whether biological risk factors most clearly relate to crime and violence in those with relatively benign home backgrounds. Again there are initial empirical findings which suggest that this may be true, at least on this occasion for *nonviolent* crime. One general theme to emerge from reviews on biosocial research into crime is that especially where nonviolent forms of antisocial behavior are concerned, psychophysiological factors relate most strongly to antisocials from relatively *benign* home environments (Raine, 1988; Raine & Mednick, 1989). For example, although resting HRL is lower in antisocials, it is a particularly strong characteristic of antisocials from higher social classes (Raine & Venables, 1984b), those from privileged middle class backgrounds attending private schools in England (Maliphant, Hume, & Furnham, 1990a), and those from intact but not broken homes (Wadsworth, 1976). Similarly, reduced skin conductance activity characterizes antisocial adolescents from high but not low social classes (Raine & Venables, 1981), schizoid criminals from intact but not broken early home environments (Raine, 1987), criminals *without* a childhood history broken by parental absence and disharmony (Hemming, 1981), and "privileged" (high socioeconomic status) offenders who commit crimes of evasion (Buikhuisen *et al.*, 1985). One explanation for this pattern of results is that where the "social push" toward antisocial behavior is lower (high-socioeconomic status, intact homes), psychophysiological determinants of such behavior assume greater importance (Mednick & Christiansen, 1977, Raine & Venables, 1981). Conversely social causes of criminal behavior may be more important explanations of antisociality in those exposed to adverse early home conditions. The importance of this third scenario regarding the interface between social and psychophysiological risk factors is that it suggest different processes operating in violent versus nonviolent forms of offending. The previous literature in this area has paid very little attention to processes specific to violent versus nonviolent forms of offending, even though such information is crucial to a better understanding of violence per se.

A fourth question concerns whether *good* psychophysiological functioning can in certain circumstances protect an otherwise predisposed individual from the development of crime. There has been no previous research on psychophysiological protective factors for crime, even though this issue is clearly an important one. This line of research, while involving biological risk factors, could paradoxically be of greater significance to socially based research on crime than psychophysiological research. The starting point for this line of thinking is the fact that social predispositional factors for violence and crime cannot explain all variance associated with such behavior. Indeed, the variance accounted for by major social and familial risk factors for crime and violence to date has not been high (e.g., Loeber & Stouthamer-Loeber, 1986; Farrington, 1989). It is clear that while some individuals who are predisposed to antisocial and criminal behavior by virtue of, for example, poor parental supervision, lack of parental involvement, or poor parent–child relationships, do become violent or antisocial, there are many who possess such factors yet do not succumb to violence. Many of these "false positives" may be explained by the fact that they possess, for example, *higher* arousal, which serves to protect them from developing criminal behavior. For example, poor parental supervision may not result in a pathway toward later adult crime in an individual who has physiological high levels of arousal and who may consequently be more sensitive to albeit infrequent socializing punishments for associating with delinquent peer groups. High arousal would also result in such individuals being more likely to avoid the types of "arousal-jag" environments associated with offending, and thus help avoid delinquent peer associations. Such psychophysiological functioning may contribute to success in school and occupational training, which may again result in that individual deviating from a life pathway to crime and violence.

This analysis can also be reversed. That is, psychophysiological risk factors for crime do not to date account for an extensive proportion of variance in violent behavior. This may be because those who possess a psychophysiological risk factor for crime (e.g., low arousal) may be protected by virtue of possessing a familial protective factor (e.g., high parental supervision, family intactness). The promise of this type of analysis is that it illustrates the fallacy of equating biological risk factors with a destiny for crime, it underlies the point that any biological risk factor cannot operate in an environmental vacuum, and it emphasizes a more dynamic interplay between biological and environmental factors.

The obvious limitation of these lines of thinking is that such notions are clearly speculative and so far without empirical foundation. They may also be overly simplistic as currently stated. Nevertheless, the promise is that such an analysis may make social risk factors much more powerful predictors of crime by isolating a subgroup (those who possess the social risk factor but not the putative biological protective factor) in whom such social factors are more strongly predictive of later violent and antisocial behavior.

X. SUMMARY

This chapter has reviewed research on psychophysiological correlates of antisocial and criminal behavior, with special reference to studies that have been conducted since one major review in 1978. The current review focuses on three main psychophysiological response systems which have been most frequently studied in antisocials, that is, electrodermal, cardiovascular, and cortical. The review of skin conductance indicates that (1) there is some evidence for underarousal in antisocials, particularly with respect to crimes of evasion; (2) orienting deficits seem to be specific to antisocials with concomitant features of schizotypal personality; (3) prior findings up to 1978 of reduced SC responsiveness to aversive stimuli have not been observed in more recent studies, in either psychopathic or nonpsychopathic antisocials; and (4) psychopaths may, however, be more responsive to speech stimuli but less responsive to socially meaningful stimuli. The strongest findings for SC activity lie with respect to reduced classical conditioning and longer SC half-recovery time.

In contrast to studies on institutionalized adult offenders, who show no differences in resting heart rate, all studies conducted to date on younger and predominantly noninstitutionalized, nonclinical samples show reduced resting heart rate levels in antisocials. This is probably the best replicated and most robust biological finding on antisocial behavior reported to date. Reduced heart rate may reflect underarousal or alternatively fearlessness to novel situations.

EEG studies indicate that abnormalities exist in resting EEG in criminal populations, but interpretation of many of these studies is clouded by methodological limitations. The predominant deficit of excessive slow-wave activity supports the notion of generalized underarousal in antisocials and may be consistent with reduced heart rate levels reflecting excessive vagal tuning.

The most consistent finding from event-related potential studies consists of enhanced P300 amplitudes to target stimuli. This finding is incorporated into a stimulation-seeking theory of antisocial and psychopathic behavior and is taken as consistent with the notion that antisocials have enhanced short-term attentional processing in active attend situations.

Prospective psychophysiological research has confirmed electrodermal, cardiovascular, and cortical underarousal as a predisposition for the development of criminal behavior. Autonomic arousal also appears to underpin a disinhibited temperament early in life which may act as a forerunner of conduct disorder and delinquency. Finally, several differing models of the interaction between social and psychophysiological variables are briefly laid out, and it is hypothesized that psychophysiological protective factors against the development of crime (e.g., high arousal) may help explain why some who are at risk for crime by virtue of possessing negative psychosocial factors do not develop such an outcome; such a perspective could help potentiate findings from psychosocial research on crime.

8

Other Biological Factors: Head Injury, Pregnancy and Birth Complications, Physical Appearance, Hormones, Diet, and Lead

I. INTRODUCTION

Many of the previous chapters have focused on the relationships between one main biological factor or set of factors and criminal behavior. There are many other biological processes that have been related to crime, and this chapter will attempt to introduce these literatures to the reader. Factors were selected for inclusion in this chapter on the grounds that while there is clear evidence of their link to crime and antisocial behavior, the empirical literature for these factors may not have been as extensive as for other factors that have been discussed in the preceding chapters. Some of these factors, such as obstetric ones, are relatively new and represent a developing field. Others such as body build are older and represent a static but still potentially important research field. In all cases, however, there is sufficient empirical evidence for a relationship with crime to warrant closer and serious scrutiny.

It is important to emphasize that many of these biological factors are likely to be determined by *environmental* factors. There is a substantial number of social scientists who equate biological factors with genetics alone and who do not consider the possibility that many biological predispositional factors for crime can be determined directly by the environment. This is a different argument from those made in Chapter 3 that (1) genetic factors need an environment within which to be expressed, and (2) genetic factors may interact with environmental factors in the development of crime. Rather, many of the biological factors here are directly caused by environmental influences. For example, many cases of head injury (which can be equated with CNS damage) are caused by environmental accidents or violent interpersonal encounters. Exposure to the neurotoxin lead occurs in the environment. Diet is clearly an environmental factor. Birth complications also represent an environmental hazard, although they may also be in part genetically determined. These environmentally caused biological factors are important in that they illustrate very clearly the fallacy of equating biology with destiny. Clearly, these factors can be avoided or reduced by environmental modifications. If we ignore their possible relevance to criminal behavior we run the great risk of ignoring possible ways of reducing crime rates; such a mistake could be a major loss to society.

This chapter does not include all biological factors that have been related to crime. For example, one recent study by Gottschalk, Rebello, Buchsbaum, Tucker, and Hodges (1991) has observed high levels of manganese in hair samples of violent criminals. The focus in this chapter will instead be on some of the main biological factors related to crime that have not been covered in other chapters. Such factors to be discussed include head injury, birth complications, minor physical anomalies, physical attraction, disabilities and amelioration through plastic surgery, body build, cortisol, testosterone, progesterone and premenstrual syndrome, hypoglycemia and diet, and lead exposure.

II. HEAD INJURY

Having sustained a significant head injury may represent one factor that predisposes the individual to later crime and violence. A number of studies have found a greater history of head injury in a variety of offender populations. In one relatively extreme population consisting of 14 seriously violent juveniles condemned to death, all had a reported history of relatively severe head injury, and in 8 cases these were severe enough to result in hospitalization (Lewis, Pincus, Bard, Richardson, Prichep, Feldman, & Yeager, 1988). Similarly, all violent adult offenders on death row studied by Lewis, Pincus, Bard, Richardson, Prichep, Feldman, and Yeager (1986) had a history of severe head injury. Head trauma has also been associated with general delinquency (Lewis, 1976; Pincus & Tucker, 1978), while Mark and Ervin (1970) reported that 75% of a sample of adult prisoners had histories of head injury severe enough to result in periods of unconsciousness. Head injury has also been found to characterize aggressive adults in the community; Rosenbaum and Hodge (1989) found that 61.3% of males with problems of aggression in marital and dating relationships had a history of head injury severe enough to result in concussion or loss of consciousness. Rosenbaum (1991) reports data from a second study in which he finds that 52% of wife batterers have a history of head injury compared to 22% of nonbatterers. Finally, patient groups characterized by episodic dyscontrol (characterized by attacks of aggression and violence) are also found to have raised levels of head injury (Elliott, 1982).

These studies indicated a raised incidence of head injury in antisocial populations. The reverse is also true, that is, head-injured populations are also found to show raised levels of antisocial and violent behavior. For example, McKinlay, Brooks, Bond, Martinage, and Marshall (1981) found aggression and irritability to follow serious head injury in 70% of cases. An overview of this area may be found in Miller (1990).

Again, the critical question in this literature concerns whether there is a causal relationship between head injury and violence. It is possible, for example, that violence and crime cause head injury, in that head injury is an occupational risk of adopting a violent criminal career. Alternatively, it is possible that the same factors that cause crime and violence also predispose an individual to head injury. For example, criminal parents may cause head injuries in offspring through rough physical treatment; the cause of the resulting violent and criminal behavior in these offspring may, however, be the result of genetic or environmental consequences of parental criminality rather than head injury per se. There are, however, a number of reasons to believe that, although these scenarios may be partly true, they cannot fully account for the head injury–crime link, and that instead head injury may partly predispose to the development of crime.

First, Rosenbaum (1991) found that in 92% of cases, a history of head injury preceded marital aggression in time. Although this does not in itself prove a causal relationship, it at least tends to rule out the alternative possibility that marital violence causes head injury. Second, epidemiological data on head injuries for whites show that the highest rates of head injury occur in the 15–19 year age group or the 10–20 year age group, with rates at those ages being nearly twice the overall occurrence (Whitman, Coonley-Hoganson, & Desai, 1984; Jagger, Levine, Jane, & Rimel, 1984). This major elevation in the age curve occurs at an earlier age than the peak for violent offending, which tends to occur in the late teens and early twenties, as opposed to property offenses, which peak earlier (Farrington, 1986). Again, these data do not prove a causal link, but they are at least consistent with a model that suggests that head injury precedes violence and crime. Third, 74% of all suburban head injuries result from causes other than interpersonal attacks (e.g., motorist and pedestrian accidents, falls, recreational accidents) (Whitman *et al.*, 1984), while 89% of all rural head injuries result from causes other than interpersonal violence (Jagger *et al.*, 1984). Even when head injuries occurring only in inner cities are considered, 60% do not result from interpersonal violence (Whitman *et al.*, 1984). Supporting this notion, 12 of the 14 causes of head injury reported above in juveniles on death row were caused by falls or traffic accidents; only two were caused by interpersonal violence (Lewis, Pincus, Bard, Richardson, Prichep, Feldman, & Yeager, 1988). These data are not consistent with the notion that most cases of head injury are produced from involvement in crime and violence. Fourth, epidemiological correlates of head injury show parallels to the epidemiology of crime; for example, head injuries are much more common in males, adolescents/young adults, blacks, and those living in inner cities. Again, while these data are consistent with a causal model linking head injury to crime, they do not prove such a model.

While these data are suggestive of a direct link between head injury and crime, there are other alternative models that are also generally consistent with head injury lying on a causal pathway to crime. One such model is the possibility that neurological or neuropsychological deficits occurring early in life (e.g., caused by obstetric factors) may predispose an individual to have an accident resulting in head injury, and that the combination of the preexisting neuropsychological deficits and the CNS deficits caused by the later head injury combine to more strongly predispose the individual to crime and violence. For example, some early neuropsychological deficits may result in motor deficits that may make the individual more clumsy, resulting in more falling accidents. Similarly, neuropsychological deficits resulting in perceptual deficits may lead to more pedestrian or vehicle accidents due to lack of attention to traffic and pedestrians. Both of these factors are major causes of head injury both in city and in rural environments (Whitman *et al.*, 1984; Jagger *et al.*, 1984).

If head injury is etiologically linked to later crime and violence, what are the mechanisms that may mediate the causal link? Head injury is known to increase sensitivity to the effects of alcohol, so outcome for crime and violence may be a result of head injury exacerbating the criminogenic effects of alcohol abuse. Alternatively, head injury may result in cognitive, social skills, self-esteem, problem-solving, academic, and work-related deficits which in turn predispose to crime and violence. Head injury may result in later aggression because it results in a postconcussional syndrome that includes headaches, irritability, and sensitivity to noise, which may predispose such individuals to more easily lose their temper (Elliott, 1988). Perhaps more directly, closed head injuries (i.e., those without a fracture to the skull) most frequently result in damage to the orbitofrontal region of the frontal lobe and the anterior region of the temporal lobes. Damage to the right orbitofrontal regions tends to result in edginess and anxiety while damage to left orbitofrontal regions tends to result in anger and hostility (Mattson & Levin, 1990). As outlined in Chapter 6, there are a number of pathways (neurobehavioral, cognitive, social, personality) by which such prefrontal deficits could result in criminal and violent behavior.

Head injury does not, of course, result in violence and crime in all cases, and indeed large proportions of such cases are not violent. It is likely that head injury precipitates violence in those individuals who are already predisposed to violence through other biological or social risk factors. Because head injury diminishes coping skills, judgment, and restraint (Miller, 1990), such injury may result in violence in those who already have deficits in these areas.

Finally, one important and often overlooked source of brain injury that needs to be considered is early child abuse. Rough shaking of a child by its parent or babysitter can result in whiplash injuries that cause shearing of white-matter fiber tracts, while even single blows to the head can cause multiple microscopic lesions in the brainstem, hypothalamus, and cerebral regions. Such injuries are probably much more common than might be thought because they leave no external marks and because their effects are often cumulative rather than immediate. As pointed out by Milner and Mc-Canne (1991), the majority of all infant head injuries and 95% of serious head injuries are due to child abuse.

The implications are that head injury may play a much greater role than is currently thought in predisposing an individual to delinquency and crime, and that even subjects who do not report a history of head injury may well have suffered CNS damage if they come from an abusive home. Interestingly, many studies reporting high rates of head injury in violent offenders also report high rates of severe child abuse (e.g., Lewis et al., 1986, 1988), indicating that such subjects probably have a "double dose" of CNS damage resulting in multiple rather than single deficits, and as such they are more likely to become violent or antisocial. The mechanism linking child abuse to later violence may therefore be just as much biologically based (via CNS dysfunction) as it is socially based (e.g., via modeling). Future studies of criminal behavior clearly need to pay much closer attention to a history of head injury.

III. BIRTH COMPLICATIONS

A number of studies have related perinatal factors to later criminal and violent behavior. Pasamanick, Rogers, and Lilienfield (1956) were one of the first to establish a link between obstetric complications and behavior disorders in children. Cocchi, Felici, Tonni, and Venanzi (1984) found that mothers of children showing temper tantrums were more likely to have experienced difficult deliveries than control mothers. Lewis et al. (1979) found seriously delinquent incarcerated children to be more likely to have sustained perinatal trauma than nonincarcerated delinquent children. Set against these positive findings, Szatmari, Reitsma, and Offord (1986) failed to find a relationship between adolescent antisocial behavior and pregnancy and birth complications in a sample of 58 adolescents.

Litt (1971), in a study of 1944 consecutive births in a Danish hospital between 1936 and 1938, found perinatal trauma to be predictive of impulsive criminal offenses at age 36. Similarly, Mungas (1983) found that in a group of psychiatric patients, perinatal factors were significantly related to violence. An intriguing study by Jacobson, Eklund, Hamberger, Linnarsson, and Valverius (1987) found not only that birth complications were greater in 281 suicide victims than in controls, but also that the type of birth complication was related to the method of suicide (e.g., asphyxia at birth was related to suicide by drowning or hanging). Conversely, Denno (1989) failed to find clear links between obstetric factors and later adult violence in a sample of low-income families.

More specific links with adult violent offending have been demonstrated by Kandel and Mednick (1991) using data drawn from a birth cohort of all 9125 individuals born between September 1, 1959 and December 31, 1961 at the Rigshospitalet in Copenhagen. Three groups were selected from this cohort. The first group ($N = 72$) had either a schizophrenic mother or father. The second group ($N = 72$) had either a character-disordered mother or a psychopathic father. The third group were children of parents without a psychiatric history ($N = 72$). The three groups were matched on social class, sex of child, race, multiple birth status, pregnancy number, sex of ill parent, mother's age, mother's height, and father's age. Registrations for criminal offenses were ascertained when the subjects were aged between 20 and 22 years; 15 were found to be violent offenders, 24 were property offenders, and 177 were noncriminal. The median score on an index of delivery complications was used to split subjects into groups of either high or low delivery complications. Of the violent offenders, 80% were found to have high numbers of delivery complications, relative to rates of 46.9% for noncriminals and 29.1% for property offenders. Violent offenders were found to have significantly higher rates of delivery complications relative to noncriminals ($p < .05$). Interestingly, all seven who were recidivistically violent offenders had high delivery complication scores.

Brennan, Mednick, and Kandel (1993) have recently demonstrated that this link between birth complications and later adult violence is mediated by psychopathology in the parents. Rates of violent offending in male subjects were assessed as a joint function of parental psychiatric illness (present or absent) and delivery complications (low and high). Results of these analyses are shown in Fig. 1. It can be seen that the highest rates of violent offending occurred when subjects had *both* a high number of delivery complications and a parent who was psychiatrically ill ($p < .05$). Of subjects with both parental psychiatric illness and high delivery complications, 32.3% were violent as

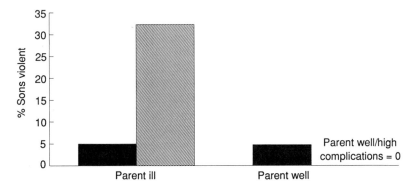

FIGURE 1   Rates of violent adult offending in offspring as a function of experiencing birth complications and having a psychiatrically ill parent. Low-complications, ■; high-complications ▨ (Brennan *et al.*, 1993).

adults compared to 5% for parental psychiatric illness only, 0% for high delivery complications only, and 4.8% with neither factor present.

Hyperactivity also appears to be an important factor when considering the link between delivery complications and later violence. Hyperactivity in the Copenhagen sample was measured between the ages of 11 and 13 years by a pediatric neurologist. Brennan *et al.* (1993) divided their sample up on the basis of hyperactivity (present/absent) and delivery complications (low/high). When both predispositional factors were present, 53% of subjects were found to be violent in adulthood compared to rates of 16.7% for high delivery complications only, 8.3% for hyperactivity only, and 3.6% when neither predispositional factor was present. Logistic regression analysis confirmed a significant interaction between hyperactivity and delivery complications in predicting adult violence ($p < .001$). The interaction between parental psychiatric status and birth complications was interpreted by Brennan *et al.* (1993) as indicating that perinatal factors may play a role in triggering what they speculate is a genetic relationship between parental psychiatric disorder and violence in the offspring.

Brennan *et al.* (1993) viewed hyperactivity as a correlate of CNS damage and interpret their pattern of findings as suggesting that where perinatal complications result in CNS damage (as reflected in hyperactivity), an increase in adult violent offending is likely. An alternative explanation is that hyperactivity, though in itself related to delivery complications and CNS damage, represents a relatively independent predispositional factor to violence which, when combined with delivery complications, results in particularly high rates of violence. This alternative view is suggested by the fact that research on anti-social behavior has generally found that the more separate behavior problems that are present in childhood, the worse is the prognosis in adulthood. More direct measures of CNS damage such as EEG, neuropsychological test data, or ideally brain imaging data would be useful in further testing the explanation offered by Brennan *et al.* (1993) regarding CNS damage.

IV. FETAL MALDEVELOPMENT AND MINOR PHYSICAL ANOMALIES

One study on prenatal factors reported by Mednick and Kandel (1988) demonstrates the importance of taking social factors into account when relating obstetric factors to violence. Minor physical anomalies (MPAs) have been associated with disorders of pregnancy (Waldrop & Halversen, 1971) and are thought to reflect fetal maldevelopment toward the end of the first trimester of pregnancy. MPAs are relatively minor physical deviations from the norm, consisting of such features as low seated ears, adherent ear lobes, furrowed tongue, curved fifth finger, single transverse palmar crease, gaps between the first and second toes, unusually long third toes, and fine hair that doesn't easily comb down. While genetic factors have been linked to MPAs, anomalies may also be caused by environmental teratogenic influences on the fetus such as anoxia, bleeding, and infection (Guy, Majorski, Wallace, & Guy, 1983).

In the study reported by Mednick and Kandel (1988), MPAs were assessed in a sample of 129 12-year-old boys by an experienced pediatrician. MPAs were found to be related to violent offending as assessed 9 years later when subjects were aged 21 years, though not to property offenses without violence. However, when subjects were divided into those from unstable, non-intact homes versus those from stable homes, the biosocial interaction illustrated in Fig. 2 was observed. MPAs only predicted violence in those individuals raised in unstable home environments. A similar interactive relationship was also observed for birth weight and family stability (Kandel *et al.*, 1990).

Mednick & Kandel (1988) suggest that pregnancy complications may indicate a degree of CNS damage that weakens control of impulsiveness early in life, leading to impulsive, violent offending in later life, a view that is consistent with repeated reports of a high incidence of brain damage in violent offenders. The finding of a relationship between MPAs and violence but not property offending would be consistent with the notion that while petty (property) offending appears to have a genetic basis, violent offending appears not to (Mednick *et al.*, 1984) and consequently may be determined more by environmental factors including the intrauterine environment.

It is interesting to note from the study of Brennan *et al.* (1993) that those subjects who have high delivery complications *and* a high number of minor physical anomalies are most likely to be at risk for adult violent offending.

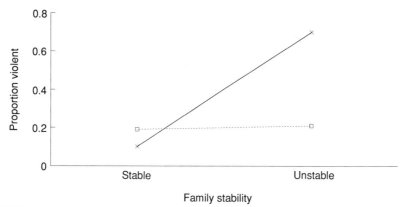

FIGURE 2   Violent offending in offspring (measured at age 21) as a function of minor physical anomalies (MPAs) (measured at age 11) and stability of home background. Low MPAs, --▫--; high MPAs, —×— (Mednick & Kandel, 1988).

Approximately 18% of this group show later adult violence (extrapolated from Figure 9 in Brennan *et al.*, 1993) compared to those with high delivery complications only (about 6%), high minor physical anomalies only (about 3%), or neither condition (about 3%). As with the preceding analyses for parental psychiatric disorder, hyperactivity, and birth complications, data for minor physical anomalies again indicate that the more detrimental factors that are present, the more likely it is that violence will result in adulthood.

These prospective biosocial findings generally implicate disruption in neural development during gestation in adult violent offending. The results of these studies are supported in an analysis carried out by Baker and Mednick (1984) on a random sample of 847 children drawn from a Copenhagen birth cohort of 9125 consecutive births. Perinatal difficulties were predictive of aggressiveness (bullying, fighting) at aged 18 years as assessed by teacher ratings, but only in those children raised in unstable early environments.

Minor physical anomalies have also been found to characterize preadult antisocial behavior and temperament. Paulus and Martin (1986) found more MPAs in aggressive and impulsive preschool boys, while Halverson and Victor (1976) also found higher levels of MPAs in elementary male schoolchildren with problem school behavior. MPAs have even been linked to peer aggression as early as age 3 years (Waldrop, Bell, McLaughlin, & Halverson, 1978). Although MPAs have generally characterized behavior disorders in children drawn from the normal population (see Pomeroy, Sprafkin, & Gadow, 1988, for a review), at least one study failed to observe a link between MPAs and conduct disorder *within* a mixed group of emotionally disturbed children (Pomeroy *et al.*, 1988).

These findings in young children are of interest in that they indicate that the link between antisocial behavior and MPAs is less likely to result from processes such as lowered self-esteem or other reactions to possessing these physical anomalies, since very young children are less likely to be affected by such processes. This interpretation is supported by the fact that MPAs are relatively mild and not easily noticed by the individual or others around them; indeed, those with MPAs appear to be no less physically attractive than others (Eysenck & Gudjonsson, 1989; Rapaport & Quin, 1975).

It seems more likely then that the processes that underlie MPAs are also the processes that lead to antisocial behavior and presumably consist of some degree of brain maldevelopment and neuropsychological impairment. The same genetic or teratogenic factors that result in MPAs also seem likely to result in CNS impairment, and there are considerable data indicating that MPAs are associated with CNS-related pathology such as poor motor coordination, learning disabilities, cognitive deficits, and hyperactivity (Waldrop, 1979). In this respect, the mechanisms that link MPAs to antisocial behavior would seem to be different from those that may link physical unattractiveness to crime (see Section V below).

These relationships between fetal neural maldevelopment in early pregnancy and birth complications on the one hand, and violence on the other, have potentially important implications for intervention. It is conceivable, for example, that one could carry out a health care intervention with mothers who (1) are at risk for pregnancy and birth complications, (2) may be at risk for bearing a child at risk for later violence (e.g., by virtue of being married to a violent criminal), and (3) are undergoing a stressful marital relationship. Such interventions could take the form of greater antenatal care, more home visits by professionals, greater education on risk to the fetus associated with smoking and alcohol consumption, and early hospitalization prior to the child's birth. Further evidence is required, however, to establish the replicability of the above association between violence and obstetric complications before such an intervention could be justified.

V. PHYSICAL ATTRACTION/DISABILITY
AND COSMETIC SURGERY

As indicated in the previous section, minor physical anomalies are indeed minor and would rarely if ever come to attention. On the other hand, general physical attractiveness is a characteristic that is very noticeable and salient in society. A number of studies have indicated that both adult and juvenile offenders are less physically attractive than controls. Attractive antisocial children are less negatively evaluated than antisocial children who are less attractive (Dion, 1972), while juvenile delinquents were found by Cavior and Howard (1973) to be rated as less attractive than controls. This latter finding applied to both white and black delinquents. In adults, one of the largest studies has been conducted by Masters and Greaves (1967). In a sample of over 11,000 criminals and 7,000 controls, it was shown that while 20% of controls had facial defects, 60% of criminals had such defects. These ratings were conducted by expert plastic surgeons, and the tripling of facial deformities was true for both female and male criminals. Kurtzberg, Safar, and Mandell (1969) estimated that approximately 50% of the prison population has at least some moderate disfigurement.

The critical question in this literature concerns whether physical unattractiveness is a cause or correlate of crime. Several experimental studies have shown that there are facial stereotypes for crime, with raters being more likely to attribute criminal offenses such as murder and armed robbery to unattractive relative to attractive individuals (e.g., Saladin, Saper, & Breen, 1988). It is possible therefore that unattractive individuals are more likely to come under police surveillance than attractive individuals, and perhaps are more likely to be prosecuted. With respect to this latter point, however, Stewart (1985) found that although physical attractiveness was negatively correlated with severity of sentence, it did not discriminate between those who were convicted or not convicted; as such physical unattractiveness in criminal populations may not necessarily be a result of bias in sentencing.

Another possibility is that crime causes unattractiveness. It is possible, for example, that criminals are more likely to get into fights than noncriminals and consequently suffer facial disfigurements. Juvenile delinquents have also been reported as more likely to have had accidents, injuries, and hospital attendances (Lewis & Shannock, 1977). Certainly, some of the facial scars and nasal deformities identified by Masters and Greaves (1967) could have occurred through fights, accidents, or early abuse. On the other hand, this scenario cannot easily account for other facial deformities identified in this study such as protruding ears and a receding chin, which are more likely to be congenital in nature. Similarly, while Thompson (1990) estimated that about half of the deformities in prison populations were acquired rather than congenital, this still leaves a significant proportion of deformities that are nonacquired, suggesting that, at least in some cases, physical unattractiveness precedes crime and delinquency.

Experimental manipulations represent the only methodology that can be used to clearly assess whether one factor is causally related to another. If, for example, correction of facial disfigurements in criminals can result in reduced crime rates, this would be relatively strong evidence for a causal relationship between unattractiveness and crime. Several such experimental studies have in fact been carried out. Thompson (1990) has systematically reviewed the results of nine plastic surgery experiments conducted on prisoners between 1959 and 1987. Of the nine studies conducted, six show that plastic surgery reduced recidivism rates, two found no significant differences, while one found higher recidivism in the plastic surgery group. One difficulty with this literature is that studies have been generally methodologically weak, particularly with respect to random assignment.

Probably the best study conducted to date is that of Kurtzberg, Mandell, Lewin, Lipton, and Shuster (1968), who employed random assignment to groups and also employed placebo conditions. The control group showed 79% recidivism at a 1-year follow-up (measured by arrests) compared to a 50% rate for a group who received plastic surgery together with social and vocational services. Although there appears to be some evidence to support the beneficial effects of plastic surgery, Thompson raises several unresolved questions about such techniques, including questions of whether juveniles are more likely to benefit than chronic adult offenders, whether there are sex differences in outcome, and what types of surgery result in better outcome.

It should be noted that although the deformities under discussion are physical in nature, the mechanism by which they result in delinquency and crime is more likely to be *social* in nature. Reduced attractiveness may result in reduced confidence and lower self-esteem which in turn could result in reduced social networks, alienation, and criminal behavior. Increased attractiveness could result in greater social acceptance and reduce the likelihood of violence in response to slights and jibes over appearance. In contrast, it is not at all clear that biological processes mediate the link between appearance and crime. In this sense, while MPAs and physical appearance are superficially similar processes, in reality they probably reflect very different mechanisms predisposing to crime. Future experimental studies that also include self-concept measures in addition to attractiveness ratings and criminal outcome measures would help further clarify (1) whether such interventions are effective, and (2) what the mechanisms are by which criminal and delinquent behavior may be reduced.

VI. BODY BUILD

There has been a long history of research into the question of whether delinquents and criminals are characterized by a specific body build. Detailed reviews of these studies may be found in Wilson and Herrnstein (1985), Eysenck and Gudjonsson (1989), and Montemayor (1985). Because there have been few if any additional studies in this area since 1989, it will not be re-reviewed here. Instead, the main empirical conclusions (as viewed by this author) from this limited literature will be outlined as follows.

1. In general, there is reasonable evidence to indicate that both juvenile delinquents and adult criminals statistically differ from controls in terms of being more mesomorphic (muscular) and mesomorphic–endomorphic (muscular–fat) and less ectomorphic (slight and thin) than controls (e.g.,

Sheldon, Hartl, & McDermott, 1949; Glueck & Glueck, 1956; Gibbens, 1963; Cortes & Galtti, 1972; Seltzer, 1951).

2. There are very few data on female offenders, but these again indicate that female delinquents are heavier and more muscular (e.g., Epps & Parnell, 1952).

3. Many studies do not use carefully matched control groups, but one large study that did carefully match delinquents on demographic factors found positive findings (Glueck & Glueck, 1956).

4. The only follow-up study (by Hartl, Monnelli, and Eldeken, 1982, of the study by Sheldon *et al.*, 1949) found that a mesomorphic body build predicts adult crime measured 30 years later.

5. While findings tend to be statistically significant, they are not large in magnitude.

6. There are some notable failures to replicate. In particular, several studies of self-report offending in noninstitutionalized samples have not found links between body size and offending (e.g., Wadsworth, 1979; West & Farrington, 1973).

Research into body build and crime has been controversial, probably because of the concern that individuals may be labeled as criminal or delinquent merely by their appearance rather than by their behavior. While understandable, this perspective misses the point that the main goal of this research has been not to label individuals as criminals merely by appearance, but to try to understand the processes and mechanisms whereby individuals become criminal. The link between body build and genetic factors has also meant that this research has come under the same fire as research on behavior genetics. Whatever the reason, the result has been that there has been little new research into body build and offending in recent years. This in turn makes it more difficult to draw safe conclusions on relatively old and sparse data.

Some of the strongest conclusions are drawn by Wilson and Herrnstein (1985) and Eysenck and Gudjonsson (1989), who suggest that these data provide good evidence that constitutional factors correlate with criminal behavior (body build is viewed as largely genetically determined) and represent a constitutional basis to crime. Similarly, most commentaries on the body build–crime literature have almost universally linked body build to genetic and constitutional interpretations of crime. It is important, however, not to ignore the fact that ultimately, the link between body build and crime/delinquency may be mediated largely through *social* mechanisms. For example, body build may be linked to delinquency because having a larger, more muscular body build allows bullying to be an effective strategy in winning social conflicts in the playground setting. Early reinforcement of this behavior may encourage the use of force and violence later in life. Consequently, body build may be linked to delinquency and crime ultimately through *social learning* mechanisms. Alternatively, a mesomorphic body build may predispose to delinquency only when combined with other social predispositional variables (e.g., attending a high-delinquency school).

Whether or not body build is truly related to crime, and whether or not the mechanism underlying this link is social or genetic, perhaps the most important point to make is that no factor linked to crime should be viewed in the anachronistic terms of genetics versus environment. Such interpretations are both divisive in disciplinary terms and overly simplistic. Instead, the field of criminology needs to move more toward integrating genetic with social risk factors for crime and attempting to understand how genetic and biological processes play out in the context of the social environment. In this context, future studies of body build should attempt to integrate this hypothesized risk factor for delinquency with social risk factors for this behavior. More specifically, there seem to have been no studies that have linked body build specifically to violent offending even though links might be expected to be stronger for this form of antisocial behavior.

VII. CORTISOL

Cortisol is an index of hypothalamic–pituitary–adrenal (HPA) axis arousal. While not under direct sympathetic control, corticotropin-releasing factor (CRF), which is a hypothalamic hormone that controls the secretion of cortisol, also affects key limbic structures that control the autonomic nervous system (Nemeroff, 1991). As such, this hormone may be of relevance to measures of autonomic arousal referred to in Chapter 7 (psychophysiology). If so, one might expect reduced cortisol levels in antisocials.

Several studies in a wide variety of groups have shown that there is such a link. McBurnett, Lahey, Frick, Risch, Loeber, Hart, Christ, and Hanson (1991) examined cortisol as an index of HPA axis arousal and found that boys with conduct disorder (CD) without comorbid anxiety disorder showed significantly lower concentrations of cortisol than did boys with CD and comorbid anxiety disorder. Clinic control groups of anxious and nonanxious boys had intermediate values that did not differ from each other or from either CD group. Cortisol has similarly been reported to be low in habitually violent incarcerated offenders (Virkkunen, 1985), in aggressive schoolchildren (Tennes & Kreye, 1985), in adolescents with conduct problems (Susman, Dorn, & Chrousos, 1991), and in disinhibited children (Kagan, Reznick, & Snidman, 1987). Susman et al. (1991) have argued from results of longitudinal and cross-sectional studies of hormones such as cortisol that such measures need to be set within the context of psychological and other factors in understanding their relationships with behavior.

Lahey and colleagues have conducted a number of important studies which indicate that anxiety may be an important moderator variable in the link between conduct disorder and cortisol levels. In a three-city longitudinal study (Lahey, Loeber, Stouthamer-Loeber, Christ, Green, Russo, Frick, & Dulcan, 1990; McBurnett *et al.*, 1991; Walker, Lahey, Russo, Frick, Christ, McBurnett, Loeber, Stouthamer-Loeber, & Green, 1991), a highly aggressive, nonanxious, conduct-disordered group has been shown to have markedly lower levels of salivary cortisol than the other two groups ($p < .04$). Interestingly, these results were virtually identical to those of an earlier study of skin conductance in subgroups of CD based on anxiety, where it was shown that nonanxious conduct-disordered subjects showed reduced SC activity (Delameter & Lahey, 1983). A more recent study (Lahey & McBurnett, 1992) has also shown that low cortisol particularly characterizes the high-aggression group of conduct-disordered children. The same low cortisol–high aggression finding was again shown in Year 4 of this study.

Anxiety may not be the only moderator variable of importance in mediating cortisol–antisocial links. There is preliminary evidence, for example, that both alcohol and testosterone may interact with cortisol. Buydens and Branchey (1992) assessed basal levels of cortisol in alcoholics with and without a history of violence and found that violent alcoholics were characterized by *increased* cortisol levels. Furthermore, this increase in cortisol was maintained 4 weeks following abstinence from alcohol. This study suggests that criminal groups may be heterogeneous with respect to cortisol and that those without a history of alcoholism may be more likely to be characterized by low levels. With respect to the mediating effects of testosterone, Dabbs, Jurkovic, and Frady (1991) related both testosterone and cortisol to violent and antisocial behavior committed by 113 young adults in a prison setting. Although there were no direct relationships between cortisol and antisocial, violent behavior, cortisol was found to moderate the relationship between testosterone and violence.

Taken together, all of these studies suggest that low HPA axis arousal, as measured by cortisol, may play a nontrivial role in mediating antisocial, violent, and criminal behavior, although clearly further empirical verification of these links is required. Importantly, future studies must be cognizant of the possible moderating effects of substance abuse and interactions with other biological risk variables. As with many other biological measures, it must also be recognized that the HPA axis that cortisol reflects is a dynamic system that is responsive to environmental changes and demands. As such, integration with social and environmental factors must be a primary aim of future studies in this area.

VIII. TESTOSTERONE

Excellent reviews and discussions of the potential role played by testosterone in both animals and man can be found in Rubin (1987), Prentky (1985), Olweus (1987), Schalling (1987), Brain (1990), and Archer (1991).

Animal research suggests that the steroid hormone testosterone plays an important role in the genesis and maintenance of some forms of aggressive behavior in rodents, and early exposure to testosterone has been found to increase aggression in a wide range of animal species (Brain, 1990). A key question generated by this literature is whether testosterone is involved in aggression and violent crime in man. Studies correlating questionnaire measures of aggression in normals to testosterone levels have generally produced weak or nonsignificant findings (Rubin, 1987). Studies of violent incarcerated inmates on the other hand have been more consistent in producing significant effects of moderate to large strength (Rubin, 1987). This theme is reiterated by Archer (1991) in a rigorous and critical review of the literature, arguing that effects are small or negligible when aggression is measured using personality inventories but strong and significant when groups high and low on behavioral measures of aggression are compared. Five studies of prisoners reviewed by Archer resulted in substantial effect sizes of 1.3, 1.4, 1.0 to 1.5, 1.6, and 0.5. This distinction between self-report and behavioral measures of violence is an important one that has not always been recognized in discussion of the testosterone–criminal violence data and helps clarify this otherwise mixed literature.

Previous studies may have had technical limitations that restricted the likelihood of obtaining significant effects. Because testosterone is secreted episodically, at least three blood samples need to be taken about 15 minutes apart and then averaged (Goldzieher, Dozier, Smith, & Steinberger, 1976), whereas most of the studies reviewed by Rubin (1987) only obtained one sample. A second significant limitation with many previous studies is that testosterone is assayed from blood samples. Of this testosterone, 98% is bound to sex hormone-binding globulin; the important consequence of this is that such testosterone is not free to enter target cells and bind with receptors. As such, only 2% is physiologically active. Relatively recently techniques have been developed to assay testosterone from saliva (Landsman, Sandford, Howland, & Dawes, 1976). Not only is this noninvasive, but such testosterone is unbound and therefore is free to act and has been found to correlate highly (.81) with free serum testosterone (Tames & Swift, 1983).

Studies by Dabbs and colleagues assessing saliva testosterone in male (Dabbs, Frady, Carr, & Besch, 1987) and female prisoners (Dabbs, Ruback, Frady, Hopper, & Sgoutas, 1988) are of particular interest. This latter study is of interest not just because female prisoners were assessed, but also because high testosterone was found to be specific to type of violence, being highest in female prisoners who committed unprovoked assault, but not in inmates who reacted violently when physically assaulted. These findings suggest that future studies assaying testosterone from saliva may obtain stronger and more consistent effects than in the past. For example, one recent study measuring free salivary testosterone found significant positive correlations between testosterone and violence *within* a group of physically aggressive bushmen (Christiansen & Winkler, 1992).

The critical question in this literature concerns whether testosterone–violence relationships are *causal*. Olweus, Mattesson, Schalling, and Low (1988) assessed their finding of higher testosterone in male adolescents with high levels of self-report aggression using path analysis. Within the context of this causal modeling, they concluded that testosterone had causal effects on both provoked and unprovoked aggressive behavior. Such modeling is consistent with a causal analysis but does not conclusively prove causality. An experimental test of the causal model would involve an intervention in violent offenders in which testosterone levels are reduced by medical intervention, and subjects are followed up on after release to assess if recidivism is reduced. One study that comes close to such an ideal experiment is reported by Wille and Beier (1989) and is worthy of report. Since 1970 a law in the then Federal Republic of Germany has allowed voluntary castration. Wille and Beier followed up 99 castrated sex offenders and 35 noncastrated sex offenders for, on average, 11 years after release from prison. Such a sample covers about 25% of all castrations in the period from 1970 to 1980 and is therefore reasonably representative of this population. Subjects were naturally not randomly assigned to experimental and control conditions, but the 35 controls had all requested castration but ended up changing their minds and as such constituted as close a control group as could be ethically achieved. The recidivism rate over an average of 11 years postrelease was 3% in castrated offenders compared to 46% in noncastrated offenders. Such low recidivism rates in castrated sex offenders are consistent with rates ranging from 0 to 11.0% in 10 studies of castrated sex offenders (see Table 1 in Wille & Beier, 1989).

These studies conducted on sex offenders with a less-than-perfect control group cannot be taken to demonstrate conclusively that high testosterone levels are causally related to criminal violence, in particular nonsexual violence. Furthermore, it should be pointed out that while 70% of castrates were satisfied with their treatment, 20% were ambivalent and 10% were not satisfied. Nevertheless, there is in addition some limited evidence that less drastic methods of reducing testosterone levels such as administration of antiandrogens and progesterone derivatives have some effect in lowering violence and sexual aggression (Rubin, 1987; Brain, 1990; Archer, 1991). Taken together with correlational data, the entire set of findings is not consistent with the view that testosterone is unrelated to violence and aggression, suggesting that a potentially causal relationship exists between testosterone and violence. The fact that testosterone levels are in part heritable (Turner, Ford, West, & Meikle, 1986) is also of interest, suggesting that the genetic predisposition to crime may in part be expressed through the hormonal system. It should be noted, however, that currently there are no solid data showing heritability for sexual violence per se.

In spite of this evidence, it is clear that one cannot assume *simple* causal relationships between single, peripheral measures of hormones and violent behavior. It seems likely that testosterone is only one of a number of hormonal factors that influence aggressive behavior, and it is likely that hormones inter-act with and are influenced by a wide range of social, perceptual, and environ-mental factors. For example, there is some initial evidence that success in competition, the perception of winning, and exposure to erotic films can in-crease circulating levels of testosterone (Brain, 1990; Archer, 1991), although one important question that remains unanswered is whether repeated success in competitive encounters can result in a sustained increase in testosterone over time. Furthermore, family variables such as poor living quality and lack of external family support have been found to correlate with amines (epinephrine, norepinephrine) and thyroid hormones that are in turn linked to recidivistic violent behavior in juvenile offenders (Schalling, 1987). In-terdisciplinary longitudinal studies are required to further assess temporal links between early social stress, changes in hormonal levels, and violent behavior.

IX. PREMENSTRUAL SYNDROME AND CRIME

Future studies must also address hormonal influences on female crime, as we know little about hormonal influences per se on such populations, although in this area there is a preexisting literature upon which to build. Hormone levels fluctuate markedly in women as a function of the menstrual cycle. During ovulation estrogen and progesterone levels are high, and females tend to be more receptive to males during this time (Clare, 1985). Progesterone levels are reduced prior to menstruation whereas other hormones such as angiotensin, prolactin, and aldosterone increase. In some cases this results in the clinical syndrome of Late Luteal Phase Dysphoric Disorder (APA, 1987) (more commonly known as premenstrual syndrome, PMS), which includes symptoms such as increased irritability, concentration problems, and emo-tional changes including depression and aggression. More controversially, it supposedly results in an increased propensity to violent and antisocial behavior.

Several correlational studies have generated testable hypotheses on the effects of hormonal changes upon female behavior. One of the first, most extensive, and influential studies was conducted by Dalton (1961), who found that in a sample of 156 newly convicted women, 46% of crimes had occurred either 4 days prior to menstruation or 4 days following menstruation, a figure higher than the expected chance rate of 29%. There have been a number of studies that support this proposition; one recent review of this literature may be found in Fishbein (1992), who argues that a subgroup of women appear to be particularly vulnerable to cyclical changes in hormone levels that cause them to be more prone to hostility during the menstruation phase.

Critics have counter suggested that stress can affect the menstrual cycle, and consequently it would be possible that the commission of the crime per se and subsequent arrest and interrogation could potentially trigger menstruation. Consequently, crime could cause menstruation rather than vice-versa (Horney, 1978), because the process of committing a crime, arrest, and police interrogation would constitute a significant degree of stress. One further complication is that there are other biochemical changes taking place during the premenstrual phase, including reduction in norepinephrine and blood glucose levels (Fishbein, 1992); because both of these factors are linked to violence (see Chapter 4 and Section X in this chapter), it is unclear which factor may be responsible for the claimed link between PMS and violence. Critics have also pointed out that Dalton's subjects had almost exclusively committed nonviolent crime and not violent offenses. This contradicts a specific link between PMS and violence, but this should not preclude follow-up research into a possible PMS–crime link, nor does it disprove a causal relationship between PMS and crime. Indeed, the fact that progesterone therapy has been reported to reduce aggressive behavior provides some limited support for the possibility of a causal link between PMS and aggression.

Since hormonal imbalances have been used as a legal defense against conviction of violent assaults, and since hormone therapy for some offenders is a controversial treatment, the role of hormones in violence has legal, ethical, and treatment implications that require careful consideration. The fact that the PMS–crime link has generated public interest far in excess of scientific research to date does not invalidate such research or constitute a good reason to discredit well-intentioned research. A better scientific basis for making statements regarding the causal relationship between hormones and violence is, however, clearly required.

X. HYPOGLYCEMIA

A number of studies have linked hypoglycemia (low blood sugar levels) to violent and aggressive behavior. The brain requires at least 80 mg of glucose/minute to function appropriately, and below this average level symptoms of panic, irritability, nervousness, and aggression can result (Marks, 1981). Increased irritability as one symptom of hypoglycemia could be the first step in the development of a full-blown aggressive outburst. The most common form of hypoglycemia, reactive hypoglycemia, is marked by symptoms occurring 2–4 hours following a meal and can be exacerbated by drugs such as alcohol.

Anthropological studies, studies of aggressive personality in "normal" subjects, and experimental studies in animals all support a link between hypoglycemia and aggression (see review in Venables & Raine, 1987). For example, Benton, Kumari, and Brain (1982) observed significant correlations between blood glucose levels and hostility scores. Acute symptoms of hypoglycemia are reported as maximal at 11:00 to 11:30 a.m. (Marks, 1981), and this time corresponds to assaults on staff and other inmates in prison, both of which peak at 11:00 to 11:30 a.m. (Davies, 1982), suggesting a possible causal relationship between hypoglycemia and violence. A number of studies have also observed that violent offenders, particularly those with a history of alcohol abuse, are characterized by reactive hypoglycemia. For example, Virkkunen (1984) found an excess of hypoglycemia in imprisoned arsonists (46%) relative to controls (17%) using a glucose tolerance test, with similar findings being observed in habitually violent offenders (Virkkunen, 1986).

Notions of a link between hypoglycemia and violence are clearly of interest, though it is equally clear that this line of research is suggestive rather than definitive. To date there is no good evidence that violent offenders are hypoglycemic at the time of committing violence (Kanareck, 1990), though it is difficult to see how this criticism can be circumvented in future research. As pointed out by Messer, Morris, and Gross (1990), glucose tolerance testing has been criticized as an inaccurate method of assessing glucose levels occurring after a normal meal, and the confounding effects of alcohol abuse have not been fully dealt with. An important area for future research concerns isolating the physiological predispositional mechanisms mediating the aggression–hypoglycemia link. Apart from the potential role of diet (see Section XI below) there is virtually no knowledge in this area. In this context, an interesting theoretical position developed by Venables (1988) attempts to link both low heart rate and EEG slowing with hypoglycemia, psychophysiological factors which themselves are thought to be linked to violent offending (Venables, 1988).

Although hypoglycemia research into violence and crime has been limited to date, it is clearly an area worthy of further consideration, particularly within the context of other biological variables. As one example, Virkkunen, DeJong, Bartko, Goodwin, and Linnoila (1989) found that when blood glucose measures were combined with 5-HIAA measures, they correctly classified 84.2% of recidivistic, alcohol-abusing violent offenders and impulsive fire setters. Interestingly, serotinergic drugs could not only counterbalance the low serotonin found in these violent offenders, but could also reduce alcohol consumption and improve abnormal glucose metabolism. This type of integrative study, combining data on violence and alcoholism on the one hand with serotonin and blood glucose on the other, has implications for the future prediction and treatment of violence. While these findings need to be replicated, they indicate the type of integration that can significantly further this field of study.

XI. DIET

The possible role of hypoglycemia in mediating violence has led to the notion that diet may influence antisocial behavior. Extreme fluctuations in blood glucose levels can be produced by diets high in refined carbohydrates. Such foods are rapidly absorbed by the gut, resulting in a large and rapid increase of glucose into the bloodstream. This in turn triggers an inappropriately large secretion of insulin and a consequent over-reduction of blood glucose levels. In contrast, reducing the sucrose content of a diet and increasing fiber intake delays gastric emptying and helps facilitate a steady regulation of glucose release into the bloodstream, preventing the extreme rise and subsequent rebound fall of blood sugar levels (Haber, Heaton, & Murphy, 1977; Monnier, Pham, Aguirre, Orsetti, & Mirouze, 1978). Such a process leads to the notion that diet may be linked to antisocial behavior and to the provocative idea that dietary manipulations may help reduce antisocial behavior.

A number of studies have claimed that dietary changes aimed at reducing sugar consumption reduce institutional antisocial behavior in juvenile offenders. Some of these claims are striking. For example, Schoenthaler (1982), in a 2-year double-blind controlled study on 12- to 18-year-old delinquents, obtained a 48% reduction in disciplinary offenses following a reduction in the diets of refined carbohydrates. Fishbein and Thatcher (1982) found that 1 month on a refined carbohydrate-free diet led to significant improvements in paranoia and depression in male adult prisoners prone to hypoglycemia relative to nonhypoglycemics and nondiet controls.

Studies such as these have been criticized on methodological and statistical grounds (Gray, 1986; Pease & Love, 1986) and as such firm conclusions cannot be confidently drawn at the present time. Nevertheless, further double-blind experimental studies into the effects of dietary manipulations on aggression and violence in institutions seem warranted, as are studies of interconnections between hypoglycemia/diet and other factors at both biological and social levels. Since alcohol increases susceptibility to hypoglycemia through its capacity to increase insulin secretion (Marks, 1981), it may well be that predispositions to both hypoglycemia and alcohol abuse, in combination with a poor diet, would make an individual particularly predisposed to violence. The fact that hyperactive children from a supportive home environment show more improvement from dietary intervention than those from an unsupportive home (Rumsey & Rapoport, 1983) also suggests a potentially important interaction between diet and family environment which could also be true for antisocial behavior. Clearly, the effects of diet and hypoglycemia should not be studied apart from interactions with factors at other levels.

XII. LEAD

There is no question that lead is a metallic neurotoxin and that sufficient exposure to it could induce brain dysfunction. It is also possible that such brain dysfunction could predispose to the development of criminal and violent behavior. The more critical question concerns whether exposure to the levels of lead found in urban environments can contribute to crime. Although exposure to lead is not an immediately obvious problem to the average person, lead exposure is insidious and all pervasive; for example, in 1992 some cities in the U.S. have been reported to have over 14 times the recommended levels of lead in their drinking water alone.

A number of studies have suggested that lead levels in the environment are related to cognitive, learning, and attentional deficits in children and that even relatively low lead levels can cause measurable deficits (see Rutter & Giller, 1983, and Loeber, 1990, for brief reviews). Needleman (1985) has argued that, although many studies have lacked statistical power and used insensitive outcome measures, even low lead levels that would not otherwise lead to medical attention can lead to significant impairment in cognitive variables such as IQ and reaction times. Nevertheless, there is currently intense debate as to whether these conclusions can be unequivocally accepted and over the accuracy of the data supporting them.

Perhaps more importantly, there has been relatively little research linking lead exposure to delinquency, violence, and criminal behavior per se. Several studies have, however, linked metallic toxins to both aggressive and antisocial behavior in children and violent criminal behavior in adults. In the U.S., Marlowe, Stellern, Moon, and Errera (1985) related lead, arsenic, mercury, cadmium, and aluminum concentrations in the hair of 80 elementary school-aged children to teacher ratings of behavior. These metals were significantly related to acting-out behavior in the children; lead was the strongest individual predictor, while cadmium also interacted with lead in predicting acting-out behavior. Similarly in the U.K., Thomson, Raab, Hepburn, & Hunter (1989) found significant relationships between lead levels assessed from blood in a large sample of 501 children aged 6–9 years and teacher and parent ratings of aggressive and antisocial behavior.

These findings in children also appear to hold up in adult violent offenders. One recent study does, however, provide evidence that exposure to lead and cadmium is related to violent criminal behavior. Pihl and Ervin (1990) used atomic absorption spectroscopy to examine levels of both lead and cadmium in the hair of 30 violent criminal offenders and 19 nonviolent psychiatrically disturbed controls. Violent offenders had significantly higher levels of lead and cadmium than nonviolent offenders. One notable strength of this study was the use of nonviolent offender controls, indicating some degree of specificity to violence.

Although these studies provide some evidence that lead exposure may indeed be related to aggressive and violent behavior in children and adults, it is also clear that research in this area is still provisional. Not only are more studies needed to critically assess the empirical link between lead and crime, but methodological and conceptual issues need to be assessed. Methodologically, future research needs to more clearly establish whether lead–antisocial links are merely the result of third factors, with those children and adults with the highest exposure to lead coming from socially disadvantaged homes in urban areas with high crime rates. At a conceptual level, future research needs to assess the mechanism or mechanisms by which lead exposure may lead to criminal and aggressive behavior. Recent animal research suggests that lead exposure may alter neurotransmitter and hormonal systems, which in turn leads to behavioral effects by making the organism less able to cope with the environment (Burright, Engellenner, & Donovick, 1989), and such a model may usefully be tested by assessing hormones and neurotransmitters together with lead levels in humans.

XIII. SUMMARY

This chapter has reviewed a number of other biological factors that have been linked to criminal behavior but have been less systematically researched than biological processes reviewed in other chapters. Both juvenile and adult violent offenders are characterized by a history of significant head injury which is likely to be caused by environmental accidents or early child abuse. Violent offenders are more likely to have suffered birth complications that may give rise to CNS deficits, particularly in those with other risk factors for violence such as hyperactivity or having parents with a mental illness. Minor physical anomalies have been found to characterize childhood behavior problems and adult violent offending and may reflect fetal neural maldevelopment occurring toward the end of the first trimester of pregnancy. Both male and female criminals have been found to be less physically attractive than controls; plastic surgery intervention provides some limited evidence suggesting that such physical disadvantages may be causally linked to crime. Adult criminals and juvenile delinquents have been found to have a mesomorphic–endomorphic body build (muscular and large); it is hypothesized that social learning and the reinforcement of aggressive behavior in individuals with this somatotype may predispose specifically to violent behavior. Low basal cortisol levels found in conduct-disordered and violent offenders may be specific to those with low levels of anxiety and may reflect one aspect of generalized autonomic underarousal in criminals. Raised testosterone levels in violent offenders may be strongly influenced by environmental factors; surgical intervention and drug therapy studies, while preliminary, are suggestive of a causal relationship. Hypoglycemia found in aggressive and violent populations may predispose to antisocial behavior by lowering the threshold for irritability and may play a particularly significant role in offenders who also abuse alcohol. Similarly, diets high in refined carbohydrates may predispose to antisocial behavior particularly when combined with alcohol abuse. While lead has been linked to cognitive deficits and behavior problems in children, there are few good studies that have demonstrated a clear link with juvenile delinquency or adult offending. Many of these biological correlates of crime are *environmentally* caused and are also hypothesized to predispose to crime through *social* mechanisms such as social rejection, reduced self-esteem, and academic failure. This highlights the mistake of adopting the simplistic and fallacious mentality of the biological versus environmental dichotomy that characterizes the approach of some criminologists, and it adds further support for the notion that criminals are handicapped by numerous biological and social deficiencies.

9 Cognitive Deficits

I. INTRODUCTION

In Chapter 1 it was outlined that impairment in functioning and efficiency was one of the more commonly cited and stronger definitions of disorder. One important aspect of functioning is cognitive functioning, which includes learning ability, intelligence, selective attention, academic ability, moral reasoning, and social information processing. Major mental disorders such as schizophrenia, depression, and alcoholism, for example, are characterized by important cognitive and information-processing deficits. In a similar manner, this chapter will argue that criminal and antisocial behavior are likewise characterized by nontrivial cognitive deficits and that the presence of such deficits fulfills this definition of disorder.

This review will first cover fundamental cognitive processes in learning, namely classical conditioning and instrumental learning. Deficits in both of these processes in antisocials will be outlined and linked to other processes including underarousal, reward dominance, and slow fear dissipation. Findings on IQ will be outlined with particular reference to the notion of specific verbal or left hemisphere dysfunction. A discussion of the link between delinquency and learning disabilities will be followed by research on moral reasoning indicating that delinquents and criminals have arrested cognitive development at the preconventional stage of moral reasoning. Finally, more recent developments on social information-processing deficits will be discussed with reference to Dodge's two-factor model of reactive and proactive aggression. It will be argued that (1) delinquents and criminals are clearly characterized by cognitive deficits, but there is considerably more doubt as to whether third factors mediate cognitive dysfunction–crime relationships and whether cognitive deficits are a cause or consequence of crime; and (2) the presence of such cognitive deficits helps to fulfill the impairment in functioning/efficiency concept of disorder.

II. CLASSICAL CONDITIONING AND CRIME

There are two fundamental learning processes: classical conditioning and instrumental learning. Although they are frequently viewed separately, the process of association is common to both. While classical conditioning involves developing an association between two events in time, instrumental learning involves learning an association between a response and later reinforcement. Research into criminal behavior and learning deficits has also tended to follow this division between classical conditioning and instrumental learning, and consequently it will be treated separately below.

The strongest proponent of a classical conditioning approach to criminal behavior has been Hans Eysenck. Eysenck (1964, 1977) has developed an influential theory of criminal behavior that rests on the notion that criminals and other antisocials are deficient with respect to classical conditioning. He argues that classical conditioning is fundamental to the whole process of socialization whereby the individual learns to withhold antisocial responses. It is argued that the crucial mechanism that stops most of us from committing criminal and antisocial acts is the concept of conscience; a well-developed conscience is what holds many of us back from not stealing even in those situations when we are almost certain of getting away with the theft undetected. Eysenck argues that what we call "conscience" is, in effect, a set of classically conditioned emotional responses. The greater the individual's ability to develop and form classically conditioned emotional responses, the

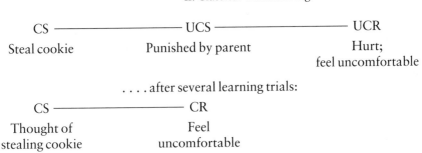

FIGURE 1   Classical conditioning model of antisocial behavior. CS, conditioned stimulus; UCS, unconditioned stimulus; UCR, unconditioned response; CR, conditioned response.

greater the conscience development, and the less likely will be the probability of becoming antisocial. Conversely, poor conditionability will result in poor conscience development and undersocialized, antisocial behavior.

Classical conditioning involves learning that an initially neutral event (a conditional stimulus or "CS"), when closely followed in time by an aversive event (unconditional stimulus or "UCS"), will develop the properties of this UCS. In the classic case of Pavlov's dogs, a bell (CS) was paired with the presentation of food (UCS). Food to hungry dogs automatically elicits an unconditional response (UCR), in this case salivation. After a sufficient number of pairings of the bell with the food, the bell by itself will come to elicit the UCR, salivation. Although conditioning has often been viewed as reflecting automatic, reflexive processes, experiments in human autonomic classical conditioning support the notion that complex cognitive processes are involved in this form of learning (see, e.g., Dawson *et al.*, 1989; Dawson & Schell, 1985).

In concrete terms, the way classical conditioning is hypothesized to relate to socialization is illustrated in Fig. 1. Taking the scenario of a small child stealing a cookie (CS) from the kitchen, punishment by the parent (scolding or physical punishment, UCS) elicits an unconditional response (UCR) whereby the child is upset and feels uncomfortable. After a number of similar "learning trials," the sight of the cookie (or even the thought of stealing the cookie) will elicit an uncomfortable feeling in the child (conditional response, CR), which acts to avert the child from enacting the "theft." Similar "conditioned emotional responses" developed relatively early in life in varying situations combine, in Eysenck's view, to represent what we call "conscience."

In this analysis, socialized individuals develop a feeling of uneasiness at even contemplating a criminal act (robbery, assault), presumably because such thoughts elicit representations or "unconscious" memories of punishment early in life for milder but related misdemeanors (theft, behaving aggressively). In this context the common response of socialized individuals to crimes committed by others such as, "I could never even *think* of doing such a thing" becomes understandable. Socialized individuals don't even contemplate such events because even the thought of such acts elicits CRs involving discomfort.

Eysenck's theory of crime involves more concepts than just conditioning. He argues that crime has a genetic basis, that personality has a genetic basis, and that genetic differences lead to individual differences in CNS and ANS functioning. Central to such differences are individual differences in arousal. These differences in arousal levels result in differing degrees of both extraversion and conditionability, with low levels of arousal predisposing to poor conditionability and high levels of extraversion. Because of links between extraversion and both arousal and conditionability, Eysenck (1964, 1977) went on to argue that criminals would be extroverts and also developed predictions concerning high neuroticism and psychoticism (Eysenck & Eysenck, 1978; Eysenck, 1987). As will be seen below, findings on classical conditioning in antisocial groups are generally supportive of Eysenck's conditioning theory of crime.

A. Evidence for Poor Classical Conditioning in Antisocials

These predictions concerning personality have generated a great deal of research, and reviews of findings may be found in Passingham (1972), Farrington, Biron, and LeBlanc (1982), Eysenck (1987), and Bartol (1991). However, the central idea in Eysenck's theory is that criminals and antisocials will be characterized by poor classical conditioning. This prediction has received less empirical attention, probably because it is much easier to assess personality than conditionability. Classical conditioning has most frequently been assessed using skin conductance: a neutral tone (CS) is presented to the subject, followed a few seconds later by either a loud tone or an electric shock (UCS). The key measure derived from this paradigm is the size of the skin conductance (SC) response elicited by the CS after a number of CS–UCS pairings. The lower the SC amplitude, the poorer the degree of conditioning. On occasions however, eye-blink classical conditionability has been assessed in which a neutral stimulus is followed by an air puff to the eye that elicits an eye blink (UCR)—the measure here is the magnitude of the eye blink to the CS alone after a number of CS–UCS pairings.

The last systematic review of conditionability was reported by Hare (1978). Of the 14 studies reported by Hare covering classical conditioning and what is termed "quasi-conditioning" (see below), 12 indicated that psychopaths, criminals, delinquents, and antisocials showed poorer SC conditioning than control groups. In one of the remaining two studies, significantly poorer conditioning was observed for a subgroup of psychopaths (those with low scores on the socialization scale). The remaining study failed to observe overall significant effects and instead observed that younger psychopaths gave

TABLE 1   Key Findings from Studies on Classical Conditioning in Antisocials, Criminals, and Psychopaths as Measured by Skin Conductance[a]

Reference	Subjects	Finding
Ziskind et al. (1978)	Psychopathic gamblers	Poor differential conditioning but verbal awareness
Aniskiewitz (1979)	Primary psychopaths	Poor vicarious conditioning
Tharp et al. (1980)	Psychopathic gamblers	Less anticipatory responding
Raine & Venables (1981)	Conduct disorder	Poor conditioning in high-social-class antisocials
Hemming (1981)	Criminals from good homes	Less conditioned discrimination in extinction
Hare (1982)	Psychopaths	Less anticipatory responding

[a]All findings were significant.

larger responses than older psychopaths. Overall therefore, this review indicates general support for the notion of poorer conditionability in antisocial groups.

In order to assess whether this general conclusion remains true, findings from conditioning studies conducted since 1978 have been assessed. These six studies and their key findings are noted in Table I. Skin conductance conditioning in these studies is assessed either by SCRs occurring to the conditional stimulus (what has been termed the conditioned "A" response) or by the SCR occurring in between the CS and the UCS (the conditioned "B" response). In two of the studies (Tharp et al., 1980; Hare, 1982) the paradigm consists of a "count-down" procedure in which the subject awaits the onset of an aversive stimulus whose onset is signaled several seconds beforehand, a paradigm referred to by Hare (1978) as "quasi-conditioning." All six of these studies showed some evidence indicating significantly poorer SC conditionability in antisocials. Not all of these studies provide unequivocal evidence for poor conditioning, however. Hemming (1981) found group differences for conditioned discrimination in extinction, but not for conditioning during acquisition. Similarly, Raine and Venables (1981) found poor conditioning specifically in antisocial children from higher social classes, but not in those from lower social classes.

B. Assessment of Conditioning Studies

The findings outlined in Table 1 are unusual in that, in one way or another, they all find significant group differences even though there are wide variations in these studies. For example, paradigms varied from a classical CS–UCS paradigm (e.g., Hemming, 1981) to vicarious conditioning where subjects watching others receive electric shocks following a CS (Aniskiewicz, 1979) to quasiconditioning count-down procedures (e.g., Tharp *et al.*, 1980). Subjects ranged from uninstitutionalized antisocial children (e.g., Raine & Venables, 1981) to adult criminals (Hemming, 1981) to institutionalized psychopaths (Tharp *et al.*, 1980) to psychopathic gamblers (Ziskind, Syndulko, & Maltzman, 1978). The fact that all studies showed significant effects in the predicted direction would indicate that poor conditioning is related to the general development of antisocial behavior.

Several of these paradigms do not control for factors such as sensitization. However, it is likely that the SC "conditioning" measures obtained are a strong correlate of true SC conditioning, since one would expect that those who sensitize easily also condition easily.

There are several interesting aspects to some of these studies. Ziskind *et al.* (1978) demonstrated that while psychopaths were able to verbalize the contingency between the CS and the UCS (i.e., they knew that the warning tone was followed by the aversive tone), they did not show conditioning. This finding suggests that conditioning deficits in antisocials are not merely a reflection of a cognitive, conscious process involving understanding the link between the CS and the UCS, but may involve more deep-seated, "unconscious" or preattentive processes.

The study by Hemming (1981) is of interest in that the subject population consisted of criminals from relatively good social backgrounds. It previously has been argued that biological predispositional variables may have greater explanatory power in antisocials from relatively benign homes where the "social push" toward antisocial behavior is low; if individuals become antisocial therefore, it may be more for biological reasons than for social reasons (Mednick, *et al.*, 1977; Raine & Venables, 1981). Hemming's findings are consistent with this analysis. An early finding by Lykken (1955) also appears to be consistent with this approach. Lykken (1955) observed that primary psychopathic inmates showed poorer SC conditioning to an electric shock that neurotic psychopaths. In commenting on Lykken's subject selection procedures, Siddle and Trasler (1981) point out that in this study subjects were excluded if they came from a "markedly sociopathic or deviant" family background (Lykken, 1955, p. 111a). As such, SC conditioning deficits were found in psychopaths from relatively good home backgrounds.

Findings from Raine and Venables (1981) are in broad agreement with the above two studies in that poorer SC conditioning was observed in children from *higher* social classes. One finding from this study that does not fit so easily with this perspective is that antisocials from lower social classes showed relatively *good* conditioning (see Fig. 2). This specific finding may be more easily explained by the process of "antisocialization." Eysenck (1977) has argued that children who are highly conditionable and who have antisocial

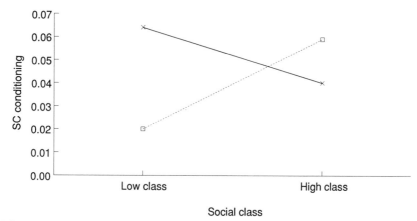

FIGURE 2   Illustration of the interaction between social class and classical conditioning as measured by skin conductance in antisocial, —×— and prosocial, ---□--- schoolboys (Adapted from Raine & Venables, 1981).

parents will become "socialized" into their parents' antisocial habits, whereas children who condition poorly would paradoxically avoid becoming antisocial. If low social class indirectly reflects a relatively criminogenic environment, then the stronger conditionability in children from low social classes found in Raine and Venables (1981) would be consistent with this analysis.

Better studies that more directly assess antisocial processes in subjects' homes and peer groups in conjunction with conditionability are needed to confirm this hypothesis because social class is likely to be only a weak correlate of family criminogenicity. Nevertheless, the important point to make is that conditionability may interact with social factors in important ways to explain antisocial behavior and provides some encouragement for a biosocial perspective on crime.

III. AVOIDANCE LEARNING AND CRIME

A. Basic Process of Avoidance Learning

An avoidance learning approach to crime starts where the classical conditioning view of crime left off. One way of viewing the stealing-the-cookie scenario described above is to view it in terms not of associations between stimuli (cookie and punishment), but in terms of an association between a behavioral response (stealing the cookie) and reinforcement (parental punishment). Figure 3 illustrates the response–reinforcement process involved in this scenario.

RESPONSE ───────────────────────── REINFORCEMENT

Steal cookie   Punished by parent

After several learning trials:

PASSIVE AVOIDANCE RESPONSE ───────── REINFORCEMENT

Inhibit antisocial response   Reduction in anxiety

FIGURE 3   The process of passive avoidance learning in the inhibition of antisocial behavior.

The basic principle behind instrumental or "operant" conditioning is that any response that is reinforced or "rewarded" will increase in frequency. Conversely, responses that are followed by punishment will decrease in frequency. Once the child has learned the association between stealing the cookie and punishment, presentation of a situation in which the child can steal the cookie again elicits a state of discomfort or anxiety, since the antisocial response is associated with punishment. If the child inhibits the response of stealing the cookie, however, anxiety will dissipate. This dissipation of fear is in itself a reinforcer, as avoidance of punishment has many of the same properties as a reward. Consequently, such "avoidance responses" will be increased in frequency because they are rewarded, and similarly stealing responses will be reduced in frequency because they are punished. This specific form of avoidance is termed "passive avoidance" learning, because simply passively inhibiting a response results in avoidance of punishment. It is this form of passive avoidance learning that has been the focus of study in criminals and psychopaths.

B. Early Findings on Avoidance Learning and the Role of Underarousal

An experiment by Lykken (1955, 1957) demonstrated that primary psychopaths are deficient with respect to passive avoidance learning. The learning paradigm consisted of a "mental maze." At each point in the maze, subjects had a choice of four responses. Choosing the correct response resulted in progression to the next step in the maze. One of the responses resulted in an electric shock. The overt task was to find the way through the maze. The interesting parameter, however, consisted of the extent to which subjects learned to passively avoid the electric shock. Although psychopaths learned the maze as well as controls, they made more punished responses, indicating a deficit in passive avoidance learning.

An experimental manipulation by Schacter and Latane (1964) demonstrated that this passive avoidance learning was reversible and also that the

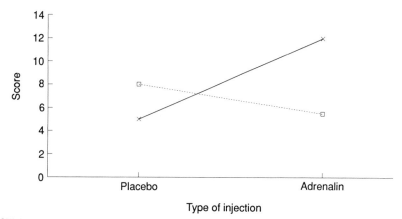

FIGURE 4   Schematic illustration of reversal of passive avoidance learning deficits in psycho-paths by increasing arousal with an injection of adrenaline. Avoidance learning scores are in arbitrary units. Psychopaths, —×—; controls, ---⊟---. (Adapted from Schacter & Latane, 1964.)

avoidance deficit may be caused by autonomic underarousal. Psychopaths and nonpsychopaths were again given a mental maze passive avoidance learning task, but this time half the subjects in each group were injected with adrenaline while half were injected with a placebo. Results of this experiment are illustrated in Fig. 4. It can be seen that under normal (placebo) conditions, psychopaths are poorer at passive avoidance learning than nonpsychopaths. In the adrenaline condition, however, psychopaths perform significantly *better* than nonpsychopaths. This experiment indicates that, when sufficiently aroused, psychopaths are capable of learning as well as, or better than, others. These data also suggest that underarousal may underlie the psychopath's deficits on this task. Such an underarousal explanation is consistent with findings reported in Chapter 7 indicating that underarousal appears to be a predisposition toward antisocial behavior in general. In passing, an unusual finding by Schacter and Latane (1964) is the fact that nonpsychopaths actually do worse in the adrenaline condition than in the control condition. One possible explanation is that nonpsychopaths are relatively highly aroused under normal circumstances, and the additional arousal produced by adrenaline interfered with performance due to overarousal.

Chesno and Kilmann (1975) also demonstrated that underarousal may be one process that underlies the poor avoidance learning in psychopaths. In this experiment, both active and passive avoidance learning using an electric shock as the reinforcer were assessed in primary (low-anxiety) psychopaths and a number of other control groups, the most critical of which was low-

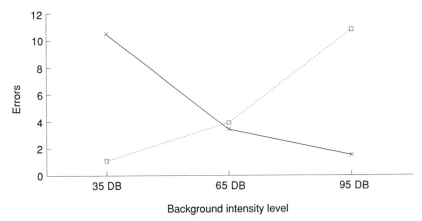

FIGURE 5   Reversal of avoidance learning deficits using white noise to increase arousal in psychopaths. Primary psychopaths, —×—; low-anxious controls, ---□---. (Adapted from Chesno & Kilmann, 1975.)

anxious nonpsychopathic criminals. The critical manipulation consisted of the background stimulation level, which consisted of either 35-, 65-, or 95-dB white noise. Results of this experiment are illustrated in Fig. 5. The primary psychopaths showed the greatest level of avoidance learning deficits in the low-arousal (35-dB) condition and made significantly fewer errors in the high-arousal condition, in which performance was nonsignificantly *better* than that of controls. This pattern of results holds for both active and passive avoidance learning. Interestingly, Chesno and Kilman (1975) found that psychopaths made more active than passive avoidance errors, suggesting that the deficit was not specific to passive avoidance but generalized to avoidance per se. Overall, findings indicate that the poorer avoidance learning in psychopaths may be attributable to lower arousal, which could be reversed through the use of highly arousing situations.

In all three of the above experiments the reinforcer was electric shock. Schmauk (1970) conducted an interesting variation on this paradigm by manipulating the type of reinforcer used in a study of primary psychopaths, neurotic psychopaths, and normal controls. In addition to the standard physical punishment condition, two other punishment conditions were introduced—social punishment (experimenter saying "wrong") and tangible punishment (loss of money). Results of this experiment are shown in Fig. 6. Primary psychopaths performed poorly in the social and physical punishment conditions, but performed significantly better in the tangible punishment condition, scoring higher than either of the other two groups. Furthermore, pri-

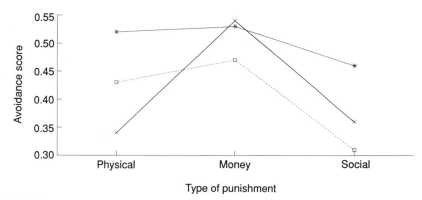

FIGURE 6   Use of monetary punishment to motivate psychopaths and abolish avoidance learning deficits in this group. Psychopaths, —✕—; prisoner controls, ---⊟---; and normal controls —✳—. (Adapted from Schmauk, 1970.)

mary psychopaths also performed as well as the other two groups with respect to number of anticipatory SCRs and awareness of the contingencies, indicating autonomic and cognitively superior performance in addition to the superior behavioral performance. This experiment again strikingly demonstrated that psychopaths are quite capable of learning to avoid a punishment, but only when sufficiently motivated to do so.

IV. OVERSENSITIVITY TO REWARDS

The previous studies suggest that underarousal may underlie the avoidance learning deficits in psychopaths and that, when psychopaths are sufficiently aroused, they may perform just as well as controls. Data presented in the chapter on psychophysiology also provided evidence that antisocials are capable of enhanced attentional performance when sufficiently motivated or when the task involves short-term active attentional processing (Hare, 1982; Jutai & Hare, 1983; Raine & Venables, 1987). Recent developments in the avoidance learning literature converge on a similar, though not identical, conclusion.

Both Newman and colleagues (Newman, Widom, & Nathan, 1985; Newman, 1987) and Quay and colleagues (Quay, 1985, 1988; Shapiro, Quay, Hogan, & Schwartz, 1988) have independently converged on the notion that psychopaths may be oversensitive to rewards. Both theoretical perspectives have been based on the influential work of Gray (1982, 1987), who argued that there are two main systems underlying the concepts of approach–avoidance, inhibition, motivation, and personality, these being the behavioral activation system (BAS) and the behavioral inhibition system (BIS). The BAS is involved in appetitive, reward-seeking behavior, while the BIS is involved in the inhibition of behavior in punishment conditions. The work of Newman, Quay, and also Fowles revolves around relative deficits in these two systems. An excellent analysis of Gray's theory as it relates to psychophysiology, arousal, motivation, and psychopathy may be found in Fowles (1980, 1988). For ease of explanation and simplification, the BAS will be referred to below as the "reward–activation" system and the BIS as the "punishment–inhibition" system.

Fowles (1980) argued that psychopaths have a deficient punishment–inhibition system but a normal activation–reward system, based on the notion that psychopaths have normal approach and active avoidance behavior and normal heart rate, but poor passive avoidance and reduced SC responses to threatening stimuli. Quay (1985) on the other hand argued that conduct-disordered children, who may be viewed as the closest childhood analog to adult psychopaths, are instead characterized by an overactive activation–reward system that predominates over the inhibition–reward system. Newman and colleagues (Newman et al., 1985; Newman, 1987) have similarly argued that psychopaths have a difficulty in inhibiting rewarded responses, that is, an overactive activation–reward system.

Newman and colleagues have intensively studied passive avoidance in psychopaths over the past decade and have generated a series of studies that provide strong support for the notion that it is specifically the presence of rewards that disrupts the passive avoidance errors in psychopaths (Newman et al., 1985; Newman, Patterson, Howland, & Nichols, 1990; Newman & Kosson, 1986; Newman et al., 1987; Newman, 1987). Passive avoidance learning deficits were especially prominent in psychopaths when the task involved rewards as well as punishments. In particular, Newman and colleagues argued that once a response set has been developed favoring rewards, psychopaths have a particular difficulty in breaking out of this reward-based response set, leading to performance deficits.

Findings from Quay's laboratory similarly indicate that undersocialized aggressive conduct-disordered children (mean age 14 years) are characterized by reward dominance. Shapiro et al. (1988) used the card-playing task of Newman et al. (1987) in which playing cards were presented to the subject. A response to some cards resulted in a reward (monetary gain) while a response to others resulted in a loss of money. Subjects could stop playing the task and keep whatever winnings they had at any point in the game. Unknown to the subject, the probability of winning a reward started off at 90% but steadily decreased to 10% by the end of the task. The key variable was the number of cards played; a rational subject would quickly gain money but then notice that losses were becoming more frequent and stop playing. A subject who could not break out of a reward-based response system would play the game longer.

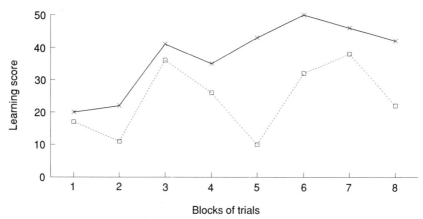

FIGURE 7   Illustration of reward dominance and ability to learn in psychopaths when sufficiently motivated. Psychopaths, —×—; nonpsychopaths, ---□--- (Adapted from Scerbo *et al.*, 1990.)

As predicted, the undersocialized aggressive conduct-disordered group played significantly more cards than a control group. These findings were later replicated in conduct-disordered children both with and without hyperactivity (Daugherty & Quay, 1989).

Scerbo, Raine, O'Brien, Chan, Rhee, and Smiley (1990) also provided support for the notion of reward dominance in psychopathic adolescents. Psychopathic and nonpsychopathic conduct-disordered adolescents were administered a passive avoidance learning task that required them to learn when to respond either to cards associated with reward (winning money) or to cards associated with punishment (losing money). The cards were dealt one at a time. Touching a card linked to reward resulted in gaining money, while touching a card linked to punishment resulted in losing money. There were eight trials in each of eight blocks. Groups did not differ in terms of passive avoidance learning, that is, nonpsychopaths were just as likely as psychopaths to respond to stimuli linked to punishment. However, psychopaths responded more to reward cards, indicating reward dominance.

This finding that psychopaths do not show deficits in passive avoidance learning when sufficiently motivated with monetary incentives is consistent with the previous findings of Schmauk (1970), while the focusing on rewards in tasks involving mixed incentives (i.e., presence of rewards and punishments) is consistent with findings of Newman and Kosson (1986) and Newman *et al.* (1985). Perhaps the most interesting aspect of these data is the fact that, overall, the psychopaths learned the task *better* than nonpsychopaths. This is illustrated most clearly with reference to Fig. 7, which shows learning curves (proportion of rewarded to punished responses) for both groups. It can be seen that the learning slope for psychopaths is steeper than for nonpsychopaths, and this impression was indicated by a Group × Blocks interaction. These data are consistent with previous psychophysiological studies showing that, when sufficiently motivated, psychopaths are capable of enhanced attentional processing (see Chapter 7) and indicate that psychopaths have latent learning abilities that could conceivably be capitalized on in clinical intervention studies (Raine & Dunkin, 1990). For example, programs that focus on reward-based interventions and that target attentional skills possessed by psychopaths may be more effective in changing behavior.

Kosson and Newman (1986) challenged the notion that psychopaths allocate a relatively large proportion of their attentional resources to matters of immediate interest (Hare, 1982) and reshaped earlier research in this area into an overfocusing hypothesis that predicted an extreme distribution of attentional resources, whereby too much attention is allocated to the primary task at the expense of a more peripheral task. Data from a divided attention task used on criminal psychopaths provided initial support for this hypothesis (Kosson & Newman, 1986). Furthermore, similar support for this position was obtained in undersocialized college students (Kosson & Newman, 1989). These initial findings are important in helping to provide some explanation of impulsive antisocial behavior in the context of an attentional impairment involving less attention to important events that occur at the same time as events of interest which are overfocused on, and they provide a potentially exciting initial basis for future cognitive information-processing perspectives on antisocial and psychopathic behavior.

V. GENERAL COMMENTS ON CLASSICAL CONDITIONING AND AVOIDANCE LEARNING DEFICITS IN CRIMINALS

The initial general conclusion of Lykken (1957) that psychopaths have a deficit in passive avoidance learning must be modified on the basis of more recent findings. Psychopaths do indeed learn poorly when the reinforcer is physical or social punishment, but they do appear to learn well when (1) their arousal is increased (Schacter & Latane, 1964), or (2) they are sufficiently motivated by financial incentives (Schmauk, 1970; Scerbo *et al.* 1990). The psychopath's deficit to physical punishment is nevertheless of key importance, since parental punishment invariably takes the form of physical and social punishment, especially in lower social class families.

The research of Quay and Newman also suggests that psychopathic and conduct-disordered subjects suffer from an oversensitivity to rewards, which may account for some aspects of antisocial behavior. In particular, the notion of response perseveration in antisocials particularly to rewards suggests that such individuals become "hooked" by rewards, regardless of associated punishment. Translated to the real world, the excitement and rewards associated with stealing and violence may be too irresistible for some adolescents, in spite of the negative consequences of such a lifestyle (parental disapproval, official sanctions). It may be that chronic underarousal is a precipitating factor that predisposes an individual to reward-seeking behavior. Although underarousal and reward dominance may be discrete, orthogonal concepts, it may be that the occurrence of both together may make an individual particularly susceptible to antisocial behavior. Future research that combines both reward dominance and CNS and ANS arousal would be capable of testing this prediction.

In spite of several demonstrated deficits, later studies indicate important exceptions to this rule, showing that there is some evidence suggesting that their performance can be *superior* when sufficiently motivated (Scerbo *et al.*, 1990). This notion could provide a building block for future intervention studies that make use of the psychopath's apparent capable learning under certain circumstances. The results of these more recent behavioral learning studies do not stand in isolation. As outlined in Chapter 7, several psychophysiological studies have also shown that psychopathic and other antisocial groups also show enhanced attentional processing under certain circumstances, usually involving short-term active attentional tasks, or where the subject is sufficiently motivated (Raine, 1989; Hare, 1982). Such findings have been observed both for autonomic variables (e.g., Hare, 1982) and also for event-related potentials (e.g., Raine & Venables, 1987, 1988b).

Regarding the research on classical conditioning, this has not been as progressive as research on avoidance learning, in that since 1981 there appear to have been few or no further studies of this topic. This may be because once a finding becomes reasonably well established, it becomes almost taken for granted and generates less interest. Alternatively, the cognitive shift that took place in psychology that started in the 1970s and developed into the 1980s may have reduced the level of interest in fundamental processes such as conditioning which originated in the earlier behavioralist tradition of psychology. Certainly these data provide good support for Eysenck's conditioning theory of crime (Eysenck, 1977). Given the strong findings from this research literature both before 1978 and after 1978, an important future step in conditioning research would be to index both of these two important forms of conditioning that would seem to play a crucial role in early socialization processes. Almost all studies have been carried out on adult antisocials. Future studies could ideally measure these learning processes at an earlier age to confirm their importance in the early learning of prosocial behavior.

VI. FEAR DISSIPATION AND SKIN CONDUCTANCE HALF-RECOVERY TIME IN CRIMINALS

Psychophysiology has played a critical role in research on both classical conditioning and instrumental learning deficits in antisocials and criminals. Data

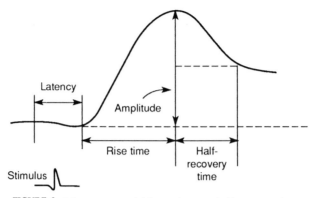

FIGURE 8 Measurement of skin conductance half-recovery time.

on another psychophysiological measure, skin conductance half-recovery time, has also provided the basis for another learning perspective on criminal behavior. Mednick (1975, 1977) has argued that fear dissipation plays a critical role in a child learning to inhibit an antisocial response. The key argument is that in order for a child to learn to passively avoid making an antisocial response, there has to be strong reinforcement. As discussed previously, the reduction in anxiety and fear that results from noncommission of the previously punished antisocial response represents an important reinforcer for passive avoidance learning. Mednick (1975, 1977) argues that the *rate* at which such anxiety or fear dissipates is of critical importance; the faster fear dissipates, the greater the level of reinforcement, since effective reinforcements must occur very soon after the response to be maximally effective.

On this basis, Mednick argued that antisocial subjects would show *slow* dissipation of fear, since slow dissipation of fear would result in reduced reinforcement for passive avoidance learning relative to fast fear dissipation. Mednick goes on to argue that SC half-recovery time indirectly indexes this process. This measure is the time it takes for an SC response to reduce to half of its amplitude (see Fig. 8). Because SC is a direct measure of autonomic nervous system activity, and because the ANS is intimately involved in emotions, Mednick argued that criminals should show *long* SC half-recovery time, indicating slow recovery from an emotional (fear) state.

In support of this theory, Mednick (1977) cited data from Siddle, Mednick, Nichol, and Foggitt (1976) that indicated that highly antisocial 16- to 18-year-old borstal boys (institutionalized offenders) had significantly slower SC half-recovery time to a 75-dB orienting stimulus relative to those with low antisocial ratings. Loeb and Mednick (1977) also found in a prospective study that slow SC recovery rate to an aversive UCS measured at age 15 was predic-

TABLE 2   Skin Conductance Half-Recovery Time (T2): Key Findings

Reference	Subjects	Findings
Significant findings		
Hinton et al. (1979)	Public offenders[a]	Long T2 (83 dB)
Levander, Schalling, Lidberg, Bartfai, and Lidberg (1980)	Undersocialized[b] criminals	Long T2 (93 dB)
Hemming (1981)	Criminals from good homes	Long T2 (100 dB)
Buikhuisen et al. (1985)	General crime	Long T2 (120 dB)
	Crimes of evasion	Long T2 (120 fB)
Buikhuisen, Eurelings-Bontekoe, and Host (1989)	Early crime	Long T2 (98 dB)
	Violence against police	Long T2 (98 dB)
Venables (1989)[c]	Fighting at age 9	Long T2 (75 dB) (at age 3)
Raine (1990)[d]	Psychopathic personality	Long T2 (65 dB)
Nonsignificant findings		
Raine & Venables (1988a)	Psychopaths	n.s.d.[e] (75 and 90 dB)

[a]Public offenders were recidivists committing offenses against strangers.
[b]Undersocialization measured by the socialization scale of the California Personality Inventory.
[c]SC measured at age 3 and related to fighting at age 9 in a normal sample.
[d]SC measured at age 15 and related to psychopathic personality also measured at age 15 in a group who had developed a criminal record by age 24 years.
[e]No significant differences.

tive of crime assessed 5–14 years later. Hare (1975) reported that while psychopaths did not differ from nonpsychopaths in SC half-recovery to orienting stimuli, psychopaths did show slower half-recovery time to a change in the orienting stimulus.

In order to further assess this theory, a review has been conducted of studies since 1977 that have reported SC half-recovery time in antisocial groups. Results from these studies are reported in Table 2. Out of the eight studies since Mednick's review in 1977 that report data on SC half-recovery time, seven observe statistically significant group differences in the predicted direction. Only one study that assessed adult institutionalized psychopaths (Raine & Venables, 1988a) failed to observe this effect. This may be because stimulus intensity was relatively low (90 dB) relative to other studies, which tended to use intensities of 100 dB or above, although some studies did obtain significant effects with lower stimulus intensities. Findings are not specific to aversive stimuli, since three studies find effects using intensities (65, 75, and 83 dB) not generally considered to elicit responses which, in psychophysiological terms, are viewed as "defensive." This finding is found in all types of antisocial behavior (antisocial children, young antisocial adults, public offenders, criminals characterized by low socialization scores) and in institutionalized as well as noninstitutionalized samples.

While the empirical data are supportive of Mednick's theory, several researchers have questioned how half-recovery time can be interpreted (Siddle & Trasler, 1981; Trasler, 1987). The key question concerns whether slow SC half-recovery time does in fact reflect the rate at which fear dissipates. Venables (1974) developed Edelberg's original view that recovery reflects "involvement in goal-oriented performance" (Edelberg 1972, p. 520) by suggesting that SC half-recovery time measured a dimension of "openness–closedness to the environment," with long recovery indexing closedness or "shutting out" of environmental stimuli. Similar interpretations have been made by Siddle and Trasler (1981). Such an interpretation would be consistent with other attentional deficits in antisocials and could explain undersocialization, since antisocials may be more proficient at screening out the aversive qualities of punishments. Again, these views are similar to those put forward by Hare (1978) on the basis of SC and HR responses in psychopaths.

Clear interpretations of the psychological significance of SC half-recovery time have remained elusive (see Edelberg, 1993, for a comprehensive discussion of mechanisms underlying SC amplitude and recovery), so it is difficult to fully evaluate SC recovery time data on criminals and consequently to more fully evaluate Mednick's theory. It is clear, however, from Table 2 that there are some strong empirical findings that require an explanation. It may be that fear dissipation may be more easily and acceptably measured by the time it takes SC levels to return to normal after a stressor, but no study to date appears to have measured this variable. It is suggested that future tests of Mednick's theory should measure this variable in conjunction with SC half-recovery time to help resolve this issue.

VII. INTELLIGENCE

By far the largest and perhaps the strongest evidence for cognitive deficits in criminals and delinquents comes from the hundreds of studies conducted on intelligence levels. The question of whether IQ deficits characterized delinquents and criminals used to be hotly disputed by sociologists such as Sutherland, whose influential and negative comments on the subject led to a virtual ban on the subject in textbooks (Hirschi & Hingelang, 1977; Binder, 1988). It took three important, large-scale studies by other sociologists (Hirschi, 1969; Wolfgang et al., 1972; Reiss & Rhodes, 1961) to dispel the myth that there was no link between IQ and crime and delinquency. More recent, detailed reviews of this very extensive literature may be found in Hirschi and Hingelang (1977), Rutter and Giller (1983), Wilson and Herrnstein (1985), Quay

(1987), and Binder (1988). These reviews agree in their main conclusions: Criminals and delinquents have significantly lower IQs than other control groups. This relationship also works in the other direction, that is, intellectually handicapped individuals are 3–4 times more likely to be registered for a criminal offense than those without such a handicap (Hodgins, 1992).

The extent of the IQ deficit in criminals is estimated by Wilson and Herrnstein (1985) as approximately 10 IQ points. Hirschi and Hingelang (1977) place the deficit in delinquents at approximately 8 points, as does Quay (1987). The strength of the link relative to more traditional variables researched by sociologists is indicated by the fact that Hirschi and Hingelang (1977) concluded in their review that IQ was as important in predicting juvenile delinquency as social class or race. IQ deficits cannot of course fully explain crime and delinquency, but by the same token their effects are not trivial (parenthetically, the average effect size for IQ is on the order of .5 to .7, less than the effect size of .84 calculated for low resting heart rate in Chapter 7).

Though criminals and delinquents have generally lower IQs than others, there is growing evidence for a more precise, specific deficit in IQ. IQ on the Wechsler Adult Intelligence Scale-Revised (WAIS-R) contains 11 different subtests and can be broken down into verbal IQ and performance (spatial) IQ. Studies that have analyzed verbal IQ separately from performance IQ have been reviewed by Quay (1987), who drew the following conclusions:

1. There is almost a universal finding that delinquents' verbal IQs are lower than their performance IQs.
2. This "verbal–performance" difference in IQ is not a perfect correlate of delinquency.
3. Aggressive, psychopathic individuals are most likely to show this verbal–performance difference.
4. The average verbal IQ in delinquents is about 10–12 points lower than average.

Similar conclusions are drawn in Wilson and Herrnstein's review of IQ and crime, although they estimate the verbal–performance discrepancy in criminals to be more on the order of 8 points, with performance IQs being almost normal and with verbal IQ accounting for the majority of the total IQ deficit.

Reviews to date have focused more on the empirical establishment of such deficits than on the explanation of them. One biological explanation would be that such verbal–performance discrepancies reflect relatively greater left hemisphere dysfunction in delinquents and criminals. Most individuals have a left hemisphere which, in relative terms, specializes in the type of information processing that underlies verbal skills, whereas the right hemisphere tends to specialize more in information processing that subserves visuospatial skills of the type that underlie performance IQ. As such, patients with lesions to the left hemisphere tend to have verbal IQ deficits, while patients with right hemisphere lesions tend to suffer from performance IQ deficits. Consequently, verbal IQ deficits in delinquents and criminals may be the result of left hemisphere dysfunction which may be caused by environmental factors such as head injury during childhood or trauma at birth. Alternatively, the deficit may be genetic in nature, since verbal IQ is partly heritable.

Returning to the main notions of generalized IQ deficits in delinquents and criminals, one important issue concerns whether such an association is an artifact of the fact that criminals and delinquents who are caught by the police have low IQs because they are less clever in evading detection. This possibility of an artifact between IQ and crime and delinquency is contradicted by the fact that those who admit to delinquency on self-report measures of delinquent acts in community samples (as opposed to institutional samples) are also found to have lower IQs. For example, Farrington (1989), in the Cambridge Study of Delinquent Development, found that low IQ measured at age 8 predicted self-report and official measures of violence at age 32. One study by Moffitt and Silva (1988) specifically addressed this issue by comparing a sample of caught delinquents in New Zealand with a group who had not been detected by police but who nevertheless scored just as high as the delinquent group on self-report measures of delinquency. Both groups had identical IQs, which were 6–7 points lower than those of the nondelinquent control group, thus indicating that detected delinquents do not have lower IQs than undetected delinquents.

Future research into IQ and crime needs to be less concerned with the empirical link between IQ and crime and more concerned with the *mechanisms* whereby low IQ leads to crime. There are several possible explanations for this link. Low IQ may predispose to school failure, which in turn results in negative attitudes and low self-esteem, which may later result in alienation and unemployment, which in turn may predispose to crime. Such an explanation is favored by Hirschi and Hingelang (1977) but does not account for the important fact that low IQ is related to conduct disorder early in life before school failure can result. For example, Richman, Stevenson, and Graham (1982) showed that links between low IQ and behavioral disturbances were present at age 3 years and did not develop over the following 5 years. Cognizant of such findings, Quay (1987) has speculated that low IQ early in life may make a child predisposed to poor parenting, which then in turn leads to troublesome behavior, which makes the child doubly disadvantaged by school age. Farrington (1991) speculates that the ability to manipulate abstract concepts may be the key factor underlying the IQ–crime link. Rutter and Giller (1983) raise the possibility that a negative early temperament may underlie both low IQ and antisocial behavior, but they admit that there has been no good empirical test of this hypothesis. At an empirical level, Schonfeld, Shaffer, O'Connor, and Portnoy (1988) tested three causal explanations linking IQ to conduct disorder in a 17-year longitudinal study (conduct disorder leads to school failure and low IQ, low IQ and cognitive deficits directly lead to conduct disorder, a third factor underlies both) and found evidence favoring the notion that cognitive deficits cause conduct disorder.

One "third factor" that may underlie both low IQ and delinquency and crime is early brain dysfunction. Early brain dysfunction or damage, due to either genetic or environmental factors (pregnancy complications, birth complications, early child abuse, and accidental head injury), may independently result in both low IQ and delinquency. The key question to be addressed is whether such brain dysfunction results in low IQ and crime that are causally independent of each other, or whether brain dysfunction leads to low IQ which then predisposes to crime along the lines suggested by other researchers emphasizing the educational and social implications of low IQ. Damage to the left hemisphere could, for example, result in specific verbal deficits resulting in poor communication skills in addition to general school failure, which in turn predisposes to crime. On the other hand, damage to the frontal lobes of the brain may directly predispose to crime because of the role played by this brain area in mediating planning versus impulsivity; the ensuing IQ deficits may be present but not have an etiological role in crime. Longitudinal studies that take valid measures of brain dysfunction early in life are needed to test such a hypothesis.

VIII. LEARNING DISABILITY

A concept related to low IQ is that of learning disability. Learning disability is a developmental disorder referring to those situations in which a child fails to develop to the level that would be expected given his or her intellectual ability. The lack of adequate development may be indicated by a deficit in a specific area, such as language, speech, arithmetic, reading, or motor skills. Such deficits are not attributable to a lack of education or other developmental disorders such as autism, mental retardation, or clearly delineated neurological disorders. Learning-disabled children are often (but not always) of above-average IQ but nevertheless manifest a specific learning deficit. As with crime and delinquency, boys are much more likely to have learning disabilities than girls (McGuiness, 1985), and there is also some evidence for a genetic predisposition to learning disabilities (Matheny, Dolan, & Wilson, 1976), although environmental factors such as anoxia at birth have also been implicated.

There is considerable empirical support for the notion that juvenile delinquents have a significantly higher proportion of learning disability than control groups. Reviews of this extensive literature on the link between delinquency and learning disabilities may be found in Brier (1989), Lombardo and Lombardo (1991), Scaret and Wilgosh (1989), Rutter (1987), Binder (1988), and Larson (1988). As one example supporting this link, Grande (1988) found that 62% of 12- to 18-year-old delinquents in a rural area showed learning disabilities, with reading and arithmetic skills at least 2 years below grade. Although there is strong evidence for the delinquency–learning disability link, it should also be emphasized that most learning-disabled adolescents do not become delinquent, in spite of the severe academic problems and frustrations that they frequently face (Lombardo & Lombardo, 1991). Furthermore, some subgroups of offenders are more likely to be learning disabled than others; for example, Nestor (1992) found that young murderers were more likely to have such a disability than older murderers.

As with the literature on IQ, the key issue facing this area is concerned with how the link is best explained, since the empirical link between delinquency and learning disability is relatively well established. The notion that learning disability leads to school failure which in turn leads to delinquency again features prominently in theoretical discussions of the link (Scaret & Wilgosh, 1989; Brier, 1989). Larson (1988) has also suggested that learning disability may contribute to the type of social–cognitive problem-solving deficits observed in antisocial children (see below). As with IQ, one could also speculate that third factors such as early brain dysfunction may underlie both delinquency and learning disabilities. Long-term developmental studies are again needed in this area to help tease out cause–effect relationships.

Biosocial theory may have important applications to the area of learning disability. Learning disability clearly does not cause delinquency in a direct fashion, since most learning-disabled children do not become delinquents and criminals. It could be hypothesized that while biological factors may in part determine learning disabilities, environmental factors play a key role in determining whether this biologically-based learning disability results in later delinquency. Learning-disabled children may suffer school failure and severe frustration but may be protected from the development of delinquency by being brought up in a supportive, caring, and intact family environment. Conversely, a more negative family environment may provide the crucial environmental trigger whereby learning disability translates itself into juvenile delinquency and then adult crime. Some current empirical data support this initial hypothesis. Grande (1988) found that most learning-disabled delinquents came from large families with divorced parents and came from a poorer economic and cultural background than nondelinquents. Further studies which additionally compare learning-disabled children from supportive homes with those from unsupportive homes over a long period of time are required, however, to test this interactive perspective.

IX. MORAL REASONING

One cognitive deficit that also bears relation to intelligence and that is related to learning disability in that it is viewed as a developmental deficit is the notion that delinquents and criminals have a cognitive impairment related to their ability to reason in moral terms. This cognitive, "moral reasoning" deficit affects their ability to tell right from wrong and to fully appreciate the rights and feelings of others.

This theory has its roots in the early work of Piaget (1948) and the later work of Kohlberg (1976), who both argued that full moral development is achieved by progressing through a developmental series of cognitive changes. In total Kohlberg postulated six cognitive stages: three primary stages (preconventional, conventional, postconventional) each divided into early and late substages. An individual must develop the skills of a lower moral stage before progressing to a higher stage. Individuals are thought to progress through these stages at different rates, with many not achieving the highest (postconventional) stage and others not developing beyond the preconventional stage.

Stage 1 is thought to develop during early middle childhood (4–8 years) and, together with Stage 2, is dominated by an individualistic, egocentric orientation. The early conventional stage (Stage 3), in contrast, is reflected by a larger social perspective and behavior directed to gaining approval, while the late conventional stage (Stage 4) is reflected in more complete conscience development and the meeting of agreed obligations. The critical division lies in the difference between Stage 2 (late preconventional) and Stage 3 (early postconventional) with respect to adolescents; delinquents were viewed by Kohlberg as having moral judgment arrested at the first two, preconventional stages, in contrast to nondelinquent adolescents, who would be more likely to have reached Stages 3 and 4 (Kohlberg & Freundlich, 1973).

Kohlberg's theory has been repeatedly tested by presenting hypothetical moral dilemmas to delinquent and control groups and categorizing their responses into the six stages. Detailed reviews of these studies may be found in Thornton (1988), Henggeler (1989), and Arbuthnot, Gordon, and Jurkovic (1987). Researchers are in general agreement that delinquents are indeed more likely to be characterized by preconventional moral thinking than controls. For example, of more than two dozen studies reviewed by Arbuthnot *et al.* (1987), only one failed to find delinquents to perform at a lower cognitive level than nondelinquents. More recent studies not included in these reviews also support this general finding (e.g., Chandler & Moran, 1990; Lee & Prentice, 1988).

As with IQ and learning disabilities, therefore, the basic finding of a link between delinquency and level of moral development is not in doubt. The more critical questions concern methodological and conceptual issues surrounding the interpretation of findings. Five criticisms can be identified in this research.

One criticism concerns the fact that verbal IQ has not been controlled for in most of these studies. Because higher levels of cognitive development require increasingly higher levels of intellectual abstraction, one would expect the two to be correlated. As such, studies need to demonstrate that level of cognitive development in Kohlberg's scheme is a variable that predicts delinquency over and above IQ in order for it to be a useful additional construct.

A second criticism is that, at one level at least, there is some degree of circularity in relating level of moral development to delinquency. Delinquents almost by definition are not particularly moral individuals, so to some extent it is not surprising that they exhibit low levels of moral reasoning.

A third conceptual issue concerns the possibility that delinquency causes low moral reasoning rather than low moral reasoning causing delinquency. Preconventional responses to moral dilemmas by a delinquent may well be a way of cognitively justifying delinquent behavior.

Fourth, most studies have been conducted using caught, institutionalized offenders. The few studies that have been conducted using self-report measures have all failed to observe a significant effect (Thornton, 1988) and consequently cast doubt on the generalizability of findings.

Fifth, some studies have looked at subtypes of offenders who show the lowest levels of cognitive moral reasoning. Thornton (1988) and Arbuthnot *et al.* (1987) both reviewed these studies and both concluded that psychopathic young offenders had the lowest moral reasoning stage of all offenders. The paradox with this finding is that, at a clinical level, psychopaths usually present as showing *good* moral reasoning when it comes to talking about hypothetical situations and about how one ought to behave (Cleckley, 1976). Because assessment of moral reasoning level is based on abstract reasoning skills about how one *ought* to behave in a given situation (as opposed to how one behaves in practice), psychopaths might be expected to actually excel in such a task. One possible explanation for this paradox is that studies on adolescents' and young adults' moral reasoning may not have employed valid and reliable measures of psychopathy.

Despite these criticisms, a strong case could be made for stage of moral reasoning being of etiological significance to delinquency and crime if interventions that raise moral ability level also result in changes in delinquent and criminal behavior. Many such interventions have been conducted on both delinquent and criminal populations. While they are generally successful in raising level of moral reasoning, few studies have examined the critical question of whether such changes have an impact on antisocial behavior. One notable study by Arbuthnot and Gordon (1986) provided training sessions on moral reasoning to students (grades 7 to 10) and found not only an increase in moral reasoning, but also better teacher ratings and reductions in police contacts relative to a control group. One year later, the experimental group showed significantly better teacher ratings relative to the control group, although surprisingly both experimental and control groups had zero scores on police and court contacts.

Regarding adult offenders, Thornton (1988) also reports results from several "just community" programs implemented in prisons in which the way that a prison unit is run is transformed by the inmates to create a more morally responsible environment. Such programs have been found to be effective in raising moral reasoning relative to control regimes, and they also change institutional behavior in the direction of reducing assaults and vandalism. However, only limited success has been reported to date for changes in recidivism rate when inmates are released into the community.

For both delinquents and criminals, therefore, the crucial unanswered question concerns whether manipulation of moral reasoning ability can result in long-term changes in antisocial behavior in juveniles and adults. Although there have been few attempts to address this question, this is a question which can be validly posed for more interventions on delinquents and criminals. Therefore, moral development theory and the consequent interventions are, on balance, still worth pursuing in spite of the criticisms raised earlier.

X. SOCIAL INFORMATION PROCESSING

Social information-processing theory provides a different perspective on violence than those described above, but it is at the same time heavily cognitive in terms of underlying processes. One early study on biases in information processing in violent subjects was carried out by Nachshon and Rotenberg (1977). In this study violent and nonviolent juvenile delinquents were shown stimuli that had previously been judged by 50% of a normal group to be violent stimuli and by 50% as nonviolent; hence these stimuli were classified as "ambiguous." One example consisted of a man who either looked like a robber with a mask shooting with a machine gun or a workman with goggles using a drill. Violent delinquents were found to be more likely to judge these ambiguous stimuli as violent, indicating that violent subjects were much more likely to view neutral events within a violence perspective.

A more detailed analysis has been developed by Dodge, who has proposed an influential social information-processing model of aggression (Dodge & Crick, 1990). This model lays out a sequence of five cognitive operations involved in the development of aggressive behavior: (1) encoding, (2) interpretation, (3) response search, (4) response decision, and (5) enactment. In the context of this model, the way a child responds to a problem social situation is a function of these five processing steps, with adept processing at each step being associated with competent processing. Conversely, deficient or biased processing is predicted to lead to deviant social behavior and aggression.

Dodge has conducted an impressive series of studies that lend support to this model. Aggressive children appear to use fewer environmental cues to mediate behavior (Dodge & Newman, 1981) and tend to interpret the behavior of a peer as more hostile (Dodge, 1980). They are also less capable in generating potential responses to conflict situations (Richard & Dodge, 1982) and are more likely to select passive and aggressive responses (Dodge, 1986). Dodge and Somberg (1987) found not only that aggressives had deficits in accurately interpreting others' intentions and a hostile attributional bias, but also that these deficits became exaggerated in conditions involving threat. The fact that aggressive children also show a bias to hostile attributions was not found to be a function of IQ, social class, or race (Dodge, Price, & Bachorowski, 1990).

Dodge (1990) has recently drawn a distinction between reactive and proactive aggression. This suggests that while some aggressive children are troubling to others and use aggression in a proactive way to meet their goals (proactive aggression), others react in an angry, volatile manner and are troubled by others (reactive aggression). This distinction is supported by similar distinctions made by ethologists and psychobiologists between "affective aggression," characterized by a high degree of autonomic arousal and "hot-blooded" frenzied anger, and "instrumental aggression," characterized by low autonomic arousal and a cold-blooded, reward-seeking form of aggression. Dodge (1990) speculates that these two forms of aggression have different neural substrates, have deficits in different stages of social information processing, and have different etiologies and developmental courses.

This two-factor model has received some support from factor-analytic studies (Dodge, 1990). While reactive aggressives at a young age are disliked by their peers, proactive aggressives are not necessarily disliked (Dodge & Coie, 1987). Proactive aggressives are also viewed as having leadership qualities and a better sense of humor than reactive aggressives (Dodge & Coie, 1987), while the use of instrumental aggression tends to be positively rated by peers (Price & Dodge, 1989). Dodge et al. (1990) has found that hostile attributional biases correlate positively with scores on reactive aggressive behavior but not with socialized aggressive behavior in 14- to 19-year-old offenders in a maximum security prison, indicating some specificity of these biases to interpersonal reactive aggression.

Although Dodge's theory has received extensive application to children and violent adolescents, an important question concerns whether it can also provide the basis for a fuller understanding of adult violence. A second question that Dodge himself has raised concerns whether the two types of aggression have separate or conversely a common neural basis. This question is of interest because it is rare for those working within a social–developmental perspective to attempt to integrate such a framework into biological research. Further research along these lines holds the promise of a potentially exciting integration between fundamental social–perceptual research and biological research into violence.

XI. SUMMARY

This chapter reviews evidence indicating that delinquents and criminals suffer significant cognitive dysfunction. There is good evidence that a wide variety of antisocial groups evidence poorer classical conditioning as measured by skin conductance activity, and there is some initial evidence suggesting that such deficits may be greatest in those from more benign social environments where the social push to antisocial behavior is weaker. Poorer classical conditioning may be linked to crime via poor conscience development. Early findings of avoidance learning deficits in psychopaths may have been a function of low arousal and lack of motivation, as later evidence suggests that psychopaths show good avoidance learning when sufficiently motivated. More recent studies have demonstrated that psychopathic criminals may be characterized by reward dominance and an inability to inhibit responses previously linked to rewards, and under certain circumstances they can show evidence of superior learning ability. Longer skin conductance half-recovery time in criminals has been interpreted as reflecting slow fear dissipation and hence poor reinforcement of passive avoidance responses, and although there remains a question of whether this skin conductance measure reflects fear dissipation, the strength of the empirical findings invites further enquiry.

One strong and consistent finding is that both delinquents and criminals have relatively lower IQs; the finding that verbal IQ in particular is compromised in antisocial groups is suggestive of left hemisphere dysfunction and a disruption of language processing. There are also good empirical links between learning disability and juvenile and adult offending, but not all learning-disabled children are delinquents, and it is hypothesized that a supportive home environment may protect a learning-disabled child from developing delinquency. Delinquents and criminals have moral reasoning ability arrested at the preconventional stage, but there are several methodological limitations to these data and intervention studies have not yet convincingly demonstrated that increasing moral reasoning skills also result in reduced antisocial behavior. Aggressive children may suffer from social information-processing deficits that contribute to the development of aggressive behavior.

It is concluded that there is little doubt that delinquents and criminals are characterized by cognitive deficits, but there is considerably more doubt as to how such relationships can be best explained, whether third factors mediate the cognitive dysfunction–crime relationships, and whether cognitive deficits are a cause or a consequence of crime. It is argued that the presence of such deficits in criminals helps to fulfill one of the more commonly cited and stronger definitions of disorder which invokes impairment in functioning/efficiency. It is hypothesized that antisocial and psychopathic individuals have "islets of cognitive skills" that have been neglected in the literature and that further research on their enhanced cognitive skills under certain circumstances may ultimately hold implications for intervention.

10 | Familial Influences

I. INTRODUCTION

Predisposition to crime has so far been viewed from the standpoint of genetic, biological, and cognitive factors. Psychologists frequently label these as "individual difference" factors, while criminologists frequently use the term "individual" factors. It is important to recognize, however, that there are strong social forces that also predispose an individual to crime, forces that are just as much beyond the immediate control of the individual as biological forces. Biological factors are often viewed in the context of "crime as destiny," but it is likely that social factors are just as much (if not more so) a destiny to crime as these biological predispositions. This particular viewpoint is rarely if ever expressed, but it is likely to be true nonetheless.

The next two chapters aim to briefly summarize the most important social factors that have been identified as predispositional factors for the development of criminal behavior. This chapter deals specifically with familial factors, while Chapter 11 will deal with extrafamilial factors such as peer influences, school factors, employment, urban living, and social class in addition to demographic factors. Detailed reviews of all social predispositional factors are beyond the scope of this book, which has instead aimed to elaborate on biological factors that have received less attention in the field. This should not be construed as suggesting that social factors are of less importance than biological factors in predisposing to crime. In fact, social factors have been much more extensively researched than biological factors, and as a result the evidence implicating some of these factors in crime is stronger than that for a number of the biological variables referred to earlier. Where possible, the reader is referred to more detailed reviews of the literature on specific social influences on crime.

This chapter will argue that negative family influences play an important role in predisposing children to later crime and delinquency. More of this research has dealt with delinquency given that long-term follow-up studies of crime have been more difficult to conduct, although findings of these latter studies will also be included. The literature linking later crime to having a criminal parent will be reviewed, followed by an analysis of the literature on child abuse as a precursor to later crime and violence. Three forms of parental absence and their influence on the child will be reviewed: (1) maternal deprivation, (2) death of a parent, and (3) divorce/separation. Family management and discipline variables that will be reviewed include parental supervision, punishment and discipline style, affective relationships, and engagement in joint activities. Finally, marital conflict and neglect of the child will be appraised as predispositions for later antisocial behavior.

In Chapter 1, reference was made to impaired social functioning as one potential characteristic or consequence of a disorder. Consequently, this chapter in conjunction with Chapter 11 will attempt to argue that criminals are socially impaired individuals characterized by poor relationships with their children and spouses, low socioeconomic status, and employment failure. It is likely that the roots of such social failures may in large part be a consequence of the social adverse conditions in which the precriminal grows up as a child, and in this sense there is a "cycle of social handicap" whereby some children growing up in a family with multiple social handicaps predisposing to crime go on to become criminals themselves and pass on this negative "social inheritance" to their children, thus perpetuating a cycle of crime.

II. PARENTAL CRIMINALITY

Probably one of the most important single predictors of whether or not a child will become criminal is whether the father of that child is criminal also. Many studies have demonstrated that antisocial and criminal parents have criminal and violent sons (Blumstein *et al.*, 1986; McCord, 1977; Reiss & Roth, 1993; Robins, 1979; Wilson & Herrnstein, 1985). Robins, West, and Herjanic (1975) found that children who had *both* parents criminal were at very high risk for later offending. Farrington (1989) found that family criminality was one of a set of six categories of variables measured at ages 8–10 years which were important predictors of later aggression and violence. Furthermore, parental conviction for crime was the only variable in a large series of variables measured at ages 8–10 in the Cambridge Study in Delinquent Development, which predicted adolescent aggression and teenage violence (Farrington, 1989). Similarly, Loeber and Dishion (1983) in an extensive review of studies of the predictors of delinquency found that, at age 10, parental criminality was highly predictive of later deliquency and that family criminality was the best predictor of recidivistic offending outside of behavioral variables such as early antisocial behavior. In a more recent review, Loeber (1990) again found parental criminality to be an important predictor of later delinquency.

The question of whether having criminal parents predisposes to crime is not in dispute. The more important issue concerns what are the specific processes whereby parental criminality results in crime and delinquency in the offspring. Although parental criminality is often viewed as a social variable, it must not be forgotten that it is also a genetic variable. Parental criminality may result in crime in the offspring not due to the social and experiential implications of having a criminal parent, but because the parent passes on genes to the offspring which predispose to crime. Findings from adoption studies reviewed in Chapter 3 provide some support for this view.

Nevertheless, it is very likely that the social interactional implications of having a parent criminal also help explain why criminal parents have criminal children. Parental criminality is a very broad variable that translates into a host of more specific social and experiential influences. Parents who are criminal are invariably bad parents, and this bad parenting, along with other social disadvantages of being criminal, translates itself into poor parental supervision, parental absence, poor discipline, child abuse and neglect, economic deprivation, city living, poor schools, and delinquent neighborhoods. These more specific factors will now be reviewed in turn. But beforehand, it should be noted that despite its importance as a predictor and potential etiological factor in crime, parental criminality still only accounts for a relatively small proportion of variance in the development of later crime and violence. For example, Farrington and Hawkins (1991) reported that while having a criminal parent by age 10 was predictive of a conviction between ages 10 and 20, this variable still accounted for less than 10% of the variance in offending, and it did not predict at all an early onset of offending. This serves to illustrate that no one single variable, social or biological, can provide a complete explanation of crime, and that instead crime is a multifactorial construct that can only be understood by considering multiple influences on crime.

III. CHILD ABUSE

There have been a large number of studies that have linked early physical and sexual abuse in childhood to later criminal and violent behavior. A comprehensive review of these studies was conducted by Widom (1989a) in an attempt to critically examine the "violence breeds violence" hypothesis, that is, that being physically abused in childhood in turn predisposes the individual to become a violent offender in adulthood. Widom identified seven different areas of research which bore on this question and noted a wide number of methodological flaws in these studies. Overreliance on self-report and retrospective data, inadequate documentation of child abuse, weak sampling techniques, and infrequent use of control groups constituted the main criticisms that future studies needed to address on this important issue.

The methodologically soundest study conducted to date on child abuse employed a large matched cohort design to study the effects of different forms of early abuse (defined by court reports) on later crime and violence (Widom, 1989b). Because this is probably the best study on child abuse conducted to date, it will be reported in some detail.

In contrast to most other retrospective studies that asked offender groups about their early social backgrounds, Widom's study directly assessed abuse from court data. All validated and substantiated cases of physical and sexual abuse and neglect that were processed in the county juvenile court in a Midwest metropolitan area were included in the study from 1967 to 1971. The experimental group of 908 abuse cases was matched as closely as possible on age, sex, and race with 667 nonabused controls. These subjects were then followed up into adulthood to a mean age of 26 years, and criminal histories of the subjects were assessed from law enforcement records.

Findings for crime in general indicated that abused and neglected children grow up to commit more crime than controls (28.6 versus 21.1%, respectively). For outcomes for violent offending in particular, key findings are illustrated in Fig. 1. When age, sex, and race were controlled, the physical abuse and the neglect groups were found to have higher rates of violent offending in adulthood. Widom (1989b) concluded that being abused or neglected as a child increased the individual's risk for criminal and violent behavior, though she also cautioned that most abused children do not become criminal. Widom also highlighted limitations in the study, consisting of the reliance on official data from a period when only a small proportion of abuse cases were likely

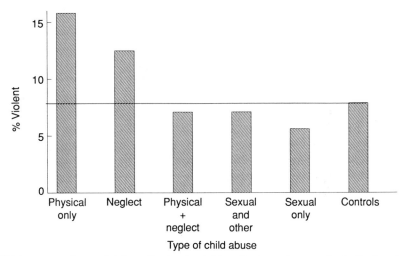

FIGURE 1   Increased rates of violent offending in adulthood in those who were physically abused or neglected as children (Adapted from Widom, 1989b).

to have been reported and the fact that subjects were largely of lower social class origin.

The "cycle of violence" hypothesis proposes that experiencing violence as a child predisposes the individual to becoming violent as an adult. Widom (1989b) commented that "the experience of child abuse and neglect has a substantial impact even on individuals with otherwise little likelihood of engaging in officially recorded criminal behavior" (p. 164). Interestingly, what is illustrated in Fig. 1 is that having been neglected represents almost as strong a predisposition to later violence as having been physically abused. Consequently, experiencing violence as a child does not in itself seem to be a critical factor; being neglected is sufficient to result in later violence. This is reinforced by the fact that sexually abused children had adult violence rates which were nonsignificantly *lower* than controls, even though this group included children who experienced "assault and battery with intent to gratify sexual desires." Those who experienced sexual abuse in combination with other abuse also had lower rates of adult violence than controls. Even more surprising is that a combination of physical abuse with neglect also resulted in rates of adult violence nonsignificantly *lower* than in normal controls. These data are not easily consistent with the cycle of violence hypothesis.

Figure 2, which has been drawn up from tabulated data in Widom (1989b), also illustrates some important caveats on the notion that violence begets violence. This figure expresses rates of later adult violence as a function of sex and race and illustrates the fact that experiencing abuse predisposes to

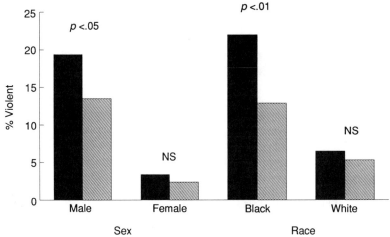

FIGURE 2   Child abuse significantly predisposes to adult violence only in males and blacks (Adapted from Widom, 1989b). ■, abused; ▨, control.

higher adult violence rates only in males and only in blacks. Effects for females and whites were not significant. Thus, the notion that "violence begets violence" only appears to apply to blacks and males in this study. These nonsignificant findings may in part be due to low base rates for violence in females and whites, and it may be that future studies capable of even larger sample sizes than those used by Widom may produce stronger effects. Alternatively, the fact that black children are five times more likely to die of physical abuse or neglect (Sedlak, 1991) suggests the possibility that blacks in Widom's study, when abused, were more severely abused relative to whites, and this may account for higher rates of later adult violence in this group.

An important alternative explanation to the notion that experiencing violence as a child predisposes to violence in adulthoood has been raised by DiLalla and Gottesman (1991). They suggest that because criminality in the families of abused children was not controlled for in Widom's study, the abused group may be more likely to have had criminal parents who passed on a genetic predisposition to crime to their offspring. Thus, genetic factors rather than experiential factors may underlie the child abuse–adult violence link. While this notion could account for raised rates of crime per se in the abused group, it cannot easily account for increased rates of violent crime for, as reviewed in Chapter 3, there is no good evidence to date that violent offending has a heritable basis.

A further important alternative that needs to be considered is that parents' abusive behavior to their children may be a result of aggressive, unruly behavior in the child. Consequently, child abuse may in part be provoked by unruly behavior in the child, whose antisocial behavior in childhood and adulthood may be caused more by biological factors and social factors rather than by child abuse.

It is clear that Widom's influential study on the cycle of violence represents more the beginning of a new phase of methodologically sounder studies into child abuse rather than a conclusive end to the debate on the cycle of violence. Clearly, the alternative explanations and limitations in the data outlined above need to be accounted for in future studies. These future studies may well be able to demonstrate that the experience of abusive violence in childhood does indeed, in and of itself, represent a predispositional factor toward violence in adulthood. Alternatively, such studies may indicate the need to incorporate biological predispositional factors in order to more fully understand the intergenerational transmission of violence (see Widom, 1991, and DiLalla & Gottesman, 1991, for a further discussion of this latter issue).

Such future studies could also usefully address several other important issues. For example, does being sexually abused in childhood lead to sexually abusive behavior in particular in adulthood? Dutton and Hart (1992) found that physically violent prisoners tended to report a specific history of childhood physical abuse, while sexual offenders reported childhood sexual abuse, suggesting that specific forms of abuse may be associated with specific forms of offending. In addition, can the mechanisms by which general neglect predisposes to adult violence be delineated more precisely? Does the *witnessing* of violence perpetrated in the family by itself predispose to later adult violence, as opposed to the *experiencing* of violence as a child? The finding by Lewis *et al.* (1988) that 12 of 14 juveniles condemned to death for capital offenses had been brutally and physically abused might suggest that experiencing serious physical abuse may predispose to serious violence, and there have been some reports that experiencing paternal violence, but not witnessing violence in the home, is linked to violent behavior in adolescent males (Truscott, 1992), findings that are not consistent with a modeling or observational learning interpretation of the abuse–violence link.

To what extent is later adult violence a result of the family disruption, labeling, and stigma associated with cases of official child abuse rather than the experiencing of violence in childhood? Child abuse is clearly a very important area of research requiring further intensive investigation (Reiss & Roth, 1993), but although the child abuse–adult violence relationship is intuitively plausible, critical scrutiny is still required in this literature.

IV. PARENTAL ABSENCE

The absence of one or both parents from the home has for a long time been associated with a raised incidence of conduct problems and eventually crime in the offspring. There are at least three ways in which this lack of parenting may arise: (1) early maternal deprivation, (2) death of a parent, or (3) divorce/ separation. This review will indicate that not all cases of parental absence have been consistently associated with risk for later antisocial behavior.

A. Maternal Deprivation

Bowlby's book on the home life of 44 juvenile thieves (Bowlby, 1946) has been influential in the controversial linking of early maternal deprivation to psychopathology in general and crime in particular. Bowlby (1946, 1969) has argued that a continuous and loving relationship between mother and infant is essential for normal personality development and the ability to form normal interpersonal relationships. Bowlby's key point in his case studies of 44 juvenile thieves was that prolonged separation from the mother early in life (and hence the absence of a warm, continuous, and intimate relationship between the mother and infant) resulted in juvenile delinquency and what he termed "affectionless psychopathy." Such affectionless psychopathy may be characterized by an uninhibited, attention-seeking, friendship-seeking individual who lacks guilt feelings, is unable to maintain interpersonal relationships, and commits offenses.

Rutter (1982) has provided an extensive reassessment and critical evaluation of the notion of disruption of the mother–infant bond in affectionless psychopathy. His critical points may be summarized as follows:

1. Affectionless psychopathy is not so much associated with prolonged separation as with *multiple* changes of the mother figure or home in infancy and childhood. Rutter based this conclusion on the fact that such frequent changes in the mother figure occurred in 7 of the 14 cases (50%) of Bowlby's thieves who were affectionless psychopaths, but in only 3 (10%) of the remaining 30 thieves. Furthermore, in the case of two of the other affectionless psychopaths, they had each spent 9 months in the hospital without any visits from parents.

2. The failure to form a bond is more critical than suffering a disruption to an existing bond. Rutter based this conclusion on the fact that affectionless psychopathy does not result in young children who have developed bonds but who have them broken or stressed by prolonged separation (e.g., hospitalization). Such failure to form a bond may be a result of repeated and persistent breaks or changes in the mother figure.

3. The key emphasis on the mother is misleading. Rather, the important factor is whether the child is able to form a bond with any person early in life, irrespective of the person's relationship to the child.

4. There may be a "critical period" during which the child must bond with another individual to develop normally. Rutter speculated that this critical period begins at approximately 6 months and ends at about 2 to 3 years of age. The end of this critical period is suggested by findings that fostered children were more likely to form a bond with their new foster parents if they had

spent less than 3 years in an orphanage compared to those who were institutionalized for longer (Goldfarb, 1945).

The focus of discussion on links between maternal deprivation and psychopathy and crime has been centered on the opportunity afforded to the child to engage in attachment formation. Conversely, there has been virtually no discussion of an alternative possibility, that the infant has full opportunity to interact with a good care-giving figure but still does not form a bond. Some of Bowlby's affectionless psychopaths did not suffer early, repeated separations from the mother; these individuals may have instead possessed some constitutional differences that made it difficult for them to form attachments with a consistent and loving mother figure. As such, biological factors might play a role in predisposing to lack of early attachment. It is also conceivable that such factors might interact with the quality of care giving. Although the child may not be physically separated from the care giver, the quality of care giving may not be good; combined with a difficult or disinhibited temperament, this may predispose to affectionless psychopathy.

Intuitively it might be expected that early maternal deprivation, with the hypothesized effects of antisocial behavior, attention seeking, lack of guilt, and poor interpersonal relationships, would be particularly characteristic of psychopathic criminals since these features also characterize the psychopath (Cleckley, 1976). There is no clear answer to this question however, largely because there have been few good studies that have provided a good test of this specific hypothesis. Hare (1970) reviewed the early literature and noted the weakness of reliance on retrospective data. Cleckley (1976), in his influential book outlining case studies of psychopaths, argued that psychopaths were not particularly characterized by early deprived family lives, although this may be due to the fact that Cleckley's samples were biased to more middle-class psychopaths. Bartol (1991) provides a short but useful review of this literature, but again, there appear to be few substantive studies that can adequately address this issue. Nevertheless, the possibility of a greater degree of early care-giving loss in psychopathic as opposed to other nonpsychopathic criminals is a reasonable hypothesis worthy of future investigation.

Similarly, there has been surprisingly little recent research on lack of bonding and its effect on later delinquency and crime. This may be partly due to the fact that it is difficult to make accurate observational assessments of the nature and quality of early attention and care given by the caretaker to the infant and then to follow such children up for 20–30 years to measure outcome for crime. Conversely, a great deal of attention has been given to factors that may cause disruption of family life, specifically death of a parent and divorce/separation.

B. Parental Death

The loss of one parent through death is a tragic event which causes severe emotional distress and which can result in economic and social hardships on a family in addition to reduced parental supervision of the children. One might easily imagine therefore that such an event would strongly predispose to later delinquency and crime. Although there is some evidence to support this proposition, it seems that the effect is relatively weak, if not absent. Wadsworth (1979) found that rates of later offending in homes broken by death were 16%, compared with 14% of those from unbroken homes, a difference of only 2 percentage points. Robins (1979), on the other hand, found that rates of later adult psychopathy in children from families broken by death or hospitalization were 2 percentage points *lower* than rates for those in the intact home control group.

West and Farrington (1973) in a prospective study found that children from homes broken by death were no more likely to offend than those from unbroken homes. Similarly, Power, Ash, Schoenberg, and Sorey (1974) found that boys aged 11–14 years from broken homes making their first court appearance were no more likely to commit a further offense than boys from intact homes. Reviews of the literature have also concluded that parental death does not seem to be a significant predisposition toward delinquency and crime (e.g., Rutter & Madge, 1976; Rutter, 1982). It seems clear that the effect of parental death on the child is an adverse event which nevertheless can be compensated for in most cases, at least with respect to outcome for crime. In contrast, the effects of divorce and separation on the child appear to be substantially worse.

C. Divorce/Separation

The notion that a home broken by divorce or separation results in delinquency and crime is one of the earliest social factors put forward as an explanation for offending, a notion that precedes Bowlby's attachment theory by over two decades. Slawson (1923) found that levels of broken homes in delinquents were twice those found in controls, while Burt (1925) found that 61% of delinquents came from broken homes compared to 25% of controls. Similar rates to Burt's were found by Glueck and Glueck (1950) in a study of 500 delinquents and 500 controls.

These early findings have also been largely substantiated in later studies. For example, a large birth cohort study by Wadsworth (1976) in Great Britain showed that in those who grew up to be convicted of serious violent offending as adults (e.g., grievous bodily harm, wounding, rape, buggery), the rates of broken homes (separation before age 4) in adult violent offenders were twice those in nonoffenders. In another English longitudinal study, Farrington (1989) showed that those who had been separated from their parents before the age of 10 for reasons other than death or hospitalization were more likely as adults to have convictions for violence. Reviews by Offord *et al.* (1978) and McCord (1982) confirm a link between parental divorce/separation and later delinquency and crime. The extent of the evidence for a link between divorce/

separation and crime can be gauged by an extensive review by Ellis (1988), who found that of a total of 116 studies, 97 reported a significant positive relationship between crime and broken homes, whereas 19 reported no significant effect.

In spite of what appears to be a strong empirical basis for the notion that divorce and separation can directly contribute to delinquency and crime, there are paradoxically as many concerns and questions about this body of literature as any other as related to crime. Some of these considerations are as follows:

1. Divorce/separation is not a *strong* predictor of delinquency and crime. Reviews of predictors of delinquency find that parental absence was only a weak predictor relative to the much stronger effects for other family variables such as poor discipline and poor parental supervision (Loeber & Stouthamer-Loeber, 1987; Loeber, 1990). Similarly Farrington (1987), in drawing conclusions on the most important predictors of crime, does not include this variable in his list of five main influences.

2. Divorce/separation may play a greater role in predisposing to more serious delinquent and criminal offending. Ellis (1988) found that nonsignificant findings tended to be present in studies of minor forms of delinquency, whereas the strongest effects were observed for the more serious and victimful offenses. Similarly, Blumstein *et al.* (1986) concluded that self-report studies that measure nonserious offenses have produced only small and inconsistent relationships between divorce/separation and delinquency. In contrast, findings for serious adult crime are different, as illustrated by the fact that Farrington (1991) found separation from parents at age 10 to be a significant predictor of both adult violent offending and adult recidivistic criminal behavior. It may also be that parental absence may help explain the continuity of aggression over time; Loeber, Tremblay, Gagnon, and Charlebois (1989) for example found that children classified as stable high fighters (whose fighting persists over time) were more likely to come from one-parent families.

3. Divorce may be a more important factor in predisposing to crime when it leads to additional changes in family relationships. A recent longitudinal study by Mednick *et al.* (1990) showed that divorce did not lead to later crime in the children when it was followed by family stability, whereas divorce followed by additional changes in family constellations significantly increased risk for crime. Similarly, Fergusson, Horwood, and Lynskey (1992), in a longitudinal study of a New Zealand birth cohort of 1265 children, found that exposure to family change taking place from birth to age 10 years did not lead to increased rates of offending at age 13 when there was no parental discord in the family.

4. Divorce and separation may not predispose to crime and violence in some groups. For example, McCord (1982) points out that crime rates are not higher for blacks who come from broken homes and cites three studies that

fail to find such effects in blacks. Wilson and Herrnstein (1985) also make the same point in their review of the broken families–crime link in blacks and whites. An additional study by Farnworth (1984) not cited in these two reviews also failed to observe an increase in delinquency in blacks from broken homes. Such findings appear to limit the explanatory significance of this variable to white crime.

5. Divorce may in some cases have the opposite effect of improving problem behavior in children. Rutter and Giller (1983) comment that when divorce leads to a cessation of marital discord, it can at times lead to better family relationships and reductions in conduct disorders in children. A violent, alcoholic, criminal father leaving the family could be a gain rather than a loss. Clearly, the nature and quality of the prior relationships between the child and the exiting parent are important factors in determining whether divorce will predispose to crime and delinquency in the children.

6. Remarriage, and therefore reestablishment of family intactness, is more likely to have deleterious rather than beneficial effects on outcome in the children. McCord (1982) reviews studies which indicate that broken homes that remain broken are less likely to result in crime and delinquency in the children than homes in which the missing parent is replaced by a surrogate. Given well-known conflicts between stepparents and their stepchildren, this may not be surprising. For example, Daly and Wilson (1985) report that preschoolers living with one natural and one stepparent were 40 times more likely to become child abuse cases than children living with two natural parents. Wadsworth (1979) also found that remarriage was associated with an increased risk of offending. Family intactness after a period of the home being broken is not therefore always a desirable feature.

7. Intact homes in which there is a lot of parental conflict appear to be more likely to result in crime and delinquency than broken homes. Wilson and Herrnstein (1985) and McCord (1982) review a number of studies which indicate that unhappy, intact homes produce more delinquents than broken homes. It seems therefore that discord and conflict are more critical variables than whether a home is intact or broken.

8. Degree of affection in mothers may be a crucial variable in mediating the broken home–crime link. McCord (1982) assessed degree of maternal affection shown by mothers to their children ($N = 253$) aged 5–13 years in a counseling program in which counselors visited homes and collected extensive data on family interactions. Subjects were then followed up for 30 years and assessed for outcome for serious crime from court records. Outcome for crime as a function of home intactness and affectionate behavior in the mother is illustrated in Fig. 3. It can be seen that whether the home was intact or broken made little difference in outcome for serious adult crime if the mothers were affectionate to their sons. Furthermore, sons with unaffectionate mothers were much more likely to become criminal ($p < .04$, $p < .0009$). Importantly, mother's affection interacted with home intactness in that the highest levels of

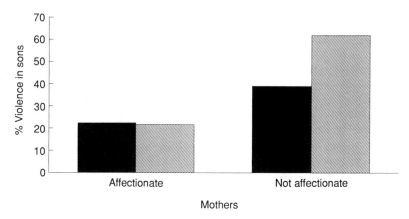

FIGURE 3   The effect of unaffectionate mothers on serious crime in sons as a function of broken homes (Adapted from McCord, 1982). ■, Intact homes; ▨, broken homes.

crime were found for those sons who had both a broken home and an unaffectionate mother. This study clearly illustrates the key importance of the quality of the home life (and mothers' level of affection in particular) in predisposing to later crime. Whether the home is intact or broken seems to be only a weak indicator of this more critical variable.

9. Age at which the home is broken does not appear to be a major factor. For example, West and Farrington (1973) found that homes broken at an early age were not more likely to lead to later delinquency than homes broken later in life.

10. The broken home does not seem to be independent of other factors such as social class and criminality in the father. B. Mednick *et al.* (1987) showed that although divorce was associated with young adult crime, a path analysis that controlled for the effects of social class and father's criminality led to an abolition of the effect for divorce. Data such as these suggest that divorce may only be linked to crime by virtue of the fact that it is a social variable correlated with other, potentially more important factors. This is an important factor which will be returned to shortly.

These caveats reveal some of the difficulties in drawing simple conclusions from the literature on divorce/separation and later delinquency and crime. If divorce/separation does play an albeit small, casual role in predisposing to later crime, what are the mechanisms by which this happens? Several possibilities come to mind.

The first is that the conflict and discord associated with the separation may have a negative impact on the child. This could take place at a number of levels: (1) Such conflict could interfere with good parenting skills such as consistent discipline; (2) aggressive encounters between parents could act as a model for the child to act out hostility and aggression at school, leading on to conduct disorder and delinquency; (3) children could develop conduct problems as a way of distracting parents from their own problems, or as a "cry for help"; and (4) conflict could have a negative impact on the love and care children receive from their parents, which could in turn negatively impact that child's relationships with others. Because parental discord and conflict could precede divorce by a considerable period of time, the impact of such discord could in theory be considerable. A second possibility is that it is the *post-divorce* environment that negatively affects the child. The absence of one parent could potentially reduce the ability of the remaining parent to adequately supervise the children and, as will be discussed below, parental supervision seems to be intimately linked with delinquency. Furthermore, there could be socioeconomic consequences of divorce whereby the children may have to live in a poorer, more criminogenic neighborhood with associated negative peer influences. The remaining parent will have much less time to spend in joint activities with the child, again negatively affecting social relationships.

In spite of the myriad of ways in which divorce and separation could contribute to later crime, the possibility has to be considered that there is no etiological link between divorce and crime. In discussions of the extensive empirical research on crime, it is easy to forget basic questions such as cause–effect relationships and to too easily make the assumption of causality from simple relationships. Rather than divorce causing delinquency and crime, it is feasible that delinquency causes divorce. Having conduct-disordered, unmanageable, and delinquent children could severely damage a marriage which may for other reasons be at risk for break up. At the least, delinquency could make a significant contribution to divorce and separation.

A perhaps more important consideration is that a third factor underlies and explains the link between divorce and crime, such that crime and divorce are causally unrelated to each other. This possibility was alluded to in the study by B. Mednick *et al.* (1987) which found that after taking into account father's criminality, the relationship between broken homes and later crime was abolished. It could be that father's criminality leads to both divorce and criminality in the offspring, and that offspring criminality is caused by either social predispositional variables such as modeling of father's antisocial behavior or biological predispositions that are inherited from the father.

An important study by Lahey, Hartdagen, Frick, McBurnett, Connor, and Hynd (1988) illustrates that this is a likely possibility at least with respect to conduct disorder. Divorce and presence of antisocial personality disorder were assessed in the fathers of children diagnosed with conduct disorder in addition to children with problems other than conduct disorder (e.g., anxiety, depression). Fathers with antisocial personality were more likely both to be divorced and to have conduct-disordered children. Critically, there was no link between divorce and conduct disorder where the father was not antisocial. As pointed out by Lahey *et al.* (1988), if parental antisociality had been ignored, it would have been concluded that there was an overall significant relationship between divorce and conduct disorder (62% conduct-disordered in divorced homes versus 34% in intact homes). Lahey *et al.* (1988) concluded that the link between divorce and separation was an artifact of antisocial personality disorder in the parents. Similarly, Robins (1978) concluded that broken homes are only correlated with outcome because antisocial parents are more likely to get divorced and produce antisocial children.

Taking all points together, it seems that the link between divorce/ separation and crime may not be as consistent as it seems and may be mediated almost entirely by a number of other important variables, including quality of family relationships and parental criminality.

V. FAMILY MANAGEMENT AND DISCIPLINE

As has become apparent from the preceding section, the quality of family life has been repeatedly implicated in the development of crime and violence (Reiss & Roth, 1993). It is unusual for hard-core criminals to come from "good" families and, when they do, their cases stand out as unusual and different. The ways in which parents interact with their children probably play a critical role in the development of criminal behavior. There have been extensive efforts over the years to identify which specific features of parenting contribute to the development of crime and delinquency, and these efforts have been successful in identifying parental supervision, parental discipline, and parental involvement with the child as being of major importance.

A. Parental Supervision

Poor parental supervision of children is probably one of the best individual family predictors of later crime and delinquency. This is illustrated repeatedly in reviews of development and risk factors for juvenile delinquency (Loeber, 1990; Loeber & Stouthamer-Loeber, 1986) that ordered individual predictor variables in terms of their predictive power. The measure of prediction accuracy used was the Relative Improvement Over Chance (RIOC), an index that ranges from 0 to 100; all values in excess of 0 indicate an increase in prediction over chance. Poor supervision had a higher RIOC than any other social predictor of delinquency, with its value of 51 comparing with values of 31 for parental uninvolvement, 31 for parental criminality, and 21 for parental absence. These comparisons support the relative strength of parental supervision not only as a predictor of general delinquency, but as a factor of potential etiological significance. A similar conclusion is drawn by the National Academy of Sciences' Panel on Research on Criminal Careers (Blumstein *et al.*, 1986), which stated that "in the panel's review of the existing literature of family influences, parental supervision, adult–child interaction, and other aspects of family management emerged as factors likely to be associated with participation in serious criminal behavior among children" (p. 43).

Both cross-section and longitudinal studies have noted the significance of parental supervision for later delinquency (e.g., Loeber & Schmaling, 1985; West & Farrington, 1973). Furthermore, parental monitoring relates to delinquency assessed by self-report as well as by official measures of crime (Wilson, 1980; West & Farrington, 1973). One study by Cernkovich and Giordano (1987) also found that poor parental supervision and control predicted self-report delinquency, particularly in single-parent families. Poor parental control has also been specifically linked to physical aggression both at home and at school (Loeber & Dishion, 1984).

While there has been more direct research on supervision and delinquency, poor supervision also predicts adult crime. Specifically, longitudinal studies by McCord (1979) and Farrington (1979, 1987) have found poor parental supervision to be a predictor of adult crime. Snyder and Patterson (1987) also review studies that indicate poor parental supervision is related to recidivistic offending and commission of more serious crimes as adults. Poor parenting may be a particularly important factor determining crime in those whose antisociality starts at an early age (before age 14), but not in those whose antisocial behavior starts after age 14 (Patterson & Yoerger, 1993).

It is not difficult to see why the construct of parental supervision should be so closely linked to crime and delinquency. Close supervision and monitoring of the child's activities involves parents setting rules for the child, monitoring whether these rules are obeyed, checking on the child's whereabouts, and supervising TV watching (Snyder & Patterson, 1987). The implications of such monitoring are that the child is likely to be denied access to delinquent peers and violent TV, to be given consistent punishment for committing antisocial acts, and to have less opportunity for school truancy. Good parental supervision is also likely to be correlated with other behaviors, such as time spent with the child and interest in the child's activities and schooling, which themselves promote prosocial behavior. Seen in this light, parental supervision is not so much one isolated variable as one general construct that encapsulates many of the features of good childhood socialization practices.

An important question that has not received a great deal of attention concerns whether poor parental monitoring relates to delinquency independently of other social factors. One step in the direction of establishing that this is the case has been taken by Weintraub and Gold (1991), who found that the relationship between poor parental monitoring and delinquency largely held up even when factors such as age, sex, perceptions of friends' delinquencies, and warmth of parent–child relationships were controlled. Future studies should attempt also to control for other important social variables to assess the independent contribution of parental monitoring to later delinquency and crime.

Although parental supervision appears to be a good correlate of crime and delinquency, and while it may be relatively independent of some other predisposing variables, it would be important to demonstrate that poor parental supervision leads to crime and delinquency in children whose parents are *not* criminal. It could be that adult criminality leads *independently* to both poor parenting and the development of criminal behavior in the child in much the same way that has been shown for conduct disorder and criminality (see previous discussions). To date, there do not appear to be studies that have assessed for this possibility. Demonstrating that poor supervision predisposes to crime and delinquency independent of parental antisocial behavior would help establish the etiological role of poor supervision with respect to crime.

B. Punishment and Discipline Style

The early literature on family influences on offending stressed the role of harsh physical punishment as an important predispositional variable for the development of crime and delinquency. Early studies by Glueck and Glueck (1968) and Gold (1970) emphasized the importance of harsh physical punishment and threats and, as noted by Snyder and Patterson (1987), such parental use of punishment has in the past been associated with both self-report and official delinquency measures. More recent studies also confirm the influence of harsh discipline. Harsh parental discipline measured at age 8 and an authoritarian style of parenting measured at age 10 have both been found by Farrington (1989) to predict violent criminal offending measured at age 32.

The more recent literature has, however, tended to emphasize the importance of erratic and inconsistent use of punishment by parents as predisposing to crime and delinquency. For example, the Panel on Research on Criminal Careers referred to previously singled out consistent, strict discipline as one of the most important aspects of parenting related to *low* rates of crime (Blumstein *et al.*, 1986). Physical child abusers in particular tend to have had parents who used punishment in unpredictable ways (Milner *et al.*, 1990).

Much of the stimulus for this view has stemmed from Patterson's influential direct observational studies of parent–child behavior measured in the home environment (Patterson, 1982). Specifically, it was demonstrated that parents of antisocial children did not set clear rules and penalties and did not consistently punish their children, but rather "nattered" to their children and intermittently administered punishments. This "nattering" communicates a general feeling of impatience, irritation, and anger to the child, but not necessarily the specifics of what the child had done wrong and why punishment was being given. The frequent punishments and "natterings" are hypothesized to form the basis for frequent coercive interchanges between parent and child and take the place of more warm and affectionate interchanges. Snyder and Patterson (1987) also argue that two different disciplinary styles characterize parents of antisocial children: an "enmeshed" style in which even trivial behaviors are punished, and a "lax" style in which few antisocial behaviors are punished.

In summary, therefore, it seems that inconsistent and either overly frequent or overly infrequent use of punishment rather than overly harsh punishment per se may be more important in predisposing to delinquency and crime (see also reviews by Henggeler, 1989, and Snyder & Patterson, 1987). Such findings would be supportive of learning theory approaches to crime, which emphasize the importance of consistent punishment for extinguishing antisocial behaviors, as opposed to inconsistent punishment which would, according to the partial reinforcement extinction effect, be inefficient in extinguishing undesirable behaviors. The fact that delinquents are more likely to be punished inconsistently might also be expected to nurture a perception that reinforcements are independent of behavior, and hence may nurture an external locus of control (Raine, Roger, & Venables, 1982).

C. Affective Relationships

As might be expected from Patterson's work which links frequent coercive parent–child interchanges with the development of antisocial behavior, the affective or emotional relationship that exists between parents and their children also appears to be predictive of antisocial behavior. Reviews of this area (e.g., Henggeler, 1989) have concluded that a wide range of negative affect characterizes the families of delinquents, including low levels of warmth and affection and high levels of hostility. An overview by Snyder and Patterson (1987) cites findings from cross-sectional studies which show that parents of delinquents are less supportive and affectionate and more rejecting and negativistic. Others have argued that emotional abuse may be even more critical than factors such as harsh parental discipline in predisposing to later delinquency (Brown, 1984). One recent study by Vissing, Straus, Gelles, and Harrop (1991) showed that experiencing frequent verbal aggression from parents is associated with delinquency in children irrespective of age or sex of the child.

Lack of warmth and acceptance also seem to be important affective features in the family lives of delinquents, criminals, and violent offenders (Reiss & Roth, 1993). Lack of affection and warmth was found to be predictive of crime in one longitudinal study by McCord (1990). Physical child abusers tend to have parents who lack warmth and are rejecting and hostile (Milner *et al.*, 1990), and they are less likely to report having had a caring adult/friend in their childhood (Milner, Robertson, & Rogers, 1990).

Snyder and Patterson (1987) comment that the proportion of variance in antisocial behavior accounted for by such factors appears to be somewhat less than that for punishment and discipline factors. Affective features of the family environment may nevertheless become more powerful predictors of delinquency and crime when employed in conjunction with other family factors. For example, the combination of lack of affection and erratic disciplinary practices was a particularly strong predictor of later crime in McCord's longitudinal study (McCord, 1990).

D. Joint Activities, Acceptance, Trust, and Support

If parents erratically punish their children, engage in prolonged hostile encounters, and are generally emotionally cold and hostile, then they would be less likely to be accepting and supportive and to spend time in joint activities with their children. Not surprisingly, these latter factors have also been found to be predictive of the absence of delinquency. Sense of belonging and involvement in family activities were found by Canter (1982) to be negatively associated with delinquency, while lack of parental care and trust have been related to higher self-report delinquency scores (Cernkovich & Giordano, 1987). Conversely, parental rejection has been found to be a nontrivial variable in relation to serious delinquency (Loeber, 1990). Low levels of both maternal and paternal acceptance have been related to aggressive behavior at home and school (Loeber & Dishion, 1984).

It may be that parent–child engagement in leisure activities may be a particularly important predictor of crime. Farrington and Hawkins (1991) report that low parental involvement with boys in leisure activities measured at age 11 was the best predictor of early onset of criminal offending (ages 10–13). Interestingly, this variable was also the best predictor of persistent offending from ages 21–32; the strength of this effect can be gauged by the fact that it was a much better predictor of later offending than self-report delinquency measured at age 18 and is illustrative of the fact that childhood events can be better predictors of adult offending than teenage behavior.

This latter finding is of particular interest because it is not intuitively obvious. Intuitively, it makes perfect sense that inconsistent discipline and cold, rejecting parental behavior should make for a delinquent child, whereas lack of shared leisure time would appear on the surface to be a much more benign variable bearing little relation to later crime. It may be that this variable is so powerful because it manages to encapsulate a wide number of other familial variables: If parents and children do not share leisure time together, this may be symptomatic of a whole host of other problems including negative affect, family conflict, lack of support, time spent with delinquent peers, paternal absence and criminality, neglect, and lack of early attachment. This variable needs to be looked at more closely in future studies that aim to predict adult offending on the basis of early behavior.

VI. MARITAL CONFLICT

Marital conflict research represents an important area for understanding not just later violence in the offspring but also for understanding the interpersonal mechanisms underlying the perpetration of family violence (Margolin, John, & Gleberman, 1988; Margolin, John, & O'Brien, 1989). The earlier section on divorce and separation made reference to the notion that the conflict that arises before and during the separation represents the key mechanism underlying any divorce–crime link. An important question, therefore, concerns whether simple exposure to parental conflict, independent of whether parents eventually separate, can in itself predispose to later crime.

There is good evidence from longitudinal studies for a link between parent–parent conflict and the development of both crime and delinquency. Farrington (1989) found that parental disagreement measured at age 8 predicted convictions for violent offenses at age 32. McCord (1979) similarly found that parental conflict predicted and preceded delinquency even after controling for socioeconomic level. Cross-sectional studies reviewed by Snyder and Patterson (1987) also confirm the link between parental conflict and juvenile delinquency.

Although the link between parental discord and crime and delinquency is not in doubt, there is doubt regarding the mechanism or mechanisms by which parental conflict translates into future crime in the offspring. One scenario is that marital conflict *directly* leads to delinquency and aggression; children who observe fighting and quarreling in their parents might use their parents' behavior as a model for problem solving with their peers and indeed with their own parents. Alternatively, marital conflict may *indirectly* predispose to crime; parent–parent conflict would be expected to result in a reduction in time for parent–child activities, time to consistently discipline the child, and time for supervision. Furthermore, a reduction in a loving relationship between parents might be expected to result in less love, affection, and emotional support for the child, who might then develop antisocial behaviors as a method for gaining parental attention. A third scenario could be that the parent conflict–crime relationship is an *artifact* of a common third variable such as parental crime/antisocial personality, much the same as illustrated previously for divorce/separation and conduct disorder (Lahey *et al.*, 1988).

Therapy intervention studies that can experimentally demonstrate that improvements in parent–parent conflict lead to long-term reductions in the likelihood of outcome for crime would effectively refute this latter possibility, although they would not differentiate between direct and indirect pathways outlined above. Particularly important in this respect would be efforts which attempt to differentiate between parent–parent conflict and parent–child conflict; the aggression and negative affect which takes place among spouses would be expected to overflow to the child. The critical question therefore is whether the witnessing of marital conflict, by itself, predisposes to aggression and crime, or whether physical and verbal aggression directed toward and experienced by the child is the critical etiological mechanism.

VII. NEGLECT

Neglect is a specific variable that has received much less attention in the literature than almost all other variables reviewed in this chapter. Consequently, it is difficult to draw any firm conclusions for a potential risk factor that is more "passive" in nature than more "active" variables such as excessive punishment or child abuse. One of the reasons for the relative neglect of the neglect variable is that studies on child abuse tend not to differentiate neglect from sexual and violent child abuse.

One exception to this is the study of Widom (1989b) described previously. This study explicitly separated neglect from other forms of abuse and found clear evidence that the experiencing of neglect alone was associated with violent offending in adulthood. In contrast, a recent study by Henggeler, McKee, and Borduin (1989) was interpreted as failing to show a substantial link between neglect and delinquency insofar as delinquents with neglect were similar to delinquents without neglect in terms of behavior problems and amounts of positive and negative family communication patterns.

The role of neglect per se in predisposing to crime requires close attention in future research. Given the findings described above for lack of shared parent–child leisure activities, it would be surprising if such future studies failed to observe an association between neglect and future crime given the wide social and familial implications of neglecting a child.

VIII. SIZE AND SIGNIFICANCE OF FAMILIAL CORRELATES OF CRIME

The voluminous number of studies that repeatedly attest to the statistical significance of the association between familial variables and delinquency and crime can give the impression that the strength of such relationships is considerable. In reality, the strength of such effects is in fact quite modest. To help illustrate this fact, Table 1 shows the average amount of variance accounted for by studies on discipline, positive parenting, parental monitoring, and family conflict, which have been computed from tables reported in Snyder and Patterson (1987). Data are tabulated separately for longitudinal and

TABLE 1 Proportion of Variance Accounted for in Delinquency by Single Familial Predictors of Delinquency and Composite Predictors in Both Longitudinal and Cross-Sectional Studies[a]

	Longitudinal	Cross-sectional
Single predictors		
Discipline	6.7%	12.0%
Positive parenting (support and affection)	6.7%	11.5%
Parental monitoring	11.6%	19.3%
Family conflict and problem solving	6.3%	4.6%
Average of single predictors	7.8%	11.9%
Combined predictors	31.4%	34.3%

[a]Values are computed from tables reported in Snyder & Patterson (1987).

cross-sectional studies. Most of these studies refer to juvenile delinquency, although some relate to adult criminal offending.

This table illustrates that, as would be expected, more variance is accounted for in cross-sectional studies where familial and antisocial measures are concurrently collected as opposed to longitudinal studies where family variables collected in childhood are related to delinquency in adolescence and criminality in adulthood. It also illustrates the importance of parental monitoring relative to other single family predictors. An additional point is that it confirms the statement made by Loeber and Dishion (1983) that composite measures of parental management techniques are substantially better predictors of delinquency than single parent variables.

The most important point to be made from this table, however, is that the average amount of variance accounted for by single family constructs is relatively modest for longitudinal studies (8%) and is not much higher for cross-sectional studies (12%). Put into correlational terms, such variables would correlate about .3 to .35 with delinquency. Consistent with this calculation, Farrington (1989) found that the best predictor of convictions at ages 10–13 was rare leisure with father measured at age 11, with the correlation between the two being .28. Consequently there is a large proportion of variance (more than 90%) unaccounted for by family variables. Some of this variance is accounted for by measurement error, but it is still clear that factors other than family variables are needed to even begin to obtain a reasonable explanation of variance in crime and delinquency. Some of these variables will be social measures, although it is widely considered that family variables are more strongly related to crime and delinquency than measures such as social class, unemployment, and urban living, which are considered in the next chapter.

Biological variables are likely to be helpful in accounting for some of the unexplained variance in crime and delinquency. It is instructive to compare values for single family variables to those obtained for biological variables. Table 4 in Chapter 7 presented effect sizes for the relationship between one single psychophysiological measure (resting heart rate) and crime/delinquency in both cross-sectional and longitudinal studies of community samples of the type reported by Snyder and Patterson (1987). Fourteen separate studies were considered, which compares well with the average number of studies (6) considered for each of the family variables in the review of Snyder and Patterson (1987). The averaged effect size (*d*) reported for the heart rate studies was .84, which translates into a correlation of .39, or approximately 16% of explained variance (Cohen, 1988). This value of 16% compares well to values of 7.8 and 11.9% reported in Table 1 above for the average of single family variables, and also compares favorably to the highest values obtained for the strongest variable, parental monitoring (11.6 and 19.3%).

These comparisons should not be viewed as indicating the superiority of psychophysiological variables over family variables in explaining crime. Further studies of heart rate and crime may well result in a lowering of the estimate of the effect size for this variable, while methodologically better studies on family variables may well result in a greater proportion of variance explained than previous studies. Rather, this comparison illustrates that neither family nor psychophysiological measures, considered individually, predicts much variance in crime. The promise and challenge awaiting future studies is to use *both* social and physiological measures to better predict and explain criminal behavior by the main effects of social factors, the main effects of biological factors, and the potentially important interaction between biological and social variables.

IX. SUMMARY

This chapter reviewed evidence demonstrating the importance of negative family factors as important social predispositions for later crime and delinquency. Parental criminality is one of the best single predictors of later crime, although it is not clear whether this link reflects genetic influences or social–familial influences such as poor parenting. Child abuse has been linked to later crime and violence, although it is unclear what the precise mechanisms linking abuse to crime are, and whether this link is independent of the genetic effect of antisocial behavior in the parent. Parental absence has been linked to crime and takes at least three forms: (1) The failure to establish a social bond with a significant other during a critical period early in life has been linked to later crime and delinquency; (2) parental death is likely to be unrelated to later crime; and (3) divorce and separation are linked to later delinquency and crime, but they are not strong predictors and may be mediated by other family variables.

The quality of family life appears to be critically important in the development of crime and delinquency. Specifically, poor parental supervision is probably the best single predictor of later crime in this class of variables. Erratic and inconsistent punishment appears to be more important in predisposing to delinquency than strength of punishment per se. Negative affective relationships including low levels of warmth, acceptance, and support and high levels of rejection predispose to later antisocial behavior, while reduced time spent in joint parent–child activities is also linked to later delinquency. Marital conflict constitutes another important family predispositional variable for later crime and delinquency, along with neglect of the child. The most critical issue facing research on family variables concerns more clearly establishing the mechanisms by which these variables translate into later delinquency and crime and establishing their independence from the genetic effect of antisocial behavior in the parents.

11 Extrafamilial Influences

I. INTRODUCTION

This chapter continues the analysis of nonbiological variables by examining links between extrafamilial factors and the development of crime. While the preceding chapter examined influences operating within the home, this chapter analyzes influences operating outside of the home environment that act as important predispositions toward the development of later crime. Another goal of this chapter is to argue for a "cycle of social dysfunction" whereby some children growing up in a family and an external environment with multiple social handicaps become criminals themselves and pass on this negative "social inheritance" to their children, thus perpetuating the cycle of crime.

This chapter starts with an examination of peer and school influences before moving on to an analysis of the role of large family size and the mechanisms whereby this factor may predispose to crime. The strength of the relationships between crime and both low social class and unemployment will be appraised from the perspective of these two factors operating in both (1) the parents, and (2) the individual. Urban living and poor housing conditions will then be viewed as potential predisposing environmental variables toward crime. Finally, the notion of a cycle of social dysfunction will be presented, together with evidence indicating that the familial and extrafamilial factors that predispose to crime in the developing individual also characterize the adult criminal. The main arguments that will be made are that (1) there are important extrafamilial influences that contribute to the development of criminal behavior, although it is not clear what the precise mechanisms are; (2) there is a cycle of social dysfunction that helps fuel the cycle of crime; and (3) there is strong support for the social dysfunction criterion of disorder in criminals.

II. PEER AND SCHOOL FACTORS

A. Peers

The notion that delinquency and crime are in part caused by association with delinquent and criminal peers has a long history. It is central to classic sociological theories such as Sutherland's differential association theory (Sutherland, 1939), which argues that crime is learned in association with others, and it is also of relevance to subculture theories of crime and delinquency (Cohen, 1955). There is certainly strong evidence to support this link. Glueck and Glueck (1950) found that 98% of delinquents had delinquent friends, while this was only true of 8% of nondelinquents. Based on more recent, strong data from self-report delinquency studies, Elliott *et al.* (1983) have argued persuasively that through observational learning and direct reinforcement, delinquent behaviors are encouraged and rewarded by the group and that such groups have an orientation that strongly reinforces delinquent behavior. Reviews tend to concur on the strength of the relationship between having delinquent friends and being delinquent oneself.

There have, however, been criticisms of the importance of peer groups. Gottfredson and Hirschi (1990) argue that measures of self-report peer delinquency are almost in effect another measure of one's own self-report delinquency. As such, the strong reported association between delinquent group membership and delinquency is somewhat circular. Wilson and Herrnstein (1985) also provide a more critical review that presents studies indicating that this link is not as strong as it is sometimes presented to be. A recent review by Loeber (1990) does not include deviant peers as a good predictor of delinquency as opposed to variables such as poor supervision and combinations of family handicaps. It also seems that peer influences may not help explain more serious offending and persistent adult crime. Blumstein *et al.* (1986) have commented that much of the data have linked negative peer influences with relatively minor forms of delinquency, and in contrast there have been few studies linking such influences with serious crime. Similarly, Farrington (1987) has argued that there is no good empirical evidence that has clearly demonstrated that association with delinquent peers precedes offending. Importantly, Farrington and Hawkins (1991) report data from the Cambridge Study in Delinquent Development which show that although association with delinquent friends at age 14 and antisocial group membership at age 18 were related to the development of criminal behavior per se, they were not related to early-onset delinquent behavior, nor were there variables related to persistent criminal offending. This suggests that peer influences may be relevant to adolescent petty delinquency but not to more serious adult crime and the more important offenders who have an early onset of offending. These data support the conclusion drawn by Wilson and Herrnstein (1985), that peer influences may be greatest for low-rate offenders and of least relevance to continuing, high-rate criminal behavior, and also the conclusion drawn by Reiss and Roth (1993) that there is uncertainty as to how important peer factors are for the development of violence in particular.

Although most attention has been given to the influence of deviant peers and gangs on the individual's delinquency, a less discussed but potentially influential aspect of peer influences concerns the quality of a child's peer relationships. For example, Parker and Asher (1987) found relationships between an individual being rejected by his/her peers and later criminal behaviors. Dodge *et al.* (1990) reported on a study of 774 6- to 8-year-old boys in which it was found that those who were socially rejected by children in the classroom were more likely to develop diadic relationships that were mutually aggressive and which produced a high degree of angry, reactive, aggressive behavior. Being disliked and rejected as a child by one's peers therefore appears to be a factor that precipitates the development of aggressive delinquent behavior in association with other aggressive and delinquent individuals. While these findings suggest that initial social rejection may cause later aggression and delinquency, the relationship could act in the other direction. Coie, Underwood, and Lochman (1991) have argued that aggressiveness is the single most important reason for a child to be rejected by peers and point to the fact that 30–40% of socially rejected children are highly aggressive. However, it is unclear whether rejection by peers causes aggressive behavior or whether aggression causes social rejection.

These early processes such as peer rejection provoke a critical question on the peer influence literature. Does differential association with delinquent peers cause delinquency, or does delinquency cause an individual to differentially associate with delinquent peers? It could easily be the case that individuals who already have a propensity to be delinquent, or who are currently delinquent, seek out like-minded individuals to act out their delinquent behaviors. This alternative "birds of a feather flock together" interpretation would suggest that delinquent peer groups per se play little or no causal role with respect to crime and delinquency, and instead that individual difference factors lead to delinquency, which lead the delinquent individual to join a delinquent group.

Parenthetically, this issue highlights the debate between "group processes" versus "individual difference" perspectives on crime. The "group processes" view argues that most crime is committed in groups and is a group phenomenon, and these groups include corporations, governments, and trade unions as well as street gangs. It is consequently argued that crime cannot be explained by individual difference factors such as low IQ, low arousal, or a sensation-seeking personality, which act independently of more "macro" group processes. This argument ignores the fact that groups are made up of individuals, and these individuals may group together because they all share the same types of predispositions or individual differences or "criminal personality" which have initially led them into a criminal or deviant way of life. This issue is discussed further in Chapter 12.

Returning to the possibility that delinquency may precede delinquent group involvement, Snyder, Dishion, and Patterson (1986) have taken the view that factors preceding entry into delinquent subculture may be more important than peer group influences per se. They suggest that family factors lead to aggressive behavior in the child, which leads him or her to be unpopular at school. Rejection by peers at school then leads these aggressive children to associate with similar children as themselves, which then allows the further development of antisocial behaviors. Dishion, Patterson, Stoolmiller, and Skinner (1991) report that factors such as poor parental discipline, poor monitoring, peer rejection, and academic failure measured at age 10 predicted delinquent peer association at age 12. Similarly, Loeber, Stouthamer-Loeber, and Green (1991) found that children rated by their mothers as not easy to deal with at ages 1–5 years displayed twice the rates of delinquency in adolescence as children rated as easy to deal with. Difficult behavior at this early age, well before association with delinquent peers can take place, certainly suggests that differential association with peers is at best only one of a number of social and temperamental factors that predispose to delinquency.

Peer influences may be more significantly related to delinquency when combined with other predispositional variables. Blumstein et al. (1986) suggest that mediating influences such as parental supervision, attachment, and involvement in conventional activities need to be controlled for in future studies. In this connection, Elliott et al. (1983) found that those with both deviant peers and poor family relations are particularly at risk for delinquency. Henggeler (1989) also reviews evidence suggesting that negative peer influences are only weakly linked to delinquency in those with supportive families. These data all suggest that the conclusion that negative peer influences by themselves lead to delinquency and later crime is overly simplistic.

Where does this leave the status of peer influences as a causal factor in crime and delinquency? It would probably be wrong to conclude that peer influences play no causal role in crime and delinquency; it is likely that delinquent groups and gangs provide an ideal medium for the expression of delinquency, and without this medium some otherwise delinquent individuals would not develop delinquency. Delinquent groups are likely to provide acceptance and powerful reinforcement for delinquency for those "outcasts" who do not succeed with other peer groups and their family. Again, it is likely that there are important interactions among individual difference factors, family factors, and peer influences. Sadly, the importance of such potential interactions has been largely ignored by most researchers who have focused on only one set of variables. Finally, it should be noted that recent evidence from Patterson and Yoerger (1993) suggests that peer influences seem to be more important in explaining antisocial behavior in those whose antisociality starts after age 14 than in early starters (before age 14); because it is believed that early starters make up the bulk of adult offenders, peer influences may be of less relevance in explaining adult criminal behavior.

B. Schools

Schools are a major social institution for the growing child which affect that individual's social, cognitive, academic, personality, and sexual development in important ways. Given their impact on children and adolescents, it would not be surprising to learn that they also influence the development of prosocial and antisocial behavior. There are at least two main ways in which experiences at school could exert their influence and predispose a child to delinquency and later crime: (1) Academic failure at school could predispose to crime and delinquency; and (2) irrespective of the child's ability, some schools could be "bad" schools that act as a breeding ground for delinquency and later crime.

1. Academic Failure

This first pathway—academic failure leading to delinquency—is very different from the second in that it emphasizes an individual difference factor (IQ or academic ability) that the child brings to school rather than an "external" environmental factor. A previous chapter on cognitive deficits outlined how both low IQ and learning disabilities predispose to later crime, and there is little doubt that low school performance and achievement are linked to later crime and violence (e.g., Blumstein *et al.* 1986; Reiss & Roth, 1993; Rutter & Giller, 1983). The more important question that is more difficult to answer concerns whether "third" factors such as brain damage underlie both crime and school failure or whether preexisting antisocial behavior produces school failure. If instead school failure is more causally related to later delinquency, is this a direct or an indirect effect? School failure may, for example, directly lead to crime by producing unemployment that in turn leads to economic deprivation and poor housing and which in turn predisposes to crime. More indirectly, school failure may result in low self-esteem, alienation, or labeling of the individual as delinquent, which in turn predisposes to delinquency.

The latter interpretation is more favored by classic sociological theories such as labeling and strain theory. Labeling theory would suggest that parents and teachers react negatively to children who do not like school and who may then play truant. Such initial behavior that is morally neutral then becomes labeled as "delinquent," which in turn leads the child to view himself as delinquent, thus predisposing to more serious delinquency. Alternatively, strain theory suggests that school failure is a result of rejection of middle-class values and a means to success by education, resulting in frustration and ultimately delinquency (Cloward & Ohlin, 1960). Such theories tend to downplay individual difference factors, however, arguing instead for a more general influence of schools per se rather than specific influences such as IQ. A more recent position put forward by Gottfredson and Hirschi (1990) argues instead that labeling theory has little empirical support. Instead, they argue that schools place important constraints on individuals and that lack of self-control leads to academic failure and a seeking out of other less restricted environments to seek rewards.

Although there are many explanations for the academic failure–delinquency link, the harsh reality is that there have been no definitive studies that have convincingly teased apart these different possibilities. The fact that aggressive and antisocial behavior precedes school suggests that school failure cannot be a complete explanation. On the other hand, one longitudinal study by Rutter and colleagues finds that the link between academic failure and delinquency is not entirely mediated by early behavior problems (Maughan, Gray, & Rutter, 1985). On balance, it seems likely that future research will instead establish that school failure *interacts* with other factors such as IQ, early conduct disorder, and family variables in predisposing to crime and delinquency. That is, school failure by itself will only rarely result in later crime, and other additional risk factors for crime are required to combine with school failure to result in long-term antisocial conduct.

2. Bad Schools

The second main way that schools may relate to crime and delinquency is through the notion that some schools are just "bad" in a qualitative sense in that, irrespective of the background of the child who enters the school, they have a negative impact on the individual. This proposition arises from the fact that numerous studies have found that there can be large differences in the amount of delinquency in schoolchildren from the same geographic areas

(Rutter & Giller, 1983). Characteristics of such poor schools would include poor-quality teachers who are less effective in exerting classroom control, the way in which academic failure is dealt with or "labeled," denial of basic rights, being too soft or strict on children's behavior, the appropriate use of rewards, teacher–student ratio, physical characteristics of the school, and administrative organization.

One of the problems facing a good test of the bad school theory is that schools are selective in who they accept. Schools labeled "bad" may be bad not because they are integrally poor, but because their intake consists largely of children with predelinquent tendencies. In a review of this area, Rutter and Giller (1983) concluded that there is good evidence for the presence of this confound. In spite of this potential confound however, some studies do find an increase in rates of delinquency in some schools even after controling for crime rates in the local communities (e.g., Hellman & Beaton, 1986). Perhaps the best study carried out to date in this area is a study of 12 London schools by Rutter, Maughan, Mortimore, Ouston, and Smith (1979). Rutter *et al.* (1979) found that school factors only accounted for a small proportion of the variance in individual behavior compared with family factors, which were found to be more important. However, they also found that intake factors did not *entirely* account for the level of problem behaviors in the children. In particular, in some schools there was a general tendency for children to be either better behaved or badly behaved, and this was a function of the academic balance of the school, with children being better behaved when there was a critical mass of more academically able students; this effect was independent of the social background of the child. Rutter *et al.* (1979) also argued, however, that the school's "ethos" also contributed to behavior, with good ethos being characterized by a teaching style that was rewarding and encouraging, emphasizing academic matters, fair and firm discipline, and giving students responsibility. As Wilson and Herrnstein (1985) point out, the type of school ethos that tends to produce well-behaved children could be labeled as "warm and restrictive"—the same type of parenting style that they argue is conducive to effective family socialization processes.

It is likely therefore that the quality of a school is not entirely unimportant with respect to delinquency. The fact that delinquency rates fall after the individual leaves school (Rutter & Giller, 1983) is also suggestive that the school environment can have a causal effect in promoting delinquency. It may be that some schools predispose to delinquency not because of their inherent quality, but because they create an environment or platform for delinquent individuals to aggregate and for peer support groups for other predelinquents to develop delinquent behavior. To put this in perspective however, even the study of Rutter *et al.* (1979) finds that such influences are not major. It seems unfortunate that few good studies into the effects of schools on delinquency have been conducted since Rutter's study. In particular, it still remains to be seen whether poor school quality has a long-term effect on predisposing to serious adult crime as opposed to the short-term effect of juvenile delinquency. The fact that Farrington (1989) failed to find that attending a school with a high rate of delinquency at age 11 predicted adult violence suggests that any such school effects may be either short lived or unrelated to serious adult offending.

The academic failure and bad school factors have been viewed above as separate and different, with the former emphasizing individual difference factors and the latter emphasizing a more global institutional effect. Although they represent two different literatures, it is possible that the most potent way that schools influence later crime and delinquency lies in the interaction between the two. That is, some individuals who have a prior predisposition to school failure stemming from either biological or social factors may need to attend a poor school with high delinquency rates in order to fulfill their potential for delinquency; without such an environment to trigger such latent traits, they may avoid later crime. Conversely, poor schools may have no effect on those who lack such a predisposition. Poor schools may also fail to trigger delinquency in those who have a social/biological predisposition but who are "protected" from later crime by high IQ, which leads to academic success and a more rewarding life experience even in the face of strong delinquent peer pressure. To date however, these hypotheses have not been empirically tested.

III. FAMILY SIZE

There is solid evidence for an empirical link between family size and crime and delinquency, in the direction that a larger family size is associated with a greater predisposition to delinquency, crime, and violence (Reiss & Roth, 1993). Reviews repeatedly substantiate this proposition. Ellis (1988) reviewed 32 studies on family size and found a significant positive relationship in 31 of these 32 studies. This global quantitative analysis therefore provides strong support for the proposed link. The strength of this link can be put into context by a review conducted by Loeber and Stouthamer-Loeber (1986), who found that the effect size in terms of RIOC for concurrent studies was 10%, a level which was significant but much lower in strength than other social correlates of delinquency, such as 35% for presence of criminal father. Interestingly, however, the RIOC from predictive studies was 33%, indicating a much more powerful effect of family size. Table 1 in Farrington (1989) indicates that large family size measured at age 10 is as good a predictor of violent criminal offending at age 32 as variables such as harsh parental discipline (age 8), parental disagreement, low verbal IQ, and high troublesomeness at ages 8–10. Such data indicate that this variable is not unimportant.

There are a number of caveats that need to be made regarding the effect of family size:

1. Two studies have indicated that large family size predisposes to crime and delinquency in children from low but not high social classes (West &

Farrington, 1973; Wadsworth, 1979). These data suggest that additional family handicap (e.g., economic deprivation) is required in order for large family size to exert an effect on delinquency or, alternatively, that high social class acts as a protective factor against the negative effects of family size.

2. The effect seems to be specific to number of *male* children in the family (Jones, Offord, & Abrams, 1980; Offord, 1982). Jones *et al.* (1980) found that while delinquency rates in boys were associated with number of male siblings, there was no relationship with number of female siblings. Interestingly, having more female siblings was associated with *lower* delinquency rates, suggesting the possibility of sisters acting as a protective factor against delinquency.

3. It is possible that the family size effect does not generalize across cultures. In India, Kodanda (1986) found that 95 male delinquents compared with 120 nondelinquent controls of the same age and sex came from *smaller* families. Because the delinquent group also suffered from parental absence, the authors speculated that loneliness in the delinquent group may have contributed to the development of delinquency. While only speculative, it is certainly feasible that lack of sibling and parent contact and support may predispose such Indian children to seek support from delinquent groups.

4. Large family size may be only a weak correlate of early onset and persistence of criminal offending. Farrington and Hawkins (1991) report that while family size at age 10 was significantly related to criminal convictions in general, its relationships with early onset of crime (at ages 10–13 years) and with persistence of criminal offending (from ages 21 to 32 years) were only marginally significant ($p < .10$).

5. There is some question as to whether family size predicts crime and delinquency independent of other social variables. Tygart (1991) found no relationship between social class and self-report measures of delinquency, but did find that family size was positively related to delinquency. Fischer (1984) also found that family size related to delinquency even when income, socioeconomic level, and parental criminality had been controled for. On the other hand, Farrington (1983) did not find family size to predict crime independent of other social predispositional variables.

What are the processes by which large family size may predispose to crime and delinquency? There are several possibilities. One is that a large family size results in economic deprivation, overcrowding in homes, and poor living conditions, which in turn result in delinquency. Alternatively, a second possibility is that a large number of siblings spread parent care resources: Under this argument family size predisposes to delinquency because children receive less supervision, attention, and support, and this provides an impetus for the child to spend more time with delinquent peer groups. These two economic and parenting explanations receive some support from the fact that it tends to be more the middle child in a large family that is predisposed to delinquency

(Tygart, 1991); such children are more likely to receive less parenting because by the time younger siblings are born, the elder children may be more likely to leave home or provide economic support for the family.

A third possibility is the "contagion" hypothesis, which suggests that the larger the family size, the more likely it is that one of the siblings will be delinquent, and the more likely that another sibling will "catch" delinquency (Robins *et al.*, 1975). Offord (1982) and Jones *et al.* (1980) have suggested a modification of this hypothesis which states instead that simply having more boys in a family, irrespective of whether any of them are delinquent, will result in "male potentiation" for delinquency through increased interaction with one another, that is, it may be easier to get up to mischief if one has a brother to act as a "companion in crime." However, the fact that having a delinquent sibling increased the chances of the subject himself becoming delinquent in small as well as large families (Robins *et al.*, 1975) suggests that contagion may be a more important process than male potentiation. A fourth possibility suggested by Rutter and Giller (1983) is that large family size is associated with educational backwardness; consequently factors like low IQ or poor reading skills may be a more central determinant of delinquency and later crime than family size per se.

One other explanation has received much less attention in the literature. This is that criminals are more likely to have larger families. As such, the offspring of such families are more likely to become criminal or delinquent either by genetic transmission of crime (see Chapter 3) or because of the negative social and familial consequences of living in a criminal family (e.g., parental absence, child abuse, poor parenting). It would be important for future studies in this area not to reiterate what is already known (i.e., that there *is* a link between family size and delinquency) but instead to see whether large family size predisposes to delinquency in homes where parents are not criminal. Large family size may, however, be a causally important variable, and it may cause economic and social deprivation and poor parenting, which in turn cause delinquency. Studies that argue that family size is unimportant because it no longer predicts crime after controling for factors such as poor parenting ignore the fact that the casual direction may flow more from large families to poor parenting rather than vice versa. Longitudinal studies that look at the increasing consequence of large family size over time may be very helpful in elucidating causal ordering of family size in relation both to other social predispositional variables and to later crime. Only when more of these studies are conducted will we be in a better position to tease apart the possible explanations for the link between family size and crime.

IV. SOCIAL CLASS

Although the question of whether social class is related to crime has been debated for over 40 years there has been little resolution to this issue. Measures of social class have been important to key sociological theories such as strain theory and social deviance theory, and this accounts for the very extensive research conducted on this variable. Certainly one is struck by the fact that crime-ridden areas tend to be poor areas in which lower social classes live rather than high social class neighborhoods, and this general link was well established in many pre-1950 studies of social ecology and crime.

Most studies since then have instead attempted to link class at an individual level to crime in preference to the more global approach of ecological studies. The data in these cases are much less convincing than the earlier data. Attempting to draw a fair summary of this very large literature is not easy. In general, the following statements appear to have reasonable support from the empirical literature.

1. There is a relationship between low social class and crime, albeit a relatively weak one (Visher & Roth, 1986); Loeber (1990) found an RIOC of only 17% for the link between low social class and delinquency in his review of the studies to date.

2. The relationship is stronger for official measures of crime as opposed to self-report measures (Rutter & Giller, 1983; Wilson & Herrnstein, 1985).

3. Low social class may be more strongly related to serious criminal and violent behavior (Blumstein *et al.*, 1986; Reiss & Roth, 1993); this is illustrated by the fact that Ellis (1988) found that all 46 studies (100%) relating class to serious victimful offenses reported significant results whereas 98 of 143 studies (68%) reporting on less serious, victimless offending reported significant findings.

One problem with positing social class as an explanatory variable for crime is paradoxically one of its strengths. This concerns the fact that it is a global variable that is correlated with other "living condition" factors (e.g., poverty and unemployment, poor housing, large family), family variables such as parental monitoring, broken homes, and inconsistent punishment, and even individual difference variables such as IQ. Indeed, social class is related to most social variables that have been implicated in crime, so much so that social class is almost universally employed as a control variable in studies of crime. Perhaps what is surprising about social class is that one might expect it to correlate more strongly with crime than it does, given its broad nature as a social variable related to so many other important measures (see also Reiss & Roth, 1993, for a detailed analysis of different dimensions of poverty and their interaction with community characteristics).

Some researchers have argued that parental social class is much less important than the *individual's* own social class in adulthood (e.g., Thornberry & Farnworth, 1982). This is well illustrated by Farrington (1992), who reports that most measures of parental social class taken when the child was aged 10 or 14 were not related to juvenile or adult convictions, whereas the subject's own social class taken at age 18 did relate to criminal offending. The relative strength of one's social class over parents' social class in relation to crime is probably due to the fact that criminals tend to be unemployed, while imprisonment will push the individual further down the social ladder. In this sense, there may be some circularity in the link between the criminal's own social class and crime, since the latter may stem directly from the former. As such, this variable may be less causally related to crime than parental social class, and as such it may be of less interest in attempts to predict crime from variables taken at an early age.

Perhaps the most neglected area of research on the link between social class and crime concerns whether this link is mediated through biological or social factors. This seems an odd question because social class is superficially so clearly a social variable rather than a biological variable. On the other hand, it is quite possible that social class is to some degree genetically determined. It must be remembered that while there are no genes for factors such as crime or social class or self-concept, there may well be genes that give rise to biological predispositions which in turn give rise to *nonbiological* concepts such as crime, social class, and vocational interests. For example, there is good evidence that ideals, goals, self-concepts, and vocational interests are all in part determined by genetic factors (Loehlin, 1992).

Only one study seems to have addressed this issue to date. Van Dusen, Mednick, Gabrielli, and Hutchings (1983) separated the genetic from the environmental influences of social class by studying crime in a very large sample of adoptees (14,427) as a function of their biological and adoptive parents' social class. The key findings from this study are summarized in Table 1, which gives the percentage of adoptees who became criminal as a function of the social class of biological and adoptive parents. Crime in the adoptees was significantly related to social class of both the adoptive and the

TABLE 1   Percentage of Crime in Male and Female Adoptees as a Function of Socioeconomic Status (SES) of Adoptive and Biological Parents[a]

	Biological SES		
Adoptive SES	High	Middle	Low
Male adoptees			
High	9.3	11.5	13.0
Middle	13.4	15.2	16.9
Low	13.8	17.2	18.0
Female adoptees			
High	0.6	2.6	2.1
Middle	0.6	1.8	3.7
Low	2.4	3.7	3.0

[a]Adapted from van Dusen *et al.* (1983).

biological parents. Model fitting indicated that genetic factors associated with low social class (biological parent) were significantly related to crime in the adoptees, even after controling for the social class of the adoptive parent (environmental influence of social class), and vice versa. These findings indicate that there is a biological factor associated with low social class and crime which may be genetically transmitted.

Two other findings are of interest from this study. First, the environmental effect of social class was stronger than the biological influence of social class in males, whereas the reverse was the case in females. Second, it can be seen from Table I that the negative biological influence exerted from low social class can be offset by being reared in a high social class environment. For example, the crime rate for sons of a biological parent with low social class is 18% if reared in a low social class environment, but this drops to 13% if they are reared in a high social class environment. Similarly, the biological influences of high social class can protect the son from crime when raised in a low social class home (13.8% for high biological social class versus 18.0% for low biological social class).

This interplay between genetic and environmental influences of social class and crime is an important issue which to date has been virtually ignored. A more recent study by Cadoret, Troughton, and Bagford (1990) of male adoptees whose biological parents were criminal and who were placed in low social class homes showed particularly high rates of antisocial personality in adulthood, illustrating the potential importance of social class as a negative environmental influence on those genetically predisposed to crime. In contrast, almost all of the hundreds of studies on crime and social class have been focused on establishing an empirical link between social class and crime. It may now be time to explore beyond this link, which is clearly present at some level, and proceed to more interesting questions on the way this effect is expressed.

V. UNEMPLOYMENT AND LOW INCOME

As with social class, there has been a long debate as to whether unemployment and economic factors are linked to crime and delinquency. Again, paralleling social class, one can either ask whether parental unemployment is linked to crime or whether unemployment in late adolescence/early adulthood in the *individual* is related to crime.

Two types of study attempt to link unemployment to crime. First, studies have attempted to link global rates of unemployment and economic recession with increases in the crime rate. Findings of these studies have been very variable, and the relationship, if any, with crime is weak. Particularly, more recent studies have tended to undermine earlier assertions of a clear relationship. Specifically, Gottfredson and Hirschi (1990) in their review of this area argue that "recent research has undercut the long-held view that unemployment leads directly to crime and that employment insulates against or prevents crime" (p. 163). Freeman (1982) also concluded that there is no good evidence that employment affects crime, while Rutter and Giller (1983) concluded in their review that ". . . it is evident that alterations in levels of unemployment over this century do *not* account for the major changes in crime rate" (p. 106). Wilson and Herrnstein (1985), in their extensive review of the labor market and crime, argue that the connection between crime and economic conditions is complex and findings are inconsistent, and they concluded that it was factors associated with unemployment (e.g., IQ) rather than unemployment itself that explained most of the link between crime and unemployment. At the most, therefore, general unemployment rates are only a weak correlate with changes in crime rates.

A second type of study has assessed whether unemployment in the *individual* or the individual's family is linked with outcome for crime in that child, rather than assessing global links in unemployment and crime. Blumstein *et al.* (1986) in their analysis of criminal careers found that such individual data gave more support for a relationship between unemployment and crime. More important to the notion of unemployment acting as a predisposition, there are also data from longitudinal studies which suggest that parental unemployment may predispose family members to crime and delinquency. West and Farrington (1973) found that an erratic parental work record and low family income were related to juvenile offending. Wikstrom (1991) showed for Swedish families that families who received social welfare and who lived in rented accommodation showed the highest rates of youth offending. The link between poor parental work record and later offending in adulthood in the sons of such families is more complicated, however. In the Cambridge Study on Delinquent Development, Farrington (1991) reported that low family income and poor parental work record measured when the child was aged 8–10 years predicted later violent offending and repeated nonviolent offending at age 32. On the other hand, low family income at age 14 did not relate to later offending in adulthood, suggesting that parental unemployment in the child's earlier years may be the most important effect.

The subject's *own* employment status at age 18 (e.g., unstable work record, sacked by age 18, six or more jobs by age 18) did however relate well to violent and frequent criminal offending at age 32 in the study of Farrington (1991). Furthermore, Farrington, Gallagher, Morley, Ledger, and West (1986) also found links between individual unemployment and crime in general, in that crime rates were higher during periods of unemployment than during periods of employment. Two particularly interesting findings from this study are that (1) unemployment was associated with crimes for material gain but not with other crimes; and (2) unemployment was linked to crime particularly in those who were already predisposed to crime for other reasons (e.g., erratic parental discipline, low IQ), whereas unemployment did not appear to turn law-abiding individuals into criminals. Taking these studies together, it seems that the subject's own employment record may show stronger links to adult criminal behavior than the employment record of the subject's parents.

Whether employment is looked at in global or individual terms, there appears to be some link between the two, albeit a relatively weak link. Is this relationship causal or correlational? A number of factors suggest that it is correlational only and that unemployment does not cause crime. First, intervention studies that attempt to give employment to offenders have produced little in the way of long-term changes in offending (Farrington *et al.*, 1986), suggesting that unemployment is not a direct cause of crime. Similarly, Gottfredson and Hirschi (1990) draw attention to the study of Glueck and Glueck (1968) of 500 delinquents and nondelinquents given military employment during World War II which showed that delinquents were 10 times more likely to be *unemployable* than nondelinquents. This finding illustrates that it is the existing characteristic of the delinquents that makes them unemployable, rather than unemployment causing delinquency.

Second, factors that precede employment are linked to both unemployment and offending. For example, aggression at ages 8–10 years predicts criminal convictions, unemployment, and not owning a house at age 32 years; such a pattern of findings is more consistent with an early predisposition for crime causing later employment failure and criminality rather than employment failure directly causing criminality. A similar conclusion is drawn by Wilson and Herrnstein (1985) on the basis of data from the Youth in Transition survey (Bachman, O'Malley, & Johnston, 1978), which showed that controling for delinquent behavior in school reduced the association between unemployment and offending. Taken together, these data suggest that third factors common to both unemployment and crime may largely account for the unemployment–crime link, although the possibility that unemployment in part contributes to crime, either directly or indirectly, cannot be entirely ruled out.

VI. URBAN LIVING/POOR HOUSING

There is little doubt that there is more crime per capita in urban city environments than in rural countryside environments. Ellis (1988) reported that all 34 studies that had looked at serious offenses involving a victim reported higher crime rates in urban than in rural areas, while even 20 of the 22 studies he reviewed on victimless criminal offending again found higher rates in urban than in rural areas. General social deprivation appears to be a predisposition to crime. As one example, Kolvin, Miller, Fleeting, and Kolvin (1988) report data on a follow-up of deprivation and criminality in 847 of the families in the Newcastle Thousand Family Study. Children who grew up in deprived backgrounds were at higher risk for delinquency and crime and also obtained more criminal convictions.

Part of the reason why crime is higher in urban areas may be because poor, disturbed, and criminal individuals may drift into poor urban areas of cities. Rutter and Giller (1983) point out, however, that this cannot be the entire reason, because West and Farrington in their longitudinal study of delinquency in London found that delinquency rates fell in those who moved away from London. It could be counterargued, however, that there was something different about those who moved away from city living which itself accounts for the lower crime rate rather than removal of the city influence per se.

Perhaps the most frustrating aspect of this area of research is that because the proposed risk factor in question is so general and global, it is difficult to tease out that aspect of urban living which contributes most directly to crime. To cite a conclusion drawn by Rutter and Giller (1983) after an extensive review of urban influences on delinquency, ". . . we have a rather limited understanding both of how high-delinquency areas are created and of the mechanisms involved in these broader sociocultural influences" (p. 220). Research in the past 10 years has done little to alter this conclusion.

Nevertheless, there is some evidence that poor housing and overcrowding, which are more specific variables than urban living, are related to crime and delinquency (Rutter & Giller, 1983). Robins (1979b) found that children from poor families living in slum housing were more likely to become offenders. Farrington (1979, 1987) reported data indicating that unsatisfactory housing predicted juvenile self-report delinquency and frequent adult offending. Effects of poor housing may be more transient for violence however. Poor housing at ages 8–10 years has been found to be related to teenage violence (even after taking into account factors such as self-report delinquency, high aggression, leaving school early) but not to adult violence (Farrington, 1989), indicating a more transient effect of poor housing on violence.

VII. THE CYCLE OF SOCIAL DYSFUNCTION IN CRIMINALS

Most of the preceding two chapters have been devoted to demonstrating that there are clear familial and extrafamilial contributions to the development of crime. Alternatively, an important consideration for the theme of this book is the idea that perpetrators of crime are themselves dysfunctional at the social level. As outlined in Chapter 1, social dysfunction represents an important defining characteristic of psychopathology. To what extent therefore do criminals suffer from familial and extrafamilial social dysfunction?

It is argued that not only do adverse familial and extrafamilial factors predispose to the later development of crime, but it is also very clear that criminals as a group possess these same dysfunctional social patterns in adulthood. For example, not only do they have bad parents as children, but they also grow up to become bad parents themselves. Indeed, when the unit of analysis is the adult criminal rather than the wider population who may be at risk for crime, the evidence for such social deficits is even stronger than for such deficits acting as predispositions. To this extent, one may speak of a "cycle of social dysfunction" whereby the social predictive factors for crime are also outcome variables. There is considerable evidence to support this view.

With respect to familial factors, children who have criminal parents are more likely to become criminal than others, and by default, criminals also play the role of being a criminal parent to their own children and are more likely to have criminal offspring. Marital conflict is an important familial predisposing factor to crime, and by the same token, adult criminals are more likely to have poor marital relationships (Farrington, 1991). Divorce/separation is another predisposing factor to crime along with having an absent father, and likewise adult criminals are more likely to be divorced and to have a child living elsewhere (Farrington, 1992). Wife battering is prevalent in the homes of children who eventually become criminals, and criminals are also more likely than noncriminals to strike their wives (Farrington, 1992). The receipt of unpredictable parental punishment is a characteristic of those who become delinquent and criminal; furthermore, such individuals are more likely to become physical child abusers (Milner et al., 1990).

With respect to extrafamilial factors, criminals not only come from larger families, but they also in turn tend to have more children than noncriminals (Robins, 1966). Parental unemployment is a predisposition to crime at least in a subgroup of criminals, and many studies have shown that adult offenders are much more likely to be unemployed and have difficulty with obtaining employment than nonoffenders (e.g., Chaiken & Chaiken, 1982; Glueck & Glueck, 1968; Ashmore & Jarvie, 1987; Blumstein et al., 1986; Farrington, 1991). While low parental social class is weakly linked to later offending, adult criminals are themselves much more likely to come from lower social class levels (e.g., Farrington, 1989); downward social mobility in itself is indicative of global social dysfunction. Growing up in a poor urban environment is linked to crime, and criminals themselves are more likely to live in poor urban areas with high crime rates (Farrington, 1992; Blumstein et al., 1986; Thornberry & Farnworth, 1982). Poor home conditions also predispose to crime, and in turn poor home conditions and not owning a home were characteristics of 32 year olds with convictions for violence in a British sample (Farrington, 1991). In Denmark, a study of 12,254 offenders by Kyvsgaard (1991) also showed that criminals lived in much poorer conditions than nonoffenders and, furthermore, within the offender sample, the more serious the sentence imposed, the poorer the conditions were. With respect to type of employment, violent offenders are much more likely in early adulthood to have unskilled manual jobs, to move from job to job, or to have been fired or be unemployed (Farrington, 1989).

Somewhat surprisingly, there have been relatively few long-term follow-ups of criminals into midlife and beyond. Nevertheless, the long-term results of the cycle of social dysfunction outlined above are nicely encapsulated in a fascinating analysis by Shover (1985) of 50 aging criminals. Shover conducted personal interviews of 50 men who had been convicted and incarcerated for offenses that were essentially property offenses (burglary, theft, and robbery) and who were all aged over 40 years. Although essentially qualitative in nature, this study provides some important insights into outcome for those who follow a criminal career. First, it should be noted that crime is not synonymous with social dysfunction in all cases. Five of the fifty criminals interviewed by Shover could be classified as "successful" in that a life of crime had resulted in life success judged in social and economic terms. These individuals might be viewed as "professional" criminals in that they received good apprenticeships in crime from older, skilled, successful thieves who acted as role models. On the other hand, this constitutes only 10% of the sample. In contrast, 36 of the 50 (72%) were classified as "unsuccessful" and clearly experienced a more debilitating lifestyle. The remaining 9 (18%) fell somewhere in between. The result of social dysfunction and general life failure and poverty characterizing the majority of the criminals in Shover's sample is aptly summed up by one of the offenders himself:

> "Look at me. I'm 52 years old. I don't have anything. I don't have a car. I don't have a place to stay. Have very few clothes, you know? And I have no job. How in the hell can I be anything but ashamed? I can't run around and bullshit myself like some people and say 'Oh, I'll have it next week.' I know that's bullshit, 'cause I'm too old to have it next week. Like I said, I ain't ever going to be president . . . I'm not going to be no success. I'm not going to set the world on fire." [Shover, 1985, p. 134]

With increasing age, economic and social deprivation lead to despair and lack of hope. These aging offenders tend to commit inept crimes that would result in little economic gain, but it also seems that they tend not to care about the consequences and even view prison as a safe refuge from a harsh world that has become alien to them and in which they have no place or chance of success. Paradoxically, many of these homeless, aged criminals compare themselves to other contemporaries and realize the extent of their social isolation and economic deprivation in a way which, if undertaken 30 years earlier, may have helped them avoid a life of crime. Again, this is aptly summed up by one of the aging criminals:

> "I say, a dude that I went to school with—my age—you know—so he's got his own house out there, you know. He's got a family, he done raised a family. He's got his home, you know. I look at him, you know, and say, 'Goddamn, this old nigger hasn't been nothing but an old square nigger, but this is what he done accomplished.' Then I

look at myself. Hey. I ain't got a mother-fucking thing. So who's the square?" [Shover, 1985, p. 135]

In summary, social disadvantage not only predisposes to crime, it also characterizes adult criminals. This social dysfunction is not trivial, but represents serious social dysfunction that is not dissimilar to that found in serious adult psychopathology. To some extent this social deprivation may in part be a result of the *consequences* of a criminal career, rather than representing an intrinsic consequence of being criminal. For example, the imprisonment that results from criminal activities would be expected to disrupt social networks, result in divorce/separation, and make it more difficult to obtain employment later. Consequently, imprisonment may contribute to the social deprivation that characterizes criminals. On the other hand, it is unlikely that such consequences of crime can fully account for social dysfunction found in criminals, particularly since such dysfunction appears relatively early in the criminal's career. Rather, most of the social dysfunction found in criminals is likely to be a result of the multiple psychosocial, cognitive, neuropsychological, psychophysiological, neurophysiological, biochemical, and other biological deficits found in adult criminals, and at an earlier age in delinquents and conduct-disordered children. Later incarceration would further exacerbate this earlier social dysfunction.

The implication of the concept of the cycle of social dysfunction is that interventions at the social level in the offspring of criminals could help to break down the vicious cycle of crime and significantly reduce the crime rate. However, there is a dearth of research studies which have focused on the transmission of social deprivation from one generation of criminals to the next, and more prospective longitudinal studies are required to more specifically map out the nature and extent of this cycle. Returning to the main theme of this book, to the extent that criminals evidence a cycle of social dysfunction, inheriting the same social and familial deficits that their parents had, the social dysfunction criterion for disorder is met.

VIII. SUMMARY

This chapter examined extrafamilial factors operating outside of the home environment acting as potentially important social predispositions toward the development of later crime. Negative peer influences may be best viewed as providing a medium within which delinquency may be expressed and seem to be of greatest relevance to early delinquency rather than later serious adult criminal behavior. Academic failure is linked to later delinquency and crime, but this link may in part be a product of early antisocial behavior, and other predispositional variables may need to be present to trigger the effects of such school failure. There is some limited evidence that attending bad schools per se can predispose to later delinquency, but these effects may be short term and not predict later serious criminal behavior. It is hypothesized that both of these school variables (academic failure and bad schools) may interact together in predisposing to later crime, that is, one may need a predisposition to academic failure in order for the effects of bad schooling to manifest themselves. There is strong evidence that a larger family size is linked to later crime, and one of a number of mechanisms linking these two variables consists of the spreading of parental care resources across children, thus reducing parental supervision. Low parental social class is only weakly related to self-report delinquency but more strongly linked to official serious criminal behavior; part of this link may be mediated by biological/genetic factors. Although there is little evidence to link general population changes in unemployment with crime, parental unemployment is linked to antisocial behavior in the offspring, while unemployment in the individual is most strongly linked to later crime; it is possible however that third factors such as early antisocial behavior and delinquency may in part cause later unemployment. Urban living, poor housing, and overcrowding are related to later crime, although selective drift of criminals into such environmental conditions suggests that much of this relationship may not be causal.

It is postulated that there is a cycle of social dysfunction and deprivation whereby the same familial and extrafamilial factors that predispose to crime in childhood and adolescence also characterize that individual in adulthood. Criminals as adults evidence marital conflict, divorce and separation, wife battering, physical abuse to their children, unemployment, low social class, poor urban environment, and poor home conditions, and they act as criminal parents. All of these characteristics of the adult criminal are found in parents of criminals. It is hypothesized that, at least in part, criminals pass on this negative "social inheritance" from their parents to their children, thus perpetuating the cycle of crime. It is also concluded that (1) there are important extrafamilial influences that contribute to the development of criminal behavior, although further work is required to elucidate their status as causal variables and the mechanisms of their effects; and (2) the significant social dysfunction found in adult criminals provides strong support for the social dysfunction criterion of disorder in criminals.

12 Is Crime a Disorder?

I. INTRODUCTION

This final chapter turns away from the empirical underpinnings of criminal behavior that have been discussed in the preceding chapters and moves back to the more conceptual issues concerning the nature of crime as a disorder. Before turning to these new issues, the way in which criminal behavior does or does not meet the definitions of disorder outlined in Chapter 1 will be briefly summarized. The extent to which a nomological network of relationships exists that could be said to extend around the concept of crime will then be assessed with reference to the key points made from the empirical reviews of criminal behavior in the last

10 chapters. Arguments that can be made against the notion that crime may be a disorder will then be raised, together with counterarguments where appropriate. The discussion then turns to the important issue of free will and the volitional nature of many disorders. If we acknowledge that absolute free will does not exist for any criminal act (and instead that individuals are in part predisposed toward certain lines of action as a function of social and biological influences over which they have no control), then there are consequent implications for the extent to which offenders should be punished. Following this analysis, the status of biological research will be examined with a focus on several misconceptions that have been linked to such research. Finally, overriding future directions for research into criminal behavior will be outlined. The main points to be drawn from this chapter are that (1) there are both conceptual and empirical grounds to conceptualize crime as a disorder; (2) there are nevertheless societal and practical constraints that make acceptance of this conclusion difficult; (3) there are also practical implications of accepting that crime is a disorder which create a barrier to this proposal; and (4) the truly major advances in understanding criminal behavior will only begin to be made when genuine attempts are made to integrate the various social and biological theories, empirical findings, and conceptual frameworks that relate to crime research.

II. FIT OF DEFINITIONS OF DISORDER TO RESEARCH FINDINGS ON CRIME

In Chapter 1 it was argued that one can adopt two approaches to defining a disorder. The first approach consisted of fitting nine criteria of what constitutes a disorder to recidivistic criminal behavior. These consisted of (1) deviation from a statistical norm, (2) deviation from ideal mental health, (3) deviation from the social norm, (4) experiencing distress and creating distress in others, (5) seeking out treatment, (6) social, occupational, behavioral, educational, and cognitive dysfunction, (7) listing in DSM-III-R, (8) presence of biological dysfunction, and (9) definition of disorder as outlined in DSM-III-R. It will be recalled that most disorders do not meet all criteria. While most individual criterion of what constitutes psychopathology have significant weaknesses, when combined they help describe a gestalt picture of psychopathology against which criminality may be viewed. A comparative analysis between criminality and other disorders listed in DSM-III-R suggested that there are grounds to believe that criminality meets these criteria just as well as many other recognized disorders.

The second approach discussed in Chapter 1 to assessing whether crime is a disorder was the construct validity approach. That is, if a clear nomological network of social, cognitive, biological, and genetic relationships can be established for criminality, this, in combination with the first approach, would suggest that criminality is a disorder. The preceding chapters have been largely concerned with establishing this body of evidence; what follows are the key conclusions that can be drawn from these reviews.

A. Evolution

(1) Criminal behavior in the guise of antisocial, "cheating" behavior has a clear evolutionary basis; (2) behaviors and emotions have also evolved as a reaction to combat this antisocial cheating; (3) this sociobiological perspective can be applied to the majority of antisocial behaviors; and (4) whether or not cheating develops will be a function of both broad and specific environmental factors; as such, antisocial behavior is viewed as a product of the dynamic interplay between environmental and sociobiological forces.

B. Genetics

(1) Summary statistics from 13 twin analyses indicate that 51.5% of MZ twins are concordant for crime compared to 20.6% for DZ twins, indicating substantial evidence for genetic influences on crime; (2) studies of twins reared apart, while few in number, support heritability for crime; and (3) adoption studies overcome some of the disadvantages of twin studies, and analysis of 14 such studies from three different countries provides strong support for conclusions drawn from twin studies. However, genetic studies also support the clear importance of environmental variables, and the interaction between these two factors may prove to be critically important.

C. Biochemistry

Antisocials are characterized by reduced central serotonin and norepinephrine, with no effect for dopamine. Norepinephrine was reduced only in antisocials with affective instability and alcoholism, while serotonin was reduced regardless of presence of a psychiatric problem and also in antisocials committing violent crimes against persons. Reduced norepinephrine and serotonin in antisocials broadly supports a behavioral disinhibition theory of antisocial behavior.

D. Neuropsychology

Some limited evidence suggests that frontal dysfunction may characterize antisocial, criminal behavior in general, and it is hypothesized that damage to orbitofrontal and dorsolateral regions of prefrontal cortex may particularly characterize antisocial or psychopathic subjects with features of schizotypal personality disorder. There is some limited evidence favoring disruption to the left hemisphere (and left fronto–temporal–limbic structures in particular) in violent and criminal populations. Adult and juvenile psychopaths are characterized by reduced lateralization for linguistic processes, while some studies suggest a higher incidence of left-handedness in criminal and delinquent populations. Psychosurgery outcome studies suggest an overall inhibitory role of the amygdala on aggression.

E. Brain Imaging

Of the 14 CT, PET, and MRI studies conducted to date, 8 suggest some specificity of findings. In all cases, selective deficits are found in the anterior region of the brain (either frontal or temporal areas). All three functional brain imaging studies that report specificity of findings indicate frontal dysfunction. Four of the fourteen imaging studies provide evidence for selective frontal dysfunction, while six studies found evidence for deficits partly localized to the temporal lobe. It was hypothesized that frontal dysfunction may be more associated with violent offending and rape, while temporal dysfunction may be more associated with sexual offending including incest and pedophilia.

F. Psychophysiology

Lower resting heart rate has been consistently found to characterize noninstitutionalized, young antisocial groups and probably represents the best replicated biological correlate of antisocial behavior, probably reflecting fearlessness and underarousal. Reduced resting arousal has also been observed in the electrodermal and cardiovascular response systems, and prospective psychophysiological research has confirmed psychophysiological underarousal as a predisposition for the development of criminal behavior. Skin conductance orienting deficits appear to be specific to antisocials with schizotypal features and may reflect frontal dysfunction. Enhanced P300 amplitudes in antisocial and psychopathic individuals reflect *enhanced* attentional processing in situations involving short-term active attention in contrast to psychophysiological deficits observed in passive attend paradigms.

G. Other Biological Factors

There is initial evidence linking various forms of criminal and violent behavior to (1) a history of significant head injury, (2) birth complications, (3) minor physical anomalies, (4) being less physically attractive than controls (plastic surgery intervention provides some limited evidence suggesting that such physical disadvantages may be causally linked to crime), (5) mesomorphic–endomorphic body build, (6) low basal cortisol levels, (7) raised testosterone levels; surgical intervention and drug therapy studies, while preliminary, are suggestive of a causal relationship, (8) hypoglycemia, (9) diets high in refined carbohydrates particularly when combined with alcohol abuse, and (10) lead exposure. Many of these biological correlates of crime are *environmentally* caused and are also hypothesized to predispose to crime through *social* mechanisms such as social rejection, reduced self-esteem, and academic failure.

H. Cognitive Factors

Substantial evidence from a number of differing sources indicates cognitive dysfunction in delinquents and criminals. Sources of evidence for impairment include (1) classical conditioning deficits, (2) passive avoidance learning deficits, (3) oversensitivity to rewards, (4) low IQ, particularly verbal IQ, (5) learning disabilities, (6) lower levels of moral reasoning ability, and (7) social information-processing deficits that contribute to the development of aggressive behavior.

I. Familial Factors

Family factors are among the most important predictors of delinquency and criminality. The following variables were found to show substantive relationships with offending: (1) parental crime, (2) child abuse, (3) maternal deprivation, (4) divorce/separation, (5) poor parental supervision, (6) erratic and inconsistent punishment, (7) negative affect, (8) marital conflict, and (9) neglect.

J. Extrafamilial Factors

Extrafamilial factors operating outside of the home environment acting as potentially important social predispositions toward the development of later crime include (1) negative peer influences, (2) academic failure, (3) bad schools, (4) large family size, (5) parental and self social class, (6) unemployment, (7) urban living, (8) poor housing, and (9) overcrowding. Criminals as adults evidence marital conflict, divorce and separation, wife battering, physical abuse to their children, unemployment, low social class, poor urban environment, and poor home conditions, and they act as criminal parents. All of these characteristics of the adult criminal are found in parents of criminals. It is hypothesized therefore that there is a cycle of social dysfunction and deprivation whereby the same familial and extrafamilial factors that predispose to crime in childhood and adolescence also characterize that individual in adulthood, thereby perpetuating the cycle of crime.

Some of these findings not only help establish a nomological network of relationships for the construct of criminal behavior, but also they speak directly to some of the various definitions of disorder that have been discussed. For example, many of these chapters support the notion of biological dysfunction in criminals, which in turn supports this (albeit imperfect) definition of disorder. Chapters 10 and 11 also provided clear evidence that criminals are characterized by social and occupational dysfunction, while Chapter 9 on cognitive factors supports the notion of educational and cognitive dysfunction in delinquents and criminals. These data support the definition of disorder based on occupation, social and cognitive dysfunction, and in part the definition of disorder outlined in DSM-III-R. Furthermore, these reviews clearly support the notion that criminals deviate from ideal mental health both in social and in biological terms.

Based on these findings, it is argued that there are good reasons to believe that a variety of social and biological factors exist that predispose the individual toward criminal behavior. In combination with the fact that criminal behavior also meets a number of the definitions of disorder, it is concluded that there is reasonable evidence either to directly support the view that crime is a disorder or alternatively to give serious consideration to this possibility. At the very least, there is sufficient evidence in favor of the notion that crime is a disorder to place the burden of proof on those wishing to disprove this position. That is, unless there are convincing arguments to the contrary, we should at least consider the possibility that crime may indeed constitute a disorder. It may be informative to reflect on the possibility that if crime was identified by any other name which was free of all societal connotations placed on it, ("ecrim" for example), then in the light of this substantive body of evidence, it is likely that ecrim would be more readily considered a disorder.

It must be acknowledged, however, that ultimately the empirical scientific approach cannot provide a clear-cut answer to questions such as whether crime is a disorder, just as it cannot answer many other "big" questions in psychiatric nosology (Kendler, 1990). This is fundamentally a value judgment on the part of society. Certainly there are many objections that society would raise against the view that crime is a disorder, and these need to be addressed in some detail.

III. ARGUMENTS AGAINST THE NOTION THAT CRIME IS A DISORDER AND THEIR ASSOCIATED COUNTERARGUMENTS

Only a minority of individuals believe crime is a disorder. In a recent survey by Bird (1992), only 35% of subjects considered repeated criminal behavior to be a disorder or illness. This rate varied somewhat as a function of whether subjects had been presented with a case description attributing criminal behavior to social factors (36%) or to biological factors (43%), but these variations were not statistically significant. Subjects in this sample were selected from a university campus, and it is quite possible that the rate endorsing crime as a disorder would be considerably lower in samples more representative of the general population. Clearly, the notion that crime may be a disorder is not a particularly popular view, though by the same token it is not altogether devoid of support in society.

There are certainly arguments that can be made against the notion that crime is a disorder, and it is important to give serious consideration to the alternative position that crime is *not* a disorder. Some of these issues have been dealt with earlier, and the reader is directed back to Chapter 1 for a discussion of these; they include among others the issue of base rates for recidivistic offending, a dimensional versus categorical approach to crime and psychopathology, and a syndrome versus prototypic approach to defining disorder. This section deals with arguments that have not been adequately covered elsewhere and will also briefly reiterate some of the points discussed in Chapter 1. Some of these arguments are substantive, while others may seem much less weighty. Nevertheless, they are all presented below because they are likely to be raised by at least a minority of those working in the field of criminology or, alternatively, they have already been brought to the attention of the author. At the same time, where appropriate, weaknesses in these criticisms and alternative counterarguments will also be provided. This listing is not definitive, but it is hoped that consideration will be given to most of the counterarguments made to the main thesis of this book.

There are at least 13 criticisms that can be made against the view that crime may constitute a disorder.

Criticism 1

There are major age, gender, and ethnic differences in rates of criminal behavior; such demographic effects are inconsistent with the view that crime is a disorder.

It is clearly the case that such demographic effects exist. Young adults are much more likely to commit crime than older adults. Males are much more likely than females to commit crime (Blumstein *et al.*, 1986). African Americans are more likely to be charged and convicted of criminal offenses, especially serious offenses such as violence, than whites (Sykes & Cullen, 1992; Wilson & Herrnstein, 1985; Reiss & Roth, 1993), although the majority of offenders are still white, and it should be noted that at least part (though not all) of this ethnic effect may be due to racial bias (Adler, Mueller, & Laufer, 1991; Sheley, 1991). Nevertheless, such demographic differences are also observed in other disorders. Schizophrenia is more common in early adulthood than late adulthood, especially for males (Flor-Henry, 1990), whereas disorders such as Alzheimer's disease occur almost exclusively in old age. Gender differences are also clearly observed in disorders such as depression, which is more common in females, while childhood disorders such as hyperactivity and dyslexia are conversely much more common in males (APA, 1987). Ethnic differences have been reported in schizophrenia, with notably higher rates being observed in the British Caribbean and in immigrants from the West

Indies in England (Glover, 1990). Consequently, the fact that demographic differences are also observed in other disorders indicates that such effects observed for criminal behavior are by no means inconsistent with the notion that crime may be a disorder.

Rather, such demographic differences may give important clues as to the causes of crime. For example, from the standpoint of social research the fact that males are much more likely to commit crime than females suggests that differential socialization processes may be important in the development of antisocial and criminal behavior. From a biological standpoint, the association between crime and maleness suggests that biological processes linked to maleness such as higher testosterone may be important in the development of crime. Eysenck and Gudjonsson (1989), for example, have used such age and sex effects to support a theory of criminal behavior which suggests that crime is in part a product of genetic factors related to brain "masculinization" and the degree to which androgens are present in the brain and which in turn result in differences in arousal, sensitivity to pain, and conditioning. With respect to the general "burn-out" of criminal behavior with increasing age, it is of interest to note that testosterone decreases with age while serotonin increases with age; such age effects on crime are therefore broadly consistent with data reviewed in previous chapters showing links between criminal behavior and both high testosterone and low serotonin. Rather than contradicting a psychopathological approach to criminal behavior therefore, such factors can help shed light on the etiology of crime as a disorder (see Ellis, 1990, for further examples of links between age and sex effects in crime and biological factors).

Criticism 2
There have been major changes in crime rates over time that are inconsistent with viewing crime as a disorder.

Crime rates have been found to vary over time. Rutter and Giller (1983) have documented changes in rates of delinquency throughout the twentieth century and provide a careful and interesting analysis of the implications of these changes for understanding the development of crime. Similar analyses for adult crime may be found in Wilson and Herrnstein (1985) and Blumstein *et al.* (1986). For example, rates for index crimes have increased threefold from 1960 to 1988 (U.S. Department of Justice, 1989). Given such changes in crime over time, is this not inconsistent with the notion that crime is a disorder?

One assumption made by this argument is that rates for psychiatric disorders do not change over time. Such an assumption is contradicted in the literature. For example, rates of conversion hysteria appear to have decreased dramatically since the last century, whereas cases of multiple personality disorder have witnessed an explosion in recent years (Davison & Neale, 1986).

As such, changes over time in the rate of crime are not inconsistent with viewing crime as a disorder, since factors that cause such a "disorder" may quite possibly change over time, thereby producing shifts in the base rate for crime.

An associated argument against the notion that crime is a disorder would be to argue that over time new crimes come into being; for example, the emergence and widespread use of credit cards and computers allows for a much greater degree of fraud than hitherto. Similarly, offenses involving drugs have been a product of the relatively recent widespread availability of such substances. Conversely, actions that used to be offenses have been decriminalized; for example, active homosexuality used to be a criminal offense but is no longer considered so in England and in many states in the U.S. Do not such factors illustrate then the artificiality of the construct of criminal behavior and therefore the absurdity of viewing such behavior as a disorder? In response, it must be borne in mind that there are also "new" psychiatric conditions that are now recognized as disorders which have never previously been officially recognized as such, such as posttraumatic stress disorder, caffeine intoxication, inhalant-induced organic mental disorder, and seasonal affective disorder (APA, 1987). Consequently, it has to be acknowledged that other psychiatric disorders are just as subject to change as crime is and that perspectives on disorder shift over time. Perhaps the most critical concept that can help resolve the apparent paradoxes associated with shifts across time in psychiatric disorders (as well as shifts in criminal behaviors) is the notion that one cannot divorce behavior from the environment. The environment provides a context within which predispositions for both criminal behavior and other psychiatric disorders become manifest. Widen or constrain the environment, and one will increase or reduce the manifestation of such disorders.

Criticism 3
There are important cross-cultural variations in the rates of crime that invalidate crime as a disorder.

Variations in crime as a function of culture have been strongly documented in the criminological literature and are relatively well established. As one example, rates of homicide in the U.S. from 1986–1987 for males aged 15–24 years were 73 times higher than those in Austria, 43.8 times higher than those in Japan, and 18.3 times higher than those in England. Can crime be considered a disorder if the rates for criminal behavior vary across countries? The answer is that it can, because other psychiatric disorders have also been found to vary across countries and cultures. As already discussed previously, schizophrenia has been found to vary across cultures within a country, but in addition rates of schizophrenia are also found to vary across countries; for example, the diagnosis of schizophrenia at the New York State Psychiatric Institute ranged from about 20% in the 1930s to about 80% in 1952, whereas rates at the Maudsley hospital in England remained relatively constant at 20% throughout this period (Kurianski, Deming, & Gurland, 1974).

Such differences may reflect differences in the way that psychopathology is defined in different countries, or they could reflect a true difference in the incidence of such disorders. If disrupted family processes predispose to crime, then countries in which the family unit is strong would be expected to have lower rates of crime. Similarly, if there are genetic, biological, and personality differences between different countries that relate to factors predisposing to crime, then again one would expect differences across countries. Wilson and Herrnstein (1985) point to the fact that the dramatically reduced rates of crime and violence in Japan may in part be a product of lower levels of extraversion and impulsivity and higher rates of IQ in Japanese, because impulsivity and low IQ have been found to be risk factors for crime. Part of these differences may also be due to the way antisocial behavior is perceived in the two countries. For example, there is some evidence that part of the reason for lower juvenile delinquency rates in Japan than the U.S. may be that juvenile delinquency in Japanese adolescents is more likely to be viewed as high-spirited sensation seeking rather than being considered intrinsically bad and destructive (Moriyama, 1990).

In summary, it would be erroneous to conclude that crime is not a disorder because crime rates vary across countries and cultures, just as it would be wrong to conclude that physical diseases are not truly diseases because their rates vary across countries.

Criticism 4
Crime is a heterogeneous concept, so it cannot represent a unitary disorder identified by a discrete cluster of traits.

The critical issue here is that criminal behavior is clearly heterogeneous, in that while some criminals may tend to commit sexual offenses, others will specialize in nonviolent property offending, while others will tend to commit nonsexual, violent acts. This argument cannot be taken too far, as the notion of specialization for crimes has not received good empirical support (Klein, 1984; Hindelang, 1971; Petersilia, 1980), though if one uses the term *specialization* more generally, there is some limited support for this notion (Farrington, Snyder, & Finnegan, 1988). At any rate, it is true that criminals do not present as a unitary group either in terms of their criminal behavior or in terms of other features such as personality (e.g. Blackburn, 1983). Because they do not represent a unitary group, can crime be considered a disorder?

The classical conception of a disorder is one in which a specific pattern of symptoms co-occurs to define a group who possesses those symptoms. As outlined in Chapter 1, the problem with this notion of disorder is that few such psychiatric disorders can be defined in such a classic way. While schizophrenia can be viewed as one disorder, the notion of "the schizophrenias" is commonly used in psychiatry because different subjects with schizophrenia can present with very different symptoms. As an example, one male schizophrenic may be characterized by the paranoid delusion that the CIA is controlling his behavior by implanting devices into his brain that disrupt his thought processes, but he may otherwise appear as relatively normal. Another male schizophrenic could present with severe thought disorder, report auditory hallucinations, and come across interpersonally as having blunted affect and very poor social skills. There may be little or no symptom overlap between these two individuals diagnosed with supposedly the same disorder. Heterogeneity within a psychiatric disorder tends to be the rule rather than the exception.

As such, heterogeneity within a group of recidivistic criminal offenders does not compromise its potential status as a disorder. Indeed, just as DSM-III-R recognizes subtypes of schizophrenia, so too could it be argued that it surreptitiously and informally recognizes subtypes of criminal behaviors (APA, 1987). As outlined in Chapter 1, DSM-III-R identifies many conditions which, taken together, would encapsulate most if not all of the population of recidivistic criminals (e.g., antisocial personality disorder, conduct disorder, pedophilia, intermittent explosive disorder, sexual sadism, psychoactive substance abuse). In a sense, therefore, it is as if DSM-III-R recognizes the "subtypes" of criminal behavior, and all it balks at recognizing is the main "umbrella" disorder of criminal behavior.

Criticism 5
Crime is a socio–political–legal construction that can be changed by changing the law, whereas psychiatric disorders are determined by biological and social forces and as such represent more fundamental, fixed concepts.

This argument suggests that crime is an artificial construct that is brought into being and modified by the forces of justice and government. Under this view, crime is artificial, a construction of the system that creates it, and as such it is in a sense "unreal." Such unreal concepts consequently cannot constitute a disorder. In contrast, disease entities are real and are based on causal factors stemming from genetic and environmental forces. As such, it would be argued that crime cannot be viewed as a disorder because it is an artificial construction that has no firm underpinning outside of the system that constructs it.

There are three important flaws to this potentially strong argument. First, it is true that criminal behavior is defined and altered by the justice system, and it can certainly be viewed as a "construction" of society. But by the same token, psychiatric disorders are equally constructions of society, brought into being by that part of society consisting of the psychiatric profession, just as that part of society constituting the justice system brings into being the concept of crime. Essentially, they are psychiatric "constructs" and are no more real or unreal in this sense than the construct of crime. Just as the laws of the land can change the way that criminal behavior is defined and construed, so too are definitions of psychiatric disorder under constant scrutiny and periodic redefinition, as witnessed, for example, in the revision of DSM-III in 1987, just 7 years after its introduction in 1980. Indeed, the major challenge to current-day psychiatric nosology lies in attempting to validate these constructs labeled as disorders against external empirical criteria. The disorder of schizophrenia is therefore no more or less real than the concept of criminal behavior.

Second, although criminal behavior is in a sense a construction of society, it has a firm basis in *behavior*. This construction is not imaginary or illusory or in some other sense unreal. The vast majority of behaviors that make up criminal acts can be defined behaviorally and psychometrically using self-report measures of delinquency and crime. These are alternative ways of measuring crime and are not bound by society and the law, except insofar as those who construct such scales are members of society. Yet such scales are still constructions and are no more real or unreal than criminal behavior or depression or schizophrenia. Anyone who claims that crime is merely a construction of society and questions that crime is a "real" concept might ask a victim of crime whether crime is real in order to obtain further clarification on this issue!

Third, part of this argument is based on the notion that crime is largely a product of wide-scale societal forces and has no basis within the individual, whereas disorders more often stem from factors within the individual. This assumption can be put to empirical test. As documented in previous chapters in this book, it is clearly the case that criminal behavior is not just determined by "macro" societal forces, but is at least in part based on genetic, neurochemical, psychophysiological, neurophysiological, cognitive, familial, and extrafamilial psychosocial factors. If crime is merely a product of global societal factors, there would be no reason to expect individual difference factors to correlate with crime. At this level of analysis, the concept of criminal behavior has much in common with other psychiatric disorders. Those who wish to deny this point must systematically attempt to demonstrate that the very large body of evidence reviewed in previous chapters is erroneous and at the same time demonstrate using the same level of criticism that the corpus of knowledge supporting broad social influences remains intact. It may be difficult to believe that a concept defined by the legal system can be in part biologically determined. For this reason, some argue that crime cannot have a genetic basis because it is a sociolegal construction. Nevertheless divorce, which is also a sociolegal construction, has also been recently shown to be in part genetically based (McGue & Lykken, 1992). Nevertheless, it must be conceded that if it can be demonstrated that social and biologically based individual difference factors play no role in predisposing to criminal behavior, this would effectively disprove the notion that crime is a disorder. Until such refutation of the social and biological evidence drawn together in this book is offered, we must seriously entertain the possibility that crime constitutes a disorder.

Criticism 6

Crime cannot be a disorder because it is so pervasive in society; we all commit crime, and the whole population cannot be viewed as "disordered."

In response to this argument, two points must be borne in mind. First, the suggestion that crime may be a disorder is here being applied to recidivistic offenders who repeatedly commit nontrivial offenses. Such a population constitutes a relatively small proportion of the population. Some estimates lie in the range of about 4 to 8% (Currie, 1993; Stattin & Magnusson, 1991) with respect to that minority of offenders who account for disproportionate amounts (e.g., 40–60%) of all offending, so an approximate figure would be around 6%, depending on how serious offending and recidivism are defined (see below). While most if not all of us have committed criminal offenses at some point in our lives, in many cases these are minor or are otherwise committed very infrequently.

Second, an analogy can be made to depression. Most people can probably report having been "depressed" at some point in their lives, but we would not draw the conclusion that the whole population has suffered from this major psychiatric disorder. People who genuinely suffer from depression have a mood disturbance that differs both in terms of severity and duration from the rest of us. Most of us might occasionally feel depressed, but this mood shift is less intense and more fleeting, lasting for perhaps a few hours or days rather than months. A legitimate question may be posed as to whether disorders like depression are best construed as representing a true category or otherwise reflect a genuine continuum running throughout the population. In the same way, one could suggest that crime is also best viewed as representing a continuum rather than a category. While the idea of a continuum for any disorder raises the question of whether we all have different degrees of that disorder, this is not a problem specific to the notion of crime as a disorder, but rather applies widely to all psychiatric disorders.

Criticism 7

The group of criminals that the disorder argument is being applied to cannot be definitively delineated; the inability to precisely identify the target population rules crime out as a disorder.

There is a very real problem in attempting to delineate the target group at a level finer than those who repeatedly commit nontrivial criminal offenses. It can with some justification be demanded that a disorder needs precise and clear boundaries. For example, how recidivistic should a criminal offender be to be included in such a category? How serious should offenses be? What about those who commit serious offenses but commit them very infrequently—are they disordered? And what about those who are recidivistic offenders but who never get caught?

Taking the last two questions first, the argument raised in this book is in theory viewed as applying to all serious, recidivistic offenders, whether they are caught or not. Because we know so little about uncaught recidivistic offenders at an empirical level, the literatures reviewed in earlier chapters of this book pertain largely to caught, "official" offenders. Whether the same biological and psychosocial attributes found in caught offenders apply to uncaught offenders remains to be seen, although there is some evidence from prospective longitudinal studies of antisocial behavior that the characteristics of caught offender populations are more clearly exemplified in noninstitutionalized groups.

This lack of knowledge is not specific to criminal behavior. A parallel can be seen in research on schizotypal personality disorder; almost all of our current knowledge of this disorder stems from schizotypals referred to hospitals for problems other than the main features of schizotypal personality (e.g., depression, borderline personality disorder). We know very little indeed about schizotypals in the community who do not approach psychiatric services for treatment for their disorder. Returning to criminal behavior, uncaught offenders may be very similar to caught offenders in terms of the underlying predisposition for crime, but it is hard to draw firm conclusions at the present time due to the major gap in our knowledge of this offender group.

The other questions raised are just as important and just as difficult to deal with, but these difficulties are again not specific to the disorder argument under scrutiny. What constitutes a "recidivistic" offender in crime research varies from study to study, and similarly what constitutes a "serious" offense is open to debate. At the extremes, however, there are far fewer arguments. One offender who commits 100 offenses a year is clearly recidivistic, while one person who only commits one criminal offense in his whole lifetime is clearly nonrecidivistic. Similarly, murder is a more serious offense than stealing a dollar. Where we draw the line for recidivism and seriousness is ultimately arbitrary and may well reflect the fact that we are dealing with continuums rather than categories.

While such lines could be drawn up, it would be clearly unwise to do so because there would currently be no sound empirical basis to support such divisions. Nevertheless, precise delineation of many psychiatric disorders is also far from ideal. As one example, DSM-III-R currently specifies that a patient must show evidence of an active phase of psychotic symptoms (e.g., hallucinations, delusions, thought disorder) for at least 1 week to be classified as schizophrenic. This time period is coming under close scrutiny, and it is likely that the next version of DSM will extend this period from 1 week to 1 month (Flaum, 1992). The precise boundaries of schizophrenia are far from clear, and it is quite possible that other classified disorders such as schizoaffective disorder and schizotypal personality disorder may be more similar than dissimilar to schizophrenia in terms of underlying etiology. Defining the precise boundaries of schizophrenia has recently come under a great deal of scrutiny (e.g., Braff & Siever, 1992), and it is not likely that this issue will be clarified quickly. The very fact that changes are made every few years to how disorders are defined attests to the fact that it is very difficult to draw very precise criteria for defining a disorder which can stand the test of time and further research. Putting forward recidivistic criminal offenders making up very roughly 6% of the general population as a target group for the disorder argument is relatively specific, but as with many other established disorders it still leaves unanswered a number of questions that can only begin to be resolved by extensive future research.

Criticism 8

Some research shows that the same factors found to underlie severe criminal behavior also characterize less severe forms of antisocial behavior; this suggests that there is no discrete category of offenders to whom the notion of a disorder can be applied.

This is an important argument that is difficult to reject outright and is related to the issue described above. To exemplify this position, violent adult criminal offenders have been found to be characterized by low resting heart rate measured at age 11 years (Wadsworth, 1976). Low resting heart rate has also been found to characterize 15-year-old schoolchildren labeled as antisocial (Davies & Maliphant, 1971). Degree of antisocial behavior as rated by schoolchildren has been found to relate to degree of resting heart rate in the expected direction (Raine & Venables, 1984b). Such findings would argue for a continuum of antisocial behavior and a continuum of a predisposition toward such antisocial, criminal behavior. Is there, therefore, a discrete cut-off? If there is no discrete cut-off in either behavior or predisposition, can there be a discrete group making up a discrete disorder?

This argument may well dictate that severe criminal behavior cannot be construed as a disorder because such behavior lies on the end of a continuum of antisocial behavior. However, it rests on the assumption that a dimensional approach is inconsistent with disorder. There are clear examples that undermine this assumption. In the domain of physical disease, hypertension is recognized as a discrete disease state, yet high blood pressure may simply represent the extreme of a continuum of biological functioning in the total population. With respect to underlying etiology in psychiatric disorder, some of the biological correlates of schizophrenia (e.g., reduced area to the prefrontal regions of the brain) have also been observed in those with mild degrees of schizotypal personality in an ostensibly normal, nonclinical sample (Raine *et al.*, 1992b). Does this mean that schizophrenia is not a disorder? Again, questions like this can be raised which cast into doubt the notion that crime can be viewed as a disorder, but these same issues also raise serious questions against much more established disorders, or rather against how we conceptualize disorder. In this regard there is a parallel to the search for a good definition of disorder which provided the focus for Chapter 1: Some definitions of disorder do not fit well with viewing criminal behavior as a disorder, yet they also do not fit well with other established psychiatric conditions.

Criticism 9

Crime is committed by groups and organizations, not by individuals; therefore, crime cannot be a disorder because organizations cannot be psychiatrically disordered.

It is certainly true that some crimes are committed in groups and that members within organizations group together to perpetrate corporate crime. This argument rests on the assumption that crime is more a product of the organization than of the individual. Because organizations cannot be viewed as being psychiatrically disordered, crime itself cannot be a disorder.

There are two main responses to this argument. First, it does not cover those criminals who do not commit crime in groups, such as the burglar operating on his own. Second and more important, however, the assumption that crime has nothing to do with the characteristics of the individual is unfounded, as extensive empirical evidence exists indicating that individual difference factors are involved in the etiology of criminal behavior (see Chapters 3 through 11). People who commit crimes in groups or within organizations probably represent those individuals who are predisposed to commit crime and who are, so to speak, "birds of a feather who flock together" to perpetrate organizational crimes. This is not to argue that there are no instances of individuals who lack predispositions to crime yet who perpetrate crimes at least in part due to situational circumstances; the unemployed, otherwise lawabiding father of seven children who must steal for food to keep his family from starving might represent one such example. Nevertheless, these instances are rare in comparison to the recidivistic criminal offenders who constitute the target population that the crime-as-disorder argument is aimed at. Furthermore, it must not be forgotten that the biological predisposition to crime cannot be divorced from the social environment and that the interaction between these two factors may well be considerable, just as situational factors may well trigger the onset of a disorder (e.g., depression) in those who are predisposed by virtue of possession of individual difference factors.

Criticism 10

Crime cannot be cured, so it probably is not a disorder.

There have been rigorous attempts to treat and "cure" criminal behavior, but decades of efforts to this end have failed to produce reliable and effective long-term treatment for such behavior. Because many disorders are treatable, the argument can be made that this failure to treat crime indicates that it is not a disorder.

The clear limitation to this argument is the fact that many conditions that were once untreatable can now be cured. Although currently we have no effective way of preventing or treating crime, this does not mean that in future years no such treatment will be developed. In this context it must be remembered that although we can treat the symptoms of schizophrenia (with varying degrees of success), even after decades of intensive research we have no way of *preventing* this debilitating disorder. In contrast to the massive research efforts made into this and other disorders, the treatment and prevention of crime have received very little research funding. In this context, it is not surprising that we cannot treat criminal behavior, although it must not be forgotten that criminal behavior is a much more complex disorder than schizophrenia and it is this complexity (in addition to lack of research funding) which also contributes to the failure to obtain a cure for crime to date.

Criticism 11
Criminal behavior differs from other psychiatric disorders in that criminals pose harm to others; this delimits it from other disorders.

It is certainly true that crime differs from many other psychiatric disorders in that criminal behavior creates harm to others in society, whereas many other disorders create much more harm to the individual. Even here, however, there are some disorders that also create considerable harm to those who interact with the disordered individual. Those with alcohol dependence and other substance-use disorders clearly create harm to others. Individuals with manic depression can also harm others in addition to themselves. Some schizophrenics are brought to the attention of hospitals not by the patients themselves, but by others such as family members, friends, or the police, at least in part because they become unmanageable or disruptive and difficult to deal with. In this context, crime is not alone as a disorder that creates disorder in society, although it is probably true that it creates more harm to others than any other disorder. If we wish to exclude crime as a disorder, we have to include in our definition of disorder the notion that all conditions that primarily create harm to others are not disorders. Yet it would be unclear what the conceptual and logical basis for such a decision would be, as well as creating major difficulties for the classification of other disorders.

Criticism 12
Crime is an aberration of behavior, whereas disorders represent aberrations of mental functioning; crime, therefore, is not a disorder in the same sense as other disorders.

Many classic disorders represent alterations in mood states (e.g., depression and anxiety), perception, and cognition (e.g., schizophrenia) and consequently are identified at least in part by alterations in these "inner" psychological processes. As such, defining criminal behavior as a disorder seems quite different in that the key feature of the disorder consists of behavioral "signs" rather than psychological "symptoms." On the other hand, many disorders are defined largely in terms of behavioral signs. Hyperactive behavior is a core feature of attention deficit/hyperactivity disorder. Psychoactive substance abuses are defined in terms of behavior, and interestingly these behavioral disorders are also clearly crimes. Conduct disorder and antisocial personality disorder are also defined almost exclusively in terms of behaviors. Indeed, the fact that antisocial personality disorder is so behaviorally defined means that it is one of the most reliably diagnosed of all of the personality disorders listed in DSM-III-R.

It must also be remembered that although crime is defined in behavioral terms, that does not mean to say that psychological, cognitive, and perceptual processes are not disturbed or that the underlying biological and psychosocial and environmental causes of this behavior are less in evidence; Chapters 2 through 11 provide evidence to support this conclusion. Furthermore, as more is uncovered about the etiology of criminal behavior, other associated features that are prominent in recidivistic criminal behavior (e.g., low IQ, impulsivity, underarousal) may come to play a more prominent role in the definiton of this putative "disorder."

Criticism 13
Criminal behavior is voluntary, whereas other disorders are involuntary.

The perceived willfulness of criminal behavior is clearly an obstacle to viewing crime as a disorder. Criminal behavior is usually volitional, whereas many psychiatric disorders are nonvolitional insofar as behaviors are not often under the control of the individual. Indeed, it is in cases where the accused is clearly shown to be suffering from a mental disorder so severe as to impair judgment and volition that the plea of not guilty by reason of insanity is most successful. "Command hallucinations" that compel the defendant to make an unprovoked and otherwise illogical attack on the victim provide dramatic examples of such cases of nonvolitional crime, but most criminal acts are viewed as volitional. The pivotal question therefore is whether criminal behavior, being volitional in nature, can be conceptualized as a disorder.

In response, it should be pointed out that there are a number of so-called "volitional disorders" where volition is not seriously impaired. Examples consist of alcohol abuse and drug abuse, but they also include other disorders such as anorexia (where the patient wants to lose weight) and bulimia in addition to all other "antisocial" disorders listed in DSM-III-R. Criminal behavior is not therefore alone as potentially constituting a disorder that is voluntary in nature. As such, the volitional nature of crime does not exclude it as a disorder. Furthermore, the notion that criminal behavior is truly volitional may be illusory, and this issue will be returned to later in the context of the discussion of free will.

Summarizing this section on arguments against the notion of crime as a disorder, there are a number of superficially strong arguments that turn out to be fairly easily rebutted. Alternatively, there are also a number of arguments that present more substantial issues. Even in these cases, counterarguments can be made that weaken their potency. Specifically, some of the best arguments against the notion of crime as a disorder are nonselective in that they also create considerable problems for other currently accepted disorders. None of these arguments can convincingly reject the notion that crime may constitute a disorder.

IV. SOCIETAL AND SOCIOBIOLOGICAL BARRIERS TO ACCEPTING CRIME AS A DISORDER

If there is no conceptually compelling reason to reject the notion of crime as a disorder, why should it be so difficult to accept this notion? To find the answer, one needs to look beyond academic arguments and toward more emotive, practical, and even sociobiological constraints on the acceptance of this argument. These constraints take three main forms, as outlined in the following sections.

A. Strong Emotional Reactions to Crime

First, it is difficult to rationally discuss the question of whether crime is a disorder because criminal actions engender a very strong emotional reaction from which it is hard to dissociate oneself from. Televised courtroom scenes that depict the strong emotions with which relatives of a murderer's victim greet a guilty verdict graphically illustrate the overriding desire for retribution that most of us feel when a serious wrong has been perpetrated. Anyone who has suffered from a nontrivial criminal act is likely to feel strongly that crime must be punished and would have very little sympathy for the notion that crime is a disorder and that criminals are not entirely responsible for their actions, no matter how heinous. Victims of crime usually feel passionately about crime and punishment, and indeed a large proportion of society, whether victims or not, feels the same way.

This is illustrated by the fact that there have been cases where murder defendants have been clearly found to be suffering from a mental illness at the time of their acts, yet have nevertheless been found guilty and sentenced to prison. Peter Sutcliffe ("the Yorkshire Ripper") terrorized Yorkshire for several years in the late 1970s, killing prostitutes and ordinary young women alike. Psychiatrists both before and after the trial have agreed that Sutcliffe was a paranoid schizophrenic, but the built-up emotions of the public were probably an important factor in the judgment that the public good would not be served by letting such a vicious killer off lightly with confinement in a secure hospital, and that instead he should be put on trial. Conversely, the public outcry and subsequent legal reforms to tighten up the insanity defense in the United States after John Hinckley was found not guilty by reason of insanity after attempting to assassinate President Reagan in 1981 also illustrate the strong public feeling against treating mentally disturbed offenders lightly.

The author is little different from most people in this regard. While holidaying in Bodrum on the west coast of Turkey in the summer of 1989 he had his throat cut by a Turk who broke into his hotel room shortly after 3:00 A.M. In the course of the struggle that ensued between the two, the blade of the knife that the intruder was using broke off, so that there were only a few millimeters of metal left on the handle of the knife when the intruder drove it into the victim's throat. Consequently, the victim only needed five stitches to his throat and lives to tell the tale. Because there was a full moon that night, the victim was able to see the face of the perpetrator and later that morning picked him out in an identity parade. Justice is swift in Turkey, and the following day both the victim and the accused were paraded through the center of Bodrum to the courthouse (the custom in Turkey is to shame the offender). Both gave their testimony, and the accused was found guilty. The judge later told the victim through the cook who was his interpreter that at a later date the defendant would receive a prison sentence. The author left Turkey immediately after the trial.

The point of this melodramatic tale is not so much that one should avoid Bodrum for one's holidays (it is in reality a delightful seaside resort with a dramatic medieval castle), but rather that at a personal, emotional level the author has little sympathy for criminals and supports the use of the death penalty. He felt angry and vengeful after his throat was cut and would have little sympathy for the notion that his attacker was suffering from a disorder, was not entirely responsible for his actions, and should not be harshly punished. Although there are exceptions, most of us feel this way when we become victims of crime. Paradoxically, these strong societal feelings are greatest toward serious, recidivistic offenders to whom the disorder argument is being applied, and they are less strong against nonserious petty property offenders who are not the target group of this argument.

B. Sociobiological Forces

What is the basis for such strong, deep-seated emotional reactions? Part of the answer lies in the fact that these strong reactions against crime probably have their bases in the same sociobiological forces that shape antisocial behavior. It will be recalled that in Chapter 2 it was argued that just as there have been evolutionary pressures for the development of antisocial behavior, there have been evolutionary pressures favoring the development of behaviors and emotions that are diametrically opposed to such antisocial "cheating" strategies. It will be recalled that just as selection favors the development of subtle cheating, so too are abilities to detect subtle cheating favored. These abilities included moralistic aggression and indignation which would develop as a strategy to "educate" the cheater, with more extreme deterrents being exile, injury, or even execution (Trivers, 1971). In this context, we have to face the possibility that, sociobiologically speaking, we are strongly motivated to oppose the notion that crime is a disorder by any means available to us, whether they be logical and academically based or more emotionally and morally based. This does not mean that the view of crime as a disorder cannot be logically and academically refuted, but it does mean that we have to be particularly sensitive to the basis for giving reasons against the notion that crime is a disorder. In one sense evolution has not only forged the weaponry of criminal behavior, but has also cast the armor against any argument that could be construed as nonpunitive against such behavior.

It could be argued that even these sociobiologically based emotions have evolved for good reason—why oppose a system that is both "natural" and that has passed the test of time until now? If we are to use this logic to oppose the notion of crime as a disorder, however, we must also acknowledge that we have abdicated the decision-making process to the selfish genes that constitute the survival machines posing as "rational" human beings. Are processes that are natural necessarily legitimate and sound at either an intellectual or a moral level? Will not society fail to evolve and instead regress by not questioning such processes?

In one sense such sociobiological counterforces to criminal behavior must inevitably lead to society rejecting the view that crime may be a disorder. Reactions against crime are literally "natural" in that we are strongly predisposed to adopt an aggressive stance against such behavior. Yet such strong reactions, no matter how natural or widely shared by others, may not provide a good logical basis on which to reject the view that crime is a disorder. Acceptance that crime may be a disorder requires an immense about-turn against a very strong emotional "gut" reaction that runs to the core of society. Nevertheless, from a scientific standpoint, crime may indeed constitute a disorder. Whether or not we are willing to accept the reality and implications of such a conclusion is a different matter.

C. Practical Implications of Crime as a Disorder Are Too Great

One significant barrier facing the notion that crime may be a disorder is that the practical implications of accepting this view are simply too great to deal with. If we accept that crime is a disorder, then at least to some degree we also have to accept the fact that the offender is not completely responsible for his criminal behavior. The practical implication is *not* that no action should be taken against such individuals. On the other hand, if we cannot currently treat offenders, what should be done with them?

Perhaps, at the least, such individuals should not be punished as harshly as they currently are. One scenario would be to place offenders deemed to be disordered into institutions that are fully secure—and which therefore pose no security threat to society at large—but which allow the individual to have as much freedom as possible given the constraints of keeping such offenders away from society, at the same time minimizing all punitive aspects of the regime. At the same time, such an environment would attempt to cultivate new treatment programs based on experimental research into treatment interventions which themselves are based on a much stronger body of basic research than is currently available. Currently, such individuals are subjected to severe restrictions on their liberty, and regimes holding criminals adopt the philosophy that one goal of incarceration is to punish the offender. Society currently practices passive eugenics on most prisoners by preventing conjugal visits, thereby reducing the reproductive capacity of the prisoner. It is important to note that despite the many evils that are claimed by some to result from genetic research on crime, this practice is not a product of such research but is a tolerated by-product of the penalty that society exacts on the imprisoned criminal. Shylock's pound of flesh is paltry meat compared to the future offspring lost to the imprisoned criminal.

Such changes to our way of dealing with criminals are not minor however. In particular, if one took a categorical approach to crime as a disorder (some criminals represent the disorder, others do not), how would the judicial system go about deciding whether a particular offender met the criteria for the crime "disorder"? Alternatively, if one took a dimensional approach (there are degrees to which a criminal can be viewed as disordered) the problems still remain: How is the degree of disorder calculated? How do psychiatrists and psychologists assess degree of disorder? How is this translated into custodial treatment? It could be argued that even disordered offenders are at least to some extent "responsible" for their actions and should be punished: How should the balance be obtained between punishment and humane containment?

There would also be a large financial cost associated with viewing crime as a disorder. Not only would there need to be substantial changes to the current infrastructure of prisons, but furthermore there would have to be a massive injection of funding for both basic and applied research on crime in order to help generate new treatment approaches that may have a more realistic chance of success. Such funding would need to make up for decades of neglect in this area and would have to be much more substantial than that currently allocated to other major disorders. Again, the strength of feeling by society against the criminal class makes allocation of such funds unlikely.

Because there are a number of substantial practical obstacles to viewing crime as a disorder, what incentive is there for pursuing such an approach?

One potentially major benefit to viewing crime as a disorder is that it may make crime more treatable. Part of the reason why criminals are so difficult to treat may be because they do not believe that they have a problem that needs treatment, and this perception may be a product of the wider perception of society that criminals are simply "bad" and not suffering from a disorder which is in need of treatment. To some extent alcoholism provides a related example. Part of the increased success in treating alcoholics arose when society began to recognize that alcoholism was a disease, whereas previously alcoholism was more likely to be attributed to individual malevolence and depravity. Recognition by society that alcoholism was a disorder may have made it easier for alcoholics themselves to recognize that they had a problem that needed treatment, and that although they had to take responsibility for their alcoholism, they could perceive that, at least in part, there were some factors beyond their direct control that contributed to their problem behavior.

The tantalizing question is whether recognition by society that crime is a disorder will similarly make criminals realize that they have a problem that requires treatment, and that this perceptual shift will make it easier for criminals to change their behavior. The ultimate promise that the concept of crime as a disorder holds for society lies in the elusive cure of crime. Perhaps it is not surprising that the criminal offender is so hard to treat given that society casts him into the role of the malignant individual who needs ostracizing for the evil behavior that he perpetrates. Placed against the backdrop of early childhood rejection by parents and peers, it is perhaps not surprising that criminals decide in turn to reject society and society's attempts to intervene. The catch 22 scenario created by this perspective is that unless we can demonstrate that criminals are treatable, society will be reluctant to accept crime as a disorder. Yet this very perspective may be an essential ingredient of the ultimate cure for crime, because by and large individuals must want to be treated for such treatment to be successful.

This section started by suggesting that one needs to look beyond the scientific data and toward more emotive, practical, and even sociobiological notions in order to understand why it is difficult to accept the notion of crime as a disorder. Society may choose to ignore the notion of crime as a disorder, but in doing so it must be intellectually honest in making this choice and acknowledge that there are more covert, nonscientific processes that help shape this view.

V. CONSTRAINTS ON FREE WILL

As outlined above, the overtly volitional nature of criminal behavior represents one important objection to the notion of crime as a disorder. The issue of volition cannot be discussed without consideration of free will. Debates on the issue of free will usually center on whether individuals have a free choice with respect to their actions. Such debates become particularly important in legal cases where there is a question mark against the defendant's sanity at the time of the crime. Even when defendants have been demonstrated to be suffering from severe early environmental and biological handicaps, they are often judged to have had free will in deciding whether or not to commit the wrongful act. Evidence that also suggests that the defendant planned the crime is usually particularly damaging.

Perhaps one erroneous assumption in these considerations is that free will is a categorical variable, that one either has free will or does not have free will at a specific point of time. Instead, it seems much more likely that free will lies on a continuum and that there are differing degrees to which each of us as individuals have a free choice in most of our daily actions as well as those more extreme acts such as killing another individual. While it is true that in most cases a criminal has a choice regarding whether or not to commit a criminal act, the decision is likely to be heavily weighted by a large number of preceding events, including the individual's social history and presence/ absence of both social and biological predispositional influences. Indeed, the whole notion of absolute free will as applied to criminal offending may be unrealistic, with consequent implications for issues such as responsibility for one's actions, consequent punishment, and justice. The following example may help illustrate these issues.

Let us suppose that we could play God and conduct an experiment that can never be executed in reality. Consider the case of Luke in the context of two very different scenarios. In the first scenario Luke is born without any birth complications. His parents are law-abiding, noncriminal, professionals who themselves are loving and supportive parents with a successful marriage. Luke has two older siblings who themselves provide caring role models for him. Luke's parents are highly educated, have superior IQs, and provide Luke with strong encouragement for school work. Luke consequently excels in school, is rewarded and encouraged by his teachers, and is well liked by his school peers. After graduating from high school he excels in university, continues on to graduate school to complete a Ph.D., and becomes a successful sociology professor at UCLA, where he earns a substantial salary. He marries a loving and supportive attorney and has three children who are themselves trouble free. Throughout his life, Luke remains law abiding and does not commit any crime.

Consider the same person, Luke, in a second scenario where we are able to play God by manipulating a number of events. Intrinsically, this is the same Luke as in the first scenario. In this second scenario, Luke's biological mother is now a prostitute. The biological father is a recidivistic criminal who has no further contact with mother or son. Luke's mother smokes, drinks, and takes cocaine during pregnancy. She has a very difficult birth, and as a result of both prenatal and perinatal adverse influences, Luke suffers some degree of brain damage at birth which contributes to hyperactivity, chronic underarousal, and significant cognitive deficits. Illness early in life causes him to be separated from his mother for the first 2 years of life, resulting in maternal deprivation and the development of an affectionless personality. Luke grows up in a crime-ridden, inner-city environment and is continually moved from one home to another. He has seven other siblings, several of whom are violent delinquents who bully and beat him. He is also physically and sexually abused by a series of temporary foster fathers. He is both neglected and rejected by his unloving mother and is also sexually abused by her. One of the foster fathers uses him as a target for firearm practice. Blows to his head from his parents exacerbate early brain dysfunction and produce new brain dysfunction. He also has a number of accidents which contribute further to this brain dysfunction. His stimulation-seeking behavior in school together with academic failure cause him to be unpopular with teachers, while his aggressive, uncontrolled, and unpredictable behavior result in rejection by his peers. His association with delinquent peers results in numerous convictions for petty offenses. Repeated accidents and physical abuse, lack of health care, and early malnutrition result in Luke tending to be physically unattractice, contributing to low self-esteem. Luke leaves school before graduating, fails to complete training schemes, and has difficulty gaining employment. His early delinquent behavior develops into adult criminal offending and he is repeatedly convicted of progressively more serious offenses. He plans and executes a hold-up of a liquor store, and in the ensuing struggle with the owner, he shoots him. The owner dies of his wounds and Luke is convicted of murder and eventually executed after waiting several years on death row.

By manipulation of events *beyond his control*, Luke has been transformed from a very law-abiding individual into a recidivistic, serious criminal offender. The critical question concerns whether Luke should be severely punished for crimes that culminated in a murderous act. While it is clearly a serious offense with devastating consequences for the victim and his/her relatives, in playing God we know that without these negative predispositions Luke would not have committed this desperate act. The scenarios are clearly extreme, but all events in the second scenario are taken from true criminal cases, and there are many offenders who share elements of the background of criminal Luke.

Are we right in taking Luke's life when in reality his biological and social predispositions (none of which he had any influence over) were virtually destined to lead him into a life of crime? Here one returns to the issue of free will. Despite his undeniable predispositions, in law it would be argued that Luke planned the crime, knew the difference between right and wrong, knew that this action in particular was wrong, was not overcome by an "irresistible impulse" to commit this specific act, and was not suffering from mental illness as currently defined. In other words, he was in control of his actions and had the freedom to decide what he would or would not do. But we need to look at this issue in terms of the shaping of freedom of will and the extent to which these background factors biased life's wheel of fortune against Luke. While in absolute terms Luke could have decided not to hold up the liquor store, his whole life's experiences had been shaped in such a way to predispose him to ultimately commit this or another similar act.

Leaving aside the issue of whether Luke meant to kill the owner before the hold-up, whether he would not have shot him if the owner had done as he was told, and whether the owner would not have died of his wounds if by chance the bullet had followed a slightly different trajectory, there is a sense in which Luke's "free will" at the time of committing this act was not subject to free expression, but was constrained by a multitude of factors in his early life. An individual may "choose" a career in accountancy, but that "free choice" is ultimately heavily shaped by factors such as previous success in mathematics at school, relative lack of success in other academic subjects, and a host of other life influences. By the same token, Luke may indeed have had a choice to either hold up the store or alternatively stay at home and watch TV, but the background predispositions over which he had no control may exert a strong "push" toward turning his decision making into an antisocial direction.

In construing free will more as a dichotomy than a dimension, law and society grossly oversimplify what in reality is a considerably more complex process. The pragmatic consideration of finding a criminal defendant guilty or not guilty is virtually a dichotomous decision process that does not do justice to the more dimensional processes (degree of predisposition, degree of free will) which in real terms bear on criminal acts.

The predispositions that have been outlined in previous chapters clearly place constraints on the individual's free will, though not in as dramatic a way as some severe mental disorders such as schizophrenia may place constraints on free will. If we accept that crime is a disorder, acknowledge that there are clear predispositions that form the basis for recidivistic crime, and acknowledge that in most cases these predispositions are beyond the individual's control, then the implication is that criminal offenders should not be punished as severely as they are currently for their actions.

VI. CRIME AS A DISORDER AND THE STATUS OF BIOLOGICAL RESEARCH

Biological research on crime at least in part challenges the notion that crime is largely caused by external environmental factors and instead suggests that individual difference factors need to be taken into account in understanding the causes of crime. Although such biological research is of relatively recent origin, it should be made clear that the question of whether there is a predisposition to crime that arises from within the individual, or alternatively is determined more by environmental factors, is not a debate of recent origin. Rather, it is a question that has been asked for thousands of years.

Jesus, for example, made his own position clear in one of his many bitter confrontations with the Pharisees. The particular clash of views described below takes place after Jesus had crossed from Bethsaida to Genesareth on the Sea of Galilee and had started to heal the sick. Pharisees who had traveled north from Jerusalem to observe him for themselves started to surround and harangue him because some of his disciples were eating meat with unwashed hands (Jewish tradition, held sacrosanct by the Pharisees, dictated that no one must eat without first washing their hands). Jesus in turn castigated the Pharisees for their hypocrisy, chastising them for developing their own traditions that he felt were taking priority over God's own commandments. He then went on to discuss the origin of sins and crimes:

> And he called the multitude to him, and said to them, Listen to me, all of you, and grasp this; nothing that finds its way into a man from outside can make him unclean; what makes a man unclean is what comes out of a man. Listen, you that have ears to hear with.
>
> When he had gone into the house, away from the multitude, his disciples asked him the meaning of the parable. And he said to them, 'Are you so slow of wit? Do you not observe that all the uncleanliness which goes into a man has no means of defiling him, because it travels, not into his heart, but into his belly, and so finds its way into the sewer?' Thus he declared all meat to be clean, and told them that what defiles a man is that which comes out of him. For it is within, from the hearts of men, that their wicked designs come, their sins of adultery, fornication, murder, theft, covetousness, malice, deceit, lasciviousness, envy, blasphemy, pride and folly. All these evils come from within, and it is these which make a man unclean. [The Holy Bible, the Gospel according to Mark, Chapter 7, vv. 14–23]

Although this seems to indicate that Jesus felt that factors internal to the individual rather than the environment were the main determinant of sins and crime, it should be made clear that his arguments are based on his insight into human nature rather than being empirically based. Furthermore, an alternative interpretation might be that Jesus is perhaps making the point that individuals are themselves *responsible* for their crimes and should not avoid responsibility by placing their blame for the crimes on external environmental factors. If Jesus is arguing for *both* positions (crime caused by nonenvironmental, constitutional factors; individuals are responsible for their actions), this view would differ from that being suggested in this book, which instead argues that (1) there are factors outside of the individual's control that act as a predisposition for later crime; (2) these factors render individuals not entirely responsible for their criminal actions; and (3) environmental factors also play a clear role in the development of crime. Furthermore, there is a political context to Jesus' statement that makes a literal interpretation potentially unsafe. Whatever Jesus really meant in this parable, the main point it illustrates is that the fundamental question of the source of criminal and antisocial behavior is not of recent origin.

More recently, in this century, the burden that biological research into crime and violence has had to bear lies with the association of biological research with four conceptions: (1) that biology implies destiny, (2) that it implicates individual difference factors in the etiology of crime, (3) more cryptically, that it is associated with the view that crime may be a disorder, and (4) that it will in some way be selectively used to justify racist policies. The first conception is erroneous for reasons previously discussed at length in Chapter 3 on genetics. The second conception is true, as attested by previous chapters dealing with biological factors on crime and violence. Nevertheless, such a conclusion is an ideological anathema to many social scientists, and given the domination of social science in the study of crime, such research has frequently been subjected to intense (and sometimes unfair) attacks.

The third conception linked to biological research, that it may help support the argument that crime is a disorder, is more surreptitious in that, to the author's knowledge, it has not been overtly stated. Nevertheless, biological findings on crime are challenging and provocative, in part because they implicitly question the notion that the individual is fully responsible for his/her actions, and this notion is only one step removed from the view that crime is a disorder. Social predispositions to crime are in reality just as important in supporting the notion that crime may be construed as a disorder, yet biological research is much more salient in the public's mind and is more traditionally linked to disorder through the medical model of illness.

VII. SUGGESTIONS OF RACIST UNDERTONES TO BIOLOGICAL RESEARCH ON CRIME

The fourth conception, that such research is linked to racist doctrines, has been illustrated most recently in the cancellation by NIH of a conference, "Genetic Factors in Crime: Findings, Uses, and Implications" on July 20, 1992. Funding for this conference was withdrawn after a psychiatrist critical of biological psychiatry on the Black Entertainment Television cable channel criticized the conference and alleged that funding of the conference by NIH was similar to "the kind of racist behavior we saw on the part of Nazi Germany" (Palca, 1992, p. 739). Paradoxically, if the conference had taken place, one goal would have been to focus on the ethical issues posed by genetic research on crime. Claims have also been made that NIH was funding research whose goal was to use drugs to control the antisocial behavior of young inner-city black children. These claims have been vigorously denied by the Health and Human Services (HHS) secretary Louis Sullivan, a black physician, who has promoted an HHS-wide program on youth violence (Barnes, 1992).

The furor over the genetics conference did not occur in isolation. As a backdrop, in February 1992, Dr. Frederick Goodwin who at that time was head of the Alcohol, Drug Abuse, and Mental Health Administration

(ADAMHA) made some remarks on violence at an NIMH advisory council meeting which were later to be misconstrued as racist. Specifically, Goodwin linked research on aggressive, hypersexual monkeys to the loss of structure in society today and stated that "maybe it isn't just the careless use of the word when people call certain areas of certain cities jungles" (APA, 1992, p. 1). Racist undertones were read into these comments, and in the turmoil that followed Goodwin resigned his post on February 27, 1992. Dr. Goodwin himself admitted that he used the word *jungle* inappropriately, but was shocked that others would interpret his comments in racist terms (APA, 1992).

One outcome of these two incidents has been a fierce attack on the violence initiative proposed by NIMH, which aims to increase research funding on understanding the origins of violence (Stone, 1992). The paradox is that although it is often mentioned that there is a disproportionately high level of crime in blacks, it must also be remembered that blacks are disproportionately the *victims* of violence and crime. Blocking research that aims to understand and control crime and violence may therefore prove to be a major disservice selective to minority groups, and in this sense attempts to block our further understanding of violence in all groups could even be construed as racially biased in itself.

It seems clear that there is very fierce opposition to any research into the biological or genetic basis of crime and violence, but the bases for this opposition are probably more imaginary than real for the following reasons. The fear is that research showing that blacks are genetically prone to violence may be used to promote racist views. However, no biological researcher of crime and violence known to the author espouses the use of such research for any form of racial bias. But perhaps more telling, there is no previous or current published research *at all* on the genetics of crime in nonwhite groups. Furthermore, the author knows of no published research that compares the biological predisposition for crime that we know exists for whites with other minority groups or, alternatively, that such predispositions are greater or less than those found in whites. Given this complete void of biological research on minority groups, one wonders if critics of a biological approach are attacking a straw man. Although many such critics may be well intentioned, care must be taken not to impute racial bias on biological research simply as a means to draw such research into disrepute.

Although there has been no research into genetic and biological research into minority groups with respect to crime and violence, it is felt that there are good scientific and pragmatic reasons why such research should take place. Apart from the more general policy issue of political interference into scientific research (Barnes, 1992; Stone, 1992), it is essential that we understand the causes of crime and violence in *all* sectors of our society, not just in privileged sectors. For example, if one found that the biological and genetic basis for crime and violence is considerably lower in nonwhites than in whites, this would constitute strong indirect evidence to suggest that any excess of violence and crime observed in a minority group may be due to economic and social deprivation and discrimination. If this were true, one practical implication would be to redouble efforts to redress such deprivation and discrimination in order to reduce levels of crime and violence in such groups. As another example, we may find that the biological bases for crime and violence in nonwhite groups is just as great as in whites, but that there is a stronger *interaction* between social and biological factors in nonwhites. Again, the implication would be to intervene at the environmental level in order to suppress the biological predisposition, and thus reduce rates of crime.

If we are to be sincere about understanding and ultimately preventing the serious harm perpetrated throughout society by offenders, society has a very important responsibility to seek out *all* forms of knowledge on the development of such behavior, including genetic and biological predispositional factors. Given the importance of these variables for fully understanding the causes of crime outlined in this book, failing to do so would ultimately result in a failure to prevent crime and potentially the unnecessary pain and suffering of the victims of crimes that otherwise may have been avoided. Previous conditions once thought to be due largely to environmental factors have, due to extensive biological research, been found to have a strong biological basis (e.g., schizophrenia). Without such research, our understanding and hopes of ultimately preventing such debilitating conditions would be today considerably reduced. While there may be a fear associated with the notion that violence may in part have biological roots, this fear must be scientifically confronted, not politically repressed.

By the same token, biological researchers have an equally important responsibility, which is to do their utmost to ensure that findings from such research are reported carefully and dispassionately to reduce the possibility of potential misinterpretations. Nevertheless, scientists should not bear the full burden of this responsibility; forces more potent than individual scientists must also be alert to misuse of scientific data by unscrupulous individuals. To leave such a responsibility solely to the scientific community would be a decided abnegation of duty by other sectors of society for the protection of vulnerable individuals. One such responsibility of society is to bring these issues more openly to *nonpartisan* public discussion and understanding if we are to truly educate society on the appropriate understanding and interpretation of biological research on crime, although clearly biological researchers must play a responsible role in this process. It is hoped that this book may make a small, initial contribution to this effort by attempting to debunk some of the myths on biological research and to have such processes viewed more within the context of important social and environmental processes where it belongs.

VIII. FUTURE DIRECTIONS IN CRIMINALITY RESEARCH

Independent of whether one does or does not accept the possibility that crime is a disorder, some comment should be made on the type of research that is most likely to advance our understanding of criminal behavior. With respect to research on social factors, family factors are clearly of major importance. Within this area, the experiencing of traumatic events such as child abuse would seem to be a particularly important avenue for future research. Although it would come as no surprise to many that child abuse may predispose to crime and violence, it has only been very recently established that such a link exists in a sound prospective study. Furthermore, we know next to nothing about the precise mechanisms by which child abuse translates itself into criminal behavior, why some but not other abused children progress on to crime while others desist, what types of interventions could prevent the development of criminal behavior in such predisposed individuals, and whether there are other traumatic events that can trigger antisocial, criminal behavior. In addition, research on interpersonal processes and their role in triggering violence within the family seems worthy of greater attention in the future.

With respect to research on biological factors, new developments in molecular genetics and neurochemistry clearly represent important areas of future research. Perhaps the most exciting developments will take place in brain imaging research. Specifically, the recent (1991) development of fast MRI (also known as MRI perfusion scanning, echo planar MRI, and fast gradient echo) allows for the assessment of both brain structure *and* function using the same noninvasive technique. The development and application of this technique, which has a temporal resolution on the order of 100 ms and a spatial resolution under 1 mm, is in its infancy at the time of this writing, but it promises to revolutionize our understanding of both normal and abnormal brain functioning. To the extent that all behavioral and thought processes originate in the brain, this technique should allow for much greater understanding of the brain mechanisms underlying antisocial, criminal behavior and its associated cognitive deficits.

It is an unfortunate reality of current academic research into criminal behavior that the majority of investigators pursue their own independent specialty lines of research, turn their backs on developments in other relevant disciplines, and closely guard their own turf. To some extent, this attitude can be justified in that interdisciplinary research cannot proceed without a sound foundation of knowledge in a variety of specialty fields, but ultimately this attitude is overly defensive and will ultimately have a net negative impact on the field.

It is likely that biologically-oriented research can contribute much to socially-oriented research, and vice versa. For example, most biological research (including that of the author) is greatly limited in terms of measurement of the independent variable in contrast to research in the field of sociology, where much greater attention tends to be placed on the measurement of crime. Similarly, the predicted advances in future brain imaging research will not be made by radiologists, but instead by collaborations involving radiologists, psychiatrists, psychologists, and sociologists. For example, sociologists can make major contributions to teams working in this field by helping to devise the uptake task which is most appropriate to this population (e.g., simulation of violence-provoking scenario), measuring self-report criminal behavior (a technique pioneered by sociologists), identifying crucial control variables, assessing potentially important demographic and environmental moderator variables, and facilitating a more sophisticated statistical analysis of such data.

In this sense, building a model of criminal behavior using knowledge from only one discipline is like trying to build a prison using only electricians. The electricians (biological and brain imaging researchers) may do an excellent job of constructing the complex internal circuitry of the prison, but without the bricklayers (social researchers) to provide the foundations and overall structure for the prison, such work is misplaced. By the same token, generating the structural basis for the prison may give a global, superficial semblance of completion but will inevitably result in a nonfunctional prison. Ultimately, the major advances in understanding crime will be derived when the leading methodologies and theories in social research are combined with those in biological research. Whether or not the artisans in the field of criminal behavior are prepared to rise to this challenge remains to be seen.

IX. CONCLUDING STATEMENT

In every society in the history of humanity, there have been tragedies and immense hardship directly resulting from criminal, antisocial acts. It seems perfectly natural that the perpetrators of these acts should suffer for their actions. However, we must face the possibility that if we close the door to even considering the notion that crime is a disorder, we may open the gates to an even greater tragedy. This tragedy is that criminals may in the future be shown not to be entirely responsible for their actions in totality and that advances in remediation and treatment of crime are foreclosed by denying this possibility.

To present-day society, the very notion that crime may be a disorder seems both unreasonable and very unlikely. It is not currently an acceptable view, it has no strong advocates, and it goes against the grain of common sense. Viewing crime as a disorder is an extreme view, and we tend to steer away from extreme views because they are usually misguided. We must not forget, however, that extreme views can be appropriate and that moderate views can be erroneous. During the days of the Spanish Inquisition a moderate view would have been not to burn too many heretics; an extreme view would have been not to burn *any* heretics.

Arguably, we live in the most scientific and intellectually advanced society in the history of the world. We must also accept the fact that every advanced society at every turn in history has viewed itself in the same fashion and has aspired to absolute knowledge and certainty. History has also shown that these same societies have made grievous misjudgments and perpetrated their own atrocities under the banner of absolute knowledge; we look back with incredulity to less than 200 years ago when mental patients were kept locked in fetters and chains and treated little better than animals because of their unacceptable behavior in society. We find it almost unthinkable that society at that time did not view mental disorders more compassionately and rationally. The criminal was permanently left behind when Pinel freed mental patients from their shackles and chains in 1793 and placed them under more humane conditions.

Ultimately, the critical question may be not so much whether crime is indeed a disorder, but whether less than 200 years from now a more advanced society will look back aghast at our current conceptualization of criminal behavior, with its concomitant incarceration and execution of prisoners, with the same incredulity with which today we look back at earlier treatment of mental patients. They may well wonder how society could have countenanced such practices. History has shown that as society becomes more ennobled and sophisticated, physical and mental disabilities such as epilepsy, psychosis, mental deficiency, and alcoholism cease to be viewed within a moral/theological context and are perceived more within the humanitarian context of treatment. It is only relatively recently that our conceptualizations of alcoholism and homosexuality have changed. Just as mental disorders were once viewed as a product of evil forces, will the evil behavior of criminals be eventually viewed as a mental disorder? Society may deny crime as a disorder in the short term, but it is predicted that a future generation *will* reconceptualize nontrivial recidivistic crime as a disorder. In the meantime, we must at least continue to ask questions such as whether crime is a disorder, even though such questions may be viewed as impertinent. For it is only when we ask impertinent questions that we find a way toward a pertinent answer.

X. SUMMARY

This final chapter argued that there is initial evidence to view crime as a disorder because (1) it meets a number of definitions of disorder as well as or better than other disorders; and (2) a nomological network of relationships can be built up around crime from the empirical literature that gives weight to the construct validity of the disorder and gives insights into the social and biological predispositions for the development of this disorder. Thirteen empirical, conceptual, and societal arguments that can be made against this conclusion were outlined, together with respective counterarguments. None of these arguments, in themselves, can convincingly reject the notion of crime as a disorder, although some raise substantive issues that also face disorders other than crime. It is suggested instead that the strongest barrier to accepting the notion of crime as a disorder resides in strong, in-built emotional reactions against crime which may be generated by the same sociobiological factors that gave rise to crime in the first place. It is argued that while criminal behavior is often viewed as volitional in nature, free will is better conceptualized as a dimension than as a dichotomy and that there are strong social and biological pressures beyond the individual's control which, to some degree at least, strongly shape that person's antisocial behavior; consequently, such offenders can be viewed in part as not being entirely responsible for their actions. If we accept that repeated, serious crime is a disorder, the implication is that such offenders should not be punished as severely for their actions, that more freedoms should be restored to incarcerated prisoners, that new, vigorous attempts should be made to increase new research and clinical efforts to understand and treat crime, and that the criminal justice system requires revision in order to take into account the consequent practical implications. It is further argued that biological research into crime is imperative in order for the scientific community to have any chance at all of developing a comprehensive understanding of the causes of crime. While such researchers are responsible for taking every care in appropriately interpreting the results of such research, it is incumbent on society at large not to allow such research to be suppressed for nonscientific reasons, because the greatest advances to be made in the forthcoming centuries clearly lie with those investigators who can successfully integrate such biological findings with the important corpus of research already established on social predispositions for crime.

References

Adams, H. E., & Sutker, P. B. (1984). *Comprehensive handbook of psychopathology.* New York: Plenum.

Adams, J. H., Mitchell, D. E., Graham, D. I., & Doyle, D. (1977). Diffuse brain damage of immediate impact type. *Brain*, **100**, 489–502.

Adler, F., Mueller, G. O. W., & Laufer, W. S. (1991). *Criminology.* New York: McGraw-Hill.

Allen, G. (1976). Scope and methodology of twin studies. *Acta Geneticae Medicae Gemellologiae*, **25**, 79–85.

Allman, L. R., & Jaffe, D. T. (1978). *Abnormal psychology in the life-cycle.* New York: Harper and Row.

Altrocchi, J. (1980). *Abnormal behavior.* New York: Harcourt Brace Jovanovich.

American Psychiatric Association (1952). *Diagnostic and statistical manual of mental disorders.* Washington, DC: American Psychiatric Association.

American Psychiatric Association (1980). *Diagnostic and statistical manual of mental disorders* (3rd ed.). Washington, DC: American Psychiatric Association.

American Psychiatric Association (1987). *Diagnostic and statistical manual of mental disorders* (3rd ed., revised). Washington, DC: American Psychiatric Association.

American Psychological Association (1992). Goodwin to take post amid campaign jitters. *APA Monitor*, **1**, May.

Andreasen, N., & Olsen, S. (1982). Negative vs positive schizophrenia. *Archives of General Psychiatry*, **39**, 789–794.

Aniskiewitz, A. (1973). Autonomic components of vicarious conditioning and psychopathy. *Journal of Clinical Psychology*, **35**, 60–67.

Arbuthnot, J., & Gordon, D. A. (1986). Behavioral and cognitive effects of a moral reasoning development intervention for high-risk behavior-disordered adolescents. *Journal of Counseling and Clinical Psychology*, **54**, 208–216.

Arbuthnot, J., Gordon, D. A., & Jurkovic, G. J. (1987). Personality. In H. C. Quay (Ed.), *Handbook of juvenile delinquency* (pp. 139–183). New York: Wiley.

Archer, J. (1991). The influence of testosterone on human aggression. *British Journal of Psychology*, **82**, 1–28.

Ashmore, Z., & Jarvie, J. (1987). Job skills for young offenders. In B. J. McGurk, D. M. Thornton, & M. Williams (Eds.), *Applying psychology to imprisonment: Theory and practice* (pp. 329–340). London: Her Majesty's Stationery Office.

Axelrod, R., & Hamilton, W. D. (1981). The evolution of cooperation. *Science*, **211**, 1390–1396.

Bach-y-Rita, G., Lion, J. R., Climent, C. E. and Ervin, F. (1971). Episodic dyscontrol: A study of 139 violent patients. *American Journal of Psychiatry*, **127**, 1473–1478.

Bachman, J. G., O'Malley, P. M., & Johnston, J. (1978). *Adolescence to adulthood—Change and stability in the lives of young men.* (Vol. 6. Youth in transition). Ann Arbor, MI: University of Michigan Institute for Social Research.

Baker, L. A. (1986). Estimating genetic correlations among discordant phenotypes: An analysis of criminal convictions and psychiatric hospital diagnoses in Danish adoptees. *Behavior Genetics*, **16**, 127–142.

Baker, L. A., Mack, W., Moffitt, T. E., & Mednick, S. A. (1989). Etiology of sex differences in criminal convictions in a Danish adoption cohort. *Behavior Genetics*, **19**, 355–370.

Baker, R. L., & Mednick, S. A. (1984). *Influences on human development: A longitudinal perspective.* Boston: Kluwer Nijhoff.

Bakhit, C., & Swerdlow, N. (1986). Behavioral changes following central injection of cysteamine in rats. *Brain Research*, **365**, 159–163.

Balasubramaniam, V., Kanaka, T. S., & Ramamurthi, B. (1970). Surgical treatment of hyperkinetic and behavior disorders. *International Surgery*, **54**, 18–23.

Barnes, D. M. (1992). Anatomy of an attempted murder: How to kill research on violent behavior (editorial). *Journal of NIH Research*, **4**, 10.

Baron, M. & Risch, N. (1987). The spectrum concept of schizophrenia: Evidence for a genetic-environmental continuum. *Journal of Psychiatric Research*, **21**, 257–267.

Bartfai, A., Edman, G., Levander, S. E., Schalling, D., & Sedvall, G. (1984). Bilateral skin conductance activity, clinical symptoms, and CSF monoamine metabolite levels in unmedicated schizophrenics, differing in rate of habituation. *Biological Psychology*, **18**, 201–218.

Bartol, C. R. (1991). *Criminal behavior: A psychosocial approach* (3rd ed.). Englewood Cliffs, NJ: Prentice Hall.

Beaumont, J. G. (1983). *Introduction to neuropsychology.* Oxford: Blackwell.

Benton, D., Kumari, N., & Brain, P. F. (1982). Mild hypoglycemia and questionnaire measures of aggression. *Biological Psychology*, **14**, 129–135.

Bice, T. (1993). Cognitive and psychophysiological differences in proactive and reactive aggressive boys. Doctoral dissertation, Department of Psychology, University of Southern California.

Binder, A. (1988). Juvenile delinquency. *Annual Review of Psychology*, **39**, 253–282.

Bird, L. (1992). *Attribution of criminal behavior to social or biological factors in undergraduates.* Unpublished manuscript, Department of Psychology, University of Southern California.

Blackburn, R. (1978). Psychopathy, arousal, and the need for stimulation. In R. D. Hare & D. Schalling (Eds.), *Psychopathic behavior: Approaches to research.* New York: Wiley.

Blackburn, R. (1979). Cortical and autonomic response arousal in primary and secondary psychopaths. *Psychophysiology,* 16, 143–150.

Blackburn, R. (1983). Psychopathy, delinquency and crime. In A. Gale & J. A. Edwards (Eds.), *Physiological correlates of human behavior* (Vol. 3, pp. 187–205). London: Academic Press.

Blakemore, C. & Cooper, G. F. (1970). Development of the brain depends on the visual environment. *Nature,* 228, 477–478.

Blashfield, R. K., & Livesley, W. J. (1991). Metaphorical analysis of psychiatric classification as a psychological test. *Journal of Abnormal Psychology,* 100, 262–270.

Blumstein, A., Cohen, J., Roth, J., & Visher, C. (1986). *Criminal careers and "career criminals."* Washington, DC: National Academy Press.

Bohman, M. (1972). A study of adopted children, their background, environment, and adjustment. *Acta Psychiatrica Scandinavica,* 61, 90–97.

Bohman, M. (1978). Some genetic aspects of alcoholism and crime: A population of adoptees. *Archives of General Psychiatry,* 35, 269–276.

Bohman, M., Cloninger, R., Sigvardsson, S., & von Knoring, A. L. (1982). Predisposition to petty criminality in Swedish adoptees. I. Genetic and environmental heterogeneity. *Archives of General Psychiatry,* 39, 1233–1241.

Borgstrom, C. A. (1939). Eine serie von Kriminellen Zwillingen. *Archiv fur Rassenbiologie.*

Bowlby, J. (1946). *Forty-four juvenile thieves: Their characters and home-life.* Baillere, England: Tindall and Cox.

Bowlby, J. (1969). *Attachment and loss* (Vol. I. *Attachment*). New York: Hogarth Press.

Boyd, R. & Lorberbaum, J. P. (1987). No pure strategy is evolutionarily stable in the repeated Prisoner's Dilemma game. *Nature,* 327, 58–59.

Braff, D. L. & Siever, L. J. (1992). Defining the boundaries of schizophrenia. Study group, *American College of Neuropsychopharmacology: 31st Annual Meeting,* San Juan, Puerto Rico, December 14–18.

Brain, P. (1990). *Hormonal aspects of aggression and violence.* Symposium on the understanding and control of violent behavior, Destin, Florida, April 1–4.

Brennan, P., Mednick, S. A., & Kandel, E. (1993). Congenital determinants of violent and property offending. In D. J. Pepler & K. H. Rubin (Eds.), *The development and treatment of childhood aggression.* (pp. 81–92). Hillsdale, NJ: Erlbaum.

Brickman, A. S., McManus, M., Grapentine, W. L., & Alessi, N. E. (1984). Neuropsychological assessment of seriously delinquent adolescents. *Journal of the American Academy of Child Psychiatry,* 23, 453–457.

Brier, N. (1989). The relationship between learning disability and delinquency: A review and reappraisal. *Journal of Learning Disabilities,* 22, 546–553.

Brinkley, J. R., Beitman, B. D., & Friedel, R. O. (1979). Low-dose neuroleptic regimens in the treatment of borderline patients. *Archives of General Psychiatry,* 36, 319.

Britten, R. J. (1986). Rates of DNA sequence evolution differ between taxonomic groups. *Science,* 231, 1393–1398.

Brizer, D. A. (1988). Psychopharmacology and the management of violent patients. *Psychiatric Clinics of North America,* 11, 551–568.

Brown, S. E. (1984). Social class, child maltreatment, and delinquent behavior. *Criminology,* 22, 259–278.

Bryant, E. T., Scott, M. L., Golden, C. J., & Tori, C. D. (1984). Neuropsychological deficits, learning disability, and violent behavior. *Journal of Consulting and Clinical Psychology,* 52, 323–324.

Bryden, M. P. (1982). *Laterality: Functional asymmetry in the intact brain*. New York: Academic Press.

Buchsbaum, M. S., Nuechterlein, K. H., Haier, R. J., Wu, J., Sicotte, N., Hazlett, E., Asarnow, R., Potkin, S., & Guich, S. (1990). Glucose metabolic rate in normals and schizophrenics during the continuous performance test assessed by positron emission tomography. *British Journal of Psychiatry*, 156, 216–227.

Buikhuisen, W., Bontekoe, E. H. M., Plas-Korenhoff, C. D., & Buuren, S. (1985). Characteristics of criminals: The privileged offender. *International Journal of Law and Psychiatry*, 7, 301–313.

Buikhuisen, W., Eurelings-Bontekoe, E. H. M., & Host, K. B. (1989). Crime and recovery time: Mednick revisited. *International Journal of Law and Psychiatry*, 12, 29–40.

Bullock, J. (1988). *Tonic heart rate, social class, and antisociality in adolescent girls*. Unpublished manuscript, University of York, England.

Burright, R. G., Engellenner, W. J., & Donovick, P. J. (1989). Postpartum aggression and plasma prolactin levels in mice exposed to lead. *Physiology and Behavior*, 46, 889–893.

Burt, C. (1925). *The young delinquent*. New York: Appleton and Co.

Buss, A. H. (1966). *Psychopathology*. New York: Wiley.

Buydens, B. L., & Branchey, M. H. (1992). Cortisol in alcoholics with a disordered aggression control. *Psychoneuroendocrinology*, 17, 45–54.

Cacioppo, J., Tassinary, L., & Fridlund, A. (1991). *Principles of psychophysiology: Physical, social, and inferential elements*. Cambridge: Cambridge University Press.

Cadoret, R. J. (1978). Psychopathology in adopted-away offspring of biological parents with antisocial behavior. *Archives of General Psychiatry*, 35, 176–184.

Cadoret, R. & Cain, C. (1980). Sex differences in predictors of antisocial behavior in adoptees. *Archives of General Psychiatry*, 37, 1171–1175.

Cadoret, R. J., Cain, C. A., & Crowe, R. R. (1983). Evidence for gene–environment interaction in the development of adolescent antisocial behavior. *Behavior Genetics*, 13, 301–310.

Cadoret, R. J., O'Gorman, T. W., Troughton, E., & Heywood, E. (1985). Alcoholism and antisocial personality: Interrelationships, genetic, and environmental factors. *Archives of General Psychiatry*, 42, 161–167.

Cadoret, R. J., Troughton, E., & O'Gorman, T. W. (1987). Genetic and environmental factors in alcohol abuse and antisocial personality. *Journal of Studies of Alcohol*, 48, 1–8.

Cadoret, R. J., Troughton, E., & Bagford, J. (1990). Genetic and environmental factors in adoptee antisocial personality. *European Archives of Psychiatry and Neurological Sciences*, 239, 231–240.

Cannon, T., Fuhrmann, M., Mednick, S. A., Machon, R. A., Parnas, J., & Schulsinger, F. (1988). Third ventricle enlargement and reduced electrodermal responsiveness. *Psychophysiology*, 25, 153–156.

Cannon, T., Raine, A., Herman, T. M., Mednick, S. A., Schulsinger, F., & Moore, M. (1992). Third ventricle enlargement and lower heart rate levels in a high risk sample. *Psychophysiology*, 29, 294–301.

Canter, R. J. (1982). Family correlates of male and female delinquency. *Criminology*, 20, 149–167.

Carey, G. (1989). *Genetics and violence: Human studies*. Commissioned paper for Panel on the Understanding and Control of Violent Behavior. Washington, DC: National Academy of Sciences.

Carey, G. (1992). Twin imitation for antisocial behavior: Implications for genetic and family environment research. *Journal of Abnormal Psychology*, 101, 18–25.

Carson, R. C. (1991). Dilemmas in the pathway of the DSM-IV. *Journal of Abnormal Psychology*, 100, 302–307.

Cavior, N., & Howard, L. R. (1973). Facial attractiveness and juvenile delinquency among black offenders and white offenders. *Journal of Abnormal Child Psychology*, 1, 202–213.

Cernkovich, S. A., & Giordano, P. C. (1987). Family relationships and delinquency. *Criminology*, 25, 295–321.

Chaiken, J. M. & Chaiken, M. (1982). *Varieties of criminal behavior* Rand report R-2814-NIJ. Santa Monica, California: Rand Corporation.

Chandler, M., & Moran, T. (1990). Psychopath and moral development: A comparative study of delinquent and nondelinquent boys. *Development and Psychopathology*, 2, 227–246.

Cherek, D., Steinberg, J., & Manno, B. (1985). Effects of alcohol on human aggressive behavior. *Journal on the Study of Alcohol*, 14, 321–328.

Chesno, F. A., & Kilmann, P. R. (1975). Effects of stimulation intensity on sociopathic avoidance learning. *Journal of Abnormal Psychology*, 84, 144–150.

Christiansen, K. O. (1977a). A review of criminality among twins. In S. A. Mednick and K. O. Christiansen (Eds.), *Biosocial bases of criminal behavior*. New York: Gardner Press.

Christiansen, K. O. (1977b). A preliminary study of criminality among twins. In S. A. Mednick & K. O. Christiansen (Eds.), *Biosocial bases of criminal behavior* (pp. 89–108). New York: Gardner Press.

Christiansen, K., & Winkler, E. M. (1992). Hormonal, anthropometrical, and behavioral correlates of physical aggression in Kung San men of Namibia. *Aggressive Behavior*, 18, 271–280.

Chronbach, L. J., & Meehl, P. E. (1955). Construct validity in psychological tests. *Psychological Bulletin*, 52, 281–302.

Clare, A. W. (1985). Hormones, behavior and the menstrual cycle. *Journal of Psychosomatic Research*, 29, 225–233.

Cleckley, H. C. (1976). *The mask of sanity*, 5th ed. St. Louis, MO: Mosby

Cleckley, H. C. (1982). *The mask of sanity*, 6th ed. St. Louis, MO: C.V. Mosby Company.

Cloninger, C. R., & Gottesman, I. I. (1987). Genetic and environmental factors in antisocial behavior disorders. In S. A. Mednick, T. E. Moffitt, & S. Stack (Eds.), *The causes of crime: New biological approaches*. Cambridge: Cambridge University Press.

Cloninger, C. R., Reich, T., and Guze, S. B. (1975). The multifactorial model of disease transmission: II. Sex differences in the familial transmission of sociopathy (antisocial personality). *British Journal of Psychiatry*, 127, 11–22.

Cloninger, C. R., Christiansen, K. O., Reich, T., and Gottesman, I. I. (1978). Implications of sex differences in the prevalences of antisocial personality, alcoholism, and criminality for familial transmission. *Archives of General Psychiatry*, 35, 941–951.

Cloninger, C. R., Sigvardsson, S., Bohman, M., & von Knorring, A. L. (1982). Predisposition to petty criminality in Swedish adoptees: II. Cross-fostering analysis of gene–environmental interactions. *Archives of General Psychiatry*, 39, 1242–1247.

Cloward, R., & Ohlin, L. (1960). *Delinquency and opportunity*. New York: The Free Press.

Cocchi, R., Felici, M., Tonni, L., & Venanzi, G. (1984). Behavior troubles in nursery school children and their possible relationship to pregnancy or delivery complications. *Acta Psychiatrica Belgica*, 84, 173–179.

Cohen, A. K. (1955). *Delinquent boys: The culture of the gang*. New York: The Free Press.

Cohen, J. (1986). Research in criminal careers: Individual frequency rates and offense seriousness. In A. Blumstein, J. Cohen, J. A. Roth, & C. A. Visher (Eds.), *Criminal careers and career criminals* (pp. 292–418). Washington, DC: National Academy Press.

Cohen, J. (1988). *Statistical power analysis for the behavioral sciences* (2nd. ed.). Hillsdale, NJ: Erlbaum.

Coie, J. D., Underwood, M., & Lochman, J. E. (1991). Programmatic intervention with aggressive children in the school setting. In D. J. Pepler & K. H. Rubin (Eds.), *The development and treatment of childhood aggression*. Hillsdale, NJ: Erlbaum.

Coleman, J. C. (1972). *Abnormal psychology and modern life* (4th ed.). Glenview, IL: Scott, Foresman and Co.

Coles, M. P. G., Donchin, E., & Porges, S. W. (1986). *Psychophysiology: Systems, processes and applications*. New York: Guilford.

Cooper, J. R., Bloom, F. E., & Roth, R. H. (1986). *The biochemical basis of neuropharmacology* (5th ed.). New York: Oxford University Press.

Cortes, J. B., & Galtti, F. M. (1972). *Delinquency and crime: A biopsychosocial approach*. New York: Seminar Press.

Craft, M. (1966). *Psychopathic disorders*. Oxford, England: Pergamon.

Crawford, C. (1987). Sociobiology: Of what value to psychology? In C. Crawford, M. Smith, & D. Krebs (Eds.), *Sociobiology and psychology: Ideas, issues and applications* (pp. 3–30). Hillsdale, NJ: Erlbaum.

Crowe, R. (1975). An adoption study of antisocial personality. *Archives of General Psychiatry*, **31**, 785–791.

Currie, E. (1993). In search of the violence initiative. *Journal of NIH Research*, **5**, 20–22.

Dabbs, J. M., Frady, R. L., Carr, T. S., & Besch, N. F. (1987). Saliva testosterone and criminal violence in young adult prison inmates. *Psychosomatic Medicine*, **49**, 174–182.

Dabbs, J. M., Ruback, R. B., Frady, R. L., Hopper, C. H., & Sgoutas, D. S. (1988). Saliva testosterone and criminal violence among women. *Personality and Individual Differences*, **9**, 269–275.

Dabbs, J. M., Jurkovic, G. J., & Frady, R. L. (1991). Salivary testosterone and cortisol among late adolescent male offenders. *Journal of Abnormal Child Psychology*, **19**, 469–478.

Dale, P. G. (1980). Lithium therapy in aggressive mentally subnormal patients. *British Journal of Psychiatry*, **137**, 469–474.

Dalgaard, O. S., & Kringlen, E. (1976). A Norwegian twin study of criminality. *British Journal of Criminal Psychology*, **16**, 213–232.

Dalton, K. (1961). Menstruation and crime. *British Medical Journal*, **2**, 1752–1753.

Daly, M., & Wilson, M. (1985). Child abuse and other risks of not living with both parents. *Ethology and Biology*, **6**, 197–210.

Daly, M., & Wilson, M. (1988a). Evolutionary social psychology and family homicide. *Science*, **242**, 519–524.

Daly, M., & Wilson, M. (1988b). *Homicide*. New York: de Gruyter.

Damasio, A. R. (1979). The frontal lobes. In K. M. Heilman & E. Valenstein (Eds.), *Clinical neuropsychology*. (pp. 339–375). New York: Oxford University Press.

Damasio, A. R. (1985). The frontal lobes. In K. M. Heilman & E. Valenstein (Eds.), *Clinical neuropsychology* (pp. 339–375). New York: Oxford University Press.

Damasio, A. R., Tranel, D., & Damasio, H. (1990). Individuals with sociopathic behavior caused by frontal damage fail to respond autonomically to social stimuli. *Behavioral Brain Research*, **41**, 81–94.

Darwin, C. R. (1859). *The origin of species*. London: John Murray.

Daugherty, T. K., & Quay, H. C. (1989). Response perseveration and delayed responding in childhood behavior disorders. *Journal of Child Psychology and Psychiatry*, **32**, 453–461.

Davies, W. (1982). Violence in prisons. In P. Feldman (Ed.), *Developments in the study of criminal behavior. Vol. 2. Violence*. London: Wiley.

Davies, J. G. V., & Maliphant, R. (1971). Autonomic responses of male adolescents exhibiting refractory behavior in school. *Journal of Child Psychology and Psychiatry*, **12**, 115–127.

Davison, G. C., & Neale, J. M. (1986). *Abnormal psychology: An experimental clinical approach* (4th ed.). New York: Wiley.

Dawkins, R. (1976). *The selfish gene*. Oxford: Oxford University Press.

Dawkins, R. (1989). *The selfish gene* (2nd ed.). Oxford: Oxford University Press.

Dawson, M. E. (1990). Psychophysiology at the interface of clinical science, cognitive science, and neuroscience: Presidential address, 1989. *Psychophysiology*, **27**, 243–255.

Dawson, M. E., & Schell, A. (1985). Information processing and human autonomic classical conditioning. In P. K. Ackles, J. R. Jennings, & M. G. H. Coles (Eds.), *Advances in psychophysiology* (Vol. 1, pp. 89–165). Greenwich, CT: JAI Press.

Dawson, M. E., Filion, D. L., & Schell, A. M. (1989). Is elicitation of the autonomic orienting response associated with allocation of processing resources? *Psychophysiology*, **26**, 560–572.

Dawson, M. E., Schell, A., & Filion, D. (1990). The electrodermal system. In J. T. Cacioppo & L. G. Tassinary (Eds.), *Principles of psychophysiology* (pp. 295–324). Cambridge: Cambridge University Press.

DeFries, J. D., & Fulker, D. W. (1985). Multiple regression analysis of twin data. *Behavior Genetics*, **15**, 467–473.

Delameter, A. M., & Lahey, B. (1983). Physiological correlates of conduct problems in hyperactive and learning disabled children. *Journal of Abnormal Child Psychology*, **11**, 85–100.

Denno, D. W. (1985). Sociological and human developmental explanations of crime: Conflict or consensus? *Criminology*, **23**, 711–741.

Denno, D. J. (1989). *Biology, crime and violence: New Evidence*. Cambridge: Cambridge University Press.

De Souza, E. B., & Van Loo, G. R. (1986). Brain catecholamine responses to repeated stress in rats. *Brain Research*, **367**, 77–86.

Devonshire, P. A., Howard, R. C., & Sellars, C. (1987). Frontal lobe functions and personality in mentally abnormal offenders. *Personality and Individual Differences*, **9**, 339–344.

DiLalla, L. F., & Gottesman, I. I. (1991). Biological and genetic contributors to violence— Widom's untold tale. *Psychological Bulletin*, **109**, 125–129.

Dion, K. (1972). Physical attractiveness and evaluations of childrens' transgressions. *Journal of Personality and Social Psychology*, **24**, 207–213.

Dishion, T. J., Patterson, G. R., Stoolmiller, M., & Skinner, M. L. (1991). Family, school, and behavioral antecedents to early adolescent involvement with antisocial peers. *Developmental Psychology*, **27**, 172–180.

Dodge, K. A. (1980). Social cognition and children's aggressive behavior. *Child Development*, **51**, 162–170.

Dodge, K. A. (1986). A social information processing model of social competence in children. In M. Perlmutter (Ed.), *Minnesota symposium in child psychology* (Vol. 18, pp. 77–125). Hillsdale, NJ: Erlbaum.

Dodge, K. A. (1990). The structure and function of reactive and proactive aggression. In D. J. Pepler & K. H. Rubin (Eds.), *The development of childhood aggression*. Hillsdale, NJ: Erlbaum.

Dodge, K. A., & Coie, J. D. (1987). Social information processing factors in reactive and proactive aggression in children's peer groups. *Journal of Personality and Social Psychology*, **53**, 1146–1158.

Dodge, K. A., & Crick, N. R. (1990). Social information processing bases of aggressive behavior in children. *Personality and Social Psychology Bulletin*, **16**, 8–22.

Dodge, K. A., & Newman, J. P. (1981). Biased decision-making processes in aggressive boys. *Journal of Abnormal Psychology*, **90**, 375–379.

Dodge, K. A., & Somberg, D. R. (1987). Hostile attributional biases among aggressive boys are exacerbated under conditions of threat to the self. *Child Development*, **58**, 213–224.

Dodge, K. A., Price, J. M., & Bachorowski, J. A. (1990). Hostile attributional biases in severely aggressive adolescents. *Journal of Abnormal Psychology*, **99**, 385–392.

Duke, M., & Nowicki, S. (1979). *Abnormal psychology*. Monterey, CA: Brooks/Cole.

Dutton, D. G., & Hart, S. D. (1992). Evidence for long-term, specific effects of childhood abuse and neglect on criminal behavior in men. *International Journal of Offender Therapy and Comparative Criminology*, **36**, 129–137.

Edelberg, R. (1972). Electrodermal recovery rate, goal-orientation, and aversion. *Psychophysiology*, **9**, 512–520.

Edelberg, R. (1993). Electrodermal mechanisms: A critique of the two-effector hypothesis and a proposed replacement. In J. C. Roy, W. Boucsein, D. C. Fowles, & J. Gruzelier (Eds.), *Electrodermal activity: From physiology to psychology*. New York: Plenum. In press.

Eichelman, B. (1986). The biology and somatic experimental treatment of aggressive disorders. In H. K. Brodie & P. A. Berger (Eds.), *The American handbook of psychiatry* (Vol. 8, pp. 651–678). New York: Basic Books.

Eichelman, B. (1993). Bridges from the animal laboratory to the study of violent or criminal individuals. In S. Hodgins (Ed.), *Mental disorder and crime* (pp. 194–207). Newbury Park, CA: Sage.

Ellingson, R. J. (1954). The incidence of EEG abnormality among patients with mental disorders of apparently nonorganic origin: A critical review. *American Journal of Psychiatry*, **111**, 263–275.

Elliott, D. S., Ageton, S. S., & Huizinga, D. (1983). The prevalence and incidence of delinquent behavior: 1976–1980. *National youth survey project* (Report no. 26). Boulder, CO: Behavioral Research Institute.

Elliott, F. A. (1978). Neurological aspects of antisocial behavior. In W. H. Reid (Ed.), *The psychopath: A comprehensive study of antisocial disorders and behavior.* New York: Brunner/Mazell.

Elliott, F. A. (1982). Neurological findings in adult minimal brain dysfunction and dyscontrol syndrome. *Journal of Nervous and Mental Disease,* **170**, 680–687.

Elliott, F. A. (1987). Neuroanatomy and neurology of aggression. Special issue: Treatment of aggressive disorders. *Psychiatric Annals,* **17**, 385–388.

Elliott, F. A. (1988). Neurological factors. In V. B. Van Hassett, R. L. Morrison, A. S. Bellack, & M. Hersen (Eds.), *Handbook of family violence* (pp. 359–382). New York: Plenum.

Ellis, L. (1988). The victimful–victimless crime distinction, and seven universal demographic correlates of victimful criminal behavior. *Personality and Individual Differences,* **9**, 525–548.

Ellis, L. (1990). Left- and mixed-handedness and criminality: Explanations for a probable relationship. In S. Coran (Ed.), *Left handedness: Behavioral implications and anomalies.* North Holland: Elsevier.

Engel, G. L. (1977). Emotional death and sudden death. *Psychology Today,* **11**, 153–154.

Epps, P., & Parnell, R. W. (1952). Physique and temperament of women delinquents compared with women undergraduates. *British Journal of Medical Psychology,* **25**, 249–255.

Eysenck, H. J. (1964). *Crime and personality* (1st ed.). London: Methuen.

Eysenck, H. J. (1977). *Crime and personality* (3rd ed.). St. Albans, England: Paladin.

Eysenck, H. J. (1987). Personality theory and problems of criminality. In B. J. McGurk, D. M. Thornton, & M. Williams (Eds.), *Applying psychology to imprisonment: Theory and practice* (pp. 29–58). London: Her Majesty's Stationery Office.

Eysenck, H. J., & Eysenck, S. G. B. (1978). Psychopathy, personality and genetics. In R. D. Hare & D. Schalling (Eds.), *Psychopathic behavior: Approaches to research* (pp. 197–224). New York: Wiley.

Eysenck, H. J., & Gudjonsson, G. H. (1989). *The causes and cures of criminality.* New York: Plenum.

Falconer, D. S. (1965). The inheritance of liability to certain diseases, estimated from the incidence among relatives. *Annals of Human Genetics,* **29**, 51–76.

Falconer, D. S. (1981). *An introduction to quantitive genetics* (2nd ed.) New York: Ronald.

Farnworth, M. (1984). Family structure, family attributes, and delinquency in a sample of low-income, minority males and females. *Journal of Youth and Adolescence,* **13**, 349–364.

Farrington, D. P. (1979). Longitudinal research on crime and delinquency. In N. Morris & M. Tonry (Eds.), *Crime and justice: An annual review of research* (Vol. 1). Chicago: Cambridge University Press.

Farrington, D. P. (1981). The prevalence of convictions. *British Journal of Criminology,* **2**, 173–175.

Farrington, D. P. (1983). *Further analyses of a longitudinal survey of crime and delinquency.* Final report to the National Institute of Justice, Washington, D.C.

Farrington, D. P. (1986). Age and crime. In M. Tonry & N. Morris (Eds.), *Crime and justice: An annual review of research.* Chicago: University of Chicago Press.

Farrington, D. P. (1987a). Implications of biological findings for criminological research. In S. A. Mednick, T. E. Moffitt, & S. A. Stack (Eds.), *The causes of crime: New biological approaches* (pp. 42–64). New York: Cambridge University Press.

Farrington, D. P. (1987b). Early precursors of frequent offending. In J. Q. Wilson & G. C. Loury (Eds.), *From children to citizens* (Vol. 3. *Families, schools, and delinquency prevention*) (pp. 27–50). London: Springer-Verlag.

Farrington, D. P. (1989). Early predictors of adolescent aggression and adult violence. *Violence and Victims,* **4**, 79–100.

Farrington, D. P. (1991). Childhood aggression and adult violence: Early precursors and later life outcomes. In D. J. Pepler & K. H. Rubin (Eds.), *The development and treatment of childhood aggression* (pp. 5–29). Hillsdale, NJ: Erlbaum.

Farrington, D. P. (1992). Explaining the beginning, progress, and ending of antisocial behavior from birth to adulthood. In J. McCord (Ed.), *Advances in criminological theory* (Vol. 3. *Crime facts, fictions, and theory*) (pp. 253–286). New Brunswick, NJ: Transaction.

Farrington, D. P., & Hawkins, J. D. (1991). Predicting participation, early onset, and later persistence in officially recorded offending. *Criminal Behavior and Mental Health*, 1, 1–33.

Farrington, D. P., & West, D. J. (1990). The Cambridge study in delinquent development: A long-term follow-up study of 411 London males. In H. J. Kerner & G. Kaiser (Eds.), *Criminality: Personality, behavior, and life history* (pp. 115–138). Berlin: Springer-Verlag.

Farrington, D. P., Biron, L., & LeBlanc, M. (1982). Personality and delinquency in London and Montreal. In J. Gunn & D. P. Farrington (Eds.), *Abnormal offenders, delinquency, and the criminal justice system*. Chichester, England: Wiley.

Farrington, D. P., Gallagher, B., Morley, L., Ledger, R. J., & West, D. G. (1986). Unemployment, school leaving, and crime. *British Journal of Criminology*, 26, 335–356.

Farrington, D. P., Snyder, H. N., & Finnegan, T. A. (1988). Specialization in juvenile court careers. *Criminology*, 26, 461–487.

Fergusson, D. M., Fleming, J., & O'Neill, D. P. (1972). *Child abuse in New Zealand*. Wellington: Government of New Zealand Printer.

Fergusson, D. M., Horwood, L. J., & Lynskey, M. T. (1992). Family change, parental discord and early offending. *Journal of Child Psychology and Psychiatry*, 33, 1059–1075.

Fischer, D. G. (1984). Family size and delinquency. *Perception and Motor Skills*, 58, 527–534.

Fischer, E. A. (1980). The relationship between mating system and simultaneous hermaphroditism in the coral reef fish, *Hypoplectrus nigricans* (Serranidae). *Animal Behavior*, 28, 620–633.

Fishbein, D. H. (1992). The psychobiology of female aggression. *Criminal Justice and Behavior*, 19, 99–126.

Fishbein, D. H., & Thatcher, R. W. (1982). *Nutritional and electrophysiological indices of maladaptive behavior*. Paper presented at the MIT Conference on Research Strategies for Assessing the Behavioral Effects of Foods and Nutrients, Cambridge, Massachusetts, November 9.

Fitten, L. J., Morley, J. E., Gross, P. L., Petry, S. D., & Cole, K. D. (1989). Depression: UCLA geriatric grand rounds. *Journal of the American Geriatric Society*, 37, 459–472.

Flaum, M. (1992). *DSM-IV: The final stage*. Paper presented at the 31st Annual Meeting of the American College of Neuropsychopharmacology, San Juan, Puerto Rico, December 14–18.

Flor-Henry, P. (1973). Psychiatric syndromes considered as manifestations of lateralized temporal-limbic dysfunction. In L. Laitiner & K. Livingston (Eds.), *Surgical approaches in psychiatry*. Lancaster, England: Medical and Technical Publishing Co.

Flor-Henry, P. (1990). Influence of gender in schizophrenia as related to other psychopathological syndromes. *Schizophrenia Bulletin*, 16, 211–227.

Forth, A., & Hare, R. D. (1990). The contingent negative variation in psychopaths. *Psychophysiology*, 26, 676–682.

Fowles, D. C. (1980). The three arousal model: Implications of Gray's two-factor learning theory for heart rate, electrodermal activity, and psychopathy. *Psychophysiology*, 17, 87–104.

Fowles, D. C. (1988). Psychophysiology and psychopathology: A motivational approach. *Psychophysiology*, 25, 373–391.

Frances, A. J., First, M. B., Widiger, T. A., Miele, G. M., Tiley, S. M., Davis, W. W., & Pincus, H. A. (1991). An A to Z guide to DSM-IV conundrums. *Journal of Abnormal Psychology*, 100, 407–412.

Frances, A., Pincus, H. A., Widiger, T. A., Davis, W. W., & First, M. B. (1990). DSM-IV: Work in progress. *American Journal of Psychiatry*, 147, 1439–1448.

Frankenhaeuser, M. (1971). Behavior and circulating catecholamines. *Brain Research*, 31, 241–262.

Frankenhaeuser, M., Lundberg, U., Von Wright, M. R., Von Wright, J., & Sedvall, G. (1986). Urinary monoamine metabolites as indices of mental stress in healthy males and females. *Pharmacology Biochemistry & Behavior*, 24, 1521–1525.

Freeman, R. B. (1982). *Crime and the labor market* (NBCR working paper no. 1031). Cambridge, MA: National Bureau of Economic Research.

Fuster, J. M. (1989). *The prefrontal cortex: Anatomy, physiology, and neuropsychology of the frontal lobe* (2nd ed.). New York: Raven Press.

Gabrielli, W. F., & Mednick, S. A. (1980). Sinistrality and delinquency. *Journal of Abnormal Psychology*, 89, 654–661.

Gale, A. (1975). *Can EEG studies make a contribution to the experimental investigation of psychopathy?* Paper presented at the NATO Advanced Study Institute on Psychopathic Behavior, Les Arc, September 5–12.

Gardner, D. L., Lucas, P. B., & Cowdry, R. W. (1990). CSF metabolite in borderline personality disorder compared with normal controls. *Biological Psychiatry*, 28(3), 247–254.

Garnett, E. S., Nahmias, C., Wortzman, G., Langevin, R., & Dickey, R. (1988). Positron emission tomography and sexual arousal in a sadist and two controls. *Annals of Sex Research*, 1, 387–399.

Gatchel, R. J., & Baum, A. (1983). *An introduction to health psychology*. Reading, MA: Addison-Wesley.

Gelder, M., Gath, D., & Mayou, R. (1989). *Oxford textbook of psychiatry* (2nd ed.). Oxford: Oxford University Press.

Gelles, R. F. (1982). Domestic criminal violence. In M. E. Wolfgang & N. A. Weiner (Eds.), *Criminal violence*. Beverly Hills, CA: Sage.

Gellhorn, E., & Loofbourrow, G. N. (1963). *Emotions and emotional disorders*. New York: Hoeber Medical Division.

Ghodsian-Carpey, J., & Baker, L. A. (1987). Genetic and environmental influences on aggression in 4- to 7-year-old twins. *Aggressive Behavior*, 13, 173–186.

Gibbens, T. C. N. (1963). *Psychiatric studies of borstal lads*. New York: Oxford University Press.

Gilbert, R. M. (1976). Caffeine as a drug of abuse. In R. J. Gibbons, Y. Israel, H. Kalant, R. E. Popham, W. Schmidt, & R. G. Smart (Eds.), *Research advances in alcohol and drug problems* (Vol. 3, pp. 49–176). New York: Wiley.

Gillstrom, B. J., & Hare, R. D. (1988). Language-related hand gestures in psychopaths. *Journal of Personality Disorders*, 2, 21–27.

Glover, G. R. (1990). *Patterns of schizophrenia in the British Caribbean*. Paper presented at the Fifth Annual Winter Workshop on Schizophrenia, Badgastein, Austria, January 28–February 3.

Glueck, S., & Glueck, E. (1968). *Delinquents and non-delinquents in perspective*. Cambridge, MA: Harvard University Press.

Glueck, S., & Glueck, T. (1950). *Unraveling juvenile delinquency*. Cambridge, MA: Harvard University Press.

Glueck, S., & Glueck, T. (1956). *Physique and delinquency*. New York: Harper.

Goffman, E. (1961). *Asylums*. Garden City, NY: Doubleday.

Gold, M. (1970). *Delinquent behavior in an American city*. Belmont, CA: Brooks-Cole.

Goldfarb, W. (1945). Effects of psychological deprivation and in infancy and subsequent stimulation. *American Journal of Psychiatry*, 102, 18–33.

Goldzieher, J. W., Dozier, T. S., Smith, K. S., & Steinberger, E. (1976). Improving the diagnostic reliability of rapidly fluctuating plasma hormone levels by optimized multiple-sampling techniques. *Journal of Clinical Endocrinology and Metabolism*, 43, 824–830.

Goodstein, L. D., & Calhoun, J. F. (1982). *Understanding abnormal behavior*. Reading, MA: Addison-Wesley.

Gorenstein, E. E. (1982). Frontal lobe functions in psychopaths. *Journal of Abnormal Psychology*, 91, 368–379.

Gorenstein, E. E. (1984). Debating mental illness: Implications for science, medicine and social policy. *American Psychologist*, 39, 50–56.

Gorenstein, E. E., & Newman, J. P. (1980). Disinhibitory psychopathology: A new perspective and a model for research. *Psychological Review*, 87, 301–315.

Gottschalk, L. A., Rebello, T., Buchsbaum, M. S., Tucker, H. G., and Hodges, E. L. (1991). Abnormalities in hair trace elements as indicators of aberrant behavior. *Comprehensive Psychiatry*, 32, 229–237.

Gottfredson, M. R., & Hirschi, T. (1990). *A general theory of crime*. Stanford, CA: Stanford University Press.

Goyer, P. (1992). *PET and personality disorders*. Paper presented at the 31st Annual Meeting of the American College of Neuropsychopharmacology, San Juan, Puerto Rico, December 14–18.

Graber, B., Hartmann, K., Coffman, J. A., Huey, C. J., & Golden, C. J. (1982). Brain damage among mentally disordered offenders. *Journal of Forensic Science*, 27, 125–134.

Grande, C. G. (1988). Delinquency: The learning disabled student's reaction to academic school failure? *Adolescence*, 23, 209–219.

Gray, G. E. (1986). Diet, crime and delinquency: A critique. *Nutrition Reviews*, 44, 89–94.

Gray, J. A. (1975). *Elements of a two-process theory of learning*. New York: Academic Press.

Gray, J. A. (1976). The neuropsychology of anxiety. In I. G. Sarason & C. D. Spielberger (Eds.), *Stress and anxiety* (Vol. 3, pp. 3–26). Washington, DC: Hemisphere.

Gray, J. A. (1981). A critique of Eysenck's theory of personality. In H. J. Eysenck (Ed.), *A model of personality* (pp. 246–276). New York: Springer.

Gray, J. A. (1982). *The neuropsychology of anxiety: An enquiry into the functions of the septo-hippocampal system*. Oxford: Oxford University Press.

Gray, J. A. (1987). Perspectives on anxiety and impulsivity: A commentary. *Journal of Research in Personality*, 21, 493–509.

Grove, W. M., Eckert, E. D., Heston, L., Bouchard, T. J., Segal, N., & Lykken, D. T. (1990). Heritability of substance abuse and antisocial behavior: A study of monozygotic twins reared apart. *Biological Psychiatry*, 27, 1293–1304.

Gur, R. E., & Gur, R. C. (1990). Gender differences in regional cerebral blood flow. *Schizophrenia Bulletin*, 16, 247–254.

Guy, J. D., Majorski, L. V., Wallace, C. J., & Guy, M. P. (1983). The incidence of minor physical anomalies in adult male schizophrenics. *Schizophrenia Bulletin*, 9, 571–582.

Haber, G. B., Heaton, K. W., & Murphy, D. (1977). Depletion and disruption of dietary fibre. Effects on society, plasma glucose and serum insulin. *Lancet*, 2, 679.

Halverson, C. F., & Victor, J. B. (1976). Minor physical anomalies and problem behavior in elementary schoolchildren. *Child Development*, 47, 281–285.

Hamilton, W. D. (1964). The genetic evolution of social behavior. *Journal of Theoretical Biology*, 7, 1–52.

Hare, R. D. (1970). *Psychopathy: Theory and practice*. New York: Wiley.

Hare, R. D. (1975). Psychophysiological studies of psychopathy. In D. C. Fowles (Ed.), *Clinical applications of psychophysiology* (pp. 77–105). New York: Cambridge University Press.

Hare, R. D. (1978). Electrodermal and cardiovascular correlates of psychopathy. In R. D. Hare & D. Schalling (Eds.), *Psychopathic behavior: Approaches to research* (pp. 107–144). New York: Wiley.

Hare, R. D. (1979). Psychopathy and laterality of cerebral function. *Journal of Abnormal Psychology*, 84, 605–610.

Hare, R. D. (1980). A research scale for the assessment of psychopathy in criminal populations. *Personality and Individual Differences*, 1, 111–119.

Hare, R. D. (1982). Psychopathy and physiological activity during anticipation of an aversive stimulus in a distraction paradigm. *Psychophysiology*, 19, 266–271.

Hare, R. D. (1983). Diagnosis of antisocial personality disorder in two prison populations. *American Journal of Psychiatry*, 140, 887–890.

Hare, R. D. (1984). Performance of psychopaths on cognitive tasks related to frontal lobe function. *Journal of Abnormal Psychology*, 93, 133–140.

Hare, R. D. (1985). Comparison of procedures for the assessment of psychopathy. *Journal of Consulting and Clinical Psychology*, 53, 7–16.

Hare, R. D., & Craigen, D. (1974). Psychopathy and physiological activity in a mixed motive game situation. *Psychophysiology*, 11, 197–206.

Hare, R. D., & Forth, A. E. (1985). Psychopathy and lateral preference. *Journal of Abnormal Psychology*, 94, 541–546.

Hare, R. D., & Jutai, J. (1988). Psychopathy and cerebral asymmetry in semantic processing. *Personality and Individual Differences*, **9**, 329–337.

Hare, R. D., & McPherson, L. M. (1984). Psychopathy and perceptual asymmetry during verbal dichotic listening. *Journal of Abnormal Psychology*, **93**, 141–149.

Hare, R. D., Frazelle, J., Bus, J., and Jutai, J. W. (1980). Psychopathy and structure of primary mental abilities. *Journal of Behavioral Assessment*, **2**, 77–88.

Hare, R. D., Frazelle, J., & Cox, D. N. (1978). Psychopathy and physiological responses to threat of an aversive stimulus. *Psychophysiology*, **15**, 165–172.

Hare, R. D., Williamson, S. E., & Harpur, T. J. (1988). Psychopathy and language. In T. E. Moffitt & S. A. Mednick (Eds.), *Biological contributions to crime causation* (pp. 68–92). Dordrecht, Holland: Martinus Nijhoff.

Hare, R. D., Hart, S. D., and Harpur, T. J. (1991). Psychopathy and DSM-IV criteria for antisocial personality disorder. *Journal of Abnormal Psychology*, **100**, 391–398.

Harlow, J. M. (1848). Passage of an iron rod through the head. *Boston Medical and Surgical Journal*, **39**, 389–393.

Haroutunian, V., Mantin, R., Campbell, G. A., and Tsuboyama, G. K. (1987). Cysteamine-induced depletion of central somatostatin-like immuno-activity: Effects on behavior, learning, memory and brain neurochemistry. *Brain Research*, **403**, 234–242.

Harpending, H., & Draper, P. (1988). Antisocial behavior and the other side of cultural evolution. In T. E. Moffitt & S. A. Mednick (Eds.), *Biological contributions to crime causation* (pp. 293–307). Dordrecht, Holland: Martinus Nijhoff.

Harpur, T. J., Williamson, S. E., Forth, A., & Hare, R. D. (1986). A quantitative assessment of resting EEG in psychopathic and non-psychopathic criminals. *Psychophysiology*, **23**, 439.

Hart, C. (1987). The relevance of a test of speech comprehension deficit to persistent aggressiveness. *Personality and Individual Differences*, **8**, 371–384.

Hartl, E., Monnelli, E., & Eldeken, R. (1982). *Physique and delinquent behavior*. New York: Academic Press.

Hawley, R. J., Major, L. F., Shulman, E. A., & Linnoila, M. (1985). Cerebrospinal fluid 3-methoxy-4-hydroxyphenylglycol and norepinephrine levels in alcohol withdrawal: Correlations with clinical signs. *Archives of General Psychiatry*, **42**, 1056–1062.

Hayashi, S. (1963). A study of juvenile delinquency by the twin method. *Acta Criminologiae et Medicinae Legalis Japanica*, **29**, 153–172.

Hazlett, E., Dawson, M., Buchsbaum, M. S., & Nuechterlein, K. (1993). Reduced regional brain glucose metabolism assessed by PET in electrodermal nonresponder schizophrenics: A pilot study. *Journal of Abnormal Psychology*, **102**, 39–46.

Hellige, J. B. (1993). *Hemisphere asymmetry: What's right and what's left?* Cambridge, MA: Harvard University Press.

Hellman, D. A., & Beaton, S. (1986). The pattern of violence in urban public schools: The influence of school and community. *Journal of Research in Crime and Delinquency*, **23**, 102–127.

Hemming, J. H. (1981). Electrodermal indices in a selected prison sample and students. *Personality and Individual Differences*, **2**, 37–46.

Henderson, M., & Hollin, C. R. (1983). A critical review of social skills training with young offenders. Criminal Justice and Behavior, **10**, 316–341.

Hendricks, S. E., Fitzpatrick, D. F., Hartmann, K., Quaife, M. A., Stratbucker, R. A., & Graber, B. (1988). Brain structure and function in sexual molesters of children and adolescents. *Journal of Clinical Psychiatry*, **49**, 108–112.

Henggeler, S. W. (1989). *Delinquency in adolescence*. Newbury Park, CA: Sage.

Henggeler, S. W., McKee, E., & Borduin, C. M. (1989). Is there a link between maternal neglect and adolescent delinquency? *Journal of Clinical Child Psychology*, **18**, 242–246.

Herzberg, J. L., & Fenwick, P. B. C. (1988). The aetiology of aggression in temporal lobe epilepsy. *British Journal of Psychiatry*, **153**, 50–55.

Heston, L. L. (1966). Psychiatric disorders in foster-home reared children of schizophrenic mothers. *British Journal of Psychiatry*, **112**, 819–825.

Hill, D., & Pond, D. A. (1952). Reflections on 100 capital cases submitted for electroencephalography. *Journal of Mental Science*, **98**, 23–43.

Hindelang, M. J. (1971). Age, sex, and versatility of delinquent involvements. *Social Problems*, **18**, 522–535.

Hinton, J., O'Neill, M., & Dishman, J. (1979). Electrodermal indices of public offending and recidivism. *Biological Psychology*, **9**, 297–309.

Hirschi, T. (1969). *Causes of delinquency*. Berkeley, CA: University of California Press.

Hirschi, T., & Hindelang, M. J. (1977). Intelligence and delinquency: A revisionist review. *American Sociological Review*, **42**, 571–587.

Hodgins, S. (1992). Mental disorder, intellectual deficiency, and crime: Evidence from a birth cohort. *Archives of General Psychiatry*, **49**, 476–483.

Hoffman, J. J., Hall, R. W., & Bartsch, T. W. (1987). On the relative importance of "Psychopathic" personality and alcoholism on neuropsychological measures of frontal lobe dysfunction. *Journal of Abnormal Psychology*, **96**, 158–160.

Horney, J. (1978). Menstrual cycles and criminal responsibility. *Law and Human Behavior*, **2**, 139–150.

Hucker, S., Langevin, R., Wortzman, G., Bain, J., Handy, L., Chambers, J., & Wright, S. (1986). Neuropsychological impairment in pedophiles. *Canadian Journal of Behavioral Science*, **18**, 440–448.

Hucker, S., Langevin, R., Wortzman, G., Dickey, R., Bain, J., Handy, L., Chambers, J., & Wright, S. (1988). Cerebral damage and dysfunction in sexually aggressive men. *Annals of Sex Research*, **1**, 33–47.

Huff, G. (1987). Social skills training. In B. J. McGurk, D. M. Thornton, & M. Williams (Eds.), *Applying psychology to imprisonment: Theory and practice* (pp. 227–238). London: Her Majesty's Stationery Office.

Hughes, J. R., Higgins, S. T., Bickel, W. K., Hunt, W. K., Fenwick, J. W., Gulliver, S. B., & Mireault, G. C. (1991). Caffeine self-administration, withdrawal, and adverse effects among coffee drinkers. *Archives of General Psychiatry*, **48**, 611–617.

Hutchings, B. (1972). *Genetic and environmental factors in psychopathology and criminality*. Unpublished master's thesis, University of London.

Hutchings, B., & Mednick, S. A. (1977). Criminality in adoptees and their adoptive and biological parents: A pilot study. In S. A. Mednick & K. O. Christiansen (Eds.), *Biosocial bases of criminal behavior*. New York: Gardner Press.

Huttenlocher, P. R. (1979). Synaptic density in human frontal cortex—developmental changes and effects of aging. *Brain Research*, **163**, 195–205.

Jacobson, B., Eklund, G., Hamberger, L., Linnarsson, G., & Valverius, M. (1987). Perinatal origin of adult self-destructive behavior. *Acta Psychiatrica Scandinavica*, **76**, 364–371.

Jagger, J., Levine, J. I., Jane, J. A., & Rimel, R. W. (1984). Epidemiologic features of head injury in a predominantly rural population. *The Journal of Trauma*, **24**, 40–44.

Jahoda, M. (1958). *Current concepts of positive mental health*. New York: Basic Books.

Jones, M. D., Offord, D. R., & Abrams, N. (1980). Brothers, sisters, and antisocial behavior. *British Journal of Psychiatry*, **136**, 139–145.

Jutai, J. W., & Hare, R. D. (1983). Psychopathy and selective attention during performance of a complex perceptual-motor task. *Psychophysiology*, **20**, 146–151.

Jutai, J., Hare, R. D., & Connolly, J. F. (1987). Psychopathy and event-related brain potentials (ERPs) associated with attention to speech stimuli. *Personality and Individual Differences*, **8**, 175–184.

Kagan, J. (1989). Temperamental contributions to social behavior. *American Psychologist*, **44**, 668–674.

Kagan, J., Reznick, J. S., & Snidman, N. (1987). The physiology and psychology of behavioral inhibition in young children. *Child Development*, **58**, 1459–1473.

Kagan, J., Reznick, J. S., & Snidman, N. (1988). Biological bases of childhood shyness. *Science,* **240,** 167–171.

Kanarek, R. B. (1990). *Nutrition and violent behavior.* Report for the National Academy of Sciences Panel on the Understanding and Control of Violent Behavior.

Kandel, E., & Freed, D. (1989). Frontal lobe dysfunction and antisocial behavior: A review. *Journal of Clinical Psychology,* **45,** 404–413.

Kandel, E., & Mednick, S. A. (1991). Perinatal complications predict violent offending. *Criminology,* **29,** 519–529.

Kandel, E., Brennan, P., & Mednick, S. A. (1990). *Minor physical anomalies and parental modeling of physical aggression predict adult violent offending.* Unpublished manuscript, University of Southern California.

Kendell, R. E. (1986). What are mental disorders? In A. M. Freedman, R. Brotman, I. Silverman, & D. Hutson (Eds.), *Issues in psychiatric classification* (pp. 23–45). New York: Human Sciences Press.

Kendler, K. S. (1983). Twin studies of schizophrenia: A current perspective. *American Journal of Psychiatry,* **140,** 1143–1425.

Kendler, K. S. (1990). Toward a scientific psychiatric nosology: Strengths and limitations. *Archives of General Psychiatry,* **47,** 969–973.

Kilo, L. G., Gye, R. S., Rushworth, R. G., Bell, D. S., & White, R. T. (1974). Stereotactic amygdaloidotomy for aggressive behavior. *Journal of Neurology, Neurosurgery, and Psychiatry,* **37,** 437–444.

Klein, D. F. (1978). A proposed definition of mental illness. In R. L. Spitzer & D. F. Klein (Eds.), *Critical issues in psychiatric diagnosis* (pp. 41–72). New York: Raven Press.

Klein, M. W. (1984). Offense specialization and versatility among juveniles. *British Journal of Criminal Psychology,* **24,** 185–194.

Klein, M. W. (1987). Watch out for that last variable. In S. A. Mednick, T. E. Moffitt, & S. Stack (Eds.), *The causes of crime: New biological approaches* (pp. 25–41). Cambridge: Cambridge University Press.

Klein, M. W. (1989). In M. W. Klein (Ed.), *Cross-national research in self-reported crime and delinquency.* Boston: Kluwer.

Kodanda, R. P. (1986). Family size and delinquency. *Indian Journal of Psychological Medicine,* **9,** 89–90.

Kohlberg, L. (1976). Moral stages and moralization: The cognitive-developmental approach. In T. Lickona (Ed.), *Moral development and behavior.* New York: Holt, Rinehart and Winston.

Kohlberg, L., & Freundlich, D. (1973). Moral judgment in youthful offenders. In L. Kohlberg & E. Turiel (Eds.), *Moralization: The cognitive developmental approach.* New York: Holt, Rinehart and Winston.

Kolb, B., & Wishaw, I. Q. (1990). *Fundamentals of human neuropsychology* (3rd ed.). New York: Freeman.

Kolb, L. C. (1977). *Modern clinical psychiatry.* Philadelphia: Saunders.

Kolvin, I., Miller, F. J., Fleeting, M., & Kolvin, P. A. (1988). Social and parenting factors affecting criminal offense rates: Findings from the Newcastle Thousand Family Study. *British Journal of Psychiatry,* **152,** 80–90.

Kosson, D. S., & Newman, J. P. (1986). Psychopathy and the allocation of attentional capacity in a divided attention situation. *Journal of Abnormal Psychology,* **95,** 257–263.

Kosson, D. S., & Newman, J. P. (1989). Socialization and attentional deficits under focusing and divided attention conditions. *Journal of Personality and Social Psychology,* **57,** 87–99.

Kranze, H. (1935). Discordant soziales Verhalten eineuger Zwillinge. *Monatschrift fur Kriminalpsychologie und Strafrechtsreform,* **26,** 511–516.

Kruesi, M. J., Rapoport, J. L., Hamburger, S., & Hibbs, E. D. (1990a). Cerebrospinal fluid monoamine metabolites, aggression, and impulsivity in disruptive behavior disorders of children and adolescents. *Archives of General Psychiatry,* **47,** 419–426.

Kruesi, M. J., Swedo, S., Leonard, H., Rubinow, D. R., & Rapoport, J. L. (1990b). CSF somato-statin in childhood psychiatric disorders: A preliminary investigation. *Psychiatry Research*, 33, 277–284.

Kurianski, J. B., Deming, W. E., & Gurland, B. J. (1974). On trends in the diagnosis of schizo-phrenia. *American Journal of Psychiatry*, 131, 402–407.

Kurtzberg, R. L., Mandell, W., Lewin, M., Lipton, D. S., & Shuster, M. (1968). Plastic surgery on offenders. In N. Johnson & L. Savitz (Eds.), *Justice and corrections* (pp. 688–700). New York: Wiley.

Kurtzberg, R. L., Safar, H., & Mandell, W. (1969). Plastic surgery in corrections. *Federal Proba-tion*, 33, 45.

Kyvsgaard, B. (1991). The living conditions of law violators in Denmark. *International Journal of Offender Therapy and Comparative Criminology*, 35, 235–247.

Lacey, B. C., & Lacey, J. I. (1974). Studies of heart rate and other bodily processes in sensorimotor behavior. In P. A. Obrist, A. H. Black, J. Brener, & L. V. DiCara (Eds.), *Cardiovascular psy-chophysiology: Current issues in response mechanisms, biofeedback and methodology* (pp. 538–564). Chicago: Aldine.

Lahey, B. B., & McBurnett, K. (1992). *Behavioral and biological correlates of aggressive conduct disorder: Temporal stability*. Paper presented at the annual meeting of the Society for Research In Child and Adolescent Psychopathology, Sarasota, FL.

Lahey, B. B., Hartdagen, S. E., Frick, P. J., McBurnett, K., Connor, R., & Hynd, G. W. (1988). Conduct disorder: Parsing the confounded relation to parental divorce and antisocial person-ality. *Journal of Abnormal Psychology*, 97, 334–337.

Lahey, B. B., Loeber, R., Stouthamer-Loeber, M., Christ, M. A. G., Green, S., Russo, M. F., Frick, P. J., & Dulcan, M. (1990). Comparison of DSM-III and DSM-III-R diagnoses for prepubertal children: Changes in prevalence and validity. *Journal of the American Academy of Child Psy-chology and Psychiatry*, 29, 620–626.

Lakosina, N. D., & Trunova, M. M. (1985). The characteristics of emotional disorders in psycho-pathic personalities. *Soviet Neurology and Psychiatry*, 18, 35–45.

Landsman, S. D., Sandford, L. M., Howland, B. E., & Dawes, C. (1976). Testosterone in human saliva. *Experientia*, 32, 940–941.

Lange, J. (1929). *Verbrechen als Schiskal*. Leipzig: Georg Thieme. English edition, 1931, London: Unwin Brothers.

Langevin, R., Bain, J., Ben-Aron, M., Coulthard, R., Day, D., Handy, L., Heasman, G., Hucker, S. J., Purins, J. E., Roper, V., Russon, A., Webster, C. D., & Wortzman, G. (1985). Sexual aggression: Constructing a predictive equation. In R. Langevin (Ed.), *Erotic preference, gender identity and aggression in men*. Hillsdale, NJ: Erlbaum.

Langevin, R., Ben-Aron, M., Wortzman, G., Dickey, R., & Handy, L. (1987). Brain damage, diagnosis, and substance abuse among violent offenders. *Behavioral Sciences and the Law*, 5, 77–94.

Langevin, R., Lang, R. A., Wortzman, G., Frenzel, R. R., & Wright, P. (1989b). An examination of brain damage and dysfunction in genital exhibitionists. *Annals of Sex Research*, 2, 77–94.

Langevin, R., Wortzman, G., Dickey, R., Wright, P., & Handy, L. (1988). Neuropsychological impairment in incest offenders. *Annals of Sex Research*, 1, 401–415.

Langevin, R., Wortzman, G., Wright, P., & Handy, L. (1989a). Studies of brain damage and dysfunction in sex offenders. *Annals of Sex Research*, 2, 163–179.

Larson, K. A. (1988). A research review and alternative hypothesis explaining the link between learning disability and delinquency. *Journal of Learning Disabilities*, 21, 357–363.

Lee, R. B., & DeVore, B. I. (Eds.). (1976). *Kalahari hunter-gatherers*. Cambridge: Harvard Uni-versity Press.

Lee, M., & Prentice, N. M. (1988). Interrelations of empathy, cognition, and moral reasoning with dimensions of juvenile delinquency. *Journal of Abnormal Child Psychology*, 16, 127–139.

Legras, A. M. (1932). *Psychese en Criminaliteit bij Twellingen*. Utrecht: Kemink en Zoon N.V.

Lehnert, H., Reinstein, D. K., Strowbridge, B. W., & Wurtman, R. (1984). Neurochemical and behavioral consequences of acute, uncontrollable stress: Effects of dietary tyrosine. *Brain Research*, 303, 215–223.

Lencz, T., Raine, A., Scerbo, A., Holt, L., Bird, L., Redmon, M., & Brodish, S. (1993). Eye tracking abnormalities in undergraduates with schizotypal personality disorder. *American Journal of Psychiatry*, 150, 152–154.

Levander, S. E., Schalling, D. S., Lidberg, L., Bartfai, A., & Lidberg, Y. (1980). Skin conductance recovery time and personality in a group of criminals. *Psychophysiology*, 17, 105–111.

Lewis, A. J. (1953). Health as a social concept. *British Journal of Sociology*, 4, 109–124.

Lewis, A. J. (1976). *Mechanisms of neurologic disease*. Boston: Little, Brown & Co.

Lewis, D. O., Pincus, J. H., Bard, B., Richardson, E., Prichep, L. S., Feldman, M., & Yeager, C. (1988). Neuropsychiatric, psycho-educational, and family characteristics of 14 juveniles condemned to death in the United States. *American Journal of Psychiatry*, 145, 584–589.

Lewis, D. O., & Shanock, S. A. (1977). Medical histories of delinquent and non-delinquent children: An epidemiological study. *American Journal of Psychiatry*, 134, 1020–1025.

Lewis, D. O., Pincus, J. H., Bard, B., Richardson, E., Prichep, L. S., Feldman, M., & Yeager, C. (1986). Psychiatric, neurological, and psycho-educational characteristics of 15 death row inmates in the United States. *American Journal of Psychiatry*, 143, 838–845.

Lewis, D. O., Pincus, J. H., Bard, B., Richardson, E., Prichep, L. S., Feldman, M., & Yeager, C. (1988). Neuropsychiatric, psychoeducational, and family characteristics of 14 juveniles condemned to death in the United States. *American Journal of Psychiatry*, 145, 584–589.

Lewis, D. O., Shanok, S. A., & Balla, D. A. (1979). Perinatal difficulties, head and face trauma, and child abuse in the medical histories of seriously delinquent children. *American Journal of Psychiatry*, 136, 419–423.

Lezack, M. D. (1983). *Neuropsychological assessment* (2nd ed.). New York: Oxford University Press.

Lidberg, L., Levander, S. E., Schalling, D., & Lidberg, Y. (1978). Necker cube reversals, arousal, and psychopathy. *British Journal of Social and Clinical Psychology*, 17, 355–361.

Litt, S. M. (1971). *Perinatal complications and criminality*. Unpublished doctoral dissertation, University of Michigan.

Little, B. (1978). *Physiological correlates of antisocial behavior in children and young adults*. Paper presented at the British Psychophysiology Society, London, December 14–17.

Loeb, J., & Mednick, S. A. (1977). A prospective study of predictors of criminality: 3. Electrodermal response patterns. In S. A. Mednick & K. O. Christiansen (Eds.), *Biosocial bases of criminal behavior* (pp. 245–254). New York: Gardner Press.

Loeber, R. (1990). Development and risk factors of juvenile antisocial behavior and delinquency. *Clinical Psychology Review*, 10, 1–41.

Loeber, R., & Dishion, T. (1983). Early predictors of male delinquency: A review. *Psychological Bulletin*, 94, 68–99.

Loeber, R., & Dishion, T. (1983). Boys who fight at home and school: Family conditions influencing cross-setting consistency. *Journal of Consulting and Clinical Psychology*, 52, 759–768.

Loeber, R., & Schmaling, K. B. (1985). The utility of differentiating between mixed and pure forms of antisocial child behavior. *Journal of Abnormal Child Psychology*, 13, 315–336.

Loeber, R., & Stouthamer-Loeber, M. (1986). Family factors as correlates and predictors of juvenile conduct problems and delinquency. In M. Tonry & N. Morris (Eds.), *Crime and justice* (Vol. 7, pp. 29–149). Chicago: Chicago University Press.

Loeber, R., & Stouthamer-Loeber, M. (1987). Prediction. In H. C. Quay (Ed.), *Handbook of juvenile delinquency* (pp. 325–382). New York: Wiley.

Loeber, R., Stouthamer-Loeber, M., & Green, S. M. (1991). Age at onset of problem behavior in boys, and later disruptive and delinquent behaviors. *Criminal Behavior and Mental Health*, 1, 229–246.

Loeber, R., Tremblay, R. E., Gagnon, C., & Charlebois, P. (1989). Continuity and desistance in disruptive boys' early fighting at school. *Development and Psychopathology*, 1, 39–50.

Loehlin, J. C. (1992). *Genes and environment in personality development*. Beverly Hills, CA: Sage.

Lombardo, V. S., & Lombardo, E. F. (1991). The link between learning disabilities and juvenile delinquency: Fact or fiction? *International Journal of Biosocial and Medical Research*, 13, 112–117.

London Home Office (1985). *Criminal careers of those born in 1953, 1958 and 1963*. Home Office statistical bulletin. London: Home Office Statistical Department.

Luria, A. R. (1980). *Higher cortical functions in man*. New York: Basic Books.

Lykken, D. T. (1955). *A study of anxiety in the sociopathic personality*. Doctoral dissertation, University of Minnesota. Ann Arbor, MI: University Microfilms, 1955, no. 55–944.

Lykken, D. T. (1957). A study of anxiety in the sociopathic personality. *Journal of Abnormal and Social Psychology*, 55, 6–10.

MacKinnon, R. A., & Yudofsky, S. C. (1986). *Psychiatric evaluation in clinical practice*. New York: Lippincott.

MacMillan, J., & Kofoed, L. (1984). Sociobiology and antisocial personality. *Journal of Nervous and Mental Disease*, 172, 701–706.

Maliphant, R., Hume, F., & Furnham, A. (1990a). Autonomic nervous system (ANS) activity, personality characteristics and disruptive behavior in girls. *Journal of Child Psychology and Psychiatry*, 31, 619–628.

Maliphant, R., Watson, S. A., & Daniels, D. (1990b). Disruptive behavior in school, personality characteristics, and heart rate (HR) levels in 7–9 year old boys. *Educational Psychology*, 10, 199–205.

Margolin, G., John, R. S., & Gleberman, L. (1988). Affective responses to conflictual discussions in violent and nonviolent couples. *Journal of Consulting and Clinical Psychology*, 56, 24–33.

Margolin, G., John, R. S., & O'Brien, M. (1989). Sequential affective patterns as a function of marital conflict style. *Journal of Social and Clinical Psychology*, 8, 45–61.

Mark, V. H., & Ervin, F. R. (1970). *Violence and the brain*. New York: Harper & Row.

Marks, V. (1981). The regulation of blood glucose. In V. Marks & F. C. Rose (Eds.), *Hypoglycemia*. Oxford: Blackwell.

Marlowe, M., Stellern, J., Moon, C., & Errera, J. (1985). Main and interactive effects of metallic toxins on aggressive classroom behavior. *Aggressive Behavior*, 11, 41–48.

Masters, F. W., & Greaves, D. C. (1967). The Quasimodo complex. *British Journal of Plastic Surgery*, 20, 204–209.

Matheny, A. P., Dolan, A. B., & Wilson, R. S. (1976). Twins with academic problems: Antecedent characteristics. *American Journal of Orthopsychiatry*, 46, 464–469.

Mattson, A. J., & Levin, H. S. (1990). Frontal lobe dysfunction following closed head injury. *Journal of Nervous and Mental Disease*, 178, 282–291.

Maughan, B., Gray, G., & Rutter, M. (1985). Reading retardation and antisocial behavior: A follow-up in employment. *Journal of Child Psychology and Psychiatry*, 26, 741–758.

Maynard, E. C. L. (1968). Cleaning symbiosis and oral grooming on the coral reef. In P. Person (Ed.), *Biology of the Month* (pp. 79–88). Washington, DC: American Association for the Advancement of Science.

Maynard Smith, J. (1976). Group selection. *Quarterly Review of Biology*, 51, 277–283.

McBurnett, K., Lahey, B. B., Frick, P. J., Risch, C., Loeber, R., Hart, E. L., Christ, M. A. G., & Hanson, K. S. (1991). Anxiety, inhibition, and conduct disorder in children: II. Relation to salivary cortisol. *Journal of the American Academy of Child and Adolescent Psychiatry*, 30, 192–196.

McCandless, B. R., Persons, W. S., & Roberts, A. (1972). Perceived opportunity, delinquency, race, and body build among delinquent youth. *Journal of Consulting and Clinical Psychology*, 38, 281–287.

McCord, J. M. (1977). A comparative study of two generations of native Americans. In R. F. Meier (Ed.), *Theory in criminology* (pp. 83–92). Beverly Hills, CA: Sage.

McCord, J. (1979). Some child-bearing antecedents of criminal behavior in adult men. *Journal of Personality and Social Psychology, 9*, 1477–1486.

McCord, J. M. (1981). Consideration of some effects of a counseling program. In S. Martin, L. Sechrest, & R. Redner (Eds.), *New directions in the rehabilitation of criminal offenders* (pp. 394–405). Washington, DC: National Academy Press.

McCord, J. M. (1982). A longitudinal view of the relationship between paternal absence and crime. In J. Gunn & D. P. Farrington (Eds.), *Abnormal offenders, delinquency, and the criminal justice system* (pp. 113–127). Chichester: Wiley.

McCord, J. (1990). Long-term perspectives on parental absence. In L. N. Robins & M. Rutter (Eds.), *Straight and devious pathways from childhood to adulthood* (pp. 116–134). Cambridge: Cambridge University Press.

McCord, W., & McCord, J. (1964). *The psychopath: An essay on the criminal mind*. Princeton, New Jersey: Van Nostrand.

McGue, M., & Lykken, D. T. (1992). Genetic influences on risk for divorce. *Psychological Science, 3*, 368–373.

McGuiness, D. (1985). *When children don't learn*. New York: Basic Books.

McGuire, M. T., Raleigh, M. J., & Brammer, G. L. (1984). Adaptation, selection, and benefit–cost balances: Implications of behavioral–physiological studies of social dominance in male vervet monkeys. *Ethology and Sociobiology, 5*, 269–277.

McGurk, B. J., & Newell, T. C. (1987). Social skills training: Case study with a sex offender. In B. J. McGurk, D. M. Thornton, & M. Williams (Eds.), *Applying psychology to imprisonment: Theory and practice* (pp. 219–226). London: Her Majesty's Stationery Office.

McKinlay, W. W., Brooks, D. N., Bond, M. R., Martinage, D. P., & Marshall, M. M. (1981). The short-term outcome of severe blunt head injury, as reported by relatives of the injured persons. *Journal of Neurology, Neurosurgery, and Psychiatry, 44*, 285–293.

McNeal, E. T., & Cimbolic, P. (1986). Antidepressants and biochemical theories of depression. *Psychological Bulletin, 99*, 361–374.

Mednick, S. A. (1975). Autonomic nervous system recovery and psychopathology. *Scandinavian Journal of Behavior Therapy, 4*, 55–68.

Mednick, S. A. (1977). A bio-social theory of the learning of law-abiding behavior. In S. A. Mednick & K. O. Christiansen (Eds.), *Biosocial bases of criminal behavior*. New York: Gardner Press.

Mednick, S. A., & Christiansen, K. O. (Eds.), (1977). *Biosocial bases of criminal behavior*. New York: Gardner Press.

Mednick, S. A., Kirkegaard-Sorensen, L., Hutchings, B., Knop, J., Rosenberg, R., and Schulsinger, F. (1977). An example of bio-social interaction research: The interplay of socioenvironmental and individual factors in the etiology of criminal behavior. In S. A. Mednick and K. O. Christiansen (Eds.), *Biosocial bases of criminal behavior* (pp. 9–24). New York: Gardner.

Mednick, S. A., & Finello, K. M. (1983). Biological factors and crime: Implications for forensic psychiatry. *International Journal of Law and Psychiatry, 6*, 1–15.

Mednick, S. A., & Kandel, E. (1988). Genetic and perinatal factors in violence. In S. A. Mednick & T. Moffitt (Eds.), *Biological contributions to crime causation* (pp. 121–134). Dordrecht, Holland: Martinus Nijhoff.

Mednick, B. R., Baker, R. L., & Carothers, L. E. (1990). Patterns of family instability and crime: The association of timing of the family's disruption with subsequent adolescent and adult criminality. *Journal of Youth and Adolescence, 19*, 201–220.

Mednick, S. A., Gabrielli, W. H., & Hutchings, B. (1984). Genetic influences in criminal convictions: Evidence from an adoption cohort. *Science, 224*, 891–894.

Mednick, S. A., Gabrielli, W. H., & Hutchings, B. (1987). Genetic factors in the etiology of criminal behavior. In S. A. Mednick, T. E. Moffitt, & S. A. Stack (Eds.), *The causes of crime: New biological approaches* (pp. 74–91). Cambridge: Cambridge University Press.

Mednick, S. A., Moffitt, T. E., & Stack, S. A. (Eds.), (1987). *The causes of crime: New biological approaches.* Cambridge: Cambridge University Press.

Mednick, B., Reznick, C., & Hocevar, D. (1987). Long-term effects of parental divorce on young adult male crime. *Journal of Youth and Adolescence,* 16, 31–45.

Mednick, S. A., Volavka, J., Gabrielli, W. F., & Itil, T. (1982). EEG as a predictor of antisocial behavior. *Criminology,* 19, 219–231.

Meehl, P. E. (1989). Schizotaxia revisited. *Archives of General Psychiatry,* 46, 935–944.

Messer, S. C., Morris, T. L., & Gross, A. M. (1990). Hypoglycemia and psychopathology: A methodological review. *Clinical Psychology Review,* 10, 631–648.

Messner, S. F. (1988). Research on cultural and socioeconomic factors in criminal violence. *Psychiatric Clinics of North America,* 11, 511–525.

Mesulam, M-M. (1986). Frontal cortex and behaviors. *Annals of Neurology,* 19, 319–323.

Mezzich, J. (1989). An empirical prototypal approach to the definition of psychiatric illness. *British Journal of Psychiatry,* 154, 21–23.

Miller, L. (1990). Major syndromes of aggressive behavior following head injury: An introduction to evaluation and treatment. *Cognitive Rehabilitation,* 8, 14–19.

Miller, M. H. (1976). Dorsolateral frontal lobe lesions and behavior in the macaque: Dissociation of threat and aggression. *Physiology and Behavior,* 17, 209–213.

Millon, T. (1991). Classification in psychopathology: Rationale, alternatives, and standards. *Journal of Abnormal Psychology,* 100, 245–261.

Milner, B. (1963). *Archives of Neurology,* 9, 90–100.

Milner, J. (1991). *Neuropsychology of aggression.* Boston: Kluwer.

Milner, J. S., & McCanne, T. R. (1991). Neuropsychological correlates of physical child abuse. In J. S. Milner (Ed.), *Neuropsychology of aggression* (pp. 131–146). Boston: Kluwer.

Milner, J. S., Robertson, K. R., & Rogers, D. L. (1990). Childhood history of abuse and child abuse potential. *Journal of Family Violence,* 5, 15–34.

Milstein, V. (1988). EEG topography in patients with aggressive violent behavior. In T. E. Moffitt and S. A. Mednick (Eds.), *Biological contributions to crime causation* (pp. 40–54). Dordrecht, North Holland: Martinus Nijhoff.

Mirkin, A. M., & Coppen, A. (1980). Electrodermal activity in depression: Clinical and biochemical correlates. *British Journal of Psychiatry,* 137, 93–97.

Mitsuda (1961). (cited in Yoshimasu, S. The criminological significance of the family in the light of the studies of criminal twins. *Acta Criminologiae et Medicinae Legalis Japanica,* 27.

Moffitt, T. E. (1984). *Genetic influence of parental psychiatric illness on violent and recidivistic criminal behavior.* Unpublished doctoral dissertation, University of Southern California.

Moffitt, T. E. (1987). Parental mental disorder and offspring criminal behavior: An adoption study. *Psychiatry: Interpersonal and Biological Processes,* 50, 346–360.

Moffitt, T. E., & Mednick, S. A. (1988). *Biological contributions to crime causation* (Eds.), Dordrecht, North Holland: Martinus Nijhoff.

Moffitt, T. E. (1988). Neuropsychology and self-reported early delinquency in an unselected birth cohort. In T. E. Moffitt & S. A. Mednick (Eds.), *Biological contributions to crime causation* (pp. 93–120). New York: Martinus Nijhoff.

Moffitt, T. E. (1990). The neuropsychology of juvenile delinquency: A critical review. In M. Tonry & N. Morris (Eds.), *Crime and justice: A review of the literature.* Chicago: University of Chicago Press.

Moffitt, T. E., & Henry, B. (1991). Neuropsychological studies of juvenile delinquency and juvenile violence. In J. S. Milner (Ed.), *Neuropsychology of aggression* (pp. 131–146). Boston: Kluwer.

Moffitt, T. E., & Silva, P. A. (1988). IQ and delinquency: A direct test of the differential detection hypothesis. *Journal of Abnormal Psychology,* 97, 227–240.

Moilanen, I. (1987). Dominance and submissiveness between twins. *Acta Geneticae Medicae et Gemellologiae,* 36, 249–255.

Molling, P. A., Lockner, A. W., Jr., Sauls, R. J., et al. (1962). Committed delinquent boys. *Archives of General Psychiatry,* 7, 70–76.

Monnier, L., Pham, T. C., Aguirre, L., Orsetti, A., & Mirouze, J. (1978). Influence of indigestible fibres on glucose tolerance. *Diabetes Care*, **1**, 83.

Monroe, R. R. (1970). *Episodic behavioral disorders—A psychodynamic and neurophysiologic analysis*. Cambridge, MA: Harvard University Press.

Monroe, R. R. (1974). Maturational lag in central nervous system development as a partial explanation of episodic violent behavior. *Psychopharmacology Bulletin*, **10**, 63–64.

Montemayor, R. (1985). Men and their bodies: The relationship between body types and behavior. In F. H. Marsh & J. Katz (Eds.), *Biology, crime and ethics*. Cincinnati: Anderson Publishing Co.

Morand, C., Young, S. N., & Ervin, F. R. (1983). Clinical response of aggressive schizophrenics to oral tryptophan. *Biological Psychiatry*, **18**, 575–578.

Morey, L. C. (1991). Classification of mental disorder as a collection of hypothetical constructs. *Journal of Abnormal Psychology*, **100**, 289–293.

Moriyama, T. (1990). *The actual phenomenon of juvenile delinquency and the response to it by formal agencies in Japan*. Paper presented at the International Comparisons of Juvenile Justice Systems, Spain, July 5–8.

Moscovich, A., & Tallafero, A. (1954). Studies on EEG and sex function orgasm. *Disease of the Nervous System*, **15**, 218–220.

Moss, H. B., Yao, J. K., & Panzak, G. L. (1990). Serotonergic responsivity and behavioral dimensions in antisocial personality disorder with substance abuse. *Biological Psychiatry*, **28**, 325–338.

Mungas, D. (1983). An empirical analysis of specific syndromes of violent behavior. *Journal of Nervous and Mental Disease*, **171**, 354–361.

Mungas, D. (1988). Psychometric correlates of episodic violent behavior: A multi-disciplinary neuropsychological approach. *British Journal of Psychiatry*, **152**, 180–187.

Murphy, Y., & Murphy, R. (1974). *Women of the forest*. New York: Columbia University Press.

Nachshon, I. (1982). Towards a biosocial approach in criminology. *Journal of Social and Biological Structures*, **5**, 1–9.

Nachshon, I. (1983). Hemisphere dysfunction in psychopathy and behavior disorders. In M. Myslobodsky (Ed.), *Hemisyndromes: Psychobiology, neurology, psychiatry*. New York: Academic Press.

Nachshon, I. (1988). Hemisphere function in violent offenders. In T. E. Moffitt & S. A. Mednick (Eds.), *Biological contributions to crime causation* (pp. 55–67). Dordrecht, Holland: Martinus Nijhoff.

Nachshon, I. (1991). Neuropsychology of violent behavior: Controversial issues and new developments in the study of hemisphere function. In J. S. Milner (Ed.), *Neuropsychology of aggression* (pp. 93–116). Boston: Kluwer.

Nachshon, I., & Denno, D. (1987). Hemisphere dysfunction in violent offenders. In S. A. Mednick, T. E. Moffitt, & S. Stack (Eds.), *The causes of crime: New biological approaches* (pp. 185–217). Cambridge: Cambridge University Press.

Nachshon, I., & Rotenberg, M. (1977). Perception of violence by institutionalized offenders. *Journal of Criminal Law and Criminology*, **68**, 454–457.

Narabayashi, H., & Uno, M. (1966). Long-range results of stereotaxic amygdalotomy for behavior disorders. *Confina Neurologica*, **27**, 168–171.

Needleman, H. L. (1985). The neurobehavioral effects of low-level exposure to lead in childhood. *International Journal of Mental Health*, **14**, 64–77.

Nemeroff, C. B. (1991). Corticotrophin-releasing factor. In C. B. Nemeroff (Ed.), *Neuropeptides and psychiatric disorders* (pp. 75–92). Washington, DC: American Psychiatric Press.

Nestor, P. G. (1992). Neuropsychological and clinical correlates of murder and other forms of extreme violence in a forensic psychiatric population. *Journal of Nervous and Mental Disease*, **180**, 418–423.

Newman, J. P. (1987). Reaction to punishment in extroverts and psychopaths: Implications for the impulsive behavior of disinhibited individuals. *Journal of Research in Personality, 21,* 464–480.

Newman, J. P., & Kosson, D. S. (1986). Passive avoidance learning in psychopathic and non-psychopathic offenders. *Journal of Abnormal Psychology, 95,* 252–256.

Newman, J. P., Patterson, C. M., Howland, E. W., & Nichols, S. L. (1990). Passive avoidance in psychopaths: The effects of reward. *Personality and Individual Differences, 11,* 1101–1114.

Newman, J. P., Patterson, C. M., & Kosson, D. S. (1987). Response perseveration in psychopaths. *Journal of Abnormal Psychology, 96,* 145–148.

Newman, J. P., Widom, C. S., & Nathan, S. (1985). Passive avoidance in syndromes of disinhibition: Psychopathy and extroversion. *Journal of Personality and Social Psychology, 48,* 1316–1327.

Obrist, P. A. (1981). *Cardiovascular psychophysiology: A perspective.* New York: Plenum.

O'Callaghan, M. A. J., & Carroll, D. (1982). *Psychosurgery: A scientific analysis.* Lancaster, England: Medical and Technical Publishing Co.

O'Callaghan, M. A. J., & Carroll, D. (1987). Psychosurgery and antisocial behavior. In S. A. Mednick, T. E. Moffitt, & S. Stack (Eds.), *The causes of crime: New biological approaches* (pp. 312–328) Cambridge: University of Cambridge Press.

O'Carroll, P. W., & Mercy, J. A. (1990). Patterns and recent trends in black homicides. In N. A. Weiner, M. A. Zahn, & R. J. Sagi (Eds.), *Violence: Pattern, causes, public policy* (pp. 55–58). San Diego: Harcourt Brace Jovanovich.

O'Connor, M., Foch, T., Sherry, T., & Plomin, R. (1980). A twin study of specific behavioral problems of socialization as viewed by parents. *Journal of Abnormal Child Psychology, 8,* 189–199.

Offord, D. R. (1982). Family background of male and female delinquents. In J. Gunn & D. P. Farrington (Eds.), *Abnormal offenders, delinquency, and the criminal justice system* (pp. 129–151). Chichester: Wiley.

Offord, D. R., Allen, N., & Abrams, N. (1978). Parental psychiatric illness, broken homes and delinquency. *Journal of the American Academy of Child Psychiatry, 17,* 224–238.

Olweus, D. (1987). Testosterone and adrenaline: Aggressive antisocial behavior in normal adolescent males. In S. A. Mednick, T. E. Moffitt, & S. A. Stack (Eds.), *The causes of crime: new biological approaches* (pp. 263–282). Cambridge: Cambridge University Press.

Olweus, D., Mattesson, A., Schalling, D., & Low, H. (1988). Circulating testosterone levels and aggression in adolescent males: A causal analysis. *Psychosomatic Medicine, 50,* 261–272.

Orne, M., Dinges, D. F., & Orbe, E. C. (1984). On the differential diagnosis of multiple personality in the forensic context. *International Journal of Experimental Hypnosis, 32,* 118–169.

Oxenstierna, G., Edman, G., Iselius, L., Oreland, L., Ross, S. B., & Sedvall, G. (1986). Concentrations of monoamine metabolites in the cerebrospinal fluid of twins and unrelated individuals: A genetic study. *Journal of Psychiatric Research, 20,* 19–29.

Palca, J. (1992). NIH wrestles with furor over conference. *Science, 257,* 739.

Parker, J. G., & Asher, S. R. (1987). Peer relationships and later personal adjustment: Are low-accepted children at risk? *Psychological Bulletin, 102,* 357–389.

Pasamanick, B., Rodgers, M. E., & Lilienfield, A. M. (1956). Pregnancy experience and the development of behavior disorders in children. *American Journal of Psychiatry, 112,* 613–618.

Passingham, R. E. (1972). Crime and personality: A review of Eysenck's theory. In V. D. Nebylitsyn & J. A. Gray (Eds.), *Biological bases of individual behavior.* New York: Academic press.

Patterson, G. R. (1982). *Coercive family process.* Eugene, OR: Castalia.

Patterson, G. R., & Yoerger, K. (1993). Developmental models for delinquent behavior. In S. Hodgins (Ed.), *Mental disorder and crime* (pp. 140–172). Newbury Park, CA: Sage.

Paulus, D. L., & Martin, C. L. (1986). Predicting adult temperament from minor physical anomalies. *Journal of Personality and Social Psychology, 50,* 1235–1239.

Pease, S. E., & Love, C. T. (1986). Optimal methods and issues in nutrition research in the correctional setting. *Nutrition Reviews*, **44**, 122–132.

Petersen, I., Matousek, M., Mednick, S. A., Volavka, J., & Pollock, V. (1982). EEG antecedents of thievery. *Criminology*, **19**, 219–229.

Petersilia, J. (1980). Criminal career research: A review of recent evidence. In M. Tonry and N. Morris (Eds.), *Crime and justice: An annual review of research*, Vol. 2. (pp. 321–379). Chicago: University of Chicago Press.

Piaget, J. (1948). *The moral judgement of the child*. New York: Free Press.

Pihl, R. O., & Ervin, F. (1990). Lead and cadmium levels in violent criminals. *Psychological Reports*, **66**, 839–844.

Pincus, J. H., & Tucker, G. J. (1978). Violence in children and adults: A neurological view. *Journal of the American Academy of Child Psychiatry*, **17**, 277–288.

Pomeroy, J. C., Sprafkin, J., & Gadow, K. D. (1988). Minor physical anomalies as a biological marker for behavior disorders. *Journal of the American Academy of Child and Adolescent Psychiatry*, **27**, 466–473.

Power, G. F., Ash, P. M., Schoenberg, E., & Sorey, E. C. (1974). Delinquency and the family. *British Journal of Social Work*, **4**, 13–38.

Prentky, R. (1985). The neurochemistry and neuroendocrinology of sexual aggression. In D. P. Farrington & J. Gunn (Eds.), *Aggression and dangerousness* (pp. 7–55). New York: Wiley.

Price, J. M., & Dodge, K. A. (1989). Reactive and proactive aggression in childhood: Relations to peer status and social context dimensions. *Journal of Abnormal Child Psychology*, **17**, 455–471.

Quay, H. C. (1965). Psychopathic personality as pathological stimulation-seeking. *American Journal of Psychiatry*, **122**, 180–183.

Quqy, H. C. (1985). *Attention deficit disorder and the behavioral inhibition system: The relevance of the neuropsychological theory of Jeffrey A. Gray*. Paper presented at the Conference on Hyperactivity as a Scientific Challenge, University of Groningen, The Netherlands.

Quay, H. C. (1987). Intelligence. In H. C. Quay (Ed.), *Handbook of juvenile delinquency* (pp. 106–117). New York: Wiley.

Quay, H. C. (1988). The behavioral reward and inhibition systems in childhood behavior disorder. In L. M. Bloomingdale (Ed.), *Attention deficit disorder* (Vol. 3, pp. 176–186). Oxford, Pergamon.

Quay, H. C., & Parsons, L. B. (1970). *The differential classification of the juvenile offender*. Washington, DC: Bureau of Prisons.

Raine, A. (1987). Effect of early environment on electrodermal and cognitive correlates of schizotypy and psychopathy in criminals. *International Journal of Psychophysiology*, **4**, 277–287.

Raine, A. (1988). Antisocial behavior and social psychophysiology. In H. Wagner (Ed.), *Social psychophysiology and emotion: Theory and clinical application* (pp. 231–253). London: Wiley.

Raine, A. (1989). Evoked potentials and psychopathy. *International Journal of Psychophysiology*, **8**, 1–16.

Raine, A. (1990). *Psychopathic personality and P300*. Unpublished data, University of Southern California.

Raine, A. (1991). *Resting heart rate in adolescent psychopaths*. Unpublished data, University of Southern California.

Raine, A. (1992). Schizotypal and borderline features in psychopathic criminals. *Personality and Individual Differences*, **13**, 717–722.

Raine, A., & Dunkin, J. J. (1990). The genetic and psychophysiological basis of antisocial behavior: Implications for counseling and therapy. *Journal of Counseling and Development*, **68**, 637–644.

Raine, A., & Jones, F. (1987). Attention, autonomic arousal, and personality in behaviorally disordered children. *Journal of Abnormal Child Psychology*, **14**, 583–599.

Raine, A., & Lencz, T. (1993). The neuroanatomy of electrodermal activity. In J. C. Roy (Ed.), *Electrodermal activity: From Physiology to psychology*. New York: Plenum. In press.

Raine, A., & Mednick, S A. (1989). Biosocial longitudinal research into antisocial behavior. *Review d'Epidemiologie et de Sante Publique*, 37, 515–524.

Raine, A., & Scerbo, A. (1991). Biological theories of violence. In J. S. Milner (Ed.), *Neuropsychology of aggression* (pp. 1–26). Boston: Kluwer.

Raine, A., & Venables, P. H. (1981). Classical conditioning and socialization—A biosocial interaction? *Personality and Individual Differences*, 2, 273–283.

Raine, A., & Venables, P. H. (1984a). Electrodermal non-responding, schizoid tendencies, and antisocial behavior in adolescents. *Psychophysiology*, 21, 424–433.

Raine, A., & Venables, P. H. (1984b). Tonic heart rate level, social class, and antisocial behavior. *Biological Psychology*, 18, 123–132.

Raine, A., & Venables, P. H. (1987). Contingent negative variation, P3 evoked potentials, and antisocial behavior. *Psychophysiology*, 24, 191–199.

Raine, A., & Venables, P. H. (1988a). Skin conductance responsivity in psychopaths to orienting, defensive, and consonant–vowel stimuli. *Journal of Psychophysiology*, 2, 221–225.

Raine, A., & Venables, P. H. (1988b). Enhanced P3 evoked potentials during a continuous performance task in psychopaths. *Psychophysiology*, 25, 30–38.

Raine, A., & Venables, P. H. (1992). Antisocial behavior: Evolution, genetics, neuropsychology, and psychophysiology. In A. Gale & M. Eysenck (Eds.), *Handbook of individual differences: Biological perspectives*. London: Wiley.

Raine, A., Buchsbaum, M. S., Stanley, J., Lottenberg, S., Abel, L., & Stoddard, J. (1993). *Selective reductions in pre-frontal glucose metabolism in murders assessed with positron emission tomography*. Manuscript under review.

Raine, A., Lencz, T., Harrison, G., Reynolds, G. P., Sheard, S., & Cooper, J. E. (1992a). An evaluation of structural and functional prefrontal deficits in schizophrenia using MRI and neuropsychological measures. *Psychiatry Research*, 45, 123–137.

Raine, A., O'Brien, M., & Scerbo, A. (1991a). *Superior performance on Wisconsin Card Sorting in adolescent psychopaths*. Unpublished manuscript, University of Southern California.

Raine, A., O'Brien, M., Smiley, N., Scerbo, A., & Chan, C. J. (1990d). Reduced lateralization in verbal dichotic listening in adolescent psychopaths. *Journal of Abnormal Psychology*, 99, 272–277.

Raine, A., Reynolds, G., & Sheard, C. (1991b). Neuroanatomical mediators of electrodermal activity in normal human subjects: A magnetic resonance imaging study. *Psychophysiology*, 28, 548–558.

Raine, A., Roger, D., & Venables, P. H. (1982). Locus of control and socialization. Journal of Research in Personality, 16, 147–156.

Raine, A., Sheard, S., & Reynolds, G. P. (1992b). Evidence for pre-frontal structural and functional deficits associated with schizotypal personality: A magnetic resonance imaging study. *Schizophrenia Research*, 7, 237–247.

Raine, A., Venables, P. H., & Williams, M. (1990a). Relationships between CNS and ANS measures of arousal at age 15 and criminality at age 24. *Archives of General Psychiatry*, 47, 1003–1007.

Raine, A., Venables, P. H., & Williams, M. (1990b). Orienting and criminality: A prospective study. *American Journal of Psychiatry*, 147, 933–937.

Raine, A., Venables, P. H., & Williams, M. (1990c). Relationships between N1, P300 and CNV recorded at age 15 and criminal behavior at age 24. *Psychophysiology*, 27, 567–575.

Rampling, D. (1978). Aggression: A paradoxical response to tricyclic antidepressants. *American Journal of Psychiatry*, 135, 117–118.

Rapaport, J. L., & Quinn, P. O. (1975). Minor physical anomalies (stigmata) and early developmental deviation: A major biologic subgroup of hyperactive children. *International Journal of Mental Health*, 4, 29–44.

Ray, W. J. (1990). The electrocortical system. In J. T. Cacioppo & L. G. Tassinary (Eds.), *Principles of psychophysiology* (pp. 385–412). Cambridge: Cambridge University Press.

Reid, W. S., & Bottlinger, J. (1979). Genetic aspects of antisocial disorders. *Hillside Journal of Clinical Psychiatry*, 1, 87–95.

Reiss, A. J., & Rhodes, A. L. (1961). The distribution of juvenile delinquency in the social class structure. *American Sociologist Review*, 26, 720–732.

Reiss, A. J., & Roth, J. A. (1993). *Understanding and preventing violence*. Washington, DC: National Academy Press.

Repp, B. H. (1977). Measuring laterality effects in dichotic listening. *Journal of the Acoustic Society of America*, 62, 720–737.

Reznick, J. S., Kagan, J., Snidman, N., Gersten, M., Baak, K., & Rosenberg, A. (1986). Inhibited and uninhibited children: A follow-up study. *Child Development*, 57, 660–680.

Richard, B. A., & Dodge, K. A. (1982). Social maladjustment and problem solving in school-aged children. *Journal of Consulting and Clinical Psychology*, 50, 226–233.

Richman, N., Stevenson, J., & Graham, P. J. (1982). *Pre-school to school: A behavioral study*. London: Academic Press.

Robins, E., & Guze, S. B. (1970). Establishment of diagnostic validity in psychiatric illness: Its application to schizophrenia. *American Journal of Psychiatry*, 126, 983–987.

Robins, L. (1966). *Deviant children grown up: A sociological and psychiatric study of sociopathic personality*. Baltimore: Williams and Wilkins.

Robins, L. N. (1978). Etiological implications in studies of childhood histories relating to antisocial personality. In R. D. Hare & D. Schalling (Eds.), *Psychopathic behavior: Approaches to research* (pp. 255–272). New York: Wiley.

Robins, L. N. (1979a). Sturdy childhood predictors of adult outcomes: Replications from longitudinal studies. In J. E. Barratt, R. M. Rose, & G. L. Klerman (Eds.), *Stress and mental disorder* (pp. 219–235). New York: Raven Press.

Robins, L. N. (1979b). Longitudinal methods in the study of normal and pathological development. In K. P. Kisker, J. E. Meyer, C. Muller, & E. Stromgren (Eds.), *Psychiatrie der Gegenwart, Band 1. Grundlagen und Methoden der Psychiatrie. 2 Auflage*. Heidelberg: Springer-Verlag.

Robins, L. N., West, P. A., & Herjanic, B. L. (1975). Arrests and delinquency in two generations: A study of black urban families and their children. *Journal of Child Psychology and Psychiatry*, 16, 125–140.

Rogeness, G. A., Cepeda, C., Macedo, C. A., Fischer, C., & Harris, W. R. (1990). Differences in heart rate and blood pressure in children with conduct disorder, major depression, and separation anxiety. *Psychiatry Research*, 33, 199–206.

Rosanoff, A. J., Handy, L. M., & Rosanoff, F. A. (1934). Criminality and delinquency in twins. *Journal of Criminal Law and Criminology*, 24, 923–934.

Rosenbaum, A. (1991). The neuropsychology of marital aggression. In J. S. Milner (Ed.), *Neuropsychology of aggression* (pp. 167–180). Boston: Kluwer.

Rosenbaum, A., & Hodge, S. K. (1989). Head injury and marital aggression. *American Journal of Psychiatry*, 146, 1048–1051.

Roth, M., & Kroll, J. (1986). *The reality of mental illness*. Cambridge: Cambridge University Press.

Rowe, D. C. (1983). Biometric genetic models of self-reported delinquent behavior: A twin study. *Behavior Genetics*, 13, 473–489.

Rowe, D. C. (1985). Sibling interaction and self-reported delinquent behavior: A study of 265 twin pairs. *Criminology*, 23, 223–240.

Roy, A., Adinoff, B., & Roehrich, L. (1988). Pathological gambling: A psychobiological study. *Archives of General Psychiatry*, 45(4), 369–373.

Rubin, R. T. (1987). The neuroendocrinology and neurochemistry of antisocial behavior. In S. A. Mednick, T. E. Moffitt, & S. A. Stack (Eds.), *The causes of crime: New biological approaches* (pp. 239–262). Cambridge: Cambridge University Press.

Rumsey, J. M., & Rapoport, J. L. (1983). In R. J. Wurtman & J. J. Wurtman (Eds.), *Nutrition and the brain* (Vol 6, pp. 101–162). New York: Raven Press.

Rutter, M. (1982). *Maternal deprivation reassessed* (2nd ed.). Harmondsworth, England: Penguin.

Rutter, M. (1987). The role of cognition in child development and disorder. *British Journal of Medical Psychology*, 60, 1–16.

Rutter, M., & Giller, H. (1983). *Juvenile delinquency: Trends and perspectives.* Harmondsworth, England: Penguin.

Rutter, M., & Madge, N. (1976). *Cycles of disadvantage: A review of research.* London, Heinemann.

Rutter, M., Boltin, P., Harrington, R., Le Couteur, A., Macdonald, H., & Simonoff, E. (1990). Genetic factors in child psychiatric disorders. I. A review of research strategies. *Journal of Child Psychology and Psychiatry*, 31, 5–37.

Rutter, M., Maughan, B., Mortimore, P., Ouston, J., & Smith, A. (1979). *Fifteen thousand hours: Secondary schools and their effects on children.* London: Open Books.

Sachser, N. (1987). Short-term responses of plasma norepinephrine, epinephrine, glucocorticoid and testosterone titers to social and non-social stressors in male guinea pigs of different social status. *Physiology & Behavior*, 39, 11–20.

Saladin, M., Saper, Z., & Breen, L. (1988). Perceived attractiveness and attributes of criminality: What is beautiful is not criminal. *Canadian Journal of Criminology*, 30, 251–259.

Scaret, D., & Wilgosh, L. (1989). Learning disabilities and juvenile delinquency: A causal relationship? *International Journal for the Advancement of Counselling*, 12, 113–123.

Scerbo, A. (1991). *Neurotransmitters and antisocial behavior.* Unpublished manuscript, University of Southern California.

Scerbo, A., & Raine, A. (1992). *Neurotransmitters and antisocial behavior: A meta-analysis.* Under review.

Scerbo, A., Raine, A., O'Brien, M., Chan, C. J., Rhee, C., & Smiley, N. (1990). Reward dominance and passive avoidance learning in adolescent psychopaths. *Journal of Abnormal Child Psychology*, 18, 451–463.

Scerbo, A., Raine, A., Venables, P. H., & Mednick, S. A. (1993a). Stability of temperament from ages 3 to 11 years in Mauritian children. *Development Psychology*, under review.

Scerbo, A., Raine, A., Venables, P. H., & Mednick, S. A. (1993b). Relationships between autonomic arousal at age 3 and temperament at ages 8 to 11 years. *Journal of Abnormal Psychology*, under review.

Schacter, S., & Latane, B. (1964). Crime, cognition, and the autonomic nervous system. In M. R. Jones (Ed.), *Nebraska symposium on motivation* (pp. 221–275). Lincoln: University of Nebraska Press.

Schacter, F. F., & Stone, R. K. (1985). Difficult sibling, easy sibling: temperament and the within-family environment. *Child Development*, 54, 424–435.

Schalling, D. (1978a). Psychopathy-related personality variables and the psychophysiology of socialization. In R. D. Hare & D. Schalling (Eds.), *Psychopathic behavior: Theory and research* (pp. 85–106). New York: Wiley.

Schalling, D. (1978b). *Psychopathy—A partial interhemispheric disconnection syndrome? A neuropsychological perspective.* Paper presented at the conference on the Psychophysiology and neuropsychology of psychopathic and antisocial behavior. Munich, August 1.

Schalling, D. (1987). Personality correlates of plasma testosterone levels in young delinquents: An example of person–situation interaction? In S. A. Mednick, T. E. Moffitt, & S. Stack (Eds.), *The causes of crime: New biological approaches* (pp. 263–282). New York: Cambridge.

Schalling, D. (1993). Neurochemical correlates of personality, impulsivity, and disinhibitory suicidality. In S. Hodgins (Ed.), *Mental disorder and crime* (pp. 208–226). Newbury Park, CA: Sage.

Schalling, D., & Rosen, A. S. (1968). Porteus maze differences between psychopathic and non-psychopathic criminals. *British Journal of Social and Clinical Psychology*, 7, 224–228.

Scheff, T. J. (1970). Schizophrenia as ideology. *Schizophrenia Bulletin*, 2, 15–19.

Schmauk, F. J. (1970). Punishment, arousal, and avoidance learning in sociopaths. *Journal of Abnormal Psychology*, 76, 325–335.

Schmidt, K., Solant, M. V., & Bridger, W. H. (1985). Electrodermal activity of undersocialized aggressive children: A pilot study. *Journal of Child Psychology and Psychiatry and Allied Disciplines*, 26, 653–660.

Schneider, E. L., & Emr, M. (1985). Research highlights. Special issue: Alzheimer's disease. *Geriatric Nursing*, 6, 136–138.

Schoenthaler, S. J. (1982). The effect of sugar on the treatment and control of anti-social behavior: A double-blind study of an incarcerated juvenile population. *International Journal of Biosocial Research*, 3, 1–9.

Schonfeld, I. S., Shaffer, D., O'Connor, P., & Portnoy, S. (1988). Conduct disorder and cognitive functioning: Testing three causal hypotheses. *Child Development*, 59, 993–1007.

Schulsinger, F. (1972). Psychopathy, heredity, and environment. *International Journal of Mental Health*, 1, 190–206.

Schwesinger, G. (1952). The effect of differential parent–child relations on identical twin resemblance in personality. *Acta Geneticae Medicae et Germellologiae*.

Scott, P. D. (1973). Fatal battered baby cases. *Medicine, Science and the Law*, 13, 197–206.

Scoville, W. B. (1972). Psychosurgery and other lesions of the brain affecting human behavior. In E. Hitchcock, L. Laitinen, & K. Vaernet (Eds.), *Psychosurgery*. Springfield, IL: Thomas.

Sedlak, A. J. (1991). *National incidence and prevalence of child abuse and neglect: 1988*. Washington, DC: Westat, Inc.

Seltzer, C. C. (1951). Constitutional aspects of juvenile delinquency. *Cold Spring Harbor Symposia on Quantitative Biology*, 15, 361–372.

Shapiro, S. K., Quay, H. C., Hogan, A. E., & Schwartz, K. P. (1988). Response perseveration and delayed responding in undersocialized aggressive conduct disorder. *Journal of Abnormal Psychology*, 97, 371–373.

Sheard, M. H. (1975). Lithium in the treatment of aggression. *Journal of Nervous and Mental Disease*, 160, 108–118.

Sheard, M. H., Marini, J. L., & Bridges, C. I. (1976). The effects of lithium in impulsive aggressive behavior in man. *American Journal of Psychiatry*, 133, 1409–1413.

Sheldon, W. H., Hartl, E. M., & McDermott, E. (1949). *Varieties of delinquent youth*. New York: Harper.

Sheley, J. F. (1991). *Criminology*. Belmont, CA: Wadsworth.

Shields, J. (1977). Polygenic influences. In M. Rutter & L. Hersov (Eds.), *Child psychiatry: Modern approaches* (pp. 22–46). Oxford: Blackwell.

Shover, N. (1985). *Aging criminals*. Beverly Hills, CA: Sage.

Siassi, I. (1982). Lithium treatment of impulsive behavior in children. *Journal of Clinical Psychiatry*, 43, 482–484.

Siddle, D. A. T. (1977). Electrodermal activity and psychopathy. In S. A. Mednick & K. O. Christiansen (Eds.), *Biosocial bases of criminal behavior* (pp. 199–212). New York: Gardner Press.

Siddle, D. A. T., & Trasler, G. (1981). The psychophysiology of psychopathic behavior. In M. J. Christie & P. G. Mellett (Eds.), *Foundations of psychosomatics* (pp. 283–303). England, Wiley.

Siddle, D. A. T., Mednick, S. A., Nichol, A. R., & Foggitt, R. H. (1976). Skin conductance recovery in antisocial adolescents. *British Journal of Social and Clinical Psychology*, 15, 425–428.

Siegel, A., & Mirsky, A. F. (1990). *The neurobiology of violence and aggression*. National Academy of Sciences' Conference on the Understanding and Control of Violent Behavior, San Destin, Florida.

Siever, L. J., Coursey, R. D., Alterman, I. S., Buchsbaum, S., & Murphy, D. L. (1984). Impaired smooth-pursuit eye movements: Vulnerability marker for schizotypal personality disorder in a normal volunteer population. *American Journal of Psychiatry*, 141, 1560–1566.

Sigvardsson, S., Cloninger, R., Bohman, M., & von Knorring, A. L. (1982). Predisposition to petty criminality in Swedish adoptees. III. Sex differences and validation of the male typology. *Archives of General Psychiatry*, 39, 1248–1253.

Silver, J. M., & Yudofsky, S. C. (1987). Aggressive behavior in patients with neuropsychiatric disorders. *Psychiatric Annals*, **17**, 367–370.

Silverton, L. (1988). Crime and the schizophrenia spectrum: A study of three Danish cohorts. In T. E. Moffitt & S. A. Mednick (Eds.), *Biological contributions to crime causation* (pp. 93–120). Dordrecht, Holland: Martinus Nijhoff.

Singh, S. D. (1976). Sociometric analysis of the effect of bilateral lesions of frontal cortex on the social behavior of rhesus Indian monkeys. *Journal of Psychology*, **51**, 144–160.

Slater, E. (1953). The incidence of mental disorder. *Annals of Eugenics*, **6**, 172.

Slawson, J. (1923). Marital relations of parents and juvenile delinquency. *Journal of Delinquency*, **8**, 280–283.

Smith, R. C., Baumgartner, R., & Calderon, M. (1987). Magnetic resonance imaging studies of the brains of schizophrenic patients. *Psychiatry Research*, **20**, 33–46.

Smith, R. C., Calderon, M., Ravichandran, G. K., Largen, J., Vroulis, G., Shvartsburd, A., Gordon, J., and Schoolar, J. C. (1984). Nuclear magnetic resonance imaging in schizophrenia: A preliminary study. *Psychiatry Research*, **12**, 137–147.

Snidman, N., Kagan, J. and McQuilkin, A. (1991). Fetal heart rate as a predictor of infant ehavior. *Psychophysiology*, **28**, 51.

Snyder, J., & Patterson, G. R. (1987). Family interaction and delinquent behavior. In H. C. Quay (Ed.), *Handbook of juvenile delinquency* (pp. 216–243). New York: Wiley.

Snyder, J., Dishion, T. J., & Patterson, G. R. (1986). Determinants and consequences of associating with deviant peers during preadolescence and adolescence. *Journal of Early Adolescence*, **6**, 29–43.

Spitzer, R. L. (1991). An outsider–insider's views about revising the DSMs. *Journal of Abnormal Psychology*, **100**, 294–296.

Spitzer, R. L., & Endicott, J. (1978). Medical and mental disorder: Proposed definition and criteria. In R. L. Spitzer & D. F. Klein (Eds.), *Critical issues in psychiatric diagnosis* (pp. 15–40). New York: Raven Press.

Stattin, H., & Magnusson, D. (1991). Stability and change in criminal behavior up to age 30. *British Journal of Criminology*, **31**, 327–346.

Stern, R. M., Ray, W. J., & Davis, C. M. (1980). *Psychophysiological recording*. New York: Oxford University Press.

Stewart, J. E. (1985). Appearance and punishment: The attraction–leniency effect in the courtroom. *Journal of Social Psychology*, **125**, 373–378.

Stone, R. (1992). HHS "violence initiative" caught in a cross-fire. *Science*, **258**, 212–213.

Stumpfl, F. (1936). *Erbanalage und Verbrechen. Charakterologische und Psychiatrische Sippenuntersuchungen.* Berlin: Julius Springer.

Stuss, D. T., & Benson, D. F. (1986). *The frontal lobes*. New York: Raven Press.

Sugmati, (1954). Psychiatric studies of the criminal by the twin method. *Twin Studies 1. Japanese Society for the Promotion of Scientific Research*, **137**.

Susman, E. J., Dorn, L. D., & Chrousos, G. P. (1991). Negative affect and hormone levels in young adolescents: Concurrent and predictive perspectives. *Journal of Youth and Adolescence*, **20**, 167–190.

Sutherland, E. (1939). *Principles of criminology*. Philadelphia: Lippincott.

Sutker, P. B., & Allain, A. N. (1983). Behavior and personality assessment in men labeled adaptive sociopaths. *Journal of Behavioral Assessment*, **5**, 65–79.

Swihart, A. A., Baskin, D. S., & Pirozzolo, F. J. (1989). Somatostatin and cognitive dysfunction in Alzheimer's disease. *Developmental Neuropsychology*, **5**, 159–168.

Sykes, G. M., & Cullen, F. T. (1992). *Criminology* (2nd ed.). San Diego: Harcourt Brace Jovanovich.

Syndulko, K. (1978). Electrocoritcal investigations of sociopathy. In R. D. Hare and D. Schalling (Eds.), *Psychopathic behavior: Approaches to research* (pp. 145–156). Chichester, England: Wiley.

Szasz, T. S. (1960). The myth of mental illness. *American Psychologist*, **15**, 5–12.

Szatmari, P., Reitsma, S. M., & Offord, D. R. (1986). Pregnancy and birth complications in antisocial adolescents and their siblings. *Canadian Journal of Psychiatry*, 31, 513–516.

Tames, F. J., & Swift, A. D. (1983). The measurement of salivary testosterone. In F. J. Tames (Ed.), *Immuno-assays for clinical chemistry* (2nd ed.). London: Churchill-Livingstone.

Tancredi, L. R., & Volkow, N. (1988). Neural substrates of violent behavior: Implications for law and public policy. *International Journal of Law and Psychiatry*, 11, 13–49.

Tarter, R. E., Hefedus, A. M., Winsten, N. E., & Alterman, A. I. (1984). Neuropsychological, personality and familial characteristics of physically abused children. *Journal of American Academy of Child Psychiatry*, 23, 668–674.

Tennes, K., & Kreye, M. (1985). Childrens' adrenocortical response to classroom activities in elementary school. *Psychosomatic Medicine*, 47, 451–460.

Tharp, V. K., Maltzman, I., Syndulko, K., & Ziskind, E. (1980). Autonomic activity during anticipation of an aversive tone in non-institutionalized sociopaths. *Psychophysiology*, 17, 123–128.

Thomson, G. O., Raab, G. M., Hepburn, W. S., & Hunter, R. (1989). Blood levels and children's behavior: Results from the Edinburgh Lead Study. *Journal of Child Psychology and Psychiatry and Allied Disciplines*, 30, 515–528.

Thompson, K. M. (1990). Refacing inmates: A critical appraisal of plastic surgery programs in prison. *Criminal Justice and Behavior*, 17, 448–466.

Thornberry, T. P., & Farnworth, M. (1982). Social correlates of criminal involvement: Further evidence on the relationship between social status and criminal behavior. *American Sociological Review*, 47, 505–518.

Thornhill, R., & Thornhill, N. W. (1983). Human rape: an evolutionary perspective. *Ethology and sociobiology*, 4, 137–173.

Thornhill, R., & Thornhill, N. M. (1987). Human rape: The strengths of the evolutionary perspective. In C. Crawford, M. Smith, & D. Krebs (Eds.), *Sociobiology and psychology*. Hillsdale, NJ: Erlbaum.

Thornton, D. M. (1988). Moral development theory. In B. J. McGurk, D. M. Thornton, & M. Williams (Eds.), *Applying psychology to imprisonment: Theory and practice*. London: Her Majesty's Stationery Office.

Timiras, P. S., Hudson, D. B., & Segall, P. E. (1984). Lifetime brain serotonin: Regional effects of age and precursor availability. *Neurobiology of Aging*, 5, 235–242.

Tonkonogy, J. M. (1991). Violence and temporal lobe lesion: Head CT and MRI data. *Journal of Neuropsychiatry*, 3, 189–196.

Trasler, G. (1978). Relations between psychopathy and persistent criminality—Methodological and theoretical issues. In R. D. Hare & D. Schalling (Eds.), *Psychopathic behavior: Approaches to research*. New York: Wiley.

Trasler, G. (1987). Biogenetic factors. In H. C. Quay (Ed.), *Handbook of juvenile delinquency* (pp. 184–216). New York: Wiley.

Trivers, R. L. (1971). The evolution of reciprocal altruism. *Quarterly Review of Biology*, 46, 35–57.

Truscott, D. (1992). Inter-generational transmission of violent behavior in adolescent males. *Aggressive Behavior*, 18, 327–335.

Turner, C. W., Ford, M. H., West, D. W., & Meikle, A. W. (1986). *Genetic influences on testosterone, hostility, and Type A behavior in adult male twins*. Paper presented at the meeting of the American Psychological Association, Washington, D.C.

Tygart, C. E. (1991). Juvenile delinquency and number of children in a family: Some empirical and theoretical updates. *Youth and Society*, 22, 525–536.

U.S. Department of Justice (1989). *Crime in the United States, 1988*. Washington, DC: U.S. Government Printing Office.

Vaernet, K., & Madsen, A. (1970). Stereotaxic amygdalotomy and baso-frontal tractotomy in psychotics and aggressive behavior. *Journal of Neurology, Neurosurgery and Psychiatry*, 33, 838–863.

van Dusen, K. T., Mednick, S. A., Gabrielli, W. F., & Hutchings, B. (1983). Social class and crime in an adoption cohort. *Journal of Criminal Law and Criminology*, **74**, 249–269.

Venables, P. H. (1974). The recovery limb of the skin conductance response. In S. A. Mednick, F. Schulsinger, J. Higgins, & B. Bell (Eds.), *Genetics, environment and psychopathology* (pp. 117–133). Oxford: North-Holland.

Venables, P. H. (1987). Autonomic and central nervous system factors in criminal behavior. In S. A. Mednick, T. Moffitt, & S. Stack (Eds.), *The causes of crime: New biological approaches* (pp. 110–136). New York: Cambridge University Press.

Venables, P. H. (1988). Psychophysiology and crime: Theory and data. In T. E. Moffitt & S. A. Mednick (Eds.), *Biological contributions to crime causation*. Dordrecht, Holland: Martinus Nijhoff.

Venables, P. H. (1989). The Emanuel Miller Memorial Lecture 1987: Childhood markers for adult disorders. *Journal of Child Psychology and Psychiatry and Allied Disciplines*, **30**, 347–364.

Venables, P. H., & Christie, M. J. (1973). Mechanisms, instrumentation, recording techniques, and quantification of responses. In W. F. Prokasy & D. C. Raskin (Eds.), *Electrodermal activity in psychological research*. New York: Wiley.

Venables, P. H., & Raine, A. (1987). Biological theory. In B. McGurk, D. Thornton, & M. Williams (Eds.), *Applying psychology to imprisonment: Theory and practice* (pp. 3–28). London: Her Majesty's Stationery Office.

Venables, P. H., Gartshore, S. A., & O'Riordan, P. W. (1980). The function of skin conductance response recovery and rise time. *Biological Psychology*, **10**, 1–6.

Virkkunen, M. (1984). Reactive hypoglycemic tendency among habitually violent offenders. *Neuropsychobiology*, **8**, 35–40.

Virkkunen, M. (1985). Urinary free cortisol excretion in habitually violent offenders. *Acta Psychiatrica Scandinavica*, **72**, 40–42.

Virkkunen, M. (1986). Reactive hypoglycemia tendency among habitually violent offenders. *Nutrition Reviews*, **44**, 94–103.

Virkkunen, M., & Linnoila, M. (1993). Serotonin in personality disorders with habitual violence and impulsivity. In S. Hodgins (Ed.), *Mental disorder and crime* (pp. 194–207). Newbury Park, CA: Sage.

Virkkunen, M., De Jong, J., Bartko, J., Goodwin, F., & Linnoila, M. (1989). Relationship of psychobiological variables to recidivism in violent offenders and impulsive fire setters. *Archives of General Psychiatry*, **46**, 600–603.

Virkkunen, M., Nuutila, A., & Huusko, S. (1976). Effect of brain injury on social adaptability. *Acta Psychiatrica Scandinavica*, **53**, 168–172.

Visher, C. A., & Roth, J. A. (1986). Participation in criminal careers. In A. Blumstein, J. Cohen, J. A. Roth, & C. A. Visher (Eds.), *Criminal careers and career criminals* (pp. 211–291). Washington, DC: National Academy Press.

Vissing, Y. M., Straus, M. A., Gelles, R. J., & Harrop, J. W. (1991). Verbal aggression by parents and psychosocial problems of children. *Child Abuse and Neglect*, **15**, 223–238.

Volavka, J. (1987). Electroencephalogram among criminals. In S. A. Mednick, T. E. Moffitt and S. Stack (Eds.), *The causes of crime: New biological approaches* (pp. 137–145). Cambridge: Cambridge University Press.

Volavka, J., Crowner, M., Brizer, D., Convit, A., Van Praag, H., & Suckow, R. F. (1990). Tryptophan treatment of aggressive psychiatric inpatients. *Biological Psychiatry*, **28**, 728–732.

Volkow, N. D., & Tancredi, L. (1987). Neural substrates of violent behavior: A preliminary study with positron emission tomography. *British Journal of Psychiatry*, **151**, 668–673.

Wadsworth, M. E. J. (1976). Delinquency, pulse rate and early emotional deprivation. *British Journal of Criminology*, **16**, 245–256.

Wadsworth, M. E. J. (1979). *Roots of delinquency*. New York: Barnes and Nobel.

Waldrop, M. F. (1979). *Minor physical anomalies—A predictor of problem behaviors*. Paper presented at the International Conference of the Association for Children with Learning Disabilities, San Francisco.

Waldrop, M. F., & Halverson, C. (1971). Minor physical anomalies and hyperactive behavior in young children. *Exceptional Infant*, **2**, 343–380.

Waldrop, M. F., Bell, R. Q., McLaughlin, B., & Halverson, C. F. (1978). Newborn minor physical anomalies predict short attention span, peer aggression, and impulsivity at age 3. *Science*, **199**, 536–564.

Walker, J. L., Lahey, B. B., Russo, M. F., Frick, P. J., Christ, M. A. G., McBurnett, K., Loeber, R., Stouthamer-Loeber, M., & Green, S. M. (1991). Anxiety, inhibition, and conduct disorder in children: I. Relations to social impairment. *Journal of the American Academy of Child and Adolescent Psychiatry*, **30**, 187–191.

Weiger, W. A., & Bear, D. M. (1988). An approach to the neurology of aggression. *Journal of Psychiatry Research*, **22**, 85–98.

Weinberger, D. R., Berman, K. F., & Zec, R. F. (1986). Physiologic dysfunction of dorsolateral prefrontal cortex in schizophrenia. *Archives of General Psychiatry*, **43**, 114–124.

Weintraub, K. J., & Gold, M. (1991). Monitoring and delinquency. *Criminal Behavior and Mental Health*, **1**, 268–281.

Weisman, R. (1986). Nutrition and neurotransmitters: The research of Richard Wurtman. *Journal of Child and Adolescent Psychotherapy*, **3**, 125–132.

Welte, J. W., & Miller, B. A. (1987). Alcohol use by violent and property offenders. *Drug and Alcohol Dependence*, **19**, 313–324.

Wessels, N. K., & Hopson, J. L. (1988). *Biology*. New York: Random House.

West, D. J., & Farrington, D. (1973). *Who becomes delinquent?* London: Heinemann.

West, D. J., & Farrington, D. (1977). *The delinquent way of life*. London: Heinemann.

Whitehead, P. L., & Clark, L. D. (1970). Effect of lithium carbonate, placebo, and thioridazine on hyperactive children. *American Journal of Psychiatry*, **127**, 824–825.

Whitman, S., Coonley-Hoganson, R., & Desai, B. T. (1984). Comparative head trauma experiences in two socio-economically different Chicago-area communities: A population study. *American Journal of Epidemiology*, **119**, 570–580.

Widiger, T. A., Frances, A. J., Pincus, H. A., Davis, W. W., & First, M. B. (1991). Toward an empirical classification for the DSM-IV. *Journal of Abnormal Psychology*, **100**, 280–288.

Widom, C. S. (1978). A methodology for studying noninstitutionalized psychopaths. In R. D. Hare & D. Schalling (Eds.), *Psychopathic behavior: Approaches to research* (pp. 71–84). Chichester: Wiley.

Widom, C. S. (1989a). Does violence beget violence? A critical examination of the literature. *Psychological Bulletin*, **106**, 3–28.

Widom, C. S. (1989b). The cycle of violence. *Science*, **244**, 160–166.

Widom, C. S. (1991). A tail on an untold tale: Response to "Biological and genetic contributors to violence—Widom's untold tale." *Psychological Bulletin*, **109**, 130–132.

Widom, C. S., & Ames, A. (1988). Biology and female crime. In T. E. Moffitt and S. A. Mednick (Eds.), *Biological contributions to crime causation* (pp. 308–331). Boston: Martinus Nijhoff.

Wikstrom, P. O. H. (1991). Housing tenure, social class and offending: The individual-level relationship in childhood and youth. *Criminal Behavior and Mental Health*, **1**, 69–89.

Wilbanks, W. (1984). *Murder in Miami* Lanham, Maryland: University Press of America.

Wilkinson, G. S. (1984). Reciprocal food-sharing in the vampire bat. *Nature*, **308**, 181–184.

Wille, R., & Beier, K. M. (1989). Castration in Germany. *Annals of Sex Research*, **2**, 103–134.

Wilson, E. O. (1975). *Sociobiology: The new synthesis*. Cambridge, MA: Harvard University Press.

Wilson, H. (1980). Parental supervision: A neglected aspect of delinquency. *British Journal of Criminology*, **20**, 203–235.

Wilson, R. S. (1983). The Louisville Twin Study: Developmental synchronies in behavior. *Child Development*, **54**, 298–316.

Wilson, J. Q., & Herrnstein, R. (1985). *Crime and human nature*. New York: Simon & Schuster.

Williams, D. (1969). Neural factors related to habitual aggression: Consideration of those differences between those habitually aggressive and others who have committed crimes of violence. *Brain*, **92**, 503–520.

Wingate, P. (1976). *Medical Encyclopedia* (2nd ed.). Harmondsworth, Middlesex: Penguin.

Witkin, H. A., Mednick, S. A., Schulsinger, F., Bakkestrom, E., Christiansen, K. O., Goodenough, D. R., Hirschhorn, K., Lundsteen, C., Owen, D. R., Philip, J., Rubin, D. B., & Stocking, M. (1977). Criminality, aggression and intelligence among XYY and XXY men. In S. A. Mednick & K. O. Christiansen (Eds.), *Biosocial bases of criminal behavior* (pp. 165–188). New York: Gardner Press.

Wolfgang, M. E., Figlio, R. F., & Sellin, T. (1972). *Delinquency in a birth cohort.* Chicago: University of Chicago Press.

Wright, P., Nobrega, J., Langevin, R., & Wortzman, G. (1990). Brain density and symmetry in pedophilic and sexually aggressive offenders. *Annals of Sex Research, 3*, 319–328.

Yamamoto, K., Arai, H., & Nakayama, S. (1990). Skin conductance response after 6-hydroxy-dopamine lesion of central noradrenaline system in cats. *Biological Psychiatry, 28*, 151–160.

Yesavage, J. A. (1984). Correlates of dangerous behavior by schizophrenics in hospital. *Journal of Psychiatric Research, 18*, 225–231.

Yeudall, L. T. (1977). Neuropsychological assessment of forensic disorders. *Canada's Mental Health, 25*, 7–16.

Yeudall, L. T. (1978). *The neuropsychology of aggression.* Clarence Hinks Memorial Lecture, University of Western Ontario, Canada.

Yeudall, L. T., & Flor-Henry, P. (1975). *Lateralized neuropsychological impairments in depression and criminal psychopathy.* Paper presented at the Conference of the Psychiatric Association of Alberta, Calgary, Alberta.

Yeudall, L. T., & Fromm-Auch, D. (1979). Neuropsychological impairments in various psychopathological populations. In J. Gruzelier and P. Flor-Henry (Eds.). *Hemisphere asymmetries of function and psychopathology* (pp. 5–13). New York: Elsevier/North Holland.

Yeudall, L. T., Fedora, O., Fedora, S., & Wardell, D. (1981). *Australian Journal of Forensic Science, 13*(4) and **14**(1).

Yeudall, L. T., Fromm-Auch, D., & Davies, P. (1982). Neuropsychological impairment of persistent delinquency. *Journal of Nervous and Mental Disease, 170*, 257–265.

Yodyingyuad, U., de la Riva, C., Abbot, D. H., Herbert, J., & Keverne, E. B. (1985). Relationship between dominance hierarchy, cerebrospinal fluid levels of amine transmitter metabolites (5-hydroxyindole acetic acid and homovanillic acid) and plasma cortisol in monkeys. *Neuroscience, 16*, 851–858.

Yoshimashu, S. (1961). The criminological significance of the family in the light of the studies of criminal twins. *Acta Criminologiae et Medicinae Legalis Japanica, 27*, 117–141.

Yudofsky, S. C., Silver, J. M., & Schneider, S. E. (1987). Pharmacologic treatment of aggression. *Psychiatric Annals, 17*, 397–407.

Zahn, T. P., (1986). Psychophysiological approaches to psychopathology. In M. G. P. Coles, E. Donchin, & S. W. Porges (Eds.), *Psychophysiology: Systems, processes, and applications* (508–610). New York: Guilford.

Ziskind, E., Syndulko, K., & Maltzman, I. (1978). Aversive conditioning in the sociopath. *Pavlovian Journal of Biological Science, 13*, 199–205.

Author Index

Subject Index

Crime (*continued*)
  aging criminals, 284–285
  biological factors and, 191–214
  brain imaging and, 129–155
  as a cheating strategy, 33–35, 45
  cognitive deficits and, 215–242
  cross-cultural variations in,
    295–296
  as a disorder, 287–320
  ethnic differences in, 293–294
  evolution and, 27–46
  extrafamilial factors and, 267–286
  family factors and, 243–266
  female, 69, 100, 111, 121, 166–168,
    203, 206, 208–209, 279
  future directions in crime research,
    317–318
  gender effects, 293–294
  genetics and, 47–79
  group crime, 302
  heterogeneity, 3, 124, 296–297
  neuropsychology and, 103–127
  neurotransmitters and, 81–102
  organizational, 302
  petty criminality, 53–54, 67
  psychophysiology and, 157–190
  population base rates, 4–5
  rate, fluctuations in, 294–295
  as socio-political-legal construct, 51,
    297–299
Crime as disorder, 287–320; *see also*
    Psychopathology
  arguments against, 292–305
  behavioral nature of crime, 303–304
  belief in view of, 292–293
  biological research and, 312–314
  conclusions on, 318–319
  cross-cultural factors and, 295–296
  curing crime and, 302–303
  defining target group, 299–300
  demographic factors, 293–294
  dimensional approach to, 301–302
  disorder definitions fitted to crime
    findings, 288–292
  emotional reactions to crime,
    305–306
  free will and, 309–312, 307–312
  harming others and, 303

  heterogeneity of crime, 296–297
  implications, 307–308
  imprisonment and, 308
  moralistic aggression and, 307
  organizational crime and, 302
  punishment of criminals and,
    307–309
  recidivistic criminals and, 299
  societal and sociobiological barriers
    against, 305–309
  sociolegal construction and,
    297–299
  voluntary nature of crime, 304–305
Criminals
  cognitive dysfunction, 12
  distress/suffering in, 9–10
  work records, 12–13
Cross-cultural variations, 295–296

Death, parental, *see* Parental death
Deformities, facial, 201
Delinquency
  academic failure and, 271–272
  birth complications and, 195–196
  body build and, 203–204
  diet and, 211
  divorce/separation and, 252–257
  family size and, 274–276
  frontal dysfunction in, 111
  head injury and, 192–195
  heritability for, 73–76
  intelligence and, 232–235
  joint family activities and, 261–262
  learning disability and, 235–236
  left handedness and, 119–120
  marital conflict and, 262–263
  maternal deprivation and, 250–251
  moral reasoning and, 237–239
  parental death and, 251–252
  parental supervision and, 257–259
  peers and, 268–271
  physical attraction and, 201–202
  psychopathic delinquents, 117
  punishment and, 259–260
  schools and, 272–274
  social information processing and,
    239

ISBN 0-12-576160-0

9 780125 761604

90065